❧❧❧❧❧❧❧❧❧❧❧❧❧❧❧❧❧❧❧❧❧❧❧❧❧❧❧❧❧❧❧❧❧

Protestant Thought in the Nineteenth Century

Volume 2, 1870–1914

❧❧❧❧❧❧❧❧❧❧❧❧❧❧❧❧❧❧❧❧❧❧❧❧❧❧❧❧❧❧

by

Claude Welch

New Haven and London

Yale University Press

Printed in the United States of America by
Murray Printing Company, Westford, Massachusetts.

Library of Congress Cataloging in Publication Data
(Revised for v. 2)

Welch, Claude.
   Protestant thought in the nineteenth century.

   Includes bibliographical references.
   Contents: v. 1. 1799–1870–v. 2. 1870–1914.
I. Title.
BT28.W394   209'.034   72–75211
ISBN 0–300–01535–6 (v. 1)
ISBN 0–300–03369–9 (v. 2)
ISBN 0–300–04201–9 (v. 2: pbk.)

10 9 8 7 6 5 4 3 2

Contents

Preface

This volume appears after a considerably greater lapse of time than I anticipated when volume 1 was published in 1972. Nonetheless, the two volumes still need to be considered parts of a single work on the development of Protestant thought (especially theology) in the nineteenth century. The introduction to volume 1 remains an introduction to the entire work, and what is said there need not be reiterated. In the present chapters I have frequently referred to relevant sections of volume 1 (which, happily, is currently being reissued).

The last third of the nineteenth century is counted here as extending from 1870 to World War I, after which a new theological generation emerged, one marked especially by the radical reaction led by Karl Barth and his associates. For this concluding period of the century, the attempt to incorporate in a single general framework the principal Protestant religious thinkers of Europe, Britain, and America seems even more appropriate than for the earlier parts of the century. Not only do the dominant problems and foci of concern cut across the national boundaries; there was also much more extensive direct interchange. The influence of German thought in Britain and America is more obvious, partly because of the translation of German works into English. But the intellectual traffic was by no means only one-way.

The extent of the commonalities of thought has led to one major difference in organization in this volume. Except for the first and last chapters, which center on thinkers uniquely representative of the beginning and end of the period, I have organized the discussion less around individual authors and movements than around problems and themes. The reasons are several. An attempt to interpret the period mainly by reference to movements or schools does not finally prove either illuminating or interesting, and no good purpose could be served by trying to establish a chronological schematization. Further, it has been necessary to venture into several nontheological areas of investigation—anthropology, psychology, sociology, and the history of science—all of which had a powerful impact on religious thinking. Hence it has seemed to me that the period can best be illumined by focusing on central issues and letting the individual thinkers appear and reappear as the occasion requires. Although this is not the only way of making sense of the variety of late-nineteenth-century theology, in view of the remarkable coalescence in the areas of theological concern it is at least one good way. This procedure also involves more assessment of the ventures than was characteristic of volume 1, though I have tried to be scrupulously fair in the interpretation of each individual.

The principal concerns of late-nineteenth-century religious thought seem to fall naturally into three categories: faith, history, and ethics, as well as their relations to one another. My interpretation is therefore ordered (mostly) in relation to those topics, not as a schema rigidly or artificially imposed, but as a way of throwing light on the principal individual efforts and debates of the period. This is not a departure from my suggestion in the introduction to volume 1 that it was the question of Christianity and culture which came especially to flower at the end of the nineteenth century. Though church and society is the special topic only of chapter 7, it should be evident that at every point of the discussion the problems of the relation of Christianity to the modern world and of the place of theology in that world are present. In each case we find an inner tension for thinkers who wanted to be Christian and an external tension with a culture that tended more and more to regard theology as not of much importance.

Again in this volume, my goal has been to give a relatively inclusive but concise account of the varieties of thought in their individualities and in their coherence with one another. But I am keenly aware of inadequacies and partialities. In a work that is intended to be useful both to readers with theological sophistication and to nontheologians, many compromises are inescapable. As noted in the preface to volume 1, while I have in each case sought to give a fresh reading of the original sources and to provide a new map of nineteenth-century theology, the final result is a general introduction, designed to encourage the reader to go further. In-depth analysis of many of the significant thinkers who appear here and well-rounded expositions of their entire works have not been possible within the scope of this study. Certain of the longer bibliographic notes have been placed in an appendix.

Further, in spite of the inclusion of a wide variety of types of thought, much selection has been inevitable. It could be said, for example, that neither here nor in volume 1 has Karl Marx received his due, though the impact of Marxism is very much in view in chapter 7 of this volume. Nor have I attempted to assess the role of Friedrich Nietzsche. Both of these figures would have to appear prominently in a more general account of nineteenth-century thought about religion. So would a variety of radically nontraditional new religious movements. But the intent of this volume is not to provide an all-inclusive account of developments in religious thinking, or to present a social history of Christianity in the late nineteenth century. My focus, within the genre of intellectual history, has rather been on what some would call the theological problematic as it developed within the broad stream of Protestantism in the West.

Yet even here it has been necessary to emphasize those thinkers and ideas that seem most important and interesting from the standpoint of the twentieth century while at the same time representing dominant concerns of the late nineteenth century. I trust that the selectivity will not seem arbitrary. Certain obvious omissions may be noted. Since the primary focus is on materials in German and English, not much is said of Protestant theological development in France, Scandinavia, or the Netherlands. Relatively little space has been given to the continuing strains of conservative or orthodox thought, because these lie at the edges of the exciting discussion. Almost nothing is said of the strong tradition, notably in Britain, of idealistic philosophies of religion represented, for example, by F. H. Bradley, B. Bosanquet, J. R. Illingworth, and A. S. Pringle-Pattison, as well as the personalistic philosophy of B. P. Bowne in the United States. Such figures might well have been discussed in either chapter 2 or chapter 7. But it seemed more important to incorporate discussions of the emerging psychology and sociology of religion, and of the history of religions. My chief regret, in this connection, is that no proper place was found for Josiah Royce, who remains the most interesting of the idealistic thinkers. Also omitted is reference to the beginnings of the Lundensian theology, which might have been dealt with either on its own or in connection with Troeltsch's idea of a religious a priori.

Finally, it might have been possible to deal full scale with some of the Roman Catholic modernists, whose concerns and problems were so much akin to those of Protestant liberalism. Indeed, for the last third of the nineteenth century, one could attempt to write a common history of Catholic and Protestant theology. Loisy and von Hügel do appear briefly here. But Tyrrell might have been usefully dealt with in the treatment of faith (chapter 2), and Murri and others

in relation to the social question (chapter 7). Yet finally I decided not
to go in this direction. Discussion of the Catholic modernists is still
highly fluid, and to treat them properly would have required an extensive analysis of the whole situation of Roman Catholicism at the
end of the century, which seemed beyond both my competence and
the feasibility of keeping the present volume within a reasonable
length. For the decisions with respect to inclusion and omission, I am
quite prepared to take responsibility, with the full awareness that
others might make different choices.

It remains only to express my thanks to those who, particularly
over the past decade, have contributed to the completion of this volume. Among the many theological colleagues who have helped me, I
count especially the faculty of the Graduate Theological Union and
my associates in the Nineteenth Century Theology Working Group
of the American Academy of Religion. For assistance in understanding the issues relative to evolution (chapter 6), I am greatly indebted
to a notable historian of science, Arthur Norberg, director of the
Charles Babbage Institute at the University of Minnesota. In practical terms, the writing of this volume was made possible by a John Simon Guggenheim Memorial Foundation Fellowship in 1976, by a
National Endowment for the Humanities Fellowship for Independent Study and Research in 1984, by leaves of absence granted by the
trustees of the Graduate Theological Union (even from presidential
and decanal responsibility), and by the hospitality of Cambridge University, especially Darwin College, in the spring of 1984.

1

Albrecht Ritschl: Faith, History,

and Ethics in Balance

The thought and role of Albrecht Ritschl (1822–89) have been the objects of greatly renewed interest in recent decades. It would be hard to contend that he, like Schleiermacher, was the founder of an epoch. Others of his time were more interesting, and among thinkers deeply influenced by Ritschl some carried on his theological impulses in more productive and decisive ways or at least gave sharper expression to the issues he posed. Yet Ritschl was far more than the mere "episode" to which Karl Barth wanted to reduce him.[1] Ritschl is the thinker with whom one must first reckon in seeking to understand the theological directions and pathos of Protestant thought in the last third of the nineteenth century, and it is appropriate to date the beginning of this period with the publication in 1870 of the first volume of his systematic theology, *Rechtfertigung und Versöhnung* (Justification and reconciliation).

Ritschl's university studies were carried on in the heyday of mediation theology: Nitzsch was his teacher at Bonn, Julius Müller and F. A. Tholuck (the highly influential figure in neopietist revival) at Halle, and Richard Rothe at Heidelberg. He grew up in the atmosphere of the Prussian Union Church, for which the best of Lutheranism was to be represented in Lutheran-Calvinist unity, in opposition to the hard-line Lutheran confessionalists. He also came out of the historical orientation and commitment of the Tübingen school, in particular of F. C. Baur, with whom his early writings were most closely associated. Thus his thought was shaped by all the major directions of German theology in the middle of the century.

What makes Ritschl important is less the power and genius of his theological construction than the representative character of his thought, which in a remarkable way encompassed the dominant

---

1. Barth, *Die protestantische Theologie im 19. Jahrhundert* (Zurich, 1946), p. 598.

1

themes of Protestant theology, especially its liberal side, toward the end of the century. He was the "characteristic" man of the period, the embodiment of the late nineteenth century's effort to hold together personal faith, scientific history, and ethical demand and so to present a view of Christianity intelligible and persuasive to modern culture. In opposition to the attack by his Göttingen orientalist colleague, Paul Lagarde, on Protestantism as a culturally ineffective misbegotten child of medieval Catholicism, Ritschl wanted to reestablish the practical relevance of justification, the center of Protestantism and indeed of all religion. Though opposed to mid-nineteenth-century mediation theology, as well as to the apologetics of orthodoxy, Ritschl was representative of a new kind of mediation, cutting loose from the speculative and metaphysical and turning to the practical and historical as a new foundation and form for theology. His thought articulated the theological mood of a rising generation, which his predecessor at Göttingen, I. A. Dorner, a prince among the mediators, had sadly recognized as emerging even before his own dogmatics could be published.[2]

The significance of Ritschl's work was that it announced changes that were immediately hailed by others, so that by the end of the 1870s Ritschl could justifiably assert that his disciples were to be found on every German theological faculty except Heidelberg.[3] In this sense it may be fairly said that Ritschl provided a new theological impulse and an alternative for his time, and set the tone for Protestant theology in imperial Germany.

The principal works in which Ritschl proclaimed the new directions—and it was through his books more than his teaching that he was influential—were his dogmatic writings of the 1870s, *Justification*

2. See Claude Welch, *Protestant Thought in the Nineteenth Century* (New Haven, 1972), 1:273 (hereafter cited as *Prot. Thought*, 1).

3. The earliest followers included Wilhelm Herrmann, Adolf Harnack, and Adolf Schürer. Others who have been counted in the Ritschlian school were Kaftan at Berlin; Haering (Ritschl's successor) and Schultz at Göttingen; Wendt at Jena; Lobstein at Strassburg; Kattenbusch and Stade at Giessen; Bornemann at Magdeburg; Loofs, Kähler, and Reischle at Halle; Gottschick at Tübingen; and Sell at Bonn. To this list one might later add even Troeltsch (who was a pupil of Ritschl and Lagarde) at Heidelberg. See, e.g., the list of Ritschl's school given by James Orr, *The Ritschlian Theology and the Evangelical Faith* (London, 1897), pp. 27–28. Of course, the extent to which these thinkers constituted a school is debatable. Among British and American thinkers with deep affinities to Ritschl, one may note P. T. Forsyth (in his early thought), A. E. Garvie, H. C. King, W. A. Brown, and W. N. Clarke (though Clarke felt he had arrived at his positions without much German influence).

and Reconciliation (1870–74), Christian Perfection (1874), and Instruction in the Christian Religion (1875), to which one may add Theology and Metaphysics, published in 1881 as a rejoinder to criticism of Justification and Reconciliation.

Yet Ritschl was equally a historian in his career at Bonn (1846–64) and Göttingen (1864–89). It is important that as a student Ritschl began with dogmatics, then moved to church history and New Testament. As a teacher he began with New Testament, then moved to church history and dogmatics. His historical interest was never far from the center, as indicated by the principles of his theological method, by the fact that the first two volumes of Justification and Reconciliation were historical and biblical studies, and by his turning after completion of his dogmatic writings to ten years of work on the history of pietism.[4]

RITSCHL AND HIS OPPONENTS

Ritschl's constructive views may be readily summarized in a few distinguishable but closely related themes: Jesus as the founder of the Church, his revelation of God's will to establish the kingdom, and his own vocation in relation to it; God's objective will for the kingdom as pure gift and man's subjective response to this gift as his own highest good; Christian existence defined by justification and reconciliation (again in a duality of gift and task); the corporate and historical nature of the Christian community; man as "spiritual personality" in contrast to nature; and the Christian religion as a way of living, a style of life expressed in ethical vocation.

The basic thrust and subsequent importance of this theological complex, however, may best be illumined by interpreting those themes in relation to the three most pervasive concerns of Protestant thought in the late nineteenth century: faith, history, and ethics —which Ritschl consciously sought to hold together in a way that he felt the Protestant tradition had failed to do. Ritschl's perspective on these concerns can be seen by looking first at what he wanted to reject, for Ritschl looked upon his work as that of a reformer seeking to recover the true Protestant impulse and to show its power for the world. Further, as Jodock has so nicely put it, "Ritschl's objections to the thinking of others are clearer than the reasons for his own."[5]

4. See pp. 303–04 for fuller bibliographic data and abbreviations.
5. Jodock, "Metaphysics and Theology in Albrecht Ritschl," p. 106.

Even in a theological world long characterized by *Auseinandersetzung*, the extent to which Ritschl developed his positions by negation is striking.

The ideas and ways of thinking that Ritschl most directly opposed can be grouped in four categories: speculative rationalism in all its varieties (or metaphysics as he thought it commonly understood); Schleiermacher's subjectivism; mysticism and pietism; and Protestant orthodoxy, especially Lutheran confessionalism.

Speculative Rationalism

Ritschl wanted to turn his back on mid-nineteenth-century mediation theology and its kind of speculative effort to harmonize Christianity with a universal and rational secular world view. This note was sounded at the beginning of *Justification and Reconciliation*, volume 3, and was taken up again directly in *Theology and Metaphysics*, which he wrote in response to critics (particularly C. E. Luthardt, F. H. R. Frank, and Hermann Weiss). In a narrow sense, turning his back meant combating a Hegelian subordination of theology to philosophy with its insistence that theology must conform to philosophical conception and judgment. But Ritschl had a far broader target in view, namely, what he called an entire false metaphysical approach to theology that had persistently infected Christian thought.

Metaphysics (or "first philosophy"), as defined by Aristotle in a way that dominated philosophy until Kant, "is devoted to an investigation of the universal grounds of all being" (*J&R*, p. 16; *T&M*, p. 154). That is, metaphysics abstracts from the distinction between nature and spirit and considers *all*, natural or spiritual, as *things*, subordinating nature and spiritual knowledge to metaphysical knowledge. It develops a theory of things in general, and then gives the name of God to the highest end of the cosmic series of ends and means. God becomes the expression of the unity of the world.

But, Ritschl asked, what right have we to speak of "God" here? This concept of God has nothing to do with the religious view of God as conscious personality. Metaphysics so understood leads only to the conception of a world unity, or to an idea of the world itself, or to an absolute which is without qualities and unrelated, an empty concept or a contentless thing. Here Ritschl was particularly concerned to oppose the orthodox attempt to adopt the absolute as a religious concept, an absoluteness lying behind love and covenant grace—as, for example, in F. H. R. Frank's description of the absoluteness of being which exists through itself (Durchsichselbstsein), in itself (Insich-selbstsein), and in full possession of itself (Seinselbstsein). God is rather, for Ritschl, to be fundamentally defined as love, love which has the attribute of almightiness, rather than almightiness or self-existence which has the attribute of love (*T&M*, pp. 162–64).[6] Ritschl judged that though Frank may not have had any inkling of it, his idea of God as the absolute implied an element of materialism (see *J&R*, p. 238).

We see here the most serious defect of the proofs for the existence of God. Not only do they fail to give the existence of God outside of thought; what they give is not the being of *God*. To be sure, Ritschl thought the moral argument developed by Kant in the *Critique of Judgment* free of the major defect of the traditional proofs. He even played with the idea of a theoretical proof, starting with "man's self-distinction from nature and his endeavors to maintain himself against it and over it," and concluding that God is the "ground and law of the coexistence of nature and spiritual life" as the necessary completion of a proper theoretical knowledge (*J&R*, pp. 214–26). But his main concern was to root out that vicious conception of God, whether in medieval or Protestant scholasticism (or in rationalism), which portrayed a "limitless being, first cause, and self-conscious end" as the outcome of "scientific" presuppositions and notions—a doctrine of God which has nothing to do with the Christian view of the world.

Metaphysical knowledge errs at the outset by lumping together nature and spirit. More precisely, it is "indifferent toward the distinctions of kind and value that exist between spirit and nature" (*T&M*, p. 157). But for religion, everything depends on the distinction. Just why this distinction is so crucial, Ritschl does not tell us clearly. It seems to have been self-evident to him. We may conjecture that it grew out of his perception of materialist threats to personal existence and freedom. At any rate, he reiterated the point constantly. The religious world view in every form "is established on the principle that the human spirit differentiates itself to some degree in value from the phenomena within its environment and from the workings of nature that press in upon it" (*J&R*, p. 17; repeated in *T&M*, p. 156). Again, "the principle of the Christian estimate of the self [is] that the

6. See, e.g., Frank's discussion of the absoluteness of God in *System der christlichen Wahrheit*, 3d ed. (Erlangen, 1894), 1:116–40.

individual is worth more than the whole world"; and "in religious cognition the idea of God is dependent on the presupposition that man opposes himself to the world of nature, and secures his position, in or over it, by faith in God" (*J&R*, pp. 211, 219).

It is not correct simply to say that Ritschl wanted to expel all metaphysics from theology. As he was careful to explain in *Theology and Metaphysics*, the real question is "which metaphysics?" and especially "which epistemology?" Here Ritschl insisted his opponents had misunderstood him. To have a correct epistemology is of prime importance, and Ritschl judged one to be currently available in the work of his Göttingen colleague Hermann Lotze.[7] The false epistemology of traditional metaphysics erred not only in its neutrality toward the distinction of spirit and nature, but also in its supposition that we can conceive the thing in itself apart from its relation to the observer. This distinction between things in themselves and the perception of them is at the root of the idea of the absolute as a thing without qualities, a God whose true being lies behind his acts and in the primacy of the inactive attributes. But it also appears in ideas of the self at rest apart from its acts; of sin as residing in some general reality behind the concrete active will; of an "objective," preexistent Godhead of Christ apart from his actuality; of the church as an entity apart from its members; and of the Spirit as a reality apart from his activity. Ritschl rejected all of these notions.

"I use a different epistemology." For Ritschl, a proper epistemology sees the reality of a thing in its activity; we know the thing in its act. "A thing 'exists' in its relationships and it is only in them that we can know the thing and only by them that we can name it" (*T&M*, p. 184; see pp. 179–87). God, then, can only be perceived in his actions toward us. With Luther, we can only speak of God *for us*. Ritschl thus associated himself with Luther's attack on the scholastic notion of the being of God, even though Luther was not fully able to carry

---

7. See Lotze, *Mikrokosmus*, 3 vols. (Leipzig, 1856–64; Eng. trans., 2 vols., Edinburgh, 1885), and *Metaphysik* (Leipzig, 1841; 2d ed., 1879; Eng. trans., 2 vols., Oxford, 1887). Lotze was also of much importance for the American philosopher of religion, Borden Parker Bowne, and the subsequent personalist tradition that centered in Boston.

Ritschl had little interest in philosophy as such. The only philosophical work he wrote was *Theology and Metaphysics*, and that was composed hastily. Like Luther, to whom he looked so much, Ritschl was primarily interested in practical religious life in church and society. Lotze had welcomed Ritschl to Göttingen, and he became his friend and philosophical mentor. Lotze's view that we know things in their relationships was particularly attractive from the standpoint of Luther's insistence that we know God only in his relation to us.

through his intention to reject scholastic methodology. A fall back into the traditional metaphysic and epistemology occurred between the first and second editions of Melanchthon's *Loci*, setting Protestant orthodoxy on the same wrong road that medieval scholasticism had taken.[8]

God is in fact known only in his revelation; in those actions toward us that correspond to his public revelation God's presence is perceived. Thus every attempt at natural theology is wrong, and even Schleiermacher finally failed at this point. Ritschl said he knew only one theologian who had broken with this whole tradition: Gottfried Menken (1768–1831). To reject natural religion means at the same time to reject "all universal concepts which one might possess prior to the particular structures of revealed religion or apart from the actuality of those structures in the founder and in the community" (*T&M*, pp. 209–10).

In the critique of metaphysics and false epistemology, we have the background for Ritschl's distinctive assertion that religious knowledge consists in value judgments (Werturteilen) or, more properly, independent value judgments. Here lies the distinction of religious from theoretical or philosophical knowledge and the protection against the collision of science and religion. Ritschl's definition of independent value judgment is tortuous, particularly in the relation of religious to other independent value judgments. But the main points are clear. The contrast with scientific judgments is not to be found in the notion that the latter are disinterested. All observation and connected knowledge of the world are interested and have value to the knower, or else they would not be pursued. But in technical observation and theoretical cognition the value judgments are necessary and operative simply as concomitant, and they are without moral effects. In religion, however, we have to do with a class of independent value judgments related to the independent value judgments that are perceptions of moral ends and effects. Here the question of worth for us is determinative rather than incidental to the nature of the judgment. Luther's insight was correct: "We know the nature of God and Christ only in their worth for us. For God and faith are inseparable conceptions" (*J&R*, p. 212; see pp. 203–211).

So far, the meaning of "value judgment" is not far from that of

8. David Lotz, *Ritschl and Luther*, is especially valuable in tracing the importance of Luther for Ritschl's thought.

"personal conviction" or "existential truth." Indeed, Ritschl's term is his way of affirming the decisive and pervasive characteristic of nineteenth-century theology, namely, a new recognition of the active involvement of the self in any genuine religious knowing.[9]

But for Ritschl there was the further essential determinant, the value of man over nature. "Knowledge of God can be demonstrated as religious knowledge only when He is conceived as securing to the believer such a position in the world as more than counterbalances its restrictions" (*J&R*, p. 212). The value in religious value judgment was for Ritschl always worth for man understood in the contrast of spirit and nature. He could say, "in every religion what is sought, with the help of the superhuman spiritual power reverenced by man, is a solution of the contradiction in which man finds himself as both a part of nature and a spiritual personality claiming to dominate nature" (*J&R*, p. 199). And he came very close to a utilitarian kind of assertion that religion is the instrument by which man can free himself from bondage to the natural conditions of life.

We shall defer to later discussion a fuller account of what Ritschl meant by the lordship over nature that Christianity brings. What is important to note here is the overwhelmingly practical character of religion as Ritschl viewed it—practical both in the sense of the practical reason in contrast to the theoretical or speculative reason and in the sense of the concrete and practical nature of human religious existence (as expressed in reconciliation and in direction of life to the highest good, the kingdom of God). Here too was the new sort of apologetic that Ritschl embodied, one not oriented to speculative or theoretical wisdom about the unity of the world but directed to Christianity's superiority in answering the practical questions that all religions ask and in its relevance to culture and society.

Schleiermacher's Subjectivism

Ritschl also found it important to define his position vis-à-vis Schleiermacher.[10] The opposition should not be overemphasized, for Ritschl was deeply indebted to Schleiermacher in many ways: in the aim of developing theology systematically around a central theme; in the insistence on the historical as well as the corporate nature of reli-

---

9. See *Prot. Thought*, 1:59–61.

10. See the discussion of Schleiermacher in chap. 9 of *R.u.V.*, 1, and his essay, *Schleiermachers Reden über die Religion und ihre Nachwirkungen auf die evangelische Kirche Deutschlands* (Bonn, 1874).

gion; in the emphasis on the function of the church; and in a real christocentrism. At the outset of volume 3 of *Justification and Reconciliation*, Ritschl expressed high appreciation for Schleiermacher's effort to identify the distinctive character of the Christian religion as "a monotheistic faith, belonging to the teleological type of religion, and essentially distinguished from other such faiths by the fact that everything in it is related to the redemption accomplished in Jesus of Nazareth" (Schleiermacher, *The Christian Faith*, §11; see *J&R*, pp. 8–9). But, Ritschl thought, Schleiermacher subsequently forgot about the teleological element and did not properly attend to the mutual relations of the mediator and the kingdom of God as the final end for God and man.

At least two kinds of antithesis to Schleiermacher can be recognized here. One, already implicit in the preceding discussion, may be described as a radical shift in emphasis from dependence to freedom. Schleiermacher spoke of utter dependence on God, distinctively qualified by the Christian experience of sin and redemption, in which human existence is in an essentially comfortable relation to a world of nature that is also utterly dependent. In Ritschl, however, the religious question has become a question of freedom vis-à-vis nature. One calls on the supernatural power to maintain oneself and provide freedom over the world. Value for the self is found in maintaining ethical existence as free self-determined person, and whatever has this value has the value of God. Thus from an outlook in which man is harmonious with nature (in Schleiermacher, as also in the Romantics generally), we move with Ritschl into a world of hostility between man and nature, or at least one in which nature is a threat to man. For Ritschl, this was plainly the threat of a scientific world view which had no special place for human freedom and dignity but swallowed the uniquely human in a universal chain of cause and effect. The problem for Ritschl was not posed particularly (if at all) by a Darwinian scientific view, but by a much more general scientific materialism—and it should be remembered that in Ritschl's day the University of Göttingen was best known as a center for the natural sciences. It was the impersonal world of mechanical causal law that generated the tension of knowing oneself to be a part of the world yet also struggling to be a free personality in God's image, and thus superior to the world (see *J&R*, pp. 209–10). So again, in contrast to Schleiermacher, there is the shift in emphasis from the utter divine causality, expressed in creation and redemption alike, to the intrinsic value of the individual. Christianity is the highest religion just because it prizes personal life above the whole world of nature.

The other major area of Ritschl's conflict with Schleiermacher, and with many of those influenced by him, was the question of the foundation and starting point for theology. In Schleiermacher, the basis was in the innermost realm of human existence, the immediate existence-relationship, which he designated by the term *Gefühl* (feeling). Doctrines were in the first instance descriptions of the religious affections. To Ritschl, this was subjectivism, even romantic sentimentalism, obscure and uncertain. To interpret religion as a feeling of utter dependence, as something lying beneath the realms of knowing and willing, is to perpetuate a false neutrality toward the distinction of spirit and nature. It represents an esthetic rather than an ethical view; it diminishes the moral feature of the community of believers and precludes a true appreciation of mercy and pardon. Our point of departure must recognize the valuing character of religious judgments, the centrality of the moral and the will. Further, in seeking to define the essentially Christian, we start not with the Christian soul in its present subjective feeling states, but with historical fact, with the givenness of revelation in Jesus Christ as set forth in the New Testament, and with the social dimension of religion. In the last point, Ritschl was particularly concerned to rebut Feuerbach's psychological explanation of religion, but the argument applied also to Schleiermacher.[11]

Mysticism and Pietism

The fundamental defect of mysticism, for Ritschl, was very like that of the metaphysics he wanted to reject. "Indeed, there is such a close relationship between mysticism and *this kind* of metaphysics that it is immaterial whether one counts certain affirmations as mysticism or as false metaphysics." In the original and classic sense of mysticism, its yearning for union with God, we find again the drive to go beyond the concrete, moral character of the spiritual life. That kind of striving can be conceptualized only in a Neoplatonic scheme that abandons the particular and the determinate in favor of universal being. In this dissolution of the concrete character of the spiritual life, "the universal being into which the mystic wants to melt" is *not*

11. See Francis S. Fiorenza, "The Response of Barth and Ritschl to Feuerbach," *Studies in Religion*, 7:2 (1978): 155–62.

the God of Christian faith (*T&M*, pp. 173–74). The Christian mystic, qua mystic, is no different from any other mystic; he is not distinctively Christian at all. Mysticism wants to dispense with a mediator and with history; it overleaps the will of God and man; it makes Christianity only a tool to something beyond itself. Mysticism must therefore be fundamentally rejected, from the standpoint of a reconciliation which involves an active realization of the ideal of life, an ethical commitment to the kingdom of God, and the acknowledgment that in the moral sphere we are children of God.

Similarly, that favorite of the Lutheran dogmaticians, the *unio mystica*, in which the faithful are united with the Father and the Son in actual being and not only in will and disposition, recapitulates the metaphysical mistake of locating an essentially indescribable and unexperienceable self behind the historical concreteness of activity and perception. So, too, in the development of pietism Ritschl saw a relapse into a monastic ideal of life, whose world-denying character is of one piece with mysticism's escape from the world.

Orthodoxy

Finally, Ritschl was constantly in conflict with the "orthodox," especially Lutheran, dogmaticians of his day. In fact, the great bulk of his polemic was directed to them, for their adoption of a false metaphysics vitiated the conceptions of God, of Christ, of the self, of sin, of reconciliation, and of the church. But equally important, and closely related, was the domination of their thinking—especially about the relation of God and man, about divine justice, punishment, atonement, and so forth—by *legal* categories, that is, by categories drawn from the pattern of civil law. They attempted, for example, to come to the doctrine of forgiveness through the idea of God as lawgiver and judge, understood by the application of criteria taken from public law. But such efforts are fraught with contradictions, and they deform Christian concepts because legal concepts are inherently narrower than concepts of moral fellowship.

The rejection of the legal was a matter of prime importance for Ritschl, since justification and reconciliation were the organizing themes of his statement of Christian doctrine. He never ceased to inveigh against the damage done by the dominant legal conceptuality, which seemed to him simply to remove the possibility of reconciliation of man to God. In the narrower sense, Ritschl was here entering into the heart of the Lutheran dogmatic development, and he had

the temerity to call Luther to his side against the Lutherans—which
helps to account for the hostility of his Lutheran opponents. Ritschl
was indeed the first, so Lotz contends, to pursue a genetic method in
Luther research in a satisfactory way, distinguishing the early from
the late Luther, and Luther from Melanchthon—in contrast, for example, to his contemporary Theodosius Harnack, who still treated
Luther's writings as a homogeneous whole. Thus Ritschl paved the
way for the new Luther research of his pupil Karl Holl in the early
twentieth century.

At the same time, Ritschl represented a much broader late-nineteenth-century move to reemphasize personal language in the interpretation of the God-man relation. In the specific reconstruction of
the Reformation idea of grace and atonement, Ritschl's shift from
the language of forensic externality to the categories of ethical inwardness had been anticipated in important ways by the Scottish
thinker John McLeod Campbell and by the American Horace Bushnell, and he was to be followed by many (for example, Walter
Moberley). What was further signaled here, as in several of Ritschl's
themes, was the pervasive sense of threat in the late nineteenth century both to the personal conception of God and to the integrity and
value of human personality. This was to lead shortly to widespread
talk about the sacredness or infinite value of human personality and
later to the popularity of "I-Thou" and "divine-human encounter"
language.

HISTORICAL THINKING AND THE ESSENCE OF CHRISTIANITY

An argument could be made for beginning the interpretation of
Ritschl's positive themes with the ethical concern expressed in his
emphasis on the kingdom of God. The kingdom of God was his first
major topic in the concentrated summary of Christian doctrine, *Instruction in the Christian Religion*, which he wrote as a lay-oriented text
for use in religion courses in the high schools.[12]

But when we look at Ritschl's procedure as a scientific theologian
and at his deepest commitments in theological method, it is the emphasis on history that makes first claim on us. Once Ritschl moved
into historical studies he never left them. He came into prominence
in debate with F. C. Baur over the development of early Christianity,

---

12. The work unfortunately proved too difficult and was little used for this purpose.
Ritschl deliberately took for the title of the work the German translation of Calvin's *Institutes of the Christian Religion* as a way of expressing the seriousness of his purpose.

and most of his major works were historical studies. He was the representative of a new historical preoccupation and served as a powerful impetus to the work of such diverse historians as Adolf Harnack (in the history of dogma), Karl Holl (in Luther research), and Ernst Troeltsch (in the history of Christian social ethics). When he wrote his own systematic theology, *Justification and Reconciliation*, the first volume was a history of the doctrine and the second an analysis of the biblical material.

For Ritschl, the essential character of Christianity can be determined only by historical study; therefore constructive theology can only grow out of historical insight. Theology does not find its basis in immediate religious experience, as it did for Schleiermacher, and after him Thomasius, Hofmann, and Lipsius. Authentic knowledge of the Christian religion and revelation can only be gained by going back to the origins, to the sources close to the epoch of the founding of the Church (see, for example, *R.u.V.*, 2:7–13). There the essential content can best be understood in what was called into existence by Jesus as the founder of the Church and maintained by the Apostles as its earliest representatives. "Back to the New Testament by way of the Reformation"—and the Reformation itself called for a return to the New Testament. Once the authentic expression of the ideas of the forgiveness of sins, of justification and reconciliation, is exposed in the origins of the Christian community, the essence and norm for all later statements have been found.

This implied, for Ritschl, a radical christocentrism. "In Christianity, revelation through God's Son is the *punctum stans* of all knowledge and religious conduct" (*J&R*, p. 202). That claim is made against all other claims to religious knowledge, whether in natural theology or in half-truths fulfilled by Christianity in such a way that general religious categories are determinative for the nature of Christianity. All assertions about the lordship of Christ are to be grounded in his historical life (*J&R*, p. 406) and in his own self-end and sonship to God, that is, in his ethical vocation—his obedience and fidelity, his perfectly fulfilling the calling laid on him as the founder of the universal ethical fellowship of mankind, his bearing of moral lordship, his finding of his end in God's end; and in his religious existence—his perfect trust in God, his unique sonship and consciousness of it as one known and loved by God as the personal vehicle of God's self-revelation.

Ritschl cannot be charged with seeking a historical Jesus who can be apprehended independently of the standpoint of the redeemed community. His was thoroughly a *church* theology and *theological* history. The theologian speaks only as a member of the religious community; theology is that community's critical self-knowledge. Everything that is said about the originating event is from the standpoint of the community. There is to be no separation of Jesus from the church, or of the gospels from the epistles. "For even if His statements might seem perfectly clear, their significance becomes completely intelligible only when we see how they are reflected in the consciousness of those who believe in Him, and how the members of the Christian community trace back their consciousness of pardon to the Person and the action and passion of Jesus." We would have no interest in Jesus' purposes apart from our membership in the community. Authentic and complete knowledge of his religious significance is given only from within the community. The historical estimate of Christ, which includes judgment of worth, does not mean divesting oneself of faith: "We can discover the full compass of His historical actuality solely from the faith of the Christian community. Not even His purpose to found the community can be quite understood historically save by one who, as a member of it, subordinates himself to His person." Indeed, the material for the doctrines of forgiveness, justification, and reconciliation is less directly to be found in the words of Christ than in the correlative expressions of the consciousness of the community (*J&R*, pp. 1, 3).

In this view of the historical grounding of Christian assertions, both the truth and the error of Schleiermacher's conception, on Ritschl's terms, become apparent. Schleiermacher was not altogether wrong in stressing the present religious self-consciousness. He did not ignore the historical figure, the indispensable Whence of the new divinely effected common life of the Christian community, nor did he make of Christ simply a backward reference of a present experience. Rather, the present religious consciousness was for him actually bound to and dependent on the event of Christ in history. But Schleiermacher took only a half-step, arriving at the figure of Jesus in a way that bypassed the considerations of historical criticism. He lacked true historical sense (see *R.u.V.*, 2:4; *Prot. Thought*, 1:82–84). Ritschl wanted to take a whole step so that the historical knowledge of Jesus in his earthly life, his sayings and his passion, and their impact on the primitive community should genuinely become the norm for Christian interpretation. In his view of redemption through

Christ, Schleiermacher had also disastrously neglected the ethical character of the kingdom of God. For Ritschl, however, the ethical as much as the redemptive was historically grounded in Jesus and in the consciousness of the original Christian community. The apostolic norm included both (equally and inseparably) religious dependence on God's grace and ethical orientation toward the kingdom of God.

Ritschl's historical work was also directed extensively to identifying what was distinctive of Reformation Christianity, that is, the Reformation of Luther, Zwingli, and Calvin, in contrast on the one hand to Latin Catholicism and on the other hand to Anabaptism or the radical Reformation.[13] At this point, Ritschl was speaking in part to the continuing nineteenth-century debate over the "formal" and "material" principles of the Reformation, which in turn was a form of the post-Reformation attempt to show continuity between the ancient church and the Reformation while distinguishing Protestant from Roman Catholic understandings. At the same time, he was able to emphasize the dimension of the ethical in the apostolic norm.

Ritschl found the usual formula of the two principles of little value in explaining the distinctiveness of the Reformation view. The formal principle of the sole authority of scripture was not decisively new. It had been significantly anticipated by Duns Scotus and the Franciscans and did not even become a special principle for Luther and his associates until their conflict with the Dominicans and the Thomists and the decisions of the Council of Trent. The material principle of justification through faith might have a better claim to distinctiveness, but Luther's assertion of justification through faith is not in itself a genuine principle of doctrine, apart from relation to other dimensions of the new understanding.

If the Reformation of Luther, Zwingli, and Calvin is more than the emergence of a new theological school, it must be viewed as having "set in motion a new phase of the Christian style of life [Lebensführung]," for that is what truly made the Reformation a new epoch in Christianity. It was distinguished from medieval Latin Christianity by its ideal of the Christian life (Ideal des christlichen Lebens), by the governing norm or image for its style of life (Lebensideal).[14] Protestantism has produced a standard of qualitative perfection which con-

13. The lines of his argument are well set forth in the "Prolegomena" to the *History of Pietism.*

14. Ibid, pp. 84–85. Ritschl's terms here may be related to Ullmann's *Lebensordnung* and to Dorner's *Lebensverhältnis.*

trasts with the dominant monastic Catholic view. As was made clear
in the Augsburg Confession, "perfection consists of fear and trust in
God through all the conditions of life; this is more fully expressed as
fear, trust in God's merciful providence, prayer, and the conscien-
tious carrying out of one's vocation." Now the decisive note in this,
which gives justification by faith its practical significance, is that
"Christians have to strive after their perfection precisely in the midst
of their regular intercourse with the world and in their vocations
within the domain of the secular society" (Prolegomena, p. 86).
Christian life is truly lived in the realm of civil society. On this point,
whatever their other divergences, Luther, Zwingli, and Calvin held a
common view.

Here is the real antithesis to Catholic Christianity, for which monasticism embodied the true and perfect Christian life. For medieval
Christianity, as in the Cluniac reform and the founding of the Franciscans, reformation was essentially only reform of monasticism,
which maintained and even intensified the ideal of renunciation of
the world (Prolegomena, pp. 60–68). The same contrast is drawn
with mysticism, which is a more pronounced phase of Catholic piety;
it teaches "escape from the world and renunciation of the world, and
it places the significance of the ethically good action and the formation of virtues far beneath ecstatic union with God" (p. 76).

But the contrast is not only with Catholic piety; it is also with Ana-
baptist reform and with pietism. Far from being a consistent
extension of the principles of the classical Reformers, said Ritschl,
the Anabaptists' ideas stood in continuity with the ascetic and mystical theology of medieval Catholicism. Their impetus for reform was
only a facade, not a more thorough reformation than that of Luther
and Zwingli but a kind of reform diametrically opposed. Similarly,
pietism, while ostensibly an attempt to counter Protestant theological
sterility and rationalism by a return to the impulse of the Reformers,
was in fact a restoration "of the thrust of the anabaptists within the
sphere of Lutheran and Reformed churches" (p. 105).

We can understand why Ritschl was willing to spend ten years on
his history of pietism and why he was so sharp in criticism. In view
not only of the role of pietism in earlier Protestantism, but also of the
neopietist revivals of the nineteenth century, it was of special importance to affirm the pietists' concern for devotion and a definite style
of life, yet to demonstrate in detail, from their own history, how

wrong the contemporary pietists were. As Hefner puts it, Ritschl rested the case "in the New Testament and in Luther, thus stealing the thunder of the pietists with one hand and attempting to eradicate them with the other."[15]

In the category of *Lebensführung* (or *Lebensideal*) Ritschl found a fundamental tool for interpreting the whole of Christianity in its development, in its continuities and discontinuities. In the second edition (1857) of *Die Entstehung der altkatholischen Kirche*, this category appeared as Ritschl's way of distinguishing his view of the movement from apostolic to Catholic Christianity from the view of F. C. Baur. For Baur—though to him also reconciliation was the central Christian theme—the process of development was the logical or dialectical movement of *Geist* or *Idee*, in which the identity or continuity of the community was located. But for Ritschl the focus was on a religious-ethical style of life. Lebensführung was a category for comparing the shape of the Christian consciousness of reconciliation in one period with its shape in another era. There is an underlying continuity in the power of reconciliation, but expressions of the new life vary. The norm is the consciousness and life-style of the apostolic community, whose relationship to Jesus was the model for the relation of all Christians to the Founder. From this norm the deviation of Catholic Christianity from the religious-ethical consciousness and life of the primitive community can be historically comprehended. Thus, for Ritschl, the concept of Lebensideal became both a tool for historical analysis and a framework for a systematic articulation of the normative expression of reconciliation, as found in the earliest Christian community and recovered in the Reformation.

ETHICS AND THE KINGDOM OF GOD

In the norm that Ritschl so confidently grounded in the history of Jesus Christ and the apostolic community, he saw a fundamental duality of religious faith and ethics. This was aptly expressed in a characteristic image (though Ritschl did not actually use it much) of Christianity as an ellipse determined by two foci: justification/reconciliation and the kingdom of God, or faith and love, or the religious and the ethical (*J&R*, p. 11). In each of these foci we find

15. Hefner, introduction to *Three Essays*, p. 32.

other persistent dualities for Ritschl's thought—not only the duality
of God's gift and man's response, but especially the dual bases of theology: in Jesus Christ as the Founder and in modern man's cultural
problem of the will to mastery over nature.

While Ritschl used justification and reconciliation as his master ru-
bric and developed this theme at length historically, biblically, and
systematically, he particularly wanted to emphasize the ethical focus.
Christianity is distinctively a moral religion of redemption through
Christ, and that moral focus can be maintained through a proper appreciation of the idea of the kingdom of God. This had not been
rightly done in Catholic Christianity, where the church was identified with the kingdom of God in the present. Nor did the Reformers
purify the idea of the kingdom as moral, but conceived it essentially
as an "inward union of Christ and believers through grace and its operations." Immanuel Kant was "the first to perceive the supreme importance for ethics of the 'Kingdom of God' as an association of men
bound together by laws of virtue" (*J&R*, p. 11; see *R.u.V.*, I, 2d ed.,
pp. 429–59). Schleiermacher first identified the teleological character of the kingdom as decisive for Christianity. For this we should be
grateful. Yet the significance of this discovery of the ethical had not
been fully exploited. That was the task which Ritschl set himself.

Because for Jesus the moral end of the religious fellowship he
founded was given in the kingdom of God, and because this meant
"the organization of humanity through action inspired by love," the
"religious" in Christianity must be perfectly balanced by the "ethical." So Ritschl defined Christianity as "the monotheistic, completely
spiritual and ethical religion, which, based on the life of its Author as
Redeemer and as Founder of the Kingdom of God, consists in the
freedom of the children of God, involves the impulse to conduct
from the motive of love, aims at the moral organization of mankind,
and grounds blessedness on the relation of sonship to God, as well as
on the Kingdom of God" (*J&R*, p. 13).

It would be a mistake, of course, to suppose that Ritschl conceived
the religious and the ethical to be independent of each other. Christianity cannot be reduced to one focus or the other, because the two,
although distinguishable, are related and inseparable. The religious
and the ethical, we might say in Coleridgean (not Ritschlian) terms,
constitute a real polarity, in which each pole calls forth and leads to
the other. Thus the kingdom of God is itself both a religious and an

ethical conception: it is a directly religious conception as an expression of the sovereignty of God, the summum bonum which God realizes in persons, and it is an ethical common task, a demand for moral action. Similarly, the religious life of the believer is doubly qualified: by justification, forgiveness, trust in God, freedom over the world, and by moral action.

These poles are distinct and not to be confused. Morally good action is not the direct aim of justification. In the idea of justification the religious function takes precedence over the moral. Even though the course of moral action is made possible by justification and reconciliation, the moral impulse is not exhausted by the religious experience. Morally good action is necessary because Christianity has the supramundane kingdom of God as its ultimate purpose. Because they did not recognize this, Luther and the Reformers generally failed to solve the problem of good works; they never seriously grasped the idea of the kingdom of God as the universal ground of moral conduct (see *J&R*, pp. 535, 511–12).

Yet the duality of the religious and the ethical is a duality in unity. In subjective experience, the religious and the ethical are inseparable, balanced and interacting. We have blessedness in the experience that all things serve for our good and blessedness in doing good. There is not only freedom from natural causes but also freedom for the final end. Thus the religious embraces the moral. Conversely, conduct animated by universal love constitutes religious freedom over the world.

It would not be fair, therefore, to accuse Ritschl of reducing the religious to the ethical. But at every point the religious had to be interpreted in relation to the ethical, and by moral categories of a distinctive sort. The centrality of the idea of the kingdom of God was Ritschl's way of emphasizing the judgment that Christianity is "the specifically moral religion" (*J&R*, p. 527). As we have already noted, when Ritschl set out to give a semipopular summary of the Christian religion he began with the doctrine of the kingdom, and in subsequent editions of *Instruction* the characterization of the kingdom as an ethical idea became even more pronounced. As the summum bonum, the kingdom of God is the final aim of both God and reconciled man. It is revealed as God's own aim, the purpose which the whole universe is designed to serve. It is both supernatural and supramundane, insofar as it transcends both the ethical forms of soci-

ety and naturally conditioned existence.[16] It is a final aim, a supreme good, a supernatural rather than a natural unity of the
human race. Since the motive of love which inspires actions is not
completely open to empirical observation, the presence of the kingdom is always "invisible and a matter of religious faith" and not identical with the institutional church (see *Instruction*, §9; *J&R*, pp.
284–290). Yet the kingdom is divinely ordained as the highest good
of the community founded in Christ, and it is this highest good "only
in the sense that it forms at the same time the ethical ideal for whose
attainment the members of the community bind themselves to each
other through a definite type of reciprocal action" (*Instruction*, §5).
In Christ the kingdom is disclosed and offered as a task for moral actualization in the world. The meaning of the kingdom becomes clear
in the imperative.

In Ritschl's characterization of the content of this imperative, the
echoes of Kant's "kingdom of ends" were strong. The task is one of
"moral unification of the human race, through action prompted by
universal love to our neighbor." It is the achievement of a unity
"through mutual and social action prompted by love" and not limited
by the natural characteristics of family, class, or nation. It consists in
achieving independent moral personality, in which spirit dominates
over nature. It is the creation of a kingdom of mutual services, a "fellowship of moral disposition and moral blessings which extends,
through all possible gradations, to the limits of the human race"
(*J&R*, pp. 281–85).

Ritschl found the idea of the kingdom of God historically
grounded in the person of Jesus. As God's final end, the kingdom is
the end Jesus came to announce and for which he founded the community. But that means, in Ritschl's language, that it was his own self-
end, "his consciously pursued personal end," whose special content
can be adequately explained only through the idea of ethical vocation. The work of Christ, ethically apprehended, is to be viewed not
under the (legal) categories of merit and satisfaction but in terms of
his obedience and fidelity, his perfectly fulfilling the vocation laid on
him as the founder of the kingdom. As the idea of ethical vocation
generally refers to that special sphere within which a person is called
to fulfill the universal moral law, that is, as one's own ethical self-end

16. See *Instruction*, §§5–10 and *J&R*, pp. 281–96, where the kingdom is treated as
part of the doctrine of God.

and the end of society, so "the business of [Christ's] vocation was the establishment of the universal ethical fellowship of mankind." This is the vocation of the kingly prophet, the highest conceivable vocation, aiming "directly at the ethical as a whole," and thus a special vocation for which he alone was qualified (*J&R*, pp. 443–49; *Instruction*, §§21–22).

Just such an ethical apprehension of Jesus leads to and is completed by the appropriate religious estimate. His moral loyalty to his vocation was based in his perfect trust in God, his unique sonship and consciousness of being known and loved by God as the personal vehicle of God's self-revelation, whereby he was God's word. What he was, he was first of all for himself. But precisely in being that, he is for us. He realizes the end for others. He is the perfect revelation of God, in whom God is revealed as love, and he is the prototype for imitation and the source of strength, the archetype of moral personality through whose impulse and direction we are able to enter his relation to God and the world, to acquire spiritual lordship, and to adopt as our supreme purpose the kingdom of God. Because of this, we apprehend that Jesus has the value of the divine for us. Personal faith is a value judgment, not merely belief in the truth of his history nor a theoretical judgment regarding his Godhead, but faith in his divine worth. Because he does for us what only God can do, he has the worth of God for us.

A properly ethical apprehension of Christ and his vocation to establish the kingdom thus led, for Ritschl, to major recasting of the traditional doctrines of Christ's person and work. The ideas of his justifying and reconciling work must be translated from legal categories into concepts appropriate to moral fellowship. The kingly or royal office, rather than the prophetic or the priestly, becomes dominant among these traditional ways of describing Christ's redeeming work (the so-called *munus triplex*). In particular, the Godhead of Christ is understood as his being the perfect revealer of God and the manifest archetype of spiritual lordship over the world. Here Ritschl's view may be set in double contrast to the scholastic views. First, the deity of Christ is not an objective doctrine, but an estimate of Christ as God for us, a trusting in him and valuing him for our salvation, and thus a doctrine in which person and work merge. Second, Ritschl attempted to move beyond the classical two-natures conception, which was always weak at the point of the relation of divinity and humanity. That concept was weak because it sought to locate the divine behind or above the historical form, whereas the divine is actually to be apprehended precisely *in* the historical form.

In the last point, Ritschl shared in the broad nineteenth-century movement toward a Christology *von unten nach oben.* He intensified the movement by the insistence that the criteria for all affirmations about Christ's person and work must come from his historical life. Otherwise we fall back into the fundamental defect of the false metaphysics which posits true being apart from its acts and relations. "The Godhead or universal lordship of Christ must be apprehended in definite features of His historical life, as an attribute of His existence in time." Otherwise, any conception of his present lordship is either meaningless or a flight of the imagination. The religious estimate of Christ must be verified in the connection between Christ's visible conduct and his religious convictions and ethical motives (*J&R*, pp. 406, 412f.). So understood, the divinity of Christ is expressed in his perfect love, which expresses the essential will of God as love; in the identity of his supreme aim with that of the Father; in his power over the world; in his patience under suffering as the real test of power over the world; and in his death in obedience to his vocation. In such ways, Jesus the man is seen as the bearer of God's ethical lordship. His whole activity forms the material of the complete revelation of God. Thus in him "the Word of God is a human person" (*J&R*, p. 451).

From the recognition of the kingdom as God's end for mankind and as Jesus' self-end, we are led to the moral action of the Christian in his vocation in the world. At this point Ritschl most clearly emerges as a theologian of culture, one who has often been accused of *Kulturprotestantismus,* indeed of the baptizing of bourgeois Prussian society. His starting point appears to be not only the New Testament witness to Jesus Christ but also a modern (and Kantian) understanding of man's ethical problem. His thinking can be viewed, as in H. R. Niebuhr's classic typology, as representing a "Christ of Culture."[17] To be sure, he does not simply identify Christ and modern culture, but (unlike Kant) seeks to hold firmly to the Christ of the New Testament and to affirm those elements of culture most in accord with Christ. Yet his understanding of humanity's vocation for the kingdom, and of the kingdom as such, is one in which the demands of Christ and of cultural values are not in conflict but in har-

17. Niebuhr, *Christ and Culture* (New York, 1951), pp. 94–100.

mony. Here he stands in contrast not only to Kierkegaard, but also to F. D. Maurice and (later) Walter Rauschenbusch and the social gospel.

Two elements can be distinguished in this harmonization. The first is the understanding of the ethical task as the achievement of independent (free) moral personality in the face of the indifference of the external natural world. This, as we have seen, is a basic principle in Ritschl's view of religion. What the religious relation to God in justification and reconciliation makes possible is a new relation and attitude to the world. That new relation is an essential ingredient in the development and maintenance of personal moral life as an end in itself. It is the attainment of personal wholeness by one who is only a tiny fraction of nature, but who as a spiritual individual is worth more than the whole of nature and "is no longer regarded as a part of the world, but as in himself a totality which can stand being compared with the world" (*J&R*, p. 502). Christianity is distinct in satisfying the universal religious impulse just because it offers this personal wholeness, and with it the idea of the moral world as a totality—for the idea of the world as a whole is a religious idea, not experienced or observed but known only in faith and trust in providence.

Second, however, the Christian moral vocation is directed to attaining the goal of a society of free moral persons in the naturally conditioned moral communities—marriage, family, civic and social life, the nation—"and according to the specific principles that govern each" (*Instruction*, §56). We recall Ritschl's idea of the distinctive nature of the classical Reformers' Lebensideal, in contrast to monasticism, Anabaptism, and pietism. The Christian's calling is exercised in a particular place and relation to the world, not in separation from it. Ritschl had no great sense of potential conflict between the universal end of the kingdom and the regular claims of activity within these narrower, naturally conditioned communities. The ethical imperative of the kingdom is universal, and the specific motive of the Christian's conduct is love for the neighbor. But the universal is realized only in the particular, and when the "regular activity incumbent upon each one in these communities is exercised in the form of an ethical vocation for the common good," our conduct is appropriately subordinated to the universal end of the kingdom (*Instruction*, §57; see *J&R*, pp. 666–69).

Ritschl's perception of the true Lebensideal thus led to no hint of conflict with the developed social structures. The human race has been educatively prepared for the influence of the idea of the kingdom of God through the development of the moral fellowship of the family, the national fellowship of the state, and even the combination of nations in world-empire (see *J&R*, pp. 309–12). For the contemporary Christian, the particular legal constitution of a state is indifferent—"yet the state is acknowledged as God's ordering, and obedience to judicial authority is prescribed as a religious duty. This is because the community of laws, being a necessary means for securing ethical freedom, is also the indispensable condition for the Christian, if he is to fulfill the imperative of the kingdom of God in all the spheres of ethical interaction" (*Instruction*, §61).

In Ritschl's own life, this sense of harmony was evident. He grew up among the cultural, ecclesiastical, and political elite of Berlin. For only a brief period (1848–49) was he an active participant in political life, supporting a movement for constitutional democracy. But after the defeat of his party in 1849 he withdrew completely from secular politics, defining his vocation more and more as that of an academic theologian (and active for university reform). We know that in the 1850s he was active in the Innere Mission, and in his 1874 essay on Schleiermacher's *Speeches* he expressed concern for the alienation of the working class. But he was constitutionally middle-class and was a supporter of Bismarck's policies as genuinely progressive, especially in contrast to the aristocratic conservatives and the social revolutionists. He was not simply uncritical of the Prussian political-social-economic system, but accepted it as the best under the circumstances, as the given within which the possibility of genuine Christian personhood might be achieved. Thus it was within this structure that Ritschl defined the religious and moral imperative. That the idea of the kingdom of God as a goal for human action might call for far greater social justice and democratization of society was a notion that appeared only after Ritschl, as others sought to develop his insistence on the ethical character of true religion (see chapter 7, below).

Within the structures of one's ethical vocation Ritschl conceived of the possibility of Christian perfection (see *Instruction*, §§47, 48, 50, 70; *J&R*, p. 647; *Die christliche Vollkommenheit*). This did not mean for him the elimination of all imperfection in dutiful actions (and in the later editions of the *Instruction* Ritschl was more cautious about the possibility than in the first). The possibility of perfection meant rather a genuine imperative to strive for the kingdom and its righteousness and for freedom over the world, and a process of fostering one's ethical vocation, a development of religious and ethical character in moral fellowship whereby moral action, however limited, is a whole. At this point Ritschl's conception of perfection could be combined paradoxically with two different sorts of late-nineteenth-century optimism about social progress: either with his own conservative satisfaction with the developing vocational structures or, from the emphasis on moral fellowship, with a movement to social reform that in another way could see progress toward the realization of the kingdom.

FAITH AND ASSURANCE

The corollary of Ritschl's rejection of the metaphysical as a basis for religious thinking was a more intense reliance on the internal witness of personal faith, as well as on the practical orientation to the ethical. Thus faith constituted the third leg of his theological tripod, along with history and ethics. Faith in Jesus Christ as the Founder and the source of our forgiveness means the personal appropriation of his worth for us, a *Werturteilung* given in the life of the community. Justification and reconciliation, as the religious focus of Christianity, are to be understood in the concrete experience of the community and of every individual, that is, in the actual life of the self in its knowing, feeling, and willing. Faith is the subjective correlate, the emotional conviction of the objective reality of justification and reconciliation as known in the experience of forgiveness, of God with us in spite of our sin, of fellowship with God as his children (*Versöhnung*: literally, being made sons), and of freedom and lordship over the world. In spite of their differences, Ritschl found a major predecessor here in Schleiermacher, in the analysis of the old formulas by reference to subjective life.

Justification, as distinguished from reconciliation, refers to pardon, the forgiveness of sins, the rendering inoperative of guilt as a hindrance to fellowship, and thus the restoring of fellowship by a judgment of God. Justification is a *Gerechtsprechung*, not a *Gerechtmachung*; it is a synthetic judgment, a resolve or act of the divine will to be with us in spite of our sins. Its objective pole is Christ's active obedience—not an innocent suffering or expiation as an independent task, for it is not God who needs to be reconciled, but a positive obedience in the overcoming of temptations and suffering in fidelity to his task. His obedience shows his intention to found a community of which forgiveness is the fundamental attribute, as his disciples are introduced into his position toward God. In this sense, Christ is properly thought of as the inclusive representative: he does first what the community is to do after him. As the head, he fully accomplished moral fellowship with God, and we are to stand alongside and with him in this relation. It is not that his active moral righteousness is as such transmitted to the community, for the formation of moral character is experienced as an act of our own wills. Yet the image of Christ persists in the church in many ways, and the author of sonship is thus operative. Because of the real relation to Christ in the community, his position in relation to God is imputed by God to those who are accounted his (*J&R*, pp. 546–62).

Reconciliation may be described as a broader concept than justification. It is justification as effective; it implies a reciprocal relation as the person pardoned enters into the relation being established. This is not only passive determination, but a formerly active contradiction now brought into harmonious direction toward God. Thus justification and reconciliation are inseparable; the removal of guilt must also involve removal of the contradiction and restoration as sons.

Justification/reconciliation, of course, presupposes sin and guilt. But forgiveness is the ground of the knowledge of sin. The order of thought is important, for in Christ is the ground of knowledge for every doctrine; one reads backward from the Christian ideal in Jesus Christ as the first full realization of the common destiny of mankind. (Thus *justitia originalis* is the assertion that the Christian ideal is an element in the conception of man.) Sin is defined in contrast to the Christian ideal. Religiously described, it is the lack of that trust in God which brings freedom from the world; ethically described, it is the failure of action prompted by love and directed toward the summum bonum.

On the one hand, sin involves separation from God as its punishment, a deprivation of sonship. The real punishment is the feeling of guilt, the sense of estrangement. Guilt includes the consciousness of guilt, not merely objective guilt, and forgiveness is the removal of that consciousness, which is the prime separation from God. On the other hand, sin is the opposite of action directed toward the kingdom of God; it is corporate, a kingdom of sin or common sin. That does not mean original sin as something apart from actual and interacting sin, for corporate sin is made up of sins of individuals, of acts out of freedom and conscious will, out of a nature which has an impulse to the good. Sin is not some prior state of the self, but the self in act, a failure to achieve moral personality. Out of such act and interaction comes common sin, sinful federation, a vast complexity of sinful action (*J&R*, pp. 327–50).

From this perspective, Ritschl drew consequences that led to his being roundly attacked for not taking sin seriously, or at least not acknowledging the dimension of tragic involvement. He thought it essential to speak explicitly of gradations within the kingdom of sin: "From the degree of wickedness which we call devilish we distinguish vice, selfish and insolent imperiousness, vain and astute indifference to moral ends, and lastly, self-seeking forms of patriotism, pride of rank, and family zeal, which indeed are based upon particular moral goods, but pursue them in a way which comes into contradiction with universal morality" (*J&R*, p. 338). There is no warrant for the idea of infinite sin, for sin is a product of limited powers of man, hence limited, finite, and quite transparent for God's judgment. Nor is there any place for a hypothesis of positive eternal condemnation. The graduated values of sin are to be seen between two limiting conceptions. At one limit there is the possibility of a sinless life, for there is nothing either a priori (original sin or evil nature) or in the conditions of existence that requires us to deny the possibility of a sinless development of life. It is only by looking at the whole of human experience that we become convinced that sin is universal. The other limiting conception appears in the distinction between sin insofar as it can be forgiven or rendered inoperative through conversion and sin "brought to its full intensity in the form of a final decision against the Christian salvation, or incorrigible selfishness" (*J&R*, p. 376). The latter is sin as final decision against recognized good, sin as thoroughgoing opposition to good, as complete hardening (sin against the Holy Spirit), and it is unredeemable, a degree of sin which can only expect to be expelled from the world order. This description, of course, cannot be taken as a judgment by us on actual persons, but only as a statement of the limiting possibility.

In this context we can understand Ritschl's assertion that sin, apart from the extreme just noted, is judged by God as ignorance. Only in that limiting case is there full awareness of the good and rejection of it; in all other cases, in which men are not looked on by God as beyond redemption, he views sin in a different light, namely, as ignorance. Ritschl did not have in mind the commonplace that ignorance is a significant factor in the development of evil and that the human

will, as a constantly growing power, does not have at first the complete knowledge of the good. His description of sin as ignorance had
a purely negative import: that "the love of God can be conceived in
relation only to such sinners as have not fallen into that degree of sin
which excludes conversion of the will . . . that the love of God to
sinners, as the motive of His purpose of redemption, and as the ultimate efficient ground of their conversion, cannot be extended to
those persons in whom the purpose of opposition to the divine order
of good has come to full consciousness and determination" (*J&R*, p.
383).

Sin, as we said, can be understood only from the standpoint of justification and reconciliation, whence we are also to view faith as trust
in God, who is known as Father rather than as judge and lawgiver.
The complete name of God, from the Christian revelation, is "God
and Father of our Lord Jesus Christ" (*J&R*, p. 273; *Instruction*, §11).

This means, first, that the primary, fundamental definition of God
is *love*. God is love who has the attribute of almightiness rather than
the reverse. He is loving will; not just will, but will defined as love. Either he is conceived as love, or he is not conceived at all. And he is
love, not wrath—either as another side of his being (his left hand) or
as an altered state of love.

Here again Ritschl undertook to correct the tradition. While we
may, in our temporality, feel as if there were changes in God's attitude toward us, no experience of evil can properly be counted as de-
structive penalty, but only as a means of our education. There is in
God no alternation from wrath to mercy; redemption traces back to
love in an unbroken line, God all along foreseeing sinners as partak-
ers in his kingdom. "Any theology which keeps to the standpoint of
the reconciled community must assert that into the life of the reconciled there can come from God's side no curse or damnatory punishment, and that God's love, as the antecedent ground of reconciliation, cannot be modified by any such feeling or action on his part
towards those who are to be reconciled" (*J&R*, p. 324). Forgiveness
is no collision with God's moral legislation, though it seems so for
those who posit a legal justice or wrath as equal or prior to love.

Faith in God, second, is faith in God as personal. As against the
threat to personal language for God that had come into nineteenth-
century theology from the pantheism and atheism controversies,
through Schleiermacher, Hegel, and especially Strauss and Biedermann—and against the drift toward materialism that he saw in the

culture of his day—Ritschl asserted unequivocally that "personality is the form in which the idea of God is given in revelation." He also thought the conception could be justified "scientifically" from the study of "independent personality" (so Lotze) as the only principle for explaining the coexistence of nature and morality. But of overriding importance is the conception of God as a Person "who establishes the kingdom of God as the final end of the world, and in it assures to every one who trusts in Him supremacy over the world" (*J&R*, pp. 237, 228–38). Faith, as trust in God, in his forgiveness and providence, is personal conviction. It is confidence in the deliverance by God, the assurance of victory, the confidence that all things serve for good. Faith is expressed in humility toward God and in the resolve to submit ourselves to him; in patience under the restrictions and sufferings from the world, seen as educative punishments under God's providence; and in prayer, for which thanksgiving is the primary form and petition a subordinate variant.[18]

In such faith a new relation to the world is given. Moral independence of natural conditionedness is made possible. The believer occupies a position of lordship over the world because he stands so near to God and belongs so peculiarly to him as to ensure independence from the elements of the world. Action motivated by love can be practiced. The content of freedom and the form of lordship are the trust in providence whereby the world is no longer a threat, but is seen as under God and for his purposes—hence as a field for action. This is, of course, not an empirical lordship, not an alteration of the mechanical conditions of sensible existence. Everyone must still submit to the laws of mechanism and organism, with only a limited range for the subjugation of nature's forces. Lordship and freedom, however, mean a change of our judgment about the value of restrictions and evils by the thought that we each, as spiritual wholes, have in God's sight a higher value than the entirety of nature (*J&R*, pp. 609–25).

Ritschl's understanding of faith brings us around again to his idea of Christian perfection, which he described as ethically the fulfillment of moral vocation and religiously the trust in God by which persons are made wholes vis-à-vis nature. Once more it appears that wherever we take hold of Ritschl's thought, we are led easily and comfortably to the other components. The concerns for faith, for

18. See *J&R*, pp. 617–44; *Instruction*, §§51, 78–80; and *Die christliche Vollkommenheit.*

moral action, and for the historical foundation are all intertwined. Whether we begin with history or ethics or personal faith, we are brought immediately to the other two. Faith is not apart from history or challenged by history, but is expressed in a historical existence that is rooted directly in the historical existence of Jesus Christ. The religious and the ethical are dual foci of the Christian religion, and these points of view can be taken up alternately; yet the religious is inseparable from the ethical and the ethical from the religious. Both the religious and the ethical are grounded in the historical perception of Christ.

Other elements as well feature in Ritschl's significance. The stress on the ethical was of decisive import for a generation of thinkers. The critique of metaphysics and the idea of lordship over nature had distinctive shape in his thought. He brought the question of the historical foundation to focus in a new way. At all of these points, he was herald of new directions and problems. He made a decisive break with the notion of a God of wrath. He ventured a radical christomonism and a rejection of natural religion that were taken up in the twentieth century even by his most vehement critic, Karl Barth. And he exploited Kant's second critique, as well as the idea of the kingdom of ends, in a new way.

Yet what is most striking about Ritschl is the way in which the ideas of the religious (faith), the ethical, and the historical recur and intertwine. These themes dominated Protestant thought among his successors. Ritschl did not exhibit the preoccupation with psychological certitude in faith that was to follow shortly (see chapter 2, below); nor did the uncertainties of historical knowledge pose any problem for him (see chapter 5, below). There was no lack of confidence as to how the ethical imperative sprang directly out of the history of Jesus and the nature of trust in God, and he had no great uneasiness about the expression of the moral demand in the given social structures (see chapter 7, below). Faith and history and ethics fitted together in a convenient harmony. But the question of that harmony is the heart of the problem of Protestant thought at the end of the nineteenth century.

2

Faith Viewed from Within:

The Problem of Certainty

Albrecht Ritschl's attempt to define a distinctive kind of religious judgment (Werturteil) that would protect the integrity of faith was both a sign and an impetus in a much broader late-nineteenth-century tendency to emphasize the internal witness of faith, or religious experience, and to consider this interior act analytically as a way of showing its autonomy and its certainty.

To isolate the question of immediate personal faith from the questions of historical judgments and of ethics is, of course, to engage in abstraction. The questions continue to intertwine. Yet each in turn may be placed at the center of attention in order to learn how it develops in harmony or in dissonance with the others, for each has its inner dynamics, its internal tensions, and its tonalities.

Much of the introspective approach to faith in the late nineteenth century is a generalized, conventional, and uninteresting affirmation of the basis of religion in religious experience, drawing heavily and consciously on Schleiermacher. Neopietism and revivalism were also in the near background (see *Prot. Thought*, 1). Some expressions sound like variations on the Ritschlian theme; others are quite un-Ritschlian.

Some of the claims for faith and religious experience seem relaxed and untroubled, but there are also many signs of a much more intense quest, a deep struggle to show the self-certifying nature of religious experience by a proper internal analysis of that experience. In this struggle two subsets of problems recur as evidence of the seriousness of the search. One is the repeated question, how can one be sure? how can one have certainty in faith? The other question treats the relation of faith acts or assertions to other sorts of human judgments, especially those of science and philosophy. For the present we leave aside the question of historical judgments, though that proved to be the most obstinate problem.

On the second question, the range of options extended all the way

31

from those which would locate faith's inner and direct apprehension in a strong positive relation to other ways of knowing (following more in the line of the traditional mediating theology) to those which would completely disjoin religious and nonreligious knowledge. We may call these soft and hard views of the independence of faith: faith as finding collateral support in the breadth of general experience, or faith as simply self-certifying; faith as correlated with or as wholly distinct from other ways of knowing. Both tendencies, however, sought for a means of describing the act (or intuition, or instinct, or experience) that would give it its own foundation and certification.

The related question was that of certainty in faith. Naturally, this was not at the center of the stage for those conservative or confessionalist or orthodox thinkers who were less touched by the broadened stream of Victorian doubt (see *Prot. Thought,* 1:184–85) and its equivalents, a stream that N. S. Talbot in 1912 called "a kind of cosmic nervousness" in a modern world in which "the assumptions of Mid-Victorian liberalism have been going bankrupt."[1] No, the traditionalists drifted, or sometimes recoiled, in a less troubled confidence, which they maintained even at the cost of retreat from the rest of the intellectual world.

But for many religious thinkers the question of certainty took on a new intensity. This was not the classical question of the personal assurance of salvation, but an anxiety over the certainty of even the most elementary affirmations and a demand for reassurance. It was the comprehensive question of being sure in belief, as even the Erlangen Lutheran F. H. R. Frank could state in 1870 at the outset of his *System der christlichen Gewissheit.* And fellow Erlanger Ludwig Ihmels spoke for many when he remarked, forty years later, "a faith that possesses no certainty is not worth talking about."[2] The question now was not the assurance of specific grace or salvation, but rather the root principle of Christian affirmation, or revelation as a whole. Here was something new, in contrast to the biblical and Reformation emphasis.[3] The question was of the security of the deepest founda-

---

1. *Foundations* (London, 1912), p. 7. The decrees of the first Vatican Council, as well as the struggles of the Catholic modernists and of early fundamentalism, have this problem in the background.

2. Ihmels, *Centralfragen der Dogmatik in der Gegenwart* (Leipzig, 1912), p. 152 (1st ed., 1910).

3. Despite the view of J. G. Tasker, "Certainty (Religious)," in *Encyclopedia of Religion and Ethics* (1908–21; hereafter cited as *ERE*), 3:325–28. It is noteworthy that this encyclopedia has a substantial entry on religious certainty, whereas the 3d ed. of the *Realencyklopädie für protestantische Theologie und Kirche* (1896–1909) has none.

tions, of an inner-experiential certainty of the whole Christian view of things, even though that certainty might arise from a specific experience, such as regeneration.

One can point to a whole literature on the theme of certainty, from Frank, *Gewissheit*, through August Carlblom, *Zur Lehre von der christlichen Gewissheit* (Leipzig, 1874), Otto Kirn, *Ueber Wesen und Begründung der religiösen Gewissheit* (Basel, 1890), to Ihmels, *Central-fragen*, as well as his *Die christliche Wahrheitsgewissheit, ihr letzter Grund und ihre Entstehung* (Leipzig, 1901; 3d ed., 1914). Wilhelm Herrmann's *Communion of the Christian with God* (1886) reveals an almost constant preoccupation with the question of certainty.

In most expressions of this concern, security is to be found in the self-certifying nature of faith, analytically considered (whether with or without positive connection to other certainties). Thus the two questions—certainty and the self-justifying nature of faith—are interwoven.

FAITH MORE OR LESS WITH SUPPORTS

Much of the late-nineteenth-century liberal or progressive theology in Britain and America seems to reflect a general and eclectic view with obvious influence from Schleiermacher. Religious experience is vaguely described as sui generis (for example, in Theodore T. Munger, *The Freedom of Faith* [Boston, 1883]). Experience is primary, as the only fundamental ground of a conviction that can endure the test of critical reason (see G. A. Gordon, *Ultimate Conceptions of Faith* [Boston, 1903]). For Egbert C. Smyth, faith is a "principle of immediateness." More fully stated, "the soul is created for religious communion, and, in this communion, attains to religious certainty." Yet this is not merely subjective. Like every "intuition of reason" or "species of knowledge founded in immediate consciousness," it is subject to verification by tests "of the understanding, of logic, of experience, of history, of life. The knowledge of faith is not grounded in those tests. The certainty is immediately given. Yet the tests guard against mistake" (*Andover Review*, I/4: 296, 308). The British Unitarian sage James Martineau found that "in the very constitution of the human soul there is provision for an immediate apprehension of God" (*Seat of Authority in Religion*, 3d ed. [London, 1891], p. 651). William Adams Brown, in his widely used textbook, points both to Schleiermacher, the first modern theologian to stress the dependence of theology on religious experience, and to Ritschl, for whom the justification of religious truths is to be found in their satisfaction of the religious needs of humanity. Yet, against Schleiermacher, he argues that the subject matter of theology is not religious experience itself, but the unseen reality that is experienced; against Ritschl, that religious judgments are not a realm artificially delimited from the theoretical judgments of science and philosophy. "In Christianity, something is offered for science to observe and for philosophy to interpret, and the result is Christian theology." The sources of theology include the world in which the theologian lives, its natural science, psychology, history, and so forth, though modern theology "begins with a consideration of the phenomena of the religious life itself." Brown is typical of much of the late-nineteenth-century appeal to religious experience in attempting to show (or assume) that it is a phenomenon, a fact, available in the same way as the phenomena with which natural science deals (see *Christian Theology in Outline*, [New York, 1906] pp. 7–23).

The move toward a sharper statement of the self-certifying nature of faith, with a more acute sense of anxiety, had earlier been made in Henry Scott Holland's essay, "What is Faith?," in *Lux Mundi* (1889), one of those summary collections of Oxford essays through which one can almost trace the story of Anglican thought.[4] "What is it to believe? Do I know what it is to believe? Have I, or have I not, that which can be called 'faith'? How can I be sure? What can I say of myself?" That is a contemporary urgent problem, practical and theoretical. Will faith "prove itself adequate to the crisis?" Such questions can be answered only by recognizing that faith stands with the "primary intuitions" of seeing, willing, and loving. "It is deeper and more elemental than them all: and therefore still less than they can it admit of translation into other conditions than its own—can still less submit itself to public observation. It can never be looked at from without. It can be known only from within itself. Belief is only intelligible by believing." Faith "is summoned to show itself on the field, in its own inner character. And this is just what it never can or may do. It can only reiterate, in response to the demand for definition, 'Faith is faith. Believing is—just believing.'" Faith is "a profound and radical act of the inner soul," a "spring of movement," an elemental energy of the soul.

4. Of at least equal importance in Holland's work was his founding, in the same year, of the Christian Social Union (see below, chap. 7). Most of his published work comprised collections of sermons. A useful selection is found in B. M. G. Reardon, *Henry Scott Holland: A Selection from His Writings* (London, 1962).

Faith, to be sure, is here on earth "a struggling and fluctuating effort in man to win for himself a valid hold upon things that exist under the conditions of eternity." Thus faith "grounds itself, solely and wholly, on an inner and vital relation of the soul to its source. . . . We stand, by the necessities of our existence, in the relationship of sons to a Father, who has poured out into us, and still pours, the vigour of His own life. This is the one basis of all faith. Unless this relationship actually exists, there could be no faith: if it exists, then faith is its essential corollary: it is bound to appear. Our faith is simply the witness to this inner bond of meaning."

So understood, faith can only be self-certifying, verifying itself through its actions. Yet for Holland faith is not isolated from the other powers of life. Rather, it "is not to be ranked by the side of the other faculties in a federation of rival powers, but is behind them all. It goes back to a deeper root; it springs from a more primitive and radical act of the central self than they. It belongs to that original spot of our being, where it adheres in God, and draws on divine resources. Out from that spot our powers divide, radiating into separate gifts—will, memory, feeling, reason, imagination, affection; but all of them are but varying expressions of that essential sonship, which is their base." The hidden activity lies behind secular life, whence it comes forward in itself and on its own account and exhibits itself as real developing religious experience, which is part of man's normal and natural experience.[5]

In *Belief and Practice* (1916), Will Spens (of Cambridge) set out a view less purely fideistic than Holland's statement, though more concerned to testify to the validity of a broadly catholic theology as a reliable map to spiritual life. (He also found himself akin to George Tyrrell in some of the latter's undeveloped views of the parallel of religion to metaphysics rather than to science.) He described the starting point as the necessity of "instinctive affirmation." Yet instinct as a ground of our belief (for example, in the existence of God) is instinct "educated in experience." And "the more fundamental a particular instinct, and the more it is an essential assumption in a large range of successful theory, the more reliable it is likely to prove, even although it is never likely to be a complete and exhaustive apprehension of final truth." We are justified, then, both "in accepting the fundamental axioms of religion in its most general form, and in as-

5. See *Lux Mundi*, ed. Charles Gore, 10th ed. (New York, 1890), pp. 3, 8, 9, 11, 12, 18.

suming the 'validity' of religious experience." Catholic theology can be affirmed as "the best guide to religious experience and the least inadequate account of the reality behind that experience. Since the most fundamental affirmation of that theology is that religious experience depends on a direct relation with a personal God, it follows that theology will represent our best picture of *ultimate* reality." Direct and indirect support for both the assumption and the resulting theology comes from the fact that "this theology proves a peculiarly successful guide to wide and various religious experience."

Obviously, here the instinctive does not bear the whole weight. While there is in both science and religion "a widespread tendency to affirm the belief in question, as a matter of instinct, antecedently to any considerable experience," the main point is not whether the instinctive affirmation is antecedent to experience, but "whether the instinct behind the affirmation does, or does not, prove a successful guide to experience where a check is possible." But is religious experience not too abstract a notion for any check to be feasible? F. R. Tennant had complained of its vagueness. To this Spens responded rather lamely that "the phrase religious experience has a meaning pretty generally accepted." The data, for those who appeal to religious experience, are

> in the first place a very general experience of certain needs and capacities, and of the possibility of their satisfaction. Among the chief of these are a sense of incompleteness, its relief by religious practice, and its removal in the experience which religion describes as communion with God; the sense of duty and vocation; the sense of sin, repentance, and forgiveness; the capacity for worship; and the experience of moral and spiritual power resulting from religious practice. This last is sufficiently different from their other experiences to lead its subjects to ascribe it, rightly or wrongly, to an external source.[6]

For Auguste Sabatier, dean of the Protestant faculty in Paris, the distinctions between faith and knowledge and between faith and belief were again to be drawn sharply.[7] Faith is no more a kind of knowledge than it is a political institution. Though knowledge always

---

6. Spens, *Belief and Practice*, 2d ed. (London, 1917), pp. 41, 68–70, 248–49, 253–54.
7. See esp. *Outlines of a Philosophy of Religion Based on Psychology and History* (Paris, 1897; Eng. trans., New York, 1902), and *Religions of Authority and the Religion of the Spirit* (Paris, 1903; Eng. trans., New York, 1904).

accompanies religious faith, this intellectual element varies continually in religious evolution and is in no sense the basis and substance of religion. Religious evolution has moved from the mythological stage (ancient paganism), through the dogmatic stage (Catholicism and orthodox Protestantism, whose dogmas are now subject to scientific criticism), to the psychological stage, that is, to an interior view, in which the truth of religion can be seen as free from the negative criticism of the modern world.

Faith, properly speaking, is "an independent, original, psychological act." As Schleiermacher showed, religion originates in a feeling of absolute dependence, which is the experimental and indestructible basis of the idea of God (though Schleiermacher failed to take due account of the element of willing response in prayer). The essence of religion is "a commerce, a conscious and willed relation into which the soul in distress enters with the mysterious power on which it feels that it and its destiny depend." This is so deeply an act of the self that the human mind "cannot believe in itself without believing in God" and cannot believe in God without finding him in itself. In contrast to the knowledge of nature, then, religious knowledge "can never pass out of subjectivity." "The object of religious knowledge only reveals itself in the subject, by the religious phenomena themselves." "Truths of the religious and moral order are known by a subjective act of what Pascal calls *the heart*," and science can know nothing about them.[8]

And in *Religions of Authority*, Sabatier asserted that faith is not to be confused with belief; these are two distinct acts of the soul, orders as different as the heart and the intelligence. Though belief is necessary (and leads to theology), the certainty of belief, especially on authority of a tradition or a witness, "is neither of the same species nor in the same degree as the certitude of faith." Faith "is God consciously felt in the heart, the inward revelation of God and his habitation in us."[9]

German theologians offered even more detailed analyses of faith and its security. In Frank, for example, the specific problem of

8. *Philosophy of Religion*, pp. 27, 291, 311.

9. See *Religions of Authority*, pp. 327–36. Compare the declaration of Henri Bois, in *La Valeur de l'expérience religieuse* (Paris, 1908), cited in J. H. Leuba, *A Psychological Study of Religion* (New York, 1912), p. 227: "The Christian feels that he believes. Yes, he feels it, and he feels also that whatever effort he may attempt to the contrary he will not succeed in not believing it. He is unable not to believe it. . . . The Christian may likewise feel authorized to say: I cannot prevent myself believing in the intervention of God. The irresistibility of my belief is the criterion I have of its truth."

Christian certainty had early begun to be an object of extensive analysis.[10] It was important for Frank, however, to set the question of
Christian certainty in the context of the question of the certainty of
knowledge in general. Certainty comes into being only in the pos-
iting of an object of which it is assured. Only insofar as the subject is
persuaded that the object is grasped as what it is, detached from the
appearance which it is not, is the subject persuaded of having certainty. That is, "certainty is the sensing of the correspondence of being with concept, or of experience with cognition." Formally speaking, then, in the relation of subject to object, Christian certainty
contains all the moments of certainty in general and is thus protected
from the charge of subjectivism. Its distinctiveness from other certainties lies in the fact that it rests on a special moral experience,
which (in the tradition of J. C. K. von Hofmann—see *Prot. Thought*,
1:221–25) is the concrete experience of regeneration and conversion—or, better, the new self that is indubitably experienced as the
innermost determination of one's personal moral life. Behind this
one cannot go, nor can one seek to base Christian certainty in any
natural condition of man or in natural truth. In contrast to appeals to
authority, Christian doctrines must be derived from the principle of
faith itself.

In the context of this understanding, Frank was prepared to turn
to the warrants of the various Christian truths. The central certainty
of the fact of rebirth "stands in indissoluble connection with the complex of objects of faith, which constitute the Christian truth." Frank
distinguished the objects of faith as being of three kinds, relating to
the unfolding of the certainty: the *immanent* objects, for which it is
not necessary to go outside the self's own certainty of self (sin, un-
freedom, habitual and actual [aktuelle] righteousness, spiritual freedom of will, hope in fulfillment); the *transcendent* objects, which are
external to the subject but which through their causality work in the
subject, coming to experience (personality of God, Trinity, God-
man, and atonement); and the *transuent* objects (church, word, scripture, miracle, revelation), which mediate the influence of the transcendent objects through creaturely realities and so form lines of
connection between the transcendent factors and the immanent con-

10. See esp. his *System der christlichen Gewissheit* (Erlangen, 1870; 2d ed., 1884; Eng. trans.,
System of the Christian Certainty [Edinburgh, 1886]). This provided the basis for a subsequent
System der christlichen Wahrheit (Erlangen, 1878; 3d ed., 1894) and a *System der christlichen
Sittlichkeit* (Erlangen, 1884–87).

dition (Tatbestand) of the Christian consciousness. Thus, beginning with the primal specific certainty of rebirth, Frank thought it possible to move to the whole range of the doctrines of confessional Lutheranism.[11]

Frank's student Ihmels (among many others) objected that one cannot get all this Lutheran orthodoxy out of the simple certainty of rebirth.[12] Frank was right that Christian certainty can only be grounded in religious experience, not in scientific investigation. He was also right that a secure starting point is essential. This is a particularly lively question for Protestantism, for in Protestant Christianity "everything is attached to personal certainty," in contrast to Roman Catholicism, where the question is relatively foreign because of reliance on the guarantees of the church. The question is, "where does the final ground of our certainty lie?" A faith without certainty is not worth having, and it cannot be a merely subjective certainty, for that is no certainty at all.[13]

But certainty, Ihmels said, has a broader base than rebirth. Christianity is personal fellowship with God and has personal certainty about this fellowship. Of course, this involves a subjectivity, as does certainty in any area of knowledge. But to be certain of something means nothing other than to come to rest in the conviction that "it cannot be conceived other than as I conceive it." Fellowship with God, or faith as trust in God, includes a quite definite knowledge. Religious knowledge is different from theoretical knowledge; it is of a practical sort, defined by practical motives and oriented to practical interests; it takes place in judgments of trust (Ihmels preferred the term *Vertrauensurteilen* to Ritschl's *Werturteilen* or Kaftan's *Wertbeurteilung*); and these judgments and this knowledge necessarily root in historical experience (Erleben). But so understood, faith's certainty is a knowledge of revelation as the self-testimony of God, his demanding and judging will (certainty that God has unconditional claim on me), a certainty of God himself, and of man's creatureliness as directed to God.

Thus religious certainty must finally be a certainty of experience; Christian certainty can and must stand on its own feet. But, Ihmels added, it is not without connections to theoretical knowledge, for it is

11. See *Gewissheit*, 2d ed., pp. 1f., 113, 58, 62, 76, 191–97.
12. See Ihmels, *Die christliche Wahrheitsgewissheit* (Leipzig, 1901; 3d ed., 1914), and *Centralfragen*, esp. lecture 6, "Die Gewissheit des Glaubens."
13. *Centralfragen*, pp. 136, 152.

not simply an isolated thing. The Christian experience of certainty does not contradict other knowledge of truth. Theoretical knowledge, insofar as it is concerned with the final ground of all events, encounters problems that either cannot be solved at all or that find their solution in Christian faith. The conversation with historical and natural science is not to be feared, but rather to be pursued, in the assurance that if the Christian certainty of experience is of the truth —and it is—the particular results of scientific study (as distinguished from science elevated to a world view) will pose no conflict with its truth.

Ihmels' last point is suggestive of a significant withdrawal from earlier patently apologetic efforts such as those of the Ritschlian Julius Kaftan, who sought to establish a congruence between the highest practical demands of reason and the central idea of Christianity.[14] In contrast to the apologetics of supranaturalism and the older mediation theology, Kaftan was explicit that any attempt at proof for the truth of Christian faith must maintain the faith character of Christian knowledge. Faith itself desires no proof. The certainty it possesses is internal to the act because the knowledge of faith involves *Wertbeurteilung*, an act of inner freedom, will, and personal judgment. (Thus, as in Ritschl, faith knowledge is sharply distinguished from objective knowledge.) Christian faith "professes to be true knowledge of the first cause and the final goal of all things."

From this stance it is possible to move to a kind of proof of Christianity by showing that "the Christian idea of the Kingdom of God as the highest good of humanity corresponds to the demands that must be made by the true, rational, universally valid idea of the highest good." There is a rational idea of the highest good, which has been the pursuit of philosophy in all ages, a highest good not to be found within the world. This idea binds the religious and moral viewpoints together. The concrete form of the Christian ideal, as the fulfillment in history of the common tendency of all moral ideals, is the conclusion of the moral development of man in the satisfaction of religious need. It meets the demands of reason, and the unity of knowledge is preserved. But this congruence—the proof that the Christian idea of the kingdom of God is the rational and universally valid idea of the highest good—is no proof of the actuality of such a kingdom. That

14. See Kaftan, *Das Wesen der christlichen Religion* (Basel, 1881; 2d ed., 1888), and *Die Wahrheit der christlichen Religion* (Basel, 1888).

can be only a postulate of reason, as the historical revelation of God is a postulate. Whether there is such a revelation of an actual supramundane kingdom can be learned only from the actualities of history. This leads us back again to an assertion that is wholly of faith. So "the *inner certainty of faith*," in its unique character of willing judgment, emerges as "the decisive witness to its correctness."[15]

THE MYSTICAL ELEMENT IN RELIGION

A special example of the concern for the internal validation of religious experience appears in the extensive literature on mysticism that emerged in the closing years of the nineteenth century and the beginning of the twentieth. This was a distinctive phenomenon in the way it cut across Protestant and Catholic lines (William James, Rufus Jones, William Inge, Evelyn Underhill, and Friedrich von Hügel). It combined the new interest in the psychology of religion (see below, chapter 3) with a historical interest in recovering elements of the Christian tradition and the classic exemplars that had generally been neglected (or attacked, for example, by Albrecht Ritschl) in Protestant interpretations.[16] But it was also powerfully informed by an apologetic interest in the justification of religious claims to truth, pointing to the self-validating character of mystical experience and the evidence it provides relative to religious experience generally. Though persons like Jones, Underhill, and von Hügel were obviously participants in at least the kind of "practical mysticism" they described, what we see in the new excitement is not a resurgence of mystical experience like that of the great mystics of the fourteenth or seventeenth centuries. Instead, it was a new burst of interest in those mystics and in the mystical tradition as definitive of the center or height of religious experience.

Important among the early documents are E. Récéjac, *Essai sur les fondements de la connaissance mystique* (Paris, 1897; trans. S. C. Upton, *Essay on the Bases of the Mystical Knowledge* [London, 1899]—a psychological study), William R. Inge, *Christian Mysticism* (London, 1899), H. Delacroix, *Essai sur le mysticisme spéculatif en Allemagne au XIV. siècle*

15. Kaftan, *Wesen*, pp. 14, 3, 506, 566.
16. For an extensive list of the many new editions of the works and lives of the mystics that appeared in the late nineteenth and early twentieth centuries, see the bibliography in Evelyn Underhill, *Mysticism: A Study in the Nature and Development of Man's Spiritual Consciousness* (London, 1930), pp. 475–95. J. Chapman describes even the nineteenth-century Roman Catholic literature on mysticism as "singularly barren" (*ERE* 9:101).

(Paris, 1900),[17] and William James's discussion in the *Varieties of Religious Experience* (see below, chapter 3). For our present interest, the two classics of the period are Baron Friedrich von Hügel, *The Mystical Element in Religion, as Studied in St. Catherine of Genoa and Her Friends* (2 vols., London, 1908), and Evelyn Underhill, *Mysticism: A Study in the Nature and Development of Man's Spiritual Consciousness* (London, 1911).[18]

Von Hügel's work, as the title suggests, was in large part a detailed and masterful account of the life and work of the sixteenth-century Italian mystic St. Catherine of Genoa. The grace and genius of the interpretation provide solid warrant for the common judgment that no modern work on mysticism has been more influential than this one. But equally important was the way in which von Hügel set the story in the context of an impressive general consideration of the role of the mystical in religion (see especially chapters 2 and 13–15). For him, the mystical is an essential element in all full religious experience, although it is not a first foundation and certainly not an exclusive basis. Exclusive mysticism is "ruinous." Rather, full religion must include the historical and the institutional, the emotional and the volitional, the analytical and the speculative. There are inevitable tensions, even hostilities, among the forces of the soul and the corresponding elements in religion, and religion must ultimately be a multiplicity in unity. There is no "specifically distinct, self-sufficing, purely mystical mode of apprehending reality" (2:283). The mystical needs to be understood as interpenetrating the other aspects of religious experience and knowing. When not set in opposition to the social and the institutional, to the analytical and the volitional, but embodied in each, mysticism emerges as the natural support of the other elements and as the crown of full human religious experience.

The characteristic balance of von Hügel's account was not lost in

17. See also Delacroix's *Etudes d'histoire et de psychologie du mysticisme: Les Grands mystiques chrétiens* (Paris, 1908).

18. Citations below are from the 1923 edition of von Hügel and the 1930 ed. of Underhill. See also Underhill, *The Mystic Way* (London, 1913), and *Practical Mysticism* (London, 1914). Other important contributions to the general study of mysticism in this period include James B. Pratt, *Psychology of Religious Belief* (New York, 1907); W. K. Fleming, *Mysticism in Christianity* (London, 1913); W. H. Dyson, *Studies in Christian Mysticism* (London, 1913); E. Lehmann, *Mysticism in Heathendom and Christendom*, trans. G. M. G. Hunt (London, 1910); Joseph Zahn, *Einführung in die christliche Mystik* (Paderborn, 1908); Rufus M. Jones, *Studies in Mystical Religion* (London, 1908), and *Spiritual Reformers in the Sixteenth and Seventeenth Centuries* (London, 1914); Percy Gardner, *The Religious Experience of St. Paul* (London, 1911); and Caroline Spurgeon, *Mysticism in English Literature* (Cambridge, 1913). See also the extensive article in *ERE*, 9:83–117, s.v. "Mysticism."

Evelyn Underhill's *Mysticism*, but she was much more concerned to accentuate the uniqueness and centrality of the mystical. Mysticism she understood to be

> the expression of the innate tendency of the human spirit towards complete harmony with the transcendental order; whatever be the theological formula under which that order is understood. This tendency, in great mystics, gradually captures the whole field of consciousness; it dominates their life, and in the experience called "mystic union," attains its end. Whether that end be called the God of Christianity, the World-soul of Pantheism, the Absolute of Philosophy, the desire to attain it and the movement towards it—so long as this is a genuine life process and not an intellectual speculation—is the proper subject of mysticism. I believe this movement to represent the true life of development of the highest form of human consciousness. (Preface to 1st ed., pp. xiv–xv)

There is, then, a natural mysticism "latent in humanity," and "only the mystic can be called a whole man" (pp. 105, 63). Mysticism is "a highly specialized form of that search for reality, for heightened and completed life, which we have found to be a constant characteristic of human consciousness" (p. 93).

Mysticism can be distinguished from the aberrations of occult philosophy and the excesses of psychic phenomena; those are subject to explanation by naturalistic psychology, while mysticism is not. The mystical type of personality is to be found in "the most highly developed branches of the human family" (p. 3). Indeed, the high points in the richness and variety of mysticism—in the third, fourteenth, and seventeenth centuries—have come as the spiritual crown of great bursts of artistic and intellectual creativity in the classical, medieval, and Renaissance periods.[19] True mysticism, whose goal is "conscious union with a Living Absolute," is (1) active and practical, an organic and not theoretical process, (2) "wholly transcendental and spiritual" in its aims, not concerned with the visible universe, (3) directed to the One who is not merely *the* reality but "a living and personal Object of Love," and (4) seeks "living union with this One [in] a definite state or form of enhanced life," attained by a hard psychological and spiritual process.[20]

19. See Underhill's chronology of mysticism, in *Mysticism*, appendix, pp. 453–73.
20. See Underhill, *Mysticism*, pp. 73, 81–92. Thus Christian mystics have characteristically emphasized a union of communion rather than a union of simple identity or loss of self (see pp. 171–75).

The experience of persons of mystical genius thus "forms a body of evidence, curiously self-consistent and often mutually explanatory, which must be taken into account before we can add up the sum of the energies and potentialities of the human spirit, or reasonably speculate on its relations to the unknown world which lies outside the boundaries of sense" (p. 3). These persons have succeeded in contact with reality and can be offered as evidence that "the spirit of man, itself essentially divine, is capable of immediate communion with God, the One reality" (p. 24). The mystic way is the true story of man's spirit. It is not only innate but also is the norm for the consciousness of reality, the high road which all normal consciousness follows at a lower level (pp. 444–45).[21]

CERTAINTY IN FAITH WITHOUT SUPPORTS: WILHELM HERRMANN

In contrast to the broad appeals to religious experience and a more or less self-certifying faith that we have described, the pinnacle of a narrowing focus on an immediate and innermost certainty of faith is surely represented by the work of Johann Wilhelm Herrmann (1846–1922).

A student, amanuensis, and, for two and a half years, house guest of the famous Tholuck at Halle (where he also studied with Julius Müller and perhaps with Martin Kähler), Herrmann was the first theologian to ally himself openly with Albrecht Ritschl, whom he had met in Tholuck's home. He became the leading theological voice in the faculty at Marburg (1879–1917) and was probably the most influential of the systematic theologians in the Ritschlian tradition.[22] With Martin Rade, he edited the *Zeitschrift für Theologie und Kirche* from 1907 to 1916. Though his writing was extensive, his impact is generally considered to have come more through the intense earnestness and seriousness of his teaching. His students included not

21. For a related view, see Jones, *Mystical Religion*: "I shall use the word mysticism to express the *type of religion which puts the emphasis on immediate awareness of relation with God, on direct and intimate consciousness of the Divine Presence. It is religion in its most acute, intense, and living sense*" (p. xv). This belongs in some degree to all religion, including primitive religion. It is no compelling proof for everyone, but a "weighty ground for believing that there is a More of Consciousness continuous with our own" (p. xxix). See James, *Varieties* (n. 33, below), to which Jones here refers.

22. In passing, we may recall others usually counted in the Ritschlian tradition: Häring and Kaftan among the more conservative and Harnack among the liberals. But to trace the variations within this group—which was no school, Herrmann insisted—is not important for us. Herrmann is the most important for the problem with which we are now concerned. Harnack will be dealt with in another connection in chap. 5

only Germans, among them both Karl Barth and Rudolf Bultmann, but also a generation of Americans who pursued graduate study in pre–World War I Germany.[23]

Herrmann's lifelong concern was the problem of the possibility of Christian faith in a modern scientific world—a world in which "our whole existence, down even to that arrangement of our habits of thought which is fixed by mere caprice, has been altered, not so much through the results of science as through the method which it follows, and which is, in point of fact, unassailable" (*Communion*, p. 1). This is no mere theologian's problem, but one of the needs of the ordinary Christian who Herrmann felt was betrayed by the prevailing directions of theology. Those needs most deeply involve certainty in faith. Terms like "full certainty," "firm assurance," "indubitable," and "overcoming every doubt" continually recur in Herrmann's writings.

Metaphysics, Lehrsätze, *and Theology*

In the early writings, the cardinal question of faith and its truth in relation to science and morality was focused sharply on the problem of metaphysics.[24] Herrmann argued more drastically than Ritschl for the exclusion of metaphysics from theology (his *Metaphysik* was itself influential for Ritschl) and thus for the dissociation of the nature of religion from all that concerns speculative theology. This does not mean that science and morality are not legitimate life-expressions, modes of being, or directions for seeking the truth of human life; we shall see that for Herrmann the ethical demand has a special place of importance in relation to religion. But the distinctions must be clear. Religion is a thing in itself, not to be confused with philosophy or science. As he wrote in the concluding sentence of *Die Metaphysik*, "When we seek to do theological work, we need not clutch at the goals of metaphysics." The object of Christian faith does not lie within the realm of knowledge of the world. Science and philosophy's methodical knowledge of reality absolutely cannot touch the reality of our God.

In coming to this insistence—in the limitation of the concepts of pure reason and on the distinction between pure reason's compre-

23. See Bibliographical Notes, p. 304.
24. See esp. *Die Metaphysik; Die Religion im Verhältnis*; and "Kants Bedeutung für das Christentum" (1884), *Schriften,* 1:104–122.

hension of experience and practical reason's relating of comprehension to the will—Kant was of particular value for Herrmann. But Kant's own attempt at a metaphysic of morals, and its implication for religion, had also to be rejected as a last vestige of the rationalism that the critical philosophy was intended to destroy. It failed to locate human willing and action in the course of historical existence.

Positively, Herrmann's rejection of metaphysics in theology meant an insistence on the indissoluble unity of the objectivity of the revealer and the subjective truthfulness of man experiencing revelation (recall Ritschl's proper epistemology). Negatively, his principle cut against both speculative philosophy of religion and orthodoxy's intellectualization of the concept of faith. Thus Herrmann attacked not only the efforts of the theologians to prove the existence of God or the truths of Christianity and the adoption of philosophical conceptions of deity (Greek in origin), but also the "mixed articles" of theology (natural theology and revealed theology) and the appeal to the two-natures theory in Christology. In this thoroughgoing rejection of the mixing of religion and knowledge of the world (Welterkennen) Herrmann saw himself in opposition to all three major directions of the regnant theologies: the positive confessionalist theology of Luthardt, Kahnis, and Frank, the *liberal-freisinnig* theology of Lipsius, Biedermann, and Pfleiderer, and the mediating theologies, including Kähler.

Closely akin to the exclusion of metaphysics and mixed theology was Herrmann's protest against the legalism of orthodoxy/confessionalism, which was a form of intellectualization. For orthodoxy, faith has its foundation in the acceptance of normative articles of doctrine (Lehrsätze), by assent to which one becomes a Christian. But no doctrine or sum of doctrines, however true they may be in themselves, can bring "the full certainty that God actually exists for us." Even though they may be recorded in Holy Scripture, thoughts about faith do not make a man a Christian. Information about God does not bring us face to face with "that reality which gives faith its certainty," and no endeavor to find certainty on the basis of doctrine can ever conquer doubt, "for it is just amid such endeavors that doubt does always arise" (*Communion*, pp. 47–48, 58–59). Not only reliance on dogma or scripture, but even the mere dependence on the teachings of Jesus (as distinct from the power of his person) is a form of legalism from which we need to be freed in a continuation of Luther's struggle against the law. Herrmann found even Ritschl relapsing into a kind of biblicism, or at least not doing everything that needed to be done to break with the principle of *Lehrgesetz*, thus remaining at this point more in the tradition of the orthodox than did the Erlangen thinkers Hofmann and Frank.[25]

History

Doctrines, scriptural assertions, even Jesus' gospel, are no more than shifting sands as a foundation for faith, not only because they are not the fact of the reality of God but also because they can be (and are) called into question by scientific historical investigation. Scientific historiography demonstrates the merely *probable* character of historical (*historisch*) judgments. Historical evidence cannot be the basis of religious certainty, because then faith would always rest with fear and trembling on only probable truth. Even the historical (*geschichtlich*) appearance of Jesus, as it is drawn into this realm of probability, is "only a part of that world with which faith is to wrestle" (*Communion*, p. 70). "The Christian who imagines that the reliability of the records as historical (*historisch*) documents gives certainty to his faith, is duly startled from his false repose by the work of the historian, which ought to make it clear to such a man that the possession of Christianity cannot be obtained so cheaply as he thinks" (*Communion*, p. 77). Hence Herrmann's anger at the contemporary confessionalists, who had sold out the ordinary believer by an impossible intellectual position. Nor is there any special theological historical method which could safeguard the veracity of the New Testament witness to Christ as a source of religious certainty.[26]

The inability of scientific historiography to provide a basis for faith, however, is not a disadvantage but a positive gain, for it destroys false props. It seems that the more radical the criticism, the more satisfied Herrmann would be, though the Bible as a source of information about the historical Jesus does not lose all value for him, and it is not at all evident that he finally solves the problem; a real tension remains.

The inadequacy of scientific history to lay hold of the objective reality for Christian faith is part and parcel of its belonging to the sphere of scientific objectivity; it falls in the general category of that knowledge of the world from which faith is to be sharply distin-

25. See the 1906 essay, "Christlich-protestantische Dogmatik," in *Schriften*, 1:338–40.
26. See "Soll es eine besondere theologische Geschichtsforschung geben?" *Die Christliche Welt*, vol. 32, no. 31–32 (1918).

guished. No alliance (mediation) can be made between the thoughts of faith and science. The effort of the ruling theology at such alliance is something "from which only a worldly, grasping church could gain anything." But "it is just as clear to the believer as it is to those who are acquainted with science, that science has no part or lot in the content of these thoughts. For these things there is no *Erkenntnistheorie*. In these thoughts the believer breaks down every bridge between his own conviction, and all that science can acknowledge to be real, simply because these thoughts have grown out of the faith awakened by God's historical revelation" (*Communion*, p. 354). Between the method of natural and historical science on the one hand and the certainty of faith on the other there is radical discontinuity. Each is true in its own realm, but neither has the right to encroach on the other.

Implicit here is Herrmann's distinction between nature and history; as direct attention to the problem of metaphysics receded, his concern with interpreting the reality of the historical came to the foreground. The duality of history and nature becomes the context for the continuing explication of the nature of religion and its relation to science and morality, and in the understanding of historical existence this duality is viewed as the foundation of the knowledge of faith, including its intimate relation to morality.[27]

Man comes to know his actuality in a dual fashion, as nature and as history, as demonstrable and as experienceable (erlebbar). These ways are to be sharply distinguished (as external versus internal history?). Religion arises only in and from historical encounter or experience. For that, Herrmann's basic term was *Erlebnis*, "das Erleben des Selbst," which is undemonstrable but indisputable (here versus Herrmann's neo-Kantian Marburg colleague Cohen). The key to religious Erlebnis is found in the concept of trust (Vertrauen): trust in persons, as of a child in its parents, trust in Jesus Christ as a personal life in relation to personal life (in which man can only be an end, never a means), and in the concept of truthfulness (Wahrhaftigkeit).

In contrast to nature, the religious and the ethical are plainly intertwined as historical act. "The reality of nature rests on the natural law; the reality of history [Geschichte] rests on the moral law. The

27. The kinship to Ritschl's concern for the freedom and rule of man over nature is evident. The history/nature distinction was to be of great importance for twentieth-century theology.

natural law compels its acknowledgement for every person who is not insane; the moral law demands its acknowledgement by free will. To live in nature is a matter of course; to live in history is our task."[28] Of the reality of the moral law, Herrmann has no doubt. He can say that there are two objective facts on which the Christian's consciousness that God communes with him rests: "the historical fact (geschichtliche Tatsache) of the Person of Jesus," and the fact that "we hear within ourselves the demand of the moral law." To Herrmann's understanding of the former fact we can return. For the present we need to attend to the latter. In the demand of the moral law, Herrmann insists, "We grasp an objective fact which must be held to be valid in any historical study of life. For historical (geschichtlich) life, i.e., all specifically human life, rests absolutely upon the assumption that men know they are unconditionally bound to obey the law of duty" (Communion, pp. 102–03).

Further, religion and morality as tasks are indissolubly connected in the concept of Wahrhaftigkeit (truthfulness), which became increasingly important as a term for Herrmann, replacing his earlier utilization of Werturteilen (in Religion im Verhältnis . . .) and reflecting an abandonment of Ritschl's elliptical model for the relation of religion and ethics. Moral earnestness is a common root in religion and ethics. Truthfulness is indeed the root of virtue. True human life means inner independence, moral autonomy; only as inwardly independent (selbständig) is man one in and with himself. And "religion is nothing else than the individual life's becoming true in pure devotion to the One" (Schriften, 2:70). Christian faith can be nothing other than unreserved obedience to the truth. Indeed, against the Feuerbachian critique of religion as wish-fulfillment, Herrmann insists, "an honest atheist stands in all circumstances closer to the Christian faith than a representative of a religion of wish, no matter how Christianly garbed" (Ethik, 1901, p. 107).

The Immediacy of Communion with God

The locus of faith, in its validity and certainty, is not to be sought in speculation or metaphysics, or in knowledge of the world generally, or in revelation understood as Lehrsatz. These are all external, artificial, and untrustworthy supports for faith. The only place to look is in the inner world of consciousness. One can truly say that God has

28. "Die Wahrheit des Glaubens" (1888), Schriften, 1:143.

been found only on the basis of an event in the present moral, historical reality of life. "Anything that has not the strength to force its way
into this inner world of consciousness as an undeniable reality is not
in a position to constitute within this inner world the fulcrum of a
new life" (*Communion*, p. 141). For a morally serious, hence sincere or
truthful, desire for God, "nothing can help except a fact (Tatsache)
of that actuality in which the self exists" (*Ethik*, 1901, p. 103).

Where can we find this utterly independent and self-certifying
faith? Herrmann's answer is most fully articulated in *The Communion
of the Christian with God*. It is precisely in the experience of "a communion of the soul with the living God through the mediation of
Christ" (*Communion*, p. 9). This is a matter of the innermost life, a se-
cret of the soul, incommunicable, a sense of possession which elicits
the assertion that God is present, that "this is God." That sounds like
mysticism, and indeed there is a positive relation to mysticism, which
in its aim of finding God himself, and not just God's gifts, grasps the
goal of all genuine religion. But mysticism as such has to be rejected,
for it is unhistorical; it seeks God simply in the inner life of the soul,
and it loses the self in God, who becomes only a hidden, inscrutable
power. In contrast, Christianity speaks of an immediate experience,
a stirring of the soul, a liberation, a nontransferable awakening of
faith, which is bound to a historical fact (geschichtliche Tatsache),
namely, the inner life of Jesus.

There is a twofold factual objectivity for the consciousness that
God communes with us: the historical fact of the person of Jesus, and
the demand within ourselves of the moral law. We have already explored the latter's role for Herrmann. It need only be added that the
situation of the ethical demand shows us the need for historical revelation as the basis of faith.[29] Thus the two objective facts are joined.
"We see that we have no inner life at all until we recognize the good
and let it rule in our hearts; and the clearer this becomes the more
painfully are we sensible that all the forces of our existence are in
conflict with the good. . . . From this inward strife (*Anfechtung*), from
this inability to live in the good which, nevertheless, we see to be the
form of the true life, we are saved when once we have come to understand the fact that Jesus belongs to this world of ours" (*Communion*, pp. 99–100).

29. See *Schriften*, 1:97, 101.

What then of the objectivity of the historical fact, the only fact of the past which we can find to be present as an undeniable element of our own experience? Herrmann wrestles with this question at length against the objection that Jesus is not given to us directly but only through the reports of others. The objection maintains that not Jesus but only tradition is part of our experience, and the past fact of history, Jesus, cannot be a means of present communion with God. Herrmann's response turns on the insistence that Jesus is not present to us as a result of scientific historical (historisch) judgments. These are only probabilities, and "what sort of a religion would that be which accepted a basis for its convictions with the consciousness that it was only probably safe? . . . It is impossible to attach religious convictions to a mere historical (historisch) decision. . . . It is a fatal error to attempt to establish the basis of faith by means of historical (historisch) investigation" (*Communion*, pp. 72, 76). We cannot rest faith even on the relative certainty that the existence of the church requires the facticity of Jesus. Here, like Kierkegaard, Herrmann draws on the famous aphorism of Lessing, but with a radically different outcome: there still remains, for Herrmann, a point of certainty in experience.

The "objective fact" indubitably present to us is "the inner life of Jesus." To be sure, in the first instance we are dependent on the Christian community and its reports for our reception of the picture of Jesus' inner life. We do see its effects on others. Herrmann was quite confident of the reliability of the main features of the portrait of Jesus in the New Testament. For him the fact "remains unquestioned that the Christ of the New Testament shows a firmness of religious conviction, a clearness of moral judgment, and a purity and strength of will, such as are combined in no other figure in history." That portrait is one of a man conscious of his calling to be Messiah, intending the messianic work of establishing the kingdom of God (though reinterpreting the Jewish hope), pointing men and women to himself (in contrast to Buddha and Socrates), conscious of not being inferior to the ideal for which he willingly sacrificed himself, laying claims on the inner life of others, and so forth (see *Communion*, pp. 84-97). (Thus the problem remains whether Herrmann took fully seriously the questions then being raised about the reliability of the portrait.)

But faith's conviction, the acknowledgment of the mediation of Christ, comes only as we are led beyond the level at which we can question the details of the narrative. It occurs only when "the enrichment of our own inner life makes us aware that we have touched the Living One." This apprehension

> sets us free from the mere record, because it presses in upon us as a power that is present through its work upon us. He who has found the inner life of Jesus through the mediation of others, in so far as he has really found it, has become free even of that mediation. . . . If we have experienced his power over us, we need no longer look for the testimony of others to enable us to hold fast to his life as a real thing . . . it must arise within ourselves as the free revelation of the living to the living. It is thus, therefore, that the inner life of Jesus becomes part of our own sphere of reality . . . Jesus himself becomes a real power to us when He reveals his inner life to us; a power which we recognize as the best thing our life contains. (*Communion*, p. 74)

The question, then, is not what we make of the story (by *historisch* study), but what the contents of the story make of us:

> And the one thing which the Gospels will give us as an overpowering reality which allows no doubt is just the most tender part of all: it is the inner life of Jesus himself. Only he who yearns after an honest fulness for his own inner life can perceive the strength and fulness of that soul of Jesus, and whenever we come to see the person of Jesus, then, under the impress of that inner life that breaks through all the veils of the story, we ask no more questions as to the trustworthiness of the Evangelists. The question whether the portrait of Jesus belongs to history (*Geschichte*) or fiction is silenced in every one who learns to see it at all, for by its help he first learns to see what is the true reality of personal life. (*Communion*, p. 75; see p. 113)

     The question may be broached here, in a preliminary way, of the relation of this view to the argument of Martin Kähler, in his famous *Der sogenannte historische Jesus und der geschichtliche, biblische Christus.*[30] The distinction between *historisch* and *geschichtlich* was obviously also important for Herrmann, although in his essay responding to Kähler, Herrmann contended not only that Kähler had undervalued historical criticism but even more that he had confused the ground of faith with the content of faith.[31] Kähler's "whole biblical Christ" is

---

    30. Leipzig, 1892; 2d ed., 1896; trans. Carl E. Braaten, *The So-Called Historical Jesus and the Historic, Biblical Christ* (Philadelphia, 1964). See below, chap. 5.

    31. "Der geschichtliche Christus der Grund unseres Glaubens" (1892), *Schriften*, 1:149–85.

Christ victorious and exalted. But while such thoughts are the content of faith and proclamation, arising in faith's maturity, they are not faith's ground. The ground of faith must be in Jesus' life on earth. It is the *man* Jesus who compels the heart of man. It is, again, the inner life of Jesus that, though distinct from me, becomes a part of my sphere of actuality and evokes my trust in God.

Further, it is exclusively in this encounter with Christ that faith is grounded, that trust in God and knowledge of God exist. "We do not merely come through Christ to God. It is truer to say that we find in God Himself nothing but Christ." "We first see clearly what God really is when we experience God's communion with us in the influence which Jesus has upon us" (*Communion*, pp. 32, 128). This is the revelation that comes to us as a gift, the beginning of the consciousness within us that there is a living God, the disclosure of actual living goodness in Jesus' person. "God makes himself known to us as the Power that is with Jesus in such a way that amid all our distractions and in the midst of doubt he can never again vanish from us" (*Communion*, p. 98). This is the true miracle—and Herrmann disdains all the traditional miracle apologetics.

Christ bestows forgiveness on us. Against theories that Christ only proclaims forgiveness, or makes it possible, it must be insisted that he gives it to us; forgiveness becomes ours as we actually behold God himself in the Christ who is an indubitable fact for us. This is the proper expression of the deity of Christ. "We come to understand Jesus to be the divine act of forgiveness, . . . we see him to be the message through which God comes into communion with us; and so we recognize in his human appearance God himself drawing us to himself. . . . In what Jesus does to us, we grasp the expression God gives us of his feeling toward us, or God himself as a personal spirit working upon us. This is the form in which every man who has been reconciled to God through Christ necessarily confesses his deity, although he may decline to adopt the formula" (*Communion*, p. 143).

In faith, then, certainty is possible as well as necessary. After Herrmann has stripped off every kind of external support as unsafe—metaphysics, science, miracle, church authority, biblical Lehrsätze, historical research—there remains faith properly understood, faith whose ground is the presence of the inner life of Jesus in our life. The validation of faith is this event in human experience. It is the inwardness of the fact of Jesus, not the subjective experience of rebirth or a general religious act. We cannot prove to others that the objective fact that encounters us is the inner life of the man Jesus. "How could we, since every one must experience for himself that the spiritual power of Jesus destroys his confidence in self, and creates in him a trust in God, that makes him a new creature?" (*Communion*, p. 124). The proof is the overwhelming power over us. For this faith we are quite ready to answer to science, which cannot endanger it. Every doubt can be overcome. The ground of our faith is simply that "in the human Jesus, we have met with a fact whose content is incomparably richer than that of any feelings which arise within ourselves—a fact, moreover, which makes us so certain of God that our conviction of being in communion with him can justify itself at the bar of reason and conscience" (*Communion*, pp. 36f.).

It would not seem possible to go beyond this point in an attempt to find the validity and certainty of faith utterly in itself.

BELIEF UTTERLY WITHOUT CERTAINTY: WILLIAM JAMES

To speak of William James (1842–1910) in immediate conjunction with Wilhelm Herrmann is unusual, to say the least. Herrmann's concerns were explicitly Christian and Protestant. He was a professional theologian writing mostly in debate with other theologians, preoccupied by the historical question, and seeking to sharpen to the utmost the distinction between faith and scientific modalities of thought. James was a scientist and philosopher concerned with combining the interests of science and personal religion, impressed by the diversity of religious experience, loosely attached to the Christian tradition—"rather hopelessly non-evangelical" as he put it—and not at all interested in the questions posed for Christian faith by historical study.

It is far from strange, of course, to treat James at length in any study of nineteenth- and twentieth-century religious thought. That is inevitable. He said of himself in 1897 that "religion is the great interest of my life."[32] Others could judge that the controlling impulse and aim of his entire life's work were religious. Whether that is an exaggeration or not, James has proved to be one of the most interesting, seminal, and influential religious thinkers of modern times as well as being a great philosopher and psychologist. The conjunction with Herrmann is illuminating, for the relation is both an *and* and an *or*. We shall emphasize the *or*. Yet the alternative James offers must

32. *Letters of William James* (Boston, 1920), 2:58.

also be viewed as part of that pervasive late-nineteenth-century striving to ground the validity of faith in a deeper understanding of the act of believing.[33]

Believing and Experience

Religious convictions, for James as much as for Herrmann or Schleiermacher or Ritschl or Emerson or Bushnell, always grow out of experience. Thought must be tied to experience. For James, the pursuit of religious truth must be carried out with a kind of personal honesty that is not at all unlike Herrmann's demand for Wahrhaftigkeit, even though *experience* for James had a much broader range than Herrmann's Erlebnis, and beliefs had to have a wider kind of legitimation.

James's own thinking about religion and philosophy was thus an intensely personal act, never an indifferent speculation. This is reflected in the mostly popular style of his philosophical and religious writings. Out of concern for the real, ordinary experience of his hearers and readers, he wrote for the public mind—though one should not let the ease and vividness of his writing obscure the seriousness and depth of the thinking.

To know James, therefore, as a thinker whose thought is not to be separated from his existence, one must know James the man. Brother of the famous novelist Henry James, he was the son of Henry James, Sr., a philosopher and theologian of wealthy Calvinist background. A profoundly religious man who came to be deeply impressed by Swedenborg and the social theorist Fourier, Henry Sr. was for the family a powerful source of religious sensitivity and concern for questions of cosmic dimensions and of man's place in the world. For William, his father's friends Emerson and Carlyle were "fairy godfathers," resonating respectively in his "acquiescent or optimistic moods" and in his activist or "warlike" moods.[34] Educated in part abroad, William James was widely traveled and read, as much at home in Europe as in America. His interests were enormously broad and included painting (an early talent and vocational option), biology, psychology, psychical research, philosophy, and religion. With a medical degree from Harvard, he taught there (1873–1907) in biology, psychology, and philosophy.

33. See Bibliographical Notes: Chapter 2 (James).
34. See Perry, p. 38.

Of special importance for James's religious and philosophical thinking was the personal crisis of 1869–70, a period of severe depression eventuating in a rejection of suicide and the decision to live and to act creatively, even unsupported by certainty.

> I think that yesterday was a crisis in my life. I finished the first part of Renouvier's second "Essais" and see no reason why his definition of Free Will—"the sustaining of a thought *because I choose to* when I might have other thoughts"—need be the definition of an illusion. At any rate, I will assume for the present—until next year—that it is no illusion. My first act of free will shall be to believe in free will. . . . Today has furnished the exceptionally passionate initiative . . . I will see to the sequel. Not in maxims, not in *Anschauungen*, but in accumulated *acts* of thought lies salvation. . . . I will go a step further with my will, not only act with it, but believe as well; believe in my individual reality and creative power. My belief, to be sure, *can't* be optimistic—but I will posit life (the real, the good) in the self-governing *resistance* of the ego to the world. Life shall be built in doing and suffering and creating.[35]

This decisive turn toward a healthy-minded zest did not mean the end of irresolution, or doubt, or persistent illness. Rather, James's inner moods continue to show alternation between activity and passivity, perceptions of subjectivity and objectivity, practical demands for intimacy (as satisfied in idealism) and for energy (as demanded by empiricism, with the postulation of new worlds to conquer). James himself participated in both the healthy-minded and the sick-soul types of religious experience, as he named them.

In James's idea of a melioristic or improvable world, he clearly reflected a late-nineteenth-century and particularly American culture.[36] Evolution through variation and selection, the processive quality of both nature and man, creativity through struggle—these were powerful themes for him. Individualism was also strong in his preoccupation with personal religious experience, though in this respect he is hardly to be contrasted with Herrmann. Moreover, he was

35. Diary, April 30, 1870. See McDermott, pp. 3–8, where the crisis texts from the diary are brought together with excerpts from hallucinatory experiences recorded both by Henry James, Sr., and by William James (the latter is the famous passage from the *Varieties*, later identified as James's own experience; it may be compared but should not be confused with his experience of 1869–70). See also the discussions in Perry, pp. 119–26, and in Allen, pp. 162–70.

36. For a sensitive interpretation of James in the American context, see William A. Clebsch, *American Religious Thought: A History* (Chicago, 1973), pp. 125–70.

self-consciously part of a generation that had ceased to believe in the kind of God that the rationalist proofs and the traditional doctrines had argued for.[37] For him transcendentalism showed its futility in its unselfcritical solemnity and its pallor. James's personal struggle was not with the tendency to believe too much, but with the possibility of believing anything. Given his abiding interest in the basis for belief and in the act of believing, he offered an almost precisely contrary alternative to Herrmann's understanding of faith and quest for certainty. James proposed a will and right to believe which, just as fully an act of the self, altogether abandoned the demand for certainty.

The Will and Right to Believe

The locus classicus for James's view is "The Will to Believe," an 1896 address to the philosophical clubs of Yale and Brown universities. The audience is important, for as he said in the introduction, he would speak quite differently to "the Salvation Army or a miscellaneous popular crowd," because "what mankind at large most lacks is criticism and caution, not faith." But academic audiences are already fed on science and have a different need. Parts of the argument of this and other essays were composed as early as 1879 in response to W. K. Clifford's views on the ethics of belief, according to which it is morally wrong, always, everywhere, and for everyone, to believe anything about which the evidence has not yet come in. "Even if evidence should eventually prove a faith true, the truth, says Clifford, would have been 'stolen,' if assumed and acted on too soon."[38]

The argument of "The Will to Believe," or the "Right to Believe," as James admitted it should be called, is succinct. The justification *of* faith, that is, the defense of "our right to adopt a believing attitude in religious matters, in spite of the fact that our merely logical intellect may not have been coerced," requires the recognition that options, choices between hypotheses, may be living or dead, forced or avoidable, and momentous or trivial.

Living options are those in which both hypotheses are live ones. For example, as James saw it, the choice between being a Christian or

37. See *Varieties*, p. 74.

38. James reviewed Clifford's *Lectures and Essays* in 1879. See also, and for the citation bove, "Faith and the Right to Believe," McDermott, pp. 735–37; also the 1874 letter to the editor of *Nation*, criticizing the speculative scientist for invoking the authority of science in relation to ultimate problems.

an agnostic was a living option, while the choice between being a Muslim or a theosophist was not one that would make any real appeal to him or his hearers. Forced options are those in which there is no standing outside the choice: either accept this truth or go without it. Doubt, or skepticism, is itself a choice. Momentous options are those in which the opportunity is unique, the stakes significant, and the decision not reversible without harm being done to the chooser.

There are many options, of course, which are not living, forced, or momentous. Most choices are of this sort. Priority should be given to the skeptical avoidance of error. The chance of gaining truth may justifiably be given away in order to avoid the chance of believing falsehood. "What difference, indeed, does it make to most of us whether we have or have not a theory of the Röntgen rays, whether we believe or not in mind-stuff, or have a conviction about the causality of conscious states? It makes no difference. Such options are not forced upon us. On every account it is better not to make them, but still keep weighing reasons *pro et contra* with an indifferent hand." In such realms, Clifford is right.

But in moral decisions, in questions of personal relations, and in religious options, the case is quite different. Moral questions cannot wait for sensible proof, for they are questions "not of what sensibly exists, but of what is good, or would be good if it did exist." Decisions of personal relations, to like or not to like, to trust or not to trust, again cannot wait for the fullness of objective evidence, and they are decisions in which faith in the fact can itself help to create the fact. Similarly in religious options, it is right to venture forth in order to find truth, to risk error for the sake of finding. This is no license to believe whatever one happens to wish, to be superstitious, but a rule for belief which shows the right to choose when the options are living, forced, and momentous, and to act on the belief.

Elsewhere James spoke of a progression of the "faith-tendencies," the "extremely active psychological forces, constantly outstripping evidence," as steps of a "faith-ladder":

1. There is nothing absurd in a certain view of the world being true, nothing self-contradictory;
2. It *might* have been true under certain conditions;
3. It *may* be true, even now;
4. It is *fit* to be true;
5. It *ought* to be true;

6. It *must* be true;

7. It *shall* be true, at any rate true for *me*.[39]

Faith, then, is the readiness to believe when doubt is still theoretically possible and to act when the favorable outcome is not certified in advance.

Granted, in these statements the argument is less than fully elaborated. A living option for one person or culture will not be alive at all for another. The momentous characteristic is not without ambiguity. And the faith-ladder, if taken as an argument, seems loose indeed. But the central point is clear enough. What James was trying to do was show how inquiring and critical persons, given the possibility of belief, do and must go about the process of deciding what beliefs to affirm and to act upon. In any complex matter our conclusions can only be probable, yet our action must be whole, and we must decide on the whole.

From this way of justifying the act of religious belief, several implications and corollaries need to be drawn. As in so many of James's theological contemporaries, religion and ethics are intertwined (as we have noted, history was not a religious problem for James). This meant both that religious and ethical decisions have much the same character and that religious truth is eminently practical truth—truth for life. This is one reason why "belief" is a strong word for James, interchangeable with "faith." Religious belief has decision and courage in it; the factor of courage that is present everywhere in the intellectual process here attains its highest degree of worth. Belief is believing "in" and not simply "about"; it has the quality of *fiducia* (even in Luther's sense); it is not unlike the "loyalty" of which Josiah Royce wrote, though it does not have the social character of Royce's loyalty.

Further, James's understanding of religious belief was deeply rooted in his basic psychological analysis. Of special significance were his original analysis of the "stream of thought," especially the role of interest in the choices of consciousness; the analysis of will (the five types of decisions) and the dependency of knowledge on will; the delineation of the universe, or subuniverses, of common experience; the indestructibility in the race of the impulse "to take life strivingly" (here the spirit of Carlyle resonates); the essential role of believing in living; and thus the view of the believing, thinking, and acting self "as

39. See McDermott, p. 737; *A Pluralistic Universe*, pp. 328–29.

the hook from which the rest dangles" in the knowing and shaping of reality.[40]

Related to all this is James's judgment that "the subconscious and non-rational . . . hold primacy in the religious realm."[41] That is only one of the ways in which "our non-intellectual nature does influence our convictions," for our very belief in truth is "but a passionate affirmation of desire, in which our social system backs us up." Yet passion is of singular importance in the choices of faith: "Our passional nature not only lawfully may, but must, decide an option between propositions, whenever it is a genuine option that cannot by its nature be decided on intellectual grounds; for to say, under such circumstances, 'Do not decide, but leave the question open,' is itself a passional decision . . . and is attended with the same risk of losing the truth."[42]

Finally we need to recall the theological tradition in which James stood in this understanding of religious believing. Most broadly, he belonged to the general nineteenth-century shift to a new and deeper emphasis on the role of the subject in whatever can be called religious knowing or thinking (see *Prot. Thought,* 1:59–60). But within that powerful stream, James moved with the current represented by Coleridge and Kierkegaard (and earlier by Pascal) much more than with the current represented by Schleiermacher, Ritschl, or Herrmann. That is, he stood with those for whom faith is essentially a matter of willing and choosing, rather than a feeling or a knowing, even the knowing of a practical reason. Pascal he knew, and he discussed the famous wager in "The Will to Believe." At one level, that of its "mechanical calculation" and its faith "in masses and holy water," Pascal's wager presented no live option for James's world. But at a deeper level, that of the "reasons of the heart" and the "passional and volitional tendencies" which run before and after belief, and of the necessity of choice in the absence of compelling evidence, James belongs with Pascal. So, too, Coleridge's Reason at its highest point—where Reason becomes one with faith in a courage of venturing, choosing, risking, where the final proof is simply "Try it!"—is not far from James. Had he known him, James might have been attracted by Kierkegaard's demand for the intensity of the

40. *Principles of Psychology,* 2:297; and on the same page, "*as thinkers with emotional reaction, we give what seems to us a still higher degree of reality to whatever things we select and emphasize and turn to* WITH A WILL."

41. *Varieties,* p. 74.

42. *Will to Believe,* pp. 199f; see McDermott, pp. 722f.

self's choosing and willing in a situation of radical uncertainty, though he could have had little sympathy for choosing the inherently paradoxical, and the Kierkegaardian notion of faith's act would require significant alteration to accommodate James's idea of the process by which belief choices are made.

Pragmatism

James's understanding of the will and right to believe involved a further major theme: the pragmatic view of truth and his radical empiricism. James could say both that there is no logical connection between radical empiricism and pragmatism, each standing on its own feet, and that "the establishment of the pragmatist theory of truth is a step of first-rate importance in making radical empiricism prevail."[43] The discrepancy need not detain us. Taking "radical empiricism" as the label for the larger outlook, or James's mature philosophical position, the pragmatist idea of truth belongs with it.

As it bears on the right to believe, the principal point of pragmatism has already appeared. Believing in something, deciding that it shall be true for us, can itself be a means of making it true (patently the case in personal relations). Belief, in other words, can generate supporting data (neither Pascal nor Kierkegaard could have said this, though Coleridge could and did).

The general idea of pragmatism as a method was launched by James in an 1898 lecture, "Philosophical Conceptions and Practical Results," though some of the ideas go back to earlier writings (such as "The Sentiment of Rationality" [1879], and "The Function of Cognition" [1885]), and James attributed the origin of the principle to an 1878 article by his friend and colleague Charles Peirce.[44] Once launched, the term spread rapidly, and similar accounts were given by John Dewey and F. C. S. Schiller, with whom James was closely associated in the movement.[45] The major and hot debate, in the United States and abroad, came with James's *Pragmatism* in 1907. James himself saw the book as "something quite like the Protestant reformation,"[46] and it did represent the introduction of a genuinely new option for religious thinking.

43. Preface to *Pragmatism*; preface to *The Meaning of Truth* (New York, 1909).

44. See James's summary in *Varieties*, pp. 444–45.

45. In the preface to *The Meaning of Truth*, James sought to interpret his views and those of Schiller and Dewey as complementary.

46. *Letters,* 2:279.

Pragmatism, James insisted, is a method and not at all any set of results. It is "primarily a method of settling metaphysical disputes that otherwise might be interminable," by trying "to interpret each notion by tracing its practical consequences."[47] Thus the question the pragmatist asks is: "Grant an idea or belief to be true, what concrete difference will its being true make in any one's actual life? . . . What, in short, is the truth's cash value in experiential terms?" The answer is immediately forthcoming: "True ideas are those that we can assimilate, validate, corroborate and verify. False ideas are those we cannot." Truth is not a stagnant property inherent in an idea. It is something that happens to an idea. "It *becomes* true, is *made* true by events. Its verity *is* in fact an event, a process." Theories become instruments of action, not answers to enigmas. One can say of an idea that has become relevant "either that 'it is useful because it is true' or that 'it is true because it is useful.' Both these phrases mean exactly the same thing, namely that here is an idea that gets fulfilled and can be verified." Truth is simply a collective name for the verification process. It is built up, proving itself by working, and is a goal rather than a beginning.[48]

The relevance for religious belief is obvious, for James's pragmatism had the same roots as his will to believe and his own moral earnestness. If belief in a statement made a difference, James was willing to judge that statement to have "truth-value." Religious truth is made in the course of experience and is eminently practical truth, though obviously in a quite different sense from Ritschl's. It is true because life is better for its being believed. "If religious hypotheses about the universe be in order at all, then the active faiths of individuals in them, freely expressing themselves in life, are the experimental tests by which they are verified, and the only means by which their truth or falsehood can be wrought out."[49] Pragmatic verification is thus an integral part of the total process through which the fittest religious ideas come to be selected and to survive and the more foolish religious faiths are weeded out in the long run of experience.

47. "What Pragmatism Means"; see McDermott, p. 377.
48. See esp. "Pragmatism's Conception of Truth," in *Pragmatism*.
49. Preface to *Will to Believe*. Though it was far from James's intention, such statements were used to defend a mere belief in belief as sufficient.

A Pluralistic Universe

The nature of religious belief and the pragmatic method are also related for James to the question of the content of belief, namely, to the kind of world and the kind of God to be believed in. The relation is one of mutual conformability. James could see the possibility and attractiveness of a world view opposite to his. But he chose an open world to match an open-ended view of truth, a world texture that fits with a will to believe and a world view toward which pragmatism inclines.

The views he opposed were both monistic: the monism of scientific naturalism, which made salvation impossible, and the monism of the absolute, which made it necessary. The latter, as developed from Spinoza through Fichte and Hegel to Bradley and Royce, he saw as the view implicit in most theological formulations, as well as dominant in the British and American philosophical scenes. Though he had a lifelong affection and respect for Royce and a high opinion of Bradley, and later moved from attacking them to tolerance, recognizing idealism as an option,[50] James's campaign against the absolute is well known. "Damn the absolute," he could exclaim to Royce, and he could describe Bradley's absolute as "a metaphysical monster," and "a will o' the wisp." The following statements from an early essay (1884) give a vivid picture of the essential defects of monism:

> The through-and-through universe seems to suffocate me with its infallible, impeccable all-pervasiveness (all rationality). Its necessity, with no possibilities; its relations, with no subjects, makes me feel . . . as if I had to live in a large seaside boarding-house with no private bedroom in which I might take refuge from the society of the place. . . . Certainly, to my personal knowledge, all Hegelians are not prigs, but I somehow feel as if all prigs ought to end, if developed, by becoming Hegelians. . . . It (the through-and-through philosophy) seems too buttoned-up and white-chokered and clean-shaven a thing to speak for the vast slow-breathing unconscious Kosmos with its dread abysses and its unknown tides. The "freedom" *we* want to see there is not the freedom, with a string tied to its leg and warranted not to fly away, of that philosophy.[51]

50. On the development of James's attitude to idealism, see esp. Perry, pp. 161–71.
51. Reprinted in *Essays in Radical Empiricism* (New York, 1912), pp. 276ff.

That the absolutist philosophy recognizes no real freedom, no real evil, and grants moral holidays, James continued to believe. "It does not account for our finite consciousness. . . . It creates a problem of evil [that is, as a theoretical rather than as a practical problem]. . . . It contradicts the character of reality as perceptually experienced. . . . It is fatalistic."[52]

In contrast, a radical empiricism seeks to interpret the world as really experienced. This interpretation is rooted in James's analysis of the stream of consciousness in the *Principles of Psychology*, according to which thought, far from springing from simple sensations, is part of a personal consciousness that is always changing but sensibly continuous, that always appears to deal with objects independent of itself, and that is interested, that is, selective—welcoming, rejecting, and choosing from among the objects. In this consciousness the existence of a world that has extra-mental reality is always assumed, but that world is known only through experience. Subject and object, thing and thought are practical distinctions of utmost importance in experience, but only in the functional and not in the ontological order.

Moreover, in such a world of pure experience as the immediate flux of life, continuities and discontinuities "are absolutely coordinate." Real relations are as much given as are terms. "Radical empiricism takes conjunctive relations at their face value, holding them to be as real as the terms united by them." "The relations that connect experience must themselves be experienced relations, and any kind of relation experienced must be accounted as 'real' as anything else in the system."[53] This means that a pluralistic view of the world is neither subjectivist nor arbitrary. As he said in *Pragmatism* (p. 205):

> Woe to him whose beliefs
> play fast and loose with
> the order which realities
> follow in his experience;
> they will lead him nowhere
> or else make false connection.

The "piece-meal" world of pluralism is not a mere aggregate, nor is it sheer randomness. In a well-known letter, James could say: "The

---

52. "The One and the Many," in *Some Problems of Philosophy* (New York, 1911); McDermott, pp. 267–68; see also *Pragmatism*.

53. *Essays in Radical Empiricism*; see McDermott, p. 195, also p. 220.

world *per se* may be likened to a cast of beans on a table. By themselves they spell nothing. An onlooker may group them as he likes. He may simply count them all and map them. He may select groups and name these capriciously, or name them to suit certain extrinsic purposes of his. Whatever he does, so long as he *takes account* of them, his account is neither false nor irrelevant. If neither, why not call it true?" (*Letters*, 2:295). Taken alone, this statement involves a fair bit of hyperbole. As James went on to say, "All that Schiller and I contend for is that there is *no* 'truth' without *some* interest, and that non-intellectual interests play a part as well as intellectual ones." Further, relations are given in experience; there are many unities (though no given grand unity in the One) as well as disjunctions; and James abjured absolute pluralism equally with absolute monism.[54] The world is, in its parts, partly "hung together." (And certainly, contra the Ritschlian view, man and nature are hung together.)

In a pluralistic world there are at least some real independence and spontaneity, chance and irrationality, the raw irrational given, real human freedom and creativity, real novelty. The universe is not static and complete. Something is doing in the world. Really new things do occur, not merely apparently. Life and experience are richer than theories about them can possibly be. Everything has an environment, something beyond all our interpretation.

And there is real evil. James did not often speak of the problem of evil directly, but the reality was ever in the background as that for which monism cannot account: "this colossal universe of concrete facts, their aweful bewilderments, their surprises and cruelties."[55] The least jot of real evil is enough to put a blemish on monism's spotless appearance. He is reported to have said to his class: "If at the last day all creation was shouting hallelujah and there remained one cockroach with unrequited love, *that* would spoil the universal harmony." Pluralism insists that the world remains still imperfectly unified. Thus the world is really in process, with novelties, struggles, losses, and gains. In this point James was delighted to discover his kinship with Henri Bergson's ideas of real duration and creative evolution.[56] The world, in a word, is unfinished.

54. See "The One and the Many," in *Pragmatism*; McDermott, p. 415.

55. *Pragmatism*, p. 22; McDermott, p. 369.

56. See Bergson, *Essai sur les données immédiates de la conscience* (Paris, 1889; Eng. trans., *Time and Free Will* [London, 1910]), and *L'Evolution créatrice* (Paris, 1907; Eng. trans., *Creative Evolution* [New York, 1911]).

Obviously such a view of the world has profound consequences for religious belief.[57] James saw the religious value of the absolutist's world, and it appealed to one side of his nature, his own participation in the sick-soul form of religious experience. Absolutism provides optimism and security, the comfort and certainty that "all are one with God and with God all is well." James could not finally reject this as a possible view for one kind of religiousness, the tender-minded. But for him a pluralistic view had the decisive advantages. It is neither pessimistic nor optimistic; it is melioristic. That is, recognizing, as empiricism must, the reality of evil and the unfinished state of things, real losses and losers, it sees salvation as neither necessary nor impossible but as a possibility. The melioristic view fits with the risk of uncertainty in faith; it engages the moral energies of humanity in the struggle; it is a liberating view. It lets loose the strenuous attitude, for it "makes the world's salvation depend upon the energizing of its several parts, among which we are." We are in the struggle along with God.

James opted candidly for a finite God—and more than anyone else he was responsible for making this conception a live theological option. His own "over-belief" was a kind of "piece-meal supernaturalism" in contrast to the "refined supernaturalism" that has all the rough edges removed and is too respectable. God must be personal, *a* reality (not the ground of all), and on our side in the moral battle. He is not the all-determiner. He must be finite in either power or knowledge or both. He is in time, and works out a history as we do, thus escaping from the foreignness to the human of a static, timeless, and perfect absolute. "My 'God of things as they are,' being part of a pluralistic system is responsible for only such of them as he knows enough and has enough power to have accomplished. . . . The 'omniscient' and 'omnipotent' God of theology I regard as a disease of the philosophy-shop" (*Letters*, 2:269; to Charles A. Strong, 1907). "'God,' in the religious life of ordinary men, is the name not of the whole of things, heaven forbid, but only of the ideal tendency in things, believed in as a superhuman person who calls us to co-operate in his purposes, and who furthers ours if they are worthy. He works in an external environment, has limits, and has enemies. When John Mill said that the notion of God's omnipotence must be given up, if God is to be kept as a religious object, he was surely accurately right; . . . I

---

57. See esp. the concluding chapter of *Pragmatism*, "Pragmatism and Religion."

believe that the only God worthy of the name must be finite."[58] God must not only be different from us, but like us. With such a God, our life can be real and earnest; we can enjoy with him an intimacy and a warmer sort of loyalty than is possible under any other system.

On pragmatic principles, "If the hypothesis of God works satisfactorily, in the widest sense of the word, it is true." James affirmed that, despite residual difficulties, the hypothesis does work. Faith is capable of generating data for its verification. There is a "more." "I firmly disbelieve, myself, that our human experience is the highest form of experience extant in the universe." Yet the verification of the hypothesis of God comes only with the actual faith ventures. James thought this type of pluralistic and moralistic religion "as good a religious synthesis as you are likely to find," as he put it in the conclusion of "Pragmatism and Religion." Even more strongly, he could say, "Let empiricism once become associated with religion, as hitherto, through some strange misunderstanding, it has been associated with irreligion, and I believe that a new era of religion as well as of philosophy will be ready to begin."[59]

58. *Pluralistic Universe*, p. 124; McDermott, p. 527.
59. Ibid., p. 314; McDermott, p. 804.

3

Faith Viewed from Without:

The "Objective" Study

of Religious Subjectivity

In Volume 1 of this work I suggested that nineteenth-century theology marked a decisive Socratic turn to the self.[1] That turn was exhibited in different ways in Schleiermacher and Coleridge, in Hegel, in Maurice and Bushnell, in the Erlangen school and Isaak Dorner, dramatically in Kierkegaard, and even in J. H. Newman. It meant a new kind of self-conscious and systematic recognition of the involvement of the religious subject—his point of view, his cognitive act, his interest, his willing and choosing, with which theological reflection has to begin. Consciousness of the truth of the religious object was peculiarly one with self-consciousness. An ineradicably subjective (though not subjectivist) viewing of the religious object emerged. Significant talk about God is talk in which the self is concerned. The religious object, God, is present for reflection only in and with the religious subject in his relation to God. Religious truth is not of a disinterested, neutral sort, but irreducibly involves the believer's being in the truth.

There were ambiguities in the nineteenth-century witness that could open the door to the religious subject's becoming the principal or even exclusive object of attention—as in Schleiermacher's limitation of the direct reference of theological assertions, or the possibility in Coleridge of making the Word dependent on the human hungering and thirsting after it. Yet, predominantly, reflection was directed toward the object of faith.

This kind of thinking is powerfully represented in Ritschl's idea of religious value judgments, in the various appeals to religious experience and the quest for certainty in faith, and in James's emphasis on

1. *Prot. Thought*, 1:59–61.

the role of interest and on the necessity for choosing and willing in belief. But at the same time we have seen hints of a new attitude and standpoint, a dialectical transition that took place toward the end of the century, namely, the emergence of an attempt at an objective view of the religious subject. Instead of the insistence on a subjective standpoint for statements about the objective reality (God), we find emerging the demand for an objective methodology to deal with the religious phenomena. Instead of the assertion that I cannot talk about God in himself, but only as I know him in my experience, without its being supposed that my statements are merely affirmations about me, the focus now swings around explicitly and directly to me in my believing (or others in their believing), and to that believing or experience viewed objectively. The prior tendency does not vanish; not at all. It persists strongly, but is now paralleled and affected by a new impulse.

The evidence of this reversal in the object of attention and this change in methodology is as varied as the forms in which it appeared. The most general symbol of the new attitude and standpoint is the term *Religionswissenschaft*. The word makes explicit that *religion* is to be dealt with. This is a science of religion sharply distinguished from the mid-nineteenth-century efforts at *wissenschaftliche Theologie*. The subject matter is man in his religiousness; the method is objective, characterized by a proper scientific detachment; conclusions are drawn on the basis of publicly verifiable data; the intent is to understand the phenomenon (or phenomena) of religion with the help of tools of study external to belief. Hence the appearance of a psychology and a sociology of religion, and the burgeoning of anthropological and comparative studies.

The quest for the historical Jesus is a related form of the program. Though much more clearly a fulfillment of earlier nineteenth-century tendencies than, say, the psychology or sociology of religion, this movement too had its culmination at the end of the century (recall Ritschl's insistence that all theological assertions about Jesus be grounded in the historical facts of his life). Here the method is a historical science directed to a historical object of faith, an objective method for dealing with the religious subject Jesus. Such a scientific historical study means deliberate abstraction from personal involvement; it means pressing back to original form and fact; it means accepting as historical actuality that which is susceptible to incorporation into a framework of historical possibility. The interest is less in looking at God from Jesus' standpoint than in examining the religion (or religiousness or religious consciousness) of Jesus—and it is assumed that objective historical study can lay bare, behind the veils of early Christian testimony, his religious consciousness. To be sure, such a program engenders powerful tensions with faith's inner judgment about Jesus. This we have observed in Wilhelm Herrmann, and the problem will occupy us in detail in chapter 5.

A similar interest in objective methodology can even be found in some systematic theological endeavors of early-twentieth-century liberal theology. Although only rarely do we find constructive theological programs claiming to be rigorously scientific, as in D. C. Macintosh's effort to establish a rigorous parallel between the levels of the theological and natural scientific assertion,[2] liberal theology as a whole was permeated both by the preoccupation with religious experience and by the hope of finding an objective foundation in it. In the late-nineteenth-century revival of interest in Schleiermacher, he was recalled as the one who had established the independence of religion as a phenomenon. The characteristic liberal appeal, both in theological construction and in apologetic, was to the "verities of religious experience," the unquestionable given that can be identified as a phenomenon like others. The bases for theology were to be the objectively established religion of Jesus and the facts of personal religious experience. Here no clear line was drawn (pace Herrmann) between the objects and methodologies of *Theologie* and *Religionswissenschaft*.

PSYCHOLOGIES OF RELIGION

James and the Varieties

It is singularly appropriate that William James should serve as the bridge from the attempt at understanding faith from within to the effort at an objective study of religious experience, for his interests were genuinely of both sorts, not in isolation from each other, but clearly distinguished. To interpret *The Will to Believe* and cognate writings as simply a disinterested empirical account of belief processes would be as violent a distortion of his intentions and accomplishments as to interpret *The Varieties of Religious Experience* as merely a selection of data for the purpose of justifying James's own

2. Macintosh, *Theology as an Empirical Science* (New York, 1919). See chap. 7, below.

religious attitudes and beliefs.[3] In James the two interests were mutually supportive—and he could freely make evaluative comments on the experiences he surveyed—but they should not be confused.

While James is not the originator of the empirical psychology of religion or wholly typical of the movement, the *Varieties* has certainly proved to be its most remarkable document. By looking at "the immediate content of the religious consciousness,"[4] James aimed to develop a rudimentary science of religion, exhibiting particularly its variations and its types as phenomena of human experience (the subtitle of the book is important: "A Study in Human Nature"). The gamut of forms ranged from St. Theresa to Wesley, Luther, "mind cure," transcendentalism, Cotton Mather, and Al-Ghazzali.

Several elements of the methodology are crucial. James assumes that there are identifiable religious experiences, though at the outset these can only be described broadly as "the feelings, acts, and experiences of individual men in their solitude, so far as they apprehend themselves to stand in relation to whatever they may consider the divine" (p. 31). The divine can mean anything that is godlike. Religious also suggests a seriousness or solemnity of experience and an emotion of "happiness in the absolute and everlasting," "an enthusiastic temper of espousal" (see pp. 37, 48).

The religious sentiment is not a single sort of mental entity, but rather a collective label, and one of the tasks is to ask what the varieties have in common. Thus James's study is an empirico-historical investigation of a species of phenomena, similar to Darwin's study (it is revelatory of Darwin's importance for James that the themes of variation and selection are prominent throughout James's work). The data, further, are not the experiences themselves, but the reports of experiences from persons of widely differing times, cultures, and beliefs. Since the inquiry is psychological, dealing with feelings and impulses, James draws mainly on "those more developed subjective

---

3. The latter was James H. Leuba's accusation; see *A Psychological Study of Religion* (New York, 1912), pp. 272–74. H. S. Levinson, in his otherwise excellent study of James, *Science, Metaphysics and the Chance of Salvation* (Missoula, Mont., 1978), tends also in this direction (see pp. 179–89).

4. *The Varieties of Religious Experience*, p. 12. Citations are from the 1928 New York edition. In the context of this quotation, James was objecting both to certain attempts to identify the religious phenomena of melancholy and conversion with adolescence and puberty, and to general causal reductionism of religious experience to organic or neurological states. He reasoned that such reduction does not really characterize the phenomenon itself, nor does it help us in evaluation.

phenomena recorded in literature produced by articulate and fully self-conscious men, in works of piety and autobiography" (p. 3). He makes frequent use of manuscript accounts provided by Starbuck, Flournoy, and Leuba, and occasionally by Coe, though James had little interest in pursuing the kind of questionnaire study already being developed by Starbuck and others.[5] James's interpretation is more historical than empirical or phenomenological. He wants to make judgments about the constitution, origin, and history of religious experience, not about causes, for this would get in the way of exhibiting the phenomena. He is concerned with the conditions under which beliefs come to be held and are changed, that is, how the varieties are selected and imitated.[6]

James is particularly interested in the extreme cases, the "religious geniuses." These are the best witnesses, the "pattern setters" for the mass of conventional religious feelings, by looking at whom one can determine the boundaries of religious experience. Since the essence of religious experiences must be "that element or quality in them which we can meet nowhere else," "such a quality will be of course most prominent and easy to notice in those religious experiences which are most one-sided, exaggerated, and intense" (p. 45). The study of the abnormal, the exaggerated, and even the perverted always leads to a better understanding of the thing itself (p. 22). Here again James's approach is distinct from that of other empirical psychologists of religion (like Starbuck) who were interested in the experience of the ordinary religious person and in statistical averages.

Finally, James deliberately chose to focus on the experiences of individuals, foregoing concern with institutional dimensions (worship and sacrifice, theology, ecclesiastical organization) in order to concentrate attention on the human aspect, and particularly on the element of feeling rather than intellect in religion.[7] He was, contrary to the charge often made against him, quite aware of the social character of religion. That followed necessarily from his understanding of the social self as one of the constituents of empirical selfhood,[8] and the social aspect is exhibited particularly in the character of saintli-

5. See his preface to Starbuck's *Psychology of Religion* (London, 1899); also his responses to a questionnaire from J. B. Pratt, in the *Letters of William James* (Boston, 1920), 2:212–15.

6. See his discussion of belief psychology in *Principles of Psychology* (New York, 1890), 2, chap. 21.

7. See *Varieties*, pp. 27–31, 501. James felt that the institutional forms were oriented to the object.

8. See *Principles of Psychology*, 1:293–96. This is not, to be sure, the social selfhood of G. H. Mead and others. For James, a person has many social selves.

ness, though all religious behavior is social because it is human behavior. But by looking at the individual, one sees best the feeling dimension, the variety, and the psychological process (for example, in
conversion).

In surveying the terrain of religious experience, James marks out
the topography in one way by his classic distinction between the two
psychological temperaments: the optimistic, or "healthy-minded,"
and the pessimistic, morbid, or "sick-soul." Of course, the two basic
types of experience regularly intermingle in the same person, so that
most religious experience is a mixture. It has been argued that the
"saintly" is a third basic type of personality, but while James does
speak of certain psychological characteristics that distinguish the
saintly person, saintliness is a different modality of religious experience that cuts across the distinction between the healthy-minded versus sick-soul or the once-born versus twice-born types.[9] Saintliness
should not be placed alongside the general distinction, but should be
understood as part of another sort of mapping of dimensions of
human religiousness similar to the examinations of conversion and
mysticism.

The religion of healthy-mindedness presents a simple kind of religious happiness, in which "happiness is congenital and irreclaima-
ble." It is optimistic. In this religious sensibility, the goodness of life
and the union with the divine predominate from the outset. Evil is
not an overwhelming threat but a challenge, an obstacle to be overcome—in the extreme forms of this religion evil can be disregarded
or put down as ignorance or falsehood. God is the giver of freedom
to overcome the sting of evil, the helper and partner in the struggle.
We see here "the presence of a temperament organically weighted
on the side of cheer and fatally forbidden to linger, as those of the
opposite temperament linger, over the darker aspects of the universe" (p. 83). Such a temperament may be involuntary, or it may be
voluntary and systematic: "In its involuntary variety, healthy-mindedness is a way of feeling happy about things immediately. In its sys-
tematical variety, it is an abstract way of conceiving things as good,"
selecting good as the essential and universal aspect of being, and
systematically cultivating healthy-mindedness as an attitude (pp.
87–90).

Examples of once-born religiousness range from the quasi-patho-

9. James borrowed his use of the terms *once-born* and *twice-born* from Francis W. Newman, *The Soul: Its Sorrows and Its Aspirations*, 3d ed. (London, 1852); see *Varieties*, p. 80.

logical optimism (anesthetized against sadness) of a Walt Whitman, to transcendentalism, to the mind-cure movements (of which Christian Science is the most extreme in dealing with evil), to unitarianism, to evolutionary optimism, to liberal theology generally, even to the psychologically equivalent experiences of regeneration by "letting go" in Lutheran justification by faith and Wesleyan acceptance of free grace and to the Catholic practice of confessions and absolution, which is "in one of its aspects little more than a systematic method of keeping healthy-mindedness on top" (p. 128). This type of religion exists where the conquering efficacy of courage, hope, and trust dominates over "doubt, fear, worry, and all nervously precautionary states of mind" (p. 95).

In contrast, the sick-soul, or morbid tendency and perspective, maximizes evil, seeing it as "an essential part of our being and the key to the interpretation of life" (p. 131). Here are melancholy and the sense of our helplessness, of failure, of wrongness or vice in our essential nature, of sin rather than sins, of the vanity of mortal things, of fear of the universe—in which "original optimism and self-satisfaction get levelled with the dust" (p. 161). At the extreme emerge psychical neuralgia and panic fear. Throughout, the sense of helplessness is joined with the need for assurance and deliverance by a power outside ourselves. For his examples, James turns especially to Tolstoy, Bunyan, and an account of fear of the universe which he later admitted to have been an experience of his own.

Between these two basic tendencies or types no final value judgment can be made. Both are valid types appropriate to differing temperaments. Despite his assertion in the *Varieties* that classic healthy-mindedness is inadequate as philosophical doctrine because it does not account for the stubborn reality of evil, and his own experiences of the sick-soul variety, James seems in his pluralism, activism, and meliorism to come down finally more on the side of healthy-mindedness. But more important, from the standpoint of an empirical account and interpretation, is his judgment that the pessimistic types of religion range over a wider scale of experience and thus provide richer material for the understanding of religious experience. The most complete religions are those of salvation (of which Buddhism and Christianity are best known to us), in which "the pessimistic elements are best developed" and in which "man must die to an unreal life before he can be born into the real life" (p. 165).

For the psychology of religious experience conversion is of particular interest, both as a great turning point in religious development and as the event in which the central issue of uneasiness and deliverance is sharply focused.[10] Both healthy-minded and sick-soul types can experience conversion—though it would seem that the absolute optimist and the absolute pessimist must be excluded, because neither has a divided self. Yet the sick-soul type of religion provides the richer examples; it is properly the religion of the twice-born. Psychologically, conversion involves the reunification of a divided self, being based on a "discordance of heterogeneity" in the self, an "incompletely unified moral and intellectual constitution," which most people exhibit in some degree or form (p. 167).

"Finding religion" is of course not the only way of attaining such unity. Religious conversion is, rather, one species of a genus characterized by the attainment of "a firmness, stability, and equilibrium succeeding a period of storm and stress and inconsistency" (p. 176). It is the process by which a divided self, "consciously wrong, inferior and unhappy, becomes unified and consciously right, superior and happy, in consequence of its firmer hold upon religious realities" (p. 189). Such a process may be gradual or sudden. It may be voluntary and conscious or it may take place in an involuntary and unconscious way (Starbuck's "volitional type" and "type by self-surrender"). But the difference, while striking, is not radical. What happens is that "religious ideas, previously peripheral in [one's] consciousness, now take a central place, and . . . religious aims form the habitual centre of his energy" (p. 196). Just how this happens is something psychology cannot give a proper account of, nor can it specify the whence of the deliverance that is sensed as received. The sometimes dramatic behavioral accompaniments of conversion, though they may make the experience memorable to the convert, are of no "essential spiritual significance" (p. 251), because it is by the fruits of the experience that its value is to be judged. The characteristic fruit is a state of assurance involving loss of worry, a sense of perceiving truths not known before, and an objective change that the world seems to undergo—a fairly constant and permanent change in attitude toward life (p. 248).

Saintliness is not actually another type of religious experience on the order of the once-born and twice-born types, though of course it is related to differing human susceptibilities of emotional excitement

---

10. Here James drew on the special studies of Starbuck, Leuba, and Coe.

and differing impulses and inhibitions. Saintliness is instead a "collective name for the ripe fruits of religion in a character" (p. 271), and James is not hesitant to say that the best fruits of religion are the best things in history. Saintliness is the genuinely strenuous, intense, uninhibited life in the religious center of personal energy. It marks the religiously fittest. Certain features seem common to the religious hero in all religions: (1) "a feeling of being in a wider life than that of this world's selfish little interests; and a conviction . . . as it were sensible, of the existence of an Ideal Power"; (2) "a sense of the friendly continuity of the ideal power with our own life, and a willing surrender to its control"; (3) "an immense elation and freedom, as the outlines of the confining selfhood melt down"; and (4) "a shifting of the emotional centre towards loving and harmonious affections, towards 'yes, yes,' and away from 'no,' where the claims of the non-ego are concerned" (pp. 272–73). From these inner conditions certain characteristic practical consequences follow. They include charity and brotherly love, an enlargement of life or strength of soul (in equanimity, resignation, fortitude, and patience), a purity of life, and ascetic practices to overrule the "ordinary inhibitions of the flesh" in the service of the higher power.

All of these fruits can be corrupted by excess and imbalance. Devoutness can be tipped over into fanaticism. Purity can become selfish withdrawal. Irresponsible tenderness and charity can breed beggars and parasites. Asceticism is well known for its liability to extravagance and excess. Though "in its spiritual meaning asceticism stands for nothing less than for the essence of the twice-born philosophy" (p. 362), it can become pathological self-mortification. Yet despite these dangers of excess and distortion, it is in the fruits that are saintliness that the value of religion for human life can be judged (that is, its social value, in lives "adapted to the highest society conceivable"). Social value, or utility, can in good empiricist and pragmatist fashion be a proper criterion for religious truth. If religion is true, its fruits will be good.

Mysticism does not really fit well into James's empiricist account of the types of experience, despite his writing that "personal religious experience has its root and centre in mystical states of consciousness" (p. 379), and the importance that his own account had in the late-nineteenth-century rise of interest in mysticism. This is not simply because of his professed constitutional inability to participate in mystical states, but because by its nature mysticism eludes the kinds of public accountability of the other dimensions and forms of religious experience. Yet James felt compelled to exhibit its varieties and its importance for some as part of the picture of religious experience (though in less than half the space devoted to saintliness). James finds mysticism to be characterized especially by claims to ineffability and yet to special noetic quality, also (though less sharply) by transiency and passivity of the subject in relation to or in identity with the divine.

Herein lie the difficulties for an empiricist account. When the question is asked whether mysticism can be taken as authoritative in religion, whether it furnishes "any *warrant for the truth*" of the generally pantheistic and optimistic view it favors, or the twice-bornness and otherworldliness it best harmonizes with, the answer has to be no. Mystical states "break down the authority of the non-mystical or rationalistic consciousness, based on the understanding and the sense alone. They show it to be only one kind of consciousness [and] open out the possibility of other orders of truth." Mystical experiences have "the right to be absolutely authoritative over the individuals to whom they come." But they can have no authority "which should make it a duty for those who stand outside of them to accept their revelations uncritically" (pp. 422–23; see pp. 422–29). In other words, the claims of validity for the mystic cannot be attacked, but neither can these play an authoritative role (which presumably the other types of experience can) in the interpretation and evaluation of religious experience, except in the negative sense of overthrowing the pretensions of nonmystical states to be the sole dictators of belief. They offer hypotheses which can be ignored, though they cannot be overthrown from outside. They may be the truest insights into the meaning of life, and at their best James thinks they "point in directions to which the religious sentiments even of non-mystical men incline" (p. 428). But no epistemic claims can be made that have validity outside the experiences.

It is evident from the problem posed by mysticism that James, in the *Varieties*, was not interested solely in a descriptive science of the manifold types and variations in religious experience. He also wanted to bring the empirical account into relation with his concern for viewing belief from the inside, for understanding the right to believe. Thus, at the end, James turns to the question of what can be concluded from the whole examination. The answer can be condensed into four points.

First, though he does not need to reiterate this at the end, is the astonishing variety of religious experience. He had said much earlier, "The whole outcome of these lectures will, I imagine, be the emphasizing to your mind of the enormous diversities which the spiritual lives of different men exhibit" (p. 109). Second is the primacy of feeling over intellectual formulation in religion. Intellectual operations are important, but they "presuppose immediate experiences as their subject matter," and if there is any possibility of a science of religions it must deal with these experiences (p. 433). James hoped for a "critical science of religion" that could stand on a par with physical science.

Third, though an emphatic "No" should be given to the question whether the elements of religion should be the same in all men, a view of the entire panorama leads to the conclusion that, "summing up in the broadest possible way the characteristics of the religious life," this life includes the beliefs: "1. That the visible world is part of a more spiritual universe from which is drawn its chief significance; 2. That union or harmonious relation with that higher universe is our true end; 3. That prayer or inner communion with the spirit thereof—be that spirit 'God' or 'law'—is a process wherein work is really done, and spiritual energy flows in and produces effects, psychological or material, within the phenomenal world." Religion also includes two psychological characteristics: "4. A new zest which adds itself like a gift to life, and takes the form either of lyrical enchantment or of appeal to earnestness and heroism. 5. An assurance of safety and a temper of peace, and, in relation to others, a preponderance of loving affections" (pp. 485–86).

Further, if we ask whether there is any common nucleus under all the discrepancies of the creeds, James does find

a certain uniform deliverance in which all religions appear to meet. It consists of two parts:
1. An uneasiness; and
2. Its solution.
1. The uneasiness, reduced to its simplest terms, is a sense that there is *something wrong about us* as we naturally stand.
2. The solution is a sense that *we are saved from the wrongness* by making proper connection with the higher powers.

In this second stage, the individual becomes conscious that the "better part of him" is his real being, and *"he becomes conscious that this higher part is coterminous and continuous with a* MORE *of the same quality, which is operative in the universe outside of him, and which he can keep in working touch with, and in a fashion get on board of and save himself when all his lower being has gone to pieces in the wreck"* (p. 508).

Fourth and finally, does the science of religion provide any warrants for the truth of this religious view? James's answer is a qualified "Yes": "We have in *the fact that the conscious person is continuous with a wider self through which saving experiences come,* a positive content of religious experience which, it seems to me, *is literally and objectively true as far as it goes"* (p. 515). Beyond that we are in the realm of permissible hypotheses and overbeliefs.

Empirical Psychology of Religion: Starbuck and Others

Wilhelm Wundt is generally accounted the founder of modern experimental psychology. His *Psychologische Institut,* established at Leipzig in 1879, was the first psychological laboratory and the training ground for many experimentalists, and his *Völkerpsychologie*[11] incorporated a great deal from anthropological studies of religion.

Yet the empirical psychology of religion was a peculiarly American phenomenon, born and flourishing best there. It was more clearly differentiated in America (and to some extent in France) from the philosophy of religion than in Britain or Germany. German interest in religious psychology tended to be heavily philosophical or theological in orientation.[12] French work rarely employed the questionnaire method (an exception is L. Arreat, *Le Sentiment religieux en France* [1903], a study of current religious consciousness). The earliest British book in the field of empirical psychology was George M. Stratton, *The Psychology of the Religious Life* (London, 1912).

The first American empirical psychologist of religion, who deserves as much as anyone to be called the originator of the movement, was Granville Stanley Hall, later president of Clark University (1889) and founder of both the *American Journal of Psychology* (1887) and the *Journal of Religious Psychology* (1904–14). A student of Wil-

11. 10 vols. (Leipzig, 1900–20). For his basic psychological outlook, see *Grundzüge der physiologischen Psychologie* (Leipzig, 1874; 6th ed., 1908–11).

12. See, for example, the attempt by Georg Wobbermin at a *Systematische Theologie nach religionspsychologischer Methode* (1: *Die Religionspsychologische Methode in Religionswissenschaft und Theologie,* [Leipzig, 1913]), in which the German contribution to the formulation of the problem of religious psychology is identified almost entirely with the late-nineteenth-century recovery of Schleiermacherian perspectives, which Wobbermin sees as strongly supported by William James.

liam James at Harvard, he was the first American Ph.D. in psychology as well as the first American student at Wundt's laboratory (from the year of its founding), and he opened his own psychological laboratory at Johns Hopkins in 1883. As early as 1881 he began to report data collected on religious conversion—a special interest of American studies, doubtless because of the great impact of revivalism in the formation of American Protestant religious life. And he initiated extensive employment of the questionnaire method for data collection.

The work of Edwin D. Starbuck is the prime instance of this new method and interest. He reflects the special interest in conversion, though also in other patterns of religious growth, and in the ordinary and common experience (in contrast to James's focus on the extremes). A student of Hall, he had started at Harvard and continued at Stanford the collection and statistical analysis of an extensive body of data, which resulted in 1899 in the first full-length book of its kind, *The Psychology of Religion: An Empirical Study of the Growth of Religious Experience*,[13] a work still looked upon as a classic.

The data used (like most of James's) were autobiographical statements, but collected in response to common sets of questions (some of them fairly general ones), in order that genuine comparability might exist. Published autobiographies were not useful because they are not susceptible to scientific comparison. This was planned as a "purely inductive study into the phenomena of religion as shown in individual experience" (p. 16). For the study of conversion, Starbuck attempted to get a broad sample of Protestant Americans, which finally totaled 1,265 persons (1,011 male and 254 female), including 192 cases with information complete enough for full analysis. For the study of religious growth not involving conversion, responses were secured from 237 persons. (In neither case was the sample representative of the whole Protestant population in any strict sense, and of this Starbuck was quite aware.)

The principles of such studies were quite clear. The psychology of religion is an effort "to carry the well-established methods of science into the analysis and organization of the facts of religious consciousness, and to ascertain the laws which determine its growth and character" (p. 1). This assumes that "there is no event in the spiritual life

---

13. (London, 1899). References are to the 1906 New York edition. It may be significant that the book was first published in England, perhaps because of the delicacy of treating "objectively" a "subjective" or inner experience (conversion) that had been of such importance in the American scene.

which does not occur in accordance with immutable laws," that "every thought or volition or emotion, every expression of consciousness, is an index of some law of life; . . . the best way to understand the mental life is to view each of its manifestations as a fact of nature, and to study such expressions objectively" (pp. 3, 4). That does not mean that psychology can resolve the mystery of religion, most of which will remain outside its grasp, but it can "bring enough into orderliness that its facts may appeal to our understanding" (p. 11). The facts have an order which, given enough wisdom, can be ascertained.

Specific data related to such matters as age and place of conversion; age of most rapid bodily growth and accession to puberty; health before, at the time, and after; permanence of effect or relapse; and present age, sex, church, vocation, nationality, place of residence. More general questions referred to such things as religious customs, youthful struggles, motives and influences, doubts, fears, inner feelings, truths embodying deepest feelings, and stages of growth. From the mass of data, laboriously tabulated and exhibited in tables and graphs, Starbuck found it possible to make statistically based physiological, psychological, and sociological generalizations on topics ranging from the most common ages of conversion (and their relation to growth and the onset of puberty) to the general characteristics of both normal and abnormal conversions, the general religion of childhood, and overall lines of religious growth with and without conversion.

Not surprisingly, since James drew on his work, Starbuck's understanding of what happens psychologically in conversion is not unlike James's description. In leading up to conversion, "there are forces in human life and its surroundings which tend to break the unity and harmony of consciousness; and its unity once destroyed, the contrast between what is, and what might be, gives birth to ideals and sets two selves in sharp opposition to each other" (p. 155). Conversion itself is "primarily an unselfing": "the person emerges from a smaller, limited world of existence into a larger world of being. . . . conversion is the surrender of the personal will to be guided by the larger forces of which it is a part. . . . the individual learns to transfer himself from a centre of self-activity into an organ of revelation of universal being, and to live a life of affection for and oneness with the larger life outside" (pp. 146–47).

It was Starbuck's view that an objective understanding of the physiological, psychological, and sociological dimensions and correlates of religious growth would make a significant contribution to the practical work of religious education. That opinion and aim were shared and developed by others, notably by George A. Coe.[14] Coe also was interested in studying conversion, particularly the temperamental factors or general personality characteristics. In a significant methodological advance, he designed for his initial work questions aimed not only at reports of experiences but also at illuminating the personalities of the respondents. These questions were pursued in interviews with subjects and their acquaintances, in the creation of a scale for "objective observation of temperamental manifestations," and in hypnotic experiments to explore suggestibility. This intensive study involved seventy-seven persons, mostly healthy college students with religious training. Some notable distinctions in temperament or personality type emerged: for example, between those who expected a transformation and had it and those who expected one but did not; and between those whose conversions were accompanied by striking phenomena (such as visions or automatic behavior) and those who experienced no such manifestations. Thus in another way the psychological mechanisms involved in religious experience were illumined, and in this kind of study, broader than that of Starbuck and culminating in *The Psychology of Religion*, Coe must be reckoned one of the pioneers.[15]

The basic question here is the relation of such objective analysis, with its disclosure of psychological dynamics in religion, to views of religious belief from within. For James these could be mutually supportive. So also for Starbuck. Similarly Coe, in a view much like that of James (and in language quoted in part by James), affirms that "the ultimate test of religious values is nothing psychological, nothing definable in terms of *how it happens*, but something ethical, definable only in terms of *what is attained*. . . . The worth of the experience depends, not upon the presence or the absence of suggestions, but

14. See esp. *The Spiritual Life: Studies in the Science of Religion* (New York, 1900), and *The Psychology of Religion* (New York, 1916). Coe later moved fully into the field of the psychology of religious education. Irving King, *The Differentiation of the Religious Consciousness* (New York, 1905), and *The Development of Religion: A Study in Anthropology and Social Psychology* (New York, 1910), also reflected this interest.

15. We may also note Edward Scribner Ames, esp. *The Psychology of Religious Experience* (Boston, 1910), though he was deeply dependent on James; and James B. Pratt, *The Psychology of Religious Belief* (New York, 1908), also indebted to James (and who was not?) and more philosophically oriented than the empiricists.

upon whether it includes a decision and renewal that reach deep into the springs of conduct."[16]

But a quite contrary view was also held. It is most sharply expressed in the attitude of Wilhelm Herrmann, for whom this sort of objective study, which belongs to scientific knowledge in general, could contribute nothing to the inner life of faith. Theology should eschew such study. That attitude was not lost on James H. Leuba, who found in the Ritschlian position evidence of a basic antagonism and a last-ditch futile attempt to save the truth of religious experience from the erosion of psychological explanation.

Psychological Reductionism: Leuba and Freud

Leuba, a Swiss graduate of the University of Neuchatel who moved with his family to New York, was another of Hall's students at Clark University. His doctoral dissertation on conversion, based on interviews as well as questionnaires and published accounts, was published in the *American Journal of Psychology* (1896). Here, as in subsequent writings, he offered a thoroughly naturalistic interpretation, according to which the process, from psychological conditions prior to conversion, through the crisis itself, to the subsequent state of "faith," can be fully accounted for in the tracing of causal sequences. Faith is seen as simply supervening on specific and always identical psychological phenomena. The religious is not different in kind from the nonreligious consciousness.

In later works, Leuba tended to draw on anthropological materials (especially Frazer and Marett) more than on questionnaire-type data.[17] He found anthropological information valuable in accounting for the origins of the ideas of impersonal powers and unseen, personal beings, and of the relations between religion and magic. But his perspective was consistent. In the *Psychological Study of Religion*, for example, he reiterated that there is no specifically religious impulse or purpose or emotion. Any impulse or desire can lead to religious activity, just as any type of emotion in religion can also be found outside it. What "makes life religious . . . is standing in relation with, or attempting to make use of, a particular kind of power" (p. 7).

---

16. Coe, *Spiritual Life*, pp. 144, 146.
17. Leuba, *A Psychological Study of Religion* (New York, 1912), *The Belief in God and Immortality* (New York, 1916), and *The Psychology of Religious Mysticism* (New York, 1925).

The real question is of the function of religion in life, not whether it is a belief or feeling or idea or attitude or relation or faculty (p. 42). All that is necessary for the function is mere belief in the existence of divinities or psychic powers, not their actual existence (p. 18). One of religion's functions is causal explanation; the major one is assistance in the struggle for life, its preservation and advancement (pp. 51, 111). What differentiates religion is "the kind of power upon which dependence is felt and the kind of behavior elicited by the power." "The reason for the existence of religion is not the objective truth of its conceptions, but its biological value" (pp. 52, 53). While fear is the most conspicuous emotion in primitive religious life, nothing entitles fear to be called a distinctive or original religious emotion (p. 129). The decline in the importance of fear, or its replacement by awe, is not a result of changes in religion, for "religion is the instrument, not the creator, of human impulses and desires" (p. 132; see pp. 134–45).

Contrary to the notions of some anthropologists, religion and magic are clearly distinguishable from each other, and both of them from science. There are three fundamental types of behavior: the mechanical (science), the coercitive (magic), and the anthropopathic (religion) (p. 5). Leuba summarized a lengthy comparative study of magic and religion thus:

1. Magic and religion have had independent origins. Neither of them need be regarded as a development from the other.
2. Magic contributed very little directly to the making of religion.
3. The simpler forms of magic probably antedated religion.
4. Because they are different ways of achieving the same ends, magical and religious practices are closely associated.
5. Religion is social and beneficial; magic is dominantly individual and often evil.
6. Magic is of shorter duration than religion.
7. Science is closely related neither to magic nor to religion, but to the mechanical type of behavior. (p. 176)

Plainly, in Leuba's judgment, religion, unlike magic, has an important social value. It performs a useful function. But its gods finally belong to the science of psychology. Belief in gods rests on inductions drawn from inner life, and inner experience or religious experience belongs entirely to psychology, just as nonreligious portions of consciousness do (p. 212). There is absolutely no legitimacy in the claim to immediacy in religious knowledge—whether in Jamesian openness to mysticism, or in Ritschlian separation of religious from theoretical judgments, or in any other claim to direct knowledge of the transcendent (see esp. pp. 207–77). "The hope to lift a theology based on inner experience out of the sphere of science is preposterous; since whatever appears in consciousness is material for psychology" (p. 242). Faith is known by psychology to be a quite ordinary phenomenon, not at all limited to religious life (p. 263).

Theology, therefore, to have any significant future must become a branch of psychology. If it is "ever to find out what beliefs work best towards self-realization and happiness, it will have to deal with inner experience according to the best scientific methods" (p. 277). The religion of the future, Leuba concludes, "will have to rest content apparently with the idea of a non-purposive Creative Force, making of the universe neither an accidental creation nor one shaped in accordance with some preconceived plan. . . . Humanity idealized and conceived as a manifestation of Creative Energy possesses surpassing qualifications for a source of religious inspiration" (pp. 334–35). Such a religion would contribute to the making of an ideal society and would perform religion's proper function.

Despite his distaste for theological truth claims, Leuba was far more sympathetic to the psychological function of religion than was Sigmund Freud. For Leuba religion properly understood can be a psychologically and socially healthy thing. For Freud, on the other hand, except insofar as the repression of instinct is a condition of civilization, religion is a hindering neurosis. His was a radically different sort of reductionism.

Freud's enormous influence on religious thinking was, of course, a post–World War II event. The story of that impact belongs to the history of contemporary theology rather than to a study of nineteenth-century religious thought—and it is a story that must take account of much more than Freud's explicit writings and views on religion. Yet it is essential to note the two early works of Freud in which his understanding of religion began to emerge clearly: the brief 1907 essay, "Obsessive Actions and Religious Practices," and *Totem and Taboo* (1913), which laid the basis for themes developed in *The Future of an Illusion* (1927) and in *Moses and Monotheism* (1939).[18]

18. "Zwangshandlungen und Religionsübungen," first published in *Zeitschrift für Religionspsychologie* 1:1 (1907): 4–12. See *The Complete Psychological Works of Sigmund Freud*, ed. James Strachey, 9 (London, 1959): 117–27. *Totem and Taboo* was first published in four issues of *Imago* (1912–13), under the title "Some Points of Agreement between the Mental

In the first paper on the psychology of religion, Freud drew a general analogy between the psychological processes of religious life, as seen in the sacred acts of religious ritual, and the neurotic ceremonials that are found as part of the clinical entity he called "obsessional neuroses." Sharp differences exist, notably the great variability and private character of the neurotic ceremonials, with their particular anxieties, prohibitions, and adjustments of everyday actions, in contrast to the public, communal, and stereotyped nature of religious observances. But the same psychological forces are at work: the anxieties about deviation from the ritual, the performance of the act without concern for its significance, the displacement of psychic values, and particularly the suppression and renunciation of instinctual impulses. Thus obsessional neurosis can be called "a travesty, half comic and half tragic, of a private religion," or "a pathological counterpart of the formation of a religion" (9:119, 126). On the other hand, religion can be described as a "universal obsessional neurosis. The most essential similarity would reside in the underlying renunciation of the activation of instincts that are constitutionally present; and the chief difference would lie in the nature of those instincts, which in the neurosis are exclusively sexual in their origin, while in religion they spring from egoistic sources" (p. 127). In this context also, Freud noted the religious process of surrendering to deity what is renounced, i.e., the projection of human qualities as divine attributes.[19]

In *Totem and Taboo*, particularly in the fourth essay, "The Return of Totemism in Childhood," the decisive element of Freud's theory of religion appears, namely, the basis in the Oedipus complex. In the preliminary essays, Freud reviews in some detail the current anthropological discussion (mainly by Frazer, but also by McLennan, Lang, Tylor, and Wundt) on primitive religion as characterized by totem-

---

Lives of Savages and Neurotics." The essays were then collected in one volume, *Totem und Tabu* (Leipzig and Vienna, 1913). See the *Complete Works*, 13 (London, 1955): 1–161. References in the text are to the *Complete Works*.

19. Comparison with Feuerbach is inevitable. While Freud does say that "all the attributes of man, along with the misdeeds that follow from them, were to an unlimited amount ascribed to the ancient gods," his concern is mainly with the "iniquities," the pleasurable and egoistic instincts (including vengeance) that are renounced and handed over to deity. Feuerbach, on the other hand, particularly in *The Essence of Christianity*, is interested in man's handing over his own goodness and knowledge to God—so that he can get them back in the end. See *Prot. Thought*, 1:170–77.

ism, rules of exogamy, taboos (especially the incest taboo), animism, and magic. He accepts the view of the original dominance of totemism in religion and of animism as the first human Weltanschauung (with magic as the technique of animistic thinking), though from the psychoanalytic view he agrees with Marett's idea of a preanimistic stage. It is significant for him that this first (animistic) picture of the world was a psychological one.

His own interest, of course, was in what a psychoanalytic view could offer for further understanding of the phenomena. In the course of the earlier essays we encounter again the principle of projection outward of internal perceptions, as in the projection of unconscious hostility onto demons in the taboo upon the dead and in the projective creation of souls and spirits (see 13:36, 64, 92f.). Obvious similarities are found between taboos and the obsessional prohibitions of neurotics (p. 26), and a survival in obsessional neurosis of magic's principle of the "omnipotence of thoughts" (pp. 85–86). The sequence of animistic (mythological), religious, and scientific stages in human history is seen as corresponding to infancy, childhood, and maturity in an individual's libidinal development (p. 90).

Not until the final essay does Freud come to his central point. He disclaims any attempt on the part of psychoanalysis to reduce the origins of religion to a single source or to give a total explanation. But in the face of the ambiguities and disagreements of the interpreters regarding the origins of totemism and the explanations of the relation between totemism and exogamy, he proposes that psychoanalysis can throw a "single ray of light." The totemic system was "a product of the conditions involved in the Oedipus complex." The totem animal, with which every clan member is identified, is looked upon as the common ancestor and primal father. And "if the totem animal is the father, then the two principal ordinances of totemism, the two taboo prohibitions which constitute its core—not to kill the totem and not to have sexual relations with a woman of the same totem—coincide in their content with the two crimes of Oedipus, who killed his father and married his mother, as well as with the two primal wishes of children, the insufficient repression or the re-awakening of which forms the nucleus of perhaps every psychoneurosis" (13:132). Here the otherwise puzzling relation of the two major taboos becomes quite clear.

Freud found further illumination in William Robertson Smith's ar-

gument for the integral role of the totem meal in the totemic system.[20] Only in this meal, in which the sacrificial animal, the god, and
the community are of the same blood and members of one clan, is
the killing of the totem animal permitted. By combining the recognition of the totem animal as substitute for the father with the fact of
the totem meal and with something of Darwin's idea of the primal
horde in which a jealous father keeps all the females to himself and
drives away the sons, we can recognize the totem meal as a reflection
and commemoration of the killing and devouring of the father by
sons who had been driven out, thus accomplishing their identification with him and gaining his strength. The deed is commemorated
in the meal, but it is also revoked by proscription of the killing of the
totem, and the gains of the deed are renounced by forfeiture of
claim to the women of the same clan. Thus again the common deri-
vation of the two great taboos in which human morality has its origin
is manifest.

It is not clear to what extent Freud wanted to think of the primordial deed as historical event. He acknowledged the difficulties in assuming a collective mind, and he did not know what to do with the
mother goddesses. But he was clear in his judgment that totemic religion arose from the filial sense of guilt and that "all later religions are
seen to be attempts at solving the same problem" of allaying the feeling and appeasing the father (13:145). Further, the ambivalence in
the father complex persists. There is not only remorse and attempt
at atonement; there is also, as in the totemic meal, remembrance and
celebration of the triumph—and nowhere more clearly than in the
Christian Eucharist, which is a fresh elimination of the father.

Though he sought to bring only "a single ray of light," Freud felt
able in conclusion to insist that the inquiry "shows that the beginnings of religion, morals, society and art converge in the Oedipus
complex," and that this is in complete agreement with the psychoanalytic finding that the same complex constitutes the nucleus of all
neuroses, "so far as our present knowledge goes" (pp. 156, 157).

Sociologies of Religion

It would be far beyond the limits of this book to attempt to give a
full and systematic account of the emergence of the sociology of reli-

20. In *Lectures on the Religion of the Semites*. Freud significantly distorted Smith's view and
showed no awareness of current criticisms of the position, or of the objections to the totemic theory.

gion as a discipline in the closing decades of the nineteenth century (1885–1915). However, the impact of this kind of approach to an objective study of religion mandates the identification of three important, innovative, and influential figures who represent types of the sociology of religion: William Robertson Smith, Emile Durkheim, and Max Weber. As is immediately evident when we look at Smith and Durkheim, no good purpose is served by trying to distinguish sharply between sociological and anthropological in this context, or by setting them over against psychological modes of analysis (as the example of Freud shows). All of these were involved in the new forms of comparative religious study.

William Robertson Smith

The Prophets of Israel (Edinburgh, 1882) has been called the least dated of the works of W. Robertson Smith,[21] who contributed well over two hundred articles on biblical and related topics to the ninth edition of the *Encyclopaedia Britannica*, of which he became the editor-in-chief. But it was not in his literary or linguistic studies that Smith was innovative. In these areas of biblical and Semitic research he was largely dependent on Continental scholarship (notably on Wellhausen, whom he came to know in Germany). What was original and decisive in his analysis of Semitic religion was the sociological or social anthropological approach. Malinowski judged him "perhaps the first clearly to recognize the sociological aspect in all human religions and also to emphasize, at times perhaps to over-emphasize, the importance of ritual as against dogma."[22] James Frazer was his protégé; he was a precursor of Durkheim; and we have seen how important Freud thought his work (even while misusing it). Smith's insights were further taken up by such later thinkers as Franz Steiner, E. E. Evans-Pritchard, E. R. Leach, and Mary Douglas.

21. A full bibliography of Smith's work, as well as a useful introduction, is given in T. O. Beidelman, *W. Robertson Smith and the Sociological Study of Religion* (Chicago, 1974). After losing his post at the Free Church Divinity School (attached to the University of Aberdeen) because of protests against his early essays, Smith became, in addition to his work on the *Britannica*, Reader (and then Professor) of Arabic at Cambridge, and also Librarian of the University.

22. B. Malinowski, *Sex, Culture, and Myth* (New York, 1962), p. 254. Beidelman concludes that "it can be claimed confidently that Smith is the founder of modern sociology of religion" (*W. Robertson Smith*, p. 68), though Smith's good friend John McLennan (on whose work he drew) might more strictly be considered the first major writer in social anthropology.

Growing out of a short essay on "Animal Tribes in the Old Testament" (1880), lectures on *Kinship and Marriage in Early Arabia* (Cambridge, 1885), and his article on "Sacrifice" in the *Britannica* (1886), the *Lectures on Religion of the Semites: First Series, The Fundamental Institutions* was Smith's decisive and culminating socioanthropological work, published in Edinburgh in 1889.[23]

The central analytical principle of the work was the social basis of religious behavior, the priority of practice over belief, of socially sanctioned ritual over myth and legend. Even (or especially) to understand the deviant person—whether the innovative prophet, whom Smith thought introduced a higher form of religion, and whom he contrasted to the priest-king, or the retrograde individual, such as the practitioner of magic—one must first understand the social organization of the time, including its cosmology and modes of thought and expression. Here ritual precedes myth. The acting out of symbolic behavior is more important than the legend or belief attached to it. The ritual is prescribed; the myth is optional and variable. Myth is derived from the ritual, not ritual from the myth. Thus the *Lectures* were subtitled *The Fundamental Institutions*. Smith could even say that "ritual and practical usage were, strictly speaking, the sum-total of ancient religions." Contrary to modern ways of thinking, primitive religion "was not a system of belief with practical applications; it was a body of fixed traditional practices, to which every member of society conformed as a matter of course." Equally important, religious and political institutions were parts of one whole of social custom. "Religion was a part of the organized social life into which a man was born, and to which he conformed through life in the same unconscious way in which men fall into any habitual practice of the society in which they live." Thus "the history of religious institutions is the history of ancient religion itself" (pp. 20, 21, 25).

Associated with this analytical principle was the assumption that developed cultures and religions may be understood by the comparative study of simpler, and presumably earlier, cultures. Behind the great positive religions—Judaism, Christianity, and Islam, which arose because of religious innovators—lay "the old unconscious reli-

---

23. A second, revised edition (London, 1894) was published just after Smith's death. The work is cited in the text with page references to the third edition, which contains an introduction and additional notes by Stanley A. Cook (New York and London, 1927). Because of his poor health, Smith was unable to publish the second and third series of lectures, which were delivered in Aberdeen in 1890 and 1891.

gious tradition" which Smith was seeking to delineate and which could be identified by "survivals" in a later period of "higher" development (the doctrine of survivals was one of the weaker elements in the method, making the result a highly conjectural historical reconstruction). The understanding of sacrifice in the Old and New Testaments, for example, requires a knowledge of the older tradition.

This did not mean for Smith that Christianity is really subject to the same sort of sociological analysis (he omitted from the second edition of the *Lectures* a paragraph on the death of the God-man and the "germ" of John xvii.19). Christianity was for him a revealed, true religion, and truer in its Protestant than in its Catholic form. Smith could regularly speak of the "heathenism" of primitive Semitic religion, and of the "lower" forms of nonrational and nonethical religion. These could properly be viewed sociologically, but Christianity could be conceived only in intellectual and absolute terms. Christianity, however, was not excluded from a further principle of comparative study, that of evolutionary development, in which both Judaism and Christianity participate. Smith could speak of the "fact" that mankind all over the world has moved in the same general direction of human progress, though at different rates. "Advanced" societies have developed on similar lines.

A general concern in the *Lectures* was the earliest form of religion —in which Smith found both common developmental principles and a psychic unity of man. As he wrote in the introduction,

> This account of the position of religion in the social system holds good, I believe, for all parts and races of the ancient world in the earlier stages of their history. The causes of so remarkable a uniformity lie hidden in the midst of prehistoric time, but must plainly have been of a general kind, operating on all parts of mankind without distinction of race and local environment; for in every region of the world, as soon as we find a nation or tribe emerging from prehistoric darkness into the light of authentic history, we find also that its religion conforms to the general type which has just been indicated. (p. 30)

Here both the evolutionism and the essentialism of Smith are clear, both an evolutionary development and essentials that can be identified by sifting out common elements that have persisted through that evolution.

On these presuppositions, Smith found the earliest form of religion to be characteristically totemic (never polytheistic or monotheistic). While he did not originate the idea, but took it over from John McLennan,[24] Smith was particularly important in the development of the theory, which was then taken up uncritically by many others, notably by Frazer, who expanded (and somewhat distorted) the idea in the enormous and influential hodgepodge of material in *The Golden Bough*, and by Freud. The central principle of the theory is the solidarity expressed in the totem "of the gods and their worshippers as part of one organic society." "In the totem stage of society each kinship or stock of savages believes itself to be physically akin to some natural kind of animate or inanimate things, most generally to some kind of animal. Every animal of this kind is looked upon as a brother, is treated with the same respect as a human clansman, and is believed to aid his human relations by a variety of friendly services" (pp. 32, 124). Thus gods and worshippers were part and parcel of the same natural community bound together in a circle of blood relations, for the god was both father (physically as well as morally) and king, ancestor and ruler of the clan, so that the unity of blood relation was "the circle of all religious and social unity" (p. 512). To be sure, the origin of totemism remained a problem, and not all the phenomena of Semitic religion could be explained by totemism, but those phenomena clearly "carry us back to totemism" (p. 139).

It follows that totem and taboo are inseparably connected. The "only duties of absolute and indefeasible sanctity" are those of blood relation (p. 47). The principle of sanctity is identical with that of kinship. The rules of avoidance, as those of sacrificial obligation, are the institutional definitions of the unity of the community in which man naturally participated in the earliest stage of religion. In taboo, Smith saw evidence of a certain ambiguity, in that the rules of holiness, which constitute the system of restrictions relating to sacred things, places, and persons, are formally just like the rules of avoidance relating to pollution and uncleanness. It is not always clear, for example, whether the eating of a given animal's flesh is proscribed because the animal is holy or because it is unclean. Smith observes that "even in some advanced societies the notions of holiness and uncleanness often touch," though he found it "a real advance above savagery"

---

24. See J. F. McLennan, *Primitive Marriage* (Edinburgh, 1865), and *Studies in Ancient History* (London, 1876). Durkheim credits Smith with the first elaboration of the fundamental notions of totemism.

that at least the northern Semites distinguished between the holy and the unclean (pp. 153–54). But in either case, the dominance of the restrictive rules testifies to the priority of institution and ritual in the earliest form of religion.

Smith's special interest, to which he devoted more than half of the *Lectures*, was in the origin and meaning of sacrifice in the totemic system. This constituted "the central problem of ancient religion," for "sacrifice is the typical form of all complete acts of worship in antique religion" (pp. 27, 214). In contrast to the then prevalent theory (for example, Tylor's) that the sacrifice was primarily a gift, Smith introduced the thesis that "the leading idea in the animal sacrifices of the Semites . . . was not that of a gift made over to the god, but of an act of communion, in which the god and his worshippers unite by partaking together of the flesh and blood of a sacred victim" (pp. 226–27). Cereal offerings can be understood as given wholly over to the god, but the earliest form of sacrifice was that of a feast in which the (ancestor) totem animal was killed and eaten. The kinship identity of god, clan, and totem is here more than symbolized; in the eating of the flesh, its nature, or life, is absorbed into that of the worshipper. Thus the ritual proscription of any killing of the sacred animal apart from the sacrifice, and the prescription of the killing and eating in the sacrificial feast.

Smith's theory of the dominance of the communion motif was subsequently brought into serious question by social anthropologists, with the recognition that all aspects can be present at all stages. In particular, expiatory oblation, or sin-offering, which Smith took to be a later and dependent development, played a larger role than he allowed. The relatively neat chronological development that he assumed (with its corollary in the doctrine of survivals) was an oversimplification. Yet the theory of sacrifice was exploited by Freud and the communion idea taken up by Durkheim and others as one aspect of sacrifice. And quite beyond the particularities of Smith's theory, his focus on sacrifice was a cornerstone in the broader emphasis on the institution, the ritual, and behavior as the key to the scientific understanding of religion as a social reality.

Emile Durkheim

In Emile Durkheim's *Elementary Forms of the Religious Life*, the analysis of totemic religion first elaborated by Smith was refined and broadened into a powerful and generalized sociological theory of religion which became a primary source for later sociology of religion and for the sociology of knowledge in general.[25] But Durkheim was not simply dependent on Smith. In his account of the development of sociology in France in the nineteenth century, Durkheim traces the lineage of sociology as a science back to Saint-Simon and Comte, and in the *Elementary Forms* he takes up an enormous range of contemporary anthropological and sociological studies. Yet the continuity with Smith's themes is impressive.

First, totemism is the primitive form of religion. For Durkheim, the richest field for study (in the light of contemporary extensive reports, notably by Baldwin Spencer, F. J. Gillen, and Carl Strehlow) is the tribal religions of interior Australia. These Australian societies are appropriately the primary focus of attention not only because they have become the most completely documented but also because they represent perfectly homogeneous groups and the simplest and most primitive forms of society it has been possible to examine (p. 115). They clearly reveal that the original or core concept in religion is not the idea of the supernatural or the mysterious. The contrast of the supernatural with the natural is a late idea; primitive religious conceptions express what is constant and regular. Nor (against Tylor) does the foundation rest with ideas of divinity or spiritual beings. Some religions do not have divinities (for example, early Buddhism and Jainism), and many rites are independent of all ideas of gods. Religious phenomena are rather a complex of beliefs and rites which presuppose the distinction between the sacred and the profane (not between the supernatural and the natural), and which, in contrast to magic, are essentially social in character. Totemism, further, cannot he reduced or traced back either to animism (as Tylor and Spencer claim) or to naturism (as in Max Müller); both of those interpretations make religion a system of hallucinations (pp. 65–100), and it is a fundamental sociological postulate that no human institution can rest only on an error or a falsehood (pp. 14, 464).

Second, though Durkheim takes up for analysis first the funda-

25. *Les Formes élémentaires de la vie religieuse* (Paris, 1912). Page references are to the 1915 translation by Joseph Ward Swain, Free Press paperback ed. (New York, 1965). The other principal works that established Durkheim as one of the founders of modern scientific sociology include especially *The Division of Labor in Society* (1893; Eng. trans., Glencoe, Ill., 1947) and *The Rules of Sociological Method* (1895; Eng. trans., Glencoe, Ill., 1958). An account of Durkheim's life and a reasonably full bibliography are given in Henry Alpert, *Emile Durkheim and His Sociology* (New York, 1939).

mental beliefs and then the ritual attitudes, since the rite can be defined only after the belief, it is also true for him, as for Smith, that the study of religion is directed to the institutional forms, and that in the positive cult (as contrasted with ascetic rites) the center of the system is the great religious institution of sacrifice, "which was destined to become one of the foundation stones of the positive cult in the superior religions" (p. 377). It was necessary, of course, to correct Smith's particular theory of sacrifice.

Third, religious phenomena are ineradicably social, and this is the primary distinction from magic (which also involves rites and beliefs). "The really religious beliefs are always common to a determined group. . . . Religion . . . is inseparable from the idea of a Church. . . . a church is not a fraternity of priests; it is a moral community formed by all the believers in a single faith, laymen as well as priests." Religion is "an eminently collective thing," which can be formally defined as "a unified system of beliefs and practices relative to sacred things, that is to say, things set apart and forbidden—beliefs and practices which unite into one single moral community called a Church, all those who adhere to them" (pp. 59–63). A proper application of this principle further requires that religious phenomena be considered and compared as parts of particular social systems. Durkheim judged Frazer's failure to recognize this as a principal error in his *Totemism*, which indiscriminately lumped together all the traces of totemism that Frazer could find.

In the elaboration of these themes, several further basic assumptions and theses are evident. One, already mentioned, is the introduction of the sacred/profane distinction. This "division of the world into two domains," which are radically opposed, having nothing in common even though a being may pass by real metamorphosis from one to the other, "is the distinctive trait of religious thought" (pp. 52–54). This distinction is very different from and far more basic than the notion of a hierarchy of beings or the contrast of good and bad, which are only opposed species of the same class.

Another principle appears in the thesis that the best way to understand the religious nature of man is to identify the simplest and most primitive forms of religious life. At its point of origin we can discover the causes and determine what religion truly is. If totemism proves to be the primitive form—and it does, even though we need not claim it to have been universal—we can find there religion's constitutive elements and its fundamental explanation; thus we have "a means of determining the ever-present causes upon which the most essential forms of religious thought and practice depend" (pp. 17–21). In this idea Durkheim continues the modern quest for the essence of religion, which goes back in quite different ways, using various methods, to David Hume's *Natural History of Religion* and Ludwig Feuerbach's *Essence of Religion* as well as to a variety of philosophical and theological interpretations, and which has a counterpart in the nineteenth-century endeavor to define the essence of Christianity (as in Adolf Harnack, among many others).

For Durkheim, of course, the method of interpretation and explanation had to be explicitly and consistently sociological rather than philosophical or historical or psychological. Though Durkheim was certainly also a philosopher and a moralist, and sought the unconscious sources of social existence as Freud sought the unconscious sources of personal existence, his is the example par excellence of the sociological pursuit of the nature of religion. A proper sociological method, as he summarized his rules in the essay "Sociology in France in the Nineteenth Century," depends on two propositions: (1) "Social facts exist *sui generis*; they have their own nature. There truly exists a social realm, as distinct from the psychic realm as the latter is from the biological realm and as this last, in its turn, is from the mineral realm." And (2) the method "must be objective. Social facts must be studied from the outside like other phenomena of nature." One does not fall back on one's own interior notions (the anthropocentric viewpoint) but approaches the social facts in the same way that a physicist approaches physical phenomena, in order to determine the (as yet unknown) nature and mode of the composition of social phenomena.[26] Durkheim contrasted his approach with that of what he frequently called the "anthropological school" of Tylor, Frazer, and others, in which, for example, the religious nature of totemism could be denied (by Frazer and Lang), and religious phenomena were not given a thoroughly social interpretation.

We can only cursorily summarize Durkheim's elaborate analysis of elementary beliefs and ritual attitudes. The basic social group is the clan, whose members are held together not by blood relation but in a special kinship bond of the same name, which is that of the particular species of thing (usually animal, sometimes an ancestor or an inanimate object) with which the clan has unique relations. This is its to-

26. See *Emile Durkheim on Morality and Society: Selected Writings*, ed. Robert N. Bellah (Chicago, 1973), pp. 16–18.

tem. It designates the clan collectively and each member individually. This kinship bond defines the duties and restrictions of the members in relation to one another and to the totemic species. From the relationships of the clans—and the larger groupings of phratries and tribes—is derived the cosmology, or classification of things in the whole of nature.

Totemism is not some sort of animal or ancestor or nature worship, and it cannot be understood as deriving from some previous kind of religion, such as an ancestor cult (contra Tylor) or a nature cult (contra Jevons). Nor is the totemism of the group explained by the personal totem of the individual (as in Frazer), where religion has its origin in the individual consciousness; rather, the individual totem presupposes the totemism of the clan. Totemism is thus the elementary religious form. "It is impossible to go lower than totemism" (p. 232). The totemic principle is the first form of the idea of religious force, a quasi-divine impersonal principle/power, immanent in certain categories of men and things. From this principle are derived the ideas of mana (in the Melanesians) and wakan (in the Omaha and Dakota Indians), as well as later personalized ideas of the divine power.

Among the various classes of sacred things in the totemic system —the totemic emblem, the totem species, and the clan—it was the emblem that Durkheim found singularly important. The totem is not only a name and a collective label, but is "the very type of sacred thing" in connection with which objects are classed as sacred or profane (p. 140). It is above all a *symbol*, "a material expression of something else." Specifically, it is "the outward and visible form of what we have called the totemic principle or god. But it is also the symbol of the determined society called the clan" (p. 236). From the recognition of this duality, Durkheim developed both his powerful conception of the creative role of the symbol in social consciousness—social life not being possible without a vast symbolism—and his ultimate thesis concerning the nature of religion, according to which the totemic principle, or the god of the clan, can be "nothing else than the clan itself, personified and represented to the imagination under the visible form of the animal or vegetable which serves as totem" (pp. 264, 236).

The culminating proof emerges in a proper understanding of sacrifice. Durkheim agreed with Smith that sacrifice is the center of the ritual act, and that it is independent of the specific ways in which the religious forces are conceived. But Smith's revolutionary idea of the centrality of communion in sacrifice needed to be revised. The alimentary communion is certainly an essential element. But Smith was wrong in denying importance to oblation. Sacrifice is communion, "but it is also, and no less essentially, a gift and an act of renouncement," a giving to the gods (p. 385). However, this presupposes that the gods, no less than the worshippers, need the cult: "Men would be unable to live without gods, but, on the other hand, the gods would die if their cult were not rendered" (p. 388). That had seemed to Smith an intolerable contradiction. But for Durkheim the scandal of the idea vanishes when we recognize the fact that "the sacred beings, though superior to men, can live only in the human consciousness," indeed, that "the sacred principle is nothing more nor less than society transfigured and personified" (p. 388). What is given here is the fundamental relation between individual and society. The individual receives from society what is best in him, a distinct and special place, an intellectual and moral character. But "society exists and lives only in and through individuals" (p. 389). Thus "the effect of the cult really is to recreate periodically a moral being upon which we depend as it depends upon us. Now this being does exist: it is society" (p. 389).

Durkheim started with the fundamental sociological postulate that no human institution can rest on falsehood or error (p. 14). He reiterates the point in conclusion: "Our entire study rests upon this postulate that the unanimous sentiment of the believers of all times cannot be purely illusory. Together with a recent apologist of the faith [William James] we admit that these religious beliefs rest upon a specific experience whose demonstrative value is, in one sense, not one bit inferior to that of scientific experiments, though different from them" (pp. 464–65). But this does not mean that the religious interpretations are, as such, valid. There is an objective foundation for religious experience, but this foundation does not necessarily conform objectively to the believer's idea of it. What the sociological study of totemism, as the elementary and primal form of religion, enables us to see is that the objective cause of the sensations forming religious experience is society (a complex notion for Durkheim, involving symbolic consciousness, collective sentiments and ideas that make its moral unity and its personality). Religion is created by and creates society. Religion "has given birth to all that is essential in society," including the fundamental categories of thought, even science—making the sociology of religion also a sociology of knowledge in general (see pp. 22–23, 479–87); but if this is so, "it is because the idea of society is the soul of religion" (p. 466). Religious representations, like the fundamental categories of thought, are thus, to use Durkheim's best-known phrase, "collective representations which express collective realities" (p. 22; see pp. 22–30, 483–87).

For Durkheim, then, while the particular religious symbols of the past, including those of Judaism and Christianity, are outmoded in the contemporary world, "there is something eternal in religion which is destined to survive" (p. 474). No society can be without the periodic ritual "of upholding and reaffirming at regular intervals the collective sentiments and the collective ideas which make its unity and personality." Just what forms this may take in the future is not clear, for we live in an age of transition and "moral mediocrity," but "a day will come when our societies will know again those hours of creative effervescence, in the course of which new ideas arise and new formulae are found which serve for a while as a guide to humanity; and when those hours shall have been passed through once, men will spontaneously feel the need of reliving them from time to time in thought, that is to say, of keeping alive their memory by means of celebrations which regularly reproduce their fruits" (p. 475).[27]

Max Weber

In Max Weber's classic work, *The Protestant Ethic and the Spirit of Capitalism*,[28] we have quite another kind of sociological study of religion. This volume is not a general systematic sociology of religion (which Weber started but never finished, in a section of his *Wirtschaft und Gesellschaft*) but a carefully circumscribed study. In contrast to Smith and Durkheim, Weber is concerned not with uncovering the

27. Here it is proper to speak of Durkheim as moralist and philosopher, even prophet, the proponent of a kind of civil religion for France and Western society generally.

28. "Die protestantische Ethik und der Geist des Kapitalismus," published as two articles in the journal Weber had begun to edit, *Archiv für Sozialwissenschaft und Sozialpolitik* 20 (1904), 21 (1905). References in the text are to the translation by Talcott Parsons (New York, 1930). With a 1906 article, "Die protestantische Sekten und der Geist des Kapitalismus," these form the first parts of a general sociology of religion, incomplete because of Weber's death in 1920, but collected and edited by his widow, Marianne Weber, in *Gesammelte Aufsätze zur Religionssoziologie*, 3 vols. (Tübingen, 1920), including (also in vol. 1) *Die Wirtschaftsethik der Weltreligionen*. Vol. 2 is *Hinduismus und Buddhismus*; vol. 3, *Das antike Judentum*.

primitive forms through which the essence of religion may be dis-
cerned, but with a highly developed form of Christianity and with
the creative role of religion in the formation of modern culture. In
what he called a "sociological and historical investigation" (p. 31),
with interests in psychological patterns and the influence of ideas,
Weber was closer to James than to Smith or Durkheim. But Weber's
emphasis was, like Smith's and Durkheim's, on the behavioral and
the social. "What to a theologian is valuable in his religion cannot
play a very large part in this study. We are concerned with what,
from a religious point of view, are often quite superficial and unrefined aspects of religious life, but which, and precisely because they
were superficial and unrefined, have often influenced outward behavior most profoundly" (p. 187, note to chapter 1; see p. 90).

We must prescind from Weber's major contributions in other writings to the sociology of religion and to sociology in general—his theory of social change; his commitment to a point of view located in
Western rationality; his understanding of religion as both creative
and legitimating; the now familiar distinctions of charismatic, traditional, and legal forms of authority; the concepts of routinization
and bureaucratization; and the new steps he took, in the studies of
Buddhism and Hinduism, in the history of religions. Their main impact belongs to the story of post–World War I thought. *The Protestant
Ethic*, however, makes it clear enough that the nature of a religious
impulse must be seen, not exclusively but truly, in the cultural forms
it supports. While Weber could say that the aspects of the Reformation to which he directed attention might appear incidental and superficial to the religious consciousness, the illumination in them of
the interconnections of belief and cultural (in this case economic)
life, hence of the reality of the religious phenomenon, inevitably
shapes the problems of theological self-understanding.

The argument of *The Protestant Ethic* is familiar. Weber starts with
the question of how to account, in a country of mixed religious composition, for occupational statistics which show that "business leaders
and owners of capital, as well as the higher grades of skilled labor,
and even more the higher technically and commercially trained personnel of modern enterprises, are overwhelmingly Protestant" (p.
35). This suggests a tendency among Protestants, more than among
Catholics, to develop economic rationalism. If that is so, the "principal explanation of this difference must be sought in the permanent

intrinsic character of their religious beliefs, and not only in their temporary external historico-political situations" (p. 40).

Weber is not proposing that capitalist forms have been absent elsewhere and previously. Nor does he claim that the spirit of the distinctive Western form of "rational capitalist organization of (formally) free labor" (p. 21) could have arisen only as a result of certain Reformation impulses. Rather, he seeks to ask "whether and at what points certain correlations between forms of religious belief and practical ethics can be worked out," to which question the answer will be that "Calvinism was historically one of the agents of education in the spirit of capitalism" (pp. 91, 200). Note that he does not say the only one. Moreover, Weber is quite well aware that much of his documentation is drawn from later Puritanism (Benjamin Franklin is offered as the archetype of the spirit of capitalism), just as he knows that the iron collectivism of Calvin's Geneva was quite different from the later individualistic secular asceticism, and that Calvin's personal position was not far distant from Luther's.

Yet, with all the needed qualifications, it appears to Weber that the triumph of the spirit of capitalism, in the face of many hostile forces of "traditionalism," cannot be accounted for without reference to "the peculiar characteristics of and the differences between those great worlds of religious thought which have existed historically in the various branches of Christianity" (pp. 56, 45). Something happened to produce the conviction that "labor must . . . be performed as if it were an absolute and in itself, a calling" (p. 62). Put in its simplest terms, what happened began with the Calvinist transformation of Luther's idea of the calling (Beruf). In Luther, *Beruf* had been given a new meaning: "the valuation of fulfillment of duty in worldly affairs as the highest form which the moral activity of the individual could assume" (p. 80).[29] For him, this assignment of profound religious significance to everyday activity was understood in what Weber calls a "traditionalist" sense: one accepted one's calling as given in whatever established station of life one found oneself. In the Calvinist variation, however, the calling came to mean one's choice of a worldly enterprise to be pursued with full religious responsibility in the most strenuous and exacting way.

29. We may recall Ritschl's idea of the new *Lebensideal* as the distinctive feature of the Reformation (see chap. 1, above).

Weber found the culmination of this worldly asceticism nowhere better exhibited than in Richard Baxter's *Saints' Everlasting Rest* and *Christian Directory*. There the acquisition of wealth is a religious duty —not for the sake of enjoyment, but because the glory of God can be enhanced only by activity. As Weber put it, "waste of time is thus the first and in principle the deadliest of sins," and "unwillingness to work is symptomatic of the lack of grace" (pp. 157, 159). The wrong in wealth is only the temptation to idleness and sinful enjoyment, but this is avoided by the man with a well-marked calling pursued in a most strenuous, systematic, and methodical way (see pp. 161–63). At the root of this asceticism, which comes to varying expression in seventeenth-century Puritanism, in Reformed Pietism, in Method-ism, and in Baptist sects, lie the peculiar psychological sanctions de-rived from the idea of predestination. It is a duty to consider oneself chosen. But how can one attain the confidence that one is in fact among the elect? The most suitable means is intense worldly activity. True faith is identified by a type of conduct that increases God's glory, and God demands "a life of good works combined into a uni-fied system." Thus the Calvinist creates his own certainty of salvation "in a systematic self-control which at every moment stands before the inexorable alternative, chosen or damned" (p. 117, 115). Here there are finally no comforts of Church or fellow. Calvinism did achieve a superiority in social organization, as a sharing "by labor in a calling which serves the mundane life of the community" (p. 108). But this was not the consequence of Calvin's idea of incorporation into the body of Christ, which lacked the power psychologically "to awaken the initiative to form such communities [or] to imbue them with the power which Calvinism possessed" (p. 224). Rather, God simply wills things, including the organization of social life, to be "objectively purposeful as a means of adding to His glory" (p. 224). Labor in the calling serves, in a quite utilitarian way, the mundane life of the com-munity. But psychologically predestination remains spiritual isola-tion. The proving of faith is a lonely affair, as one keeps spiritual ac-count books for oneself; and "the process of sanctifying life could thus almost take on the character of a business enterprise" (p. 124).

Our interest in Weber's argument is not to assess its validity with respect to the development of capitalism, or its adequacy as an ac-count of Calvinism. Instead we wish to note the emergence of an-other important kind of effort at objective analysis of religious subjectivity, an effort that cannot be ignored by religious self-understanding. Though Weber is much more directly concerned with power (especially psychological power) or belief structures than were Smith and Durkheim, for him too patterns of social behavior come to the fore as central to the understanding of religion. This is so despite his protestations that he deals with what to the truly religious consciousness must appear as incidental and even superficial. The argument as a whole belies his qualification. Religious beliefs are interpreted in relation to psychological attitudes shared with social institutions. *The Protestant Ethic* is prima facie less reductionist with respect to belief reference than is *The Elementary Forms of the Religious Life*, or even *Lectures on the Religion of the Semites* (though Smith wanted to make an exception for Judaism and Christianity), but for Weber also religious belief has to be understood in a larger, newer perspective. Henceforth a new kind of self-understanding of faith is required, which can be content neither with the securities of the received tradition nor with the internal testimony of the heart.

The full impact of the psychological and sociological study of religion emerged only in the theologies of the twentieth century. But the direction of the new impulses is already evident. If religious practice and belief cannot be isolated from their context in social, political, and economic attitudes and structures, theological articulation has to take on a new shape. The question of the truth value of theological statements becomes much more difficult to deal with. The idea of faith as its own guarantee is sharply questioned. The warrants of theological statements have to be related not only to philosophical argument (as so often previously), but to the total psychological and social life, from the realm of the unconscious to that of economic behavior. Beliefs can be seen as ideology or even epiphenomena, governed by the putatively nonreligious. Or, better, the life of thought must become a seamless robe in which the strands of affirmation about God, sin, and redemption can be understood only in their interweaving with all the other orientations and commitments of human beings.

4

Christianity and Other Faiths:

The History of Religions and

the Finality of the Christian Religion

A New Perspective

The modern study variously called comparative religion / history of religions / Religionswissenschaft / *science des religions* began to emerge almost simultaneously with the publication of Ritschl's *Justification and Reconciliation*. Its appearance may conveniently be dated from Friedrich Max Müller's London lectures of 1870,[1] the contemporary work of Emile Louis Burnouf in Paris,[2] and the major article "Religion" in the ninth edition of the *Encyclopaedia Britannica* (1875) by Cornelius Petrus Tiele of Leiden.[3]

The possibility of such a kind of study emerged from two powerful developments of the late eighteenth and early nineteenth centuries. One was the impact of the early Romantics' vision, which freed the European mind to become not only curious about other people's religions, but also appreciative of them as authentic ways of expressing the human experience. Earlier, through most of the Christian centuries, the common attitude toward nonchristian faiths had been one of exclusiveness and intolerance. Only one religion can be true, and that religion is Christianity; others are error or infidelity. The char-

---

1. Published as *Introduction to the Science of Religion* (London, 1873).

2. *La Science des religions* (Paris, 1872; Eng. trans., London, 1888). Burnouf wrote: "The present century will not expire without having witnessed the entire and comprehensive establishment of a science, whose elements are at this moment still widely scattered—a science unknown to preceding centuries and undefined, and which we for the first time now call the Science of Religion" (p. 1). Müller spoke similarly of the new science "as yet a promise rather than a fulfillment," but judged that "the fulfillment is now only a question of time" (*Introduction*, p. 35).

3. As an early sign, one might also mention James Freeman Clarke, *Ten Great Religions* (Boston, 1871), a widely read work, though without scientific merit, and explicitly intended to show the superiority of Christianity.

acteristic Enlightenment reaction to this exclusivism, as well as to the disputing factions within Christianity, was twofold. On the one hand, there was a discounting of all positive religion in the (largely philosophical) search for an underlying natural religion common to all peoples (the tradition of Lord Herbert of Cherbury). On the other hand, there were the attacks on positive religion exemplified variously by Collins and Toland (for example, Toland's idea that all religions except those of savages are the product of priestly greed for power), by Hume's *Natural History of Religion*, which cut against natural religion and against positive religion as the product of fears and "sick men's dreams" (though Hume's work was also important as an effort to draw on the meager information available about primitive religion), and by Voltaire's savage attack on Mohammed as a cunning and passionate villain.[4]

In the precursors of the Romantics, however, we find a new mood. In Herder's *Ideas for a Philosophy of the History of Mankind* (1784–87), the history of positive religion is seen as an integral part of culture, a natural development of religious ideas common to the human race. Similarly Lessing, though still holding to the idea of a fundamental natural religion, asked in the preface to *Education of the Human Race* (1780) "whether it is not wiser to see in all positive religions the course taken by the human intellect in its unfolding, rather than to make sport of, or to denounce any particular religion." Out of such beginnings of a change of spirit, reinforced by the Romantics' sense for the individual and for plenitude, could come the appreciative account of the multiplicity of religions in Schleiermacher's *Speeches* and in Hegel's *Philosophy of Religion*.[5] The striking change in mood may also be seen in Carlyle's 1840 lecture on Mohammed in the series *On Heroes, Hero Worship and the Heroic in History* (London, 1846, and many later editions), which is a particularly sensitive interpretation with historical, cultural, and psychological insight (vividly contrasting

4. See *Prot. Thought*, 1:34–44.

5. A related expression of late-eighteenth-century curiosity about religions may be seen in Christoph Meiners, *Allgemeine kritische Geschichte der Religionen* (Hannover, 1806–07), and the work of Hannah Adams, who published a series of editions (beginning in 1784) of a compendium of all sects since the beginning of Christianity, culminating in *A Dictionary of All Religions and Religious Denominations, Ancient and Modern, Jewish, Pagan, Mohametan, and Christian; also of Ecclesiastical History* (London, 1815). In both works, religion is taken seriously as a human expression to be studied seriously. Although Mrs. Adams hoped such study would show the superiority of Christianity, she sought also to be scrupulously fair in reporting information, letting each tradition speak for itself, and allowing the right of all peoples to give full homage to their convictions.

to the condemnations of Mohammed by Luther and Voltaire); and in
F. D. Maurice's Boyle lectures, *The Religions of the World, and Their Relations to Christianity* (London, 1846), which urge sympathetic treatment of variant opinions and the fullest liberty in the search for truth.

The second major factor that made possible, indeed necessitated, the attempt at a genuine Religionswissenschaft was the explosion of information. Earlier generations had had to rely largely on bits and pieces of information and misinformation about other religions reported by travelers and missionaries. By the late nineteenth century, however, a vast accumulation of new material was emerging. There was extensive editing and translating of Oriental religious texts, as in the fifty volumes of *Sacred Books of the East* (Oxford, 1879–1904), which Max Müller inaugurated and edited in an endeavor to present the sacred literature of all the great religions that purported to be founded on holy books (except Judaism and Christianity). Zoroastrianism had been rediscovered, with editions and translations of the *Zend-Avesta* from the middle of the century on. The finding of the Rosetta Stone in 1799 and its decipherment by Champollion in 1822 had opened the way to an understanding of the Egyptian pyramid, temple, tomb, and coffin hieroglyphics (including the fragments of the *Book of the Dead*), and this was augmented by the uncovering of thousands of papyrus scrolls and fragments. The compilation and publication of Greco-Roman inscriptions added immeasurably to the knowledge of common beliefs. Germanic and Celtic texts offered new insights into the religions of those peoples.

Archeological investigations in the Near East uncovered the royal libraries of Ashurbanipal and Tiglath-Pileser III, with an abundance of religious texts, especially the fragments of the Gilgamesh epic, which entranced and reshaped the world of biblical scholarship. Excavations were actively pursued in all areas of the Near East. Toward the end of the century the civilization of the Hittites was revealed by the discovery (1896) of the royal archives of Boghazkoy in Turkey. Digs in Syria and Palestine made available an elaborate collection of Semitic inscriptions. Obviously, the religion of the Bible could no longer be viewed in isolation from the culture of the ancient Near East, nor could the Bible be considered as the earliest book of religious culture.

Archeological research not only compelled a complete reconsideration of the ancient world around the eastern Mediterranean. It also,

especially through cave explorations beginning in mid-century, began to unveil the life of prehistoric (Stone Age—Paleolithic, Meso-
lithic and Neolithic) humanity.

Comparably, ethnology began to provide far more reliable accounts of presently existing primitive cultures than the accounts of
civil servants and missionaries (through the latter had tried seriously
to understand the religious ideas of the tribes). Comparative philology, exploited particularly by Max Müller in his early writings, became an essential tool.[6]

The extent to which the curiosity and openness, as well as the new
discoveries and tools of study, had grown by the end of the nineteenth century can readily be illustrated. The most dramatic event,
particularly stimulating to the American imagination, was the
World's Parliament of Religions, held in conjunction with the Columbian Exposition in Chicago in 1893,[7] to which all religious faiths
were invited to send representatives to present the best possible affirmation of their own faith and service to mankind, without controversy or attack on any other religious body or system of worship.
This was not, of course, designed as a scientific congress for religious
study, but rather as a living encounter of the traditions, though many
historians of religion attended. Another aim of the Parliament was to
unite religion against irreligion and to disclose the common aims and
substantial grounds of unity among the many religions. To be sure,
the speeches of Christian representatives regularly assume and assert
the superiority of Christianity, with not a little condescension. Yet in
the following year Max Müller could describe the Parliament as "one
of the most memorable events in the history of the world . . . [which]
. . . will be remembered, aye, will bear fruit when everything else of
the mighty Columbian Exhibition has long been swept away from the
memory of man," for such a gathering of representatives of the principal religions of the world was unique. Never before had there been
such "open and solemn recognition" of "the desire to be just to non-
Christian religions." For him, too, the Parliament "established once
for all . . . that the points on which the great religions differ are far

6. See F. Max Müller, *Lectures on the Science of Language*, 2 vols. (London, 1861–64), and
Selected Essays on Language, Mythology and Religion (London, 1881). Müller began as a student of Sanskrit, then turned to comparative language studies (and to the *Avesta* around
1845).

7. See John Henry Barrows, ed., *The World's Parliament of Religions*, 2 vols. (Chicago,
1893).

less numerous, and certainly far less important, than are the points on which they all agree."[8]

More direct evidence of the emerging discipline is the establishment of numerous chairs and programs of the history of religions (beginning in the Netherlands in 1876), the publication of general surveys and handbooks on the history of religion and on comparative religion, and the initiation of conferences and journals for the history of religions. Among the last may be noted the series of international congresses of Religionswissenschaft, beginning in Stockholm in 1897, the institution of such journals as *Revue de l'histoire des religions* (1880), *Theologisch Tijdschrift* (1867; for the first twenty years heavily oriented to the history of religions, under the influence of Tiele), and *Archiv für Religionswissenschaft* (1898). The American Society of Comparative Religion was founded in 1890, the American Lectures on the History of Religion in 1891, and the Historical Study of Religion section within the American Oriental Society in 1897. In Britain, the Hibbert Lectures (begun in 1878) were planned specifically to deal with the faiths of mankind rather than Christian doctrine. Many of the Gifford lecturers in the last two decades of the century also dealt extensively with topics in the history of religions.

Finally, the change in mood and focus may be symbolized by the contrasts between the third edition of the great Herzog *Realencyklopädie für protestantische Theologie und Kirche* [*RE*], edited by A. Hauck, 22 vols. (Leipzig, 1896–1909), and both the *Encyclopedia of Religion and Ethics* [*ERE*], edited by James Hastings, 13 vols. (Edinburgh, 1908–21) and the new *Religion in Geschichte und Gegenwart* [*RGG*], edited by Gunkel and others, 5 vols. (Tübingen, 1908–13).

Though looked upon by some[9] as a work including the general history of religions, the twenty-two volumes of the *Realencyklopädie* are clearly oriented to Christian (especially Protestant) history and thought, as the title indicates. Judaism and Islam are more or less significantly present, with an article on postbiblical Israel, numerous discussions of the Jews (mostly in relation to Christian history), and references to Mohammed and Islam in over a score of articles, though no article on either. But Buddhism, for example, appears only through reference to Buddhist concepts in some thirteen arti-

8. F. Max Müller, *Last Essays 2: Essays on the Science of Religion* (London, 1901), 324–25, 335. Unhappily, the Parliament did not have much lasting popular effect. Succeeding world's fairs did not continue the emphasis.

9. Even M. Jastrow, *The Study of Religion* (London and New York, 1902), p. 401.

cles on such topics as dualism, salvation, Jesus Christ, mysticism, and perfection. There are three brief references to Hinduism and five to Brahman and Brahmanism, plus an article on the nineteenth-century Brahmo Samaj reform movement. The article on religion, by Wilhelm Herrmann, is essentially a theological restatement of Herrmann's conception of religion (see above, chapter 2), explicitly rejecting the Troeltschian view that only through an impartial and objective study of the different religions is a genuine understanding of religion possible. *Religionsgeschichte* for Herrmann does not establish but presupposes the understanding of religion, which is known through one's own inner life.

The *RE* comes closest to a general history of religions discussion in an article on heathenism, with bibliographic reference to some current German and French Religionsgeschichte literature, but the essay is mainly devoted to ancient polytheism and types of animism (shamanism and fetishism), with some concluding brief statistical and geographical information on the distribution of Buddhism, Brahmanism, Confucianism, Shinto, animism, Christianity, Judaism, and Islam. Interestingly, there is a substantial article on the work of Tiele (19:766–75), though one looks in vain for the name of Max Müller.

With the *Encyclopedia of Religion and Ethics* we find ourselves in an entirely different world from the *RE*. Beyond the article of sixty-three columns on religion, which draws widely on the literature of the history of religions, as well as anthropology and the psychology of religion, the index requires almost eight columns to list, under "Religion," the enormous variety of references to religious groups, patterns, and places, ranging from "aborigines" and "Abyssinian" to "Zoroastrianism" and "Zuni."[10] Similarly, though perhaps not quite as extensively, since the history of religions was late in developing in Germany, the scope of *Religion in Geschichte und Gegenwart* includes serious treatment of major nonchristian religions, the evolution and levels of religions, anthropological-ethnological studies, and Religionsgeschichte and the *religionsgeschichtliche Schule*.

In both cases, the theological encyclopedia has been superseded by an encyclopedia of religion with a breadth of interest recalling the ninth edition of the *Encyclopaedia Britannica*, edited by W. Robertson

10. And, to cite a perhaps trivial example, the mid-nineteenth-century mediating theologian Justus Ludwig Jacobi, who merits two pages in *RE*, vanishes from *ERE* and is replaced, we might say, by references to the work of H. Jacobi in interpreting Vedic chronology, Patanjali, and the *Ramayana*.

Smith. That work included not only the lengthy article by Tiele on religions, which surveyed impartially the varieties from animism in preliterate peoples through Buddhism, Christianity, and Islam, but also special articles representing the major religious traditions and literatures of the world. James Frazer wrote on totemism (also taboo), Andrew Lang on mythology (the main general treatment of primitive religion appears here), and E. B. Tylor on anthropology, demonology, and magic (among other articles).

A new model for thinking about religion began to replace the theological model. This history of religions endeavor obviously reflected the turn to an objective study of religious phenomena that we discussed in chapter 3 relative to the psychology and sociology of religion. But two further motifs, or kinds of interest, of the late nineteenth century need to be interpreted. One was the quest for the origin or root of religion, usually by concentration on primitive religion, though with varying purposes. The other interest was focused much more on the high or developed religions, with a view to comparative studies. Both were concerned with historical development, and both led ultimately to the question of the finality or absoluteness of Christianity.

THE ROOT OF RELIGION: *TOTEM TO NUMEN*

The phrase *root of religion* is deliberately ambiguous. It may mean historical origin, most primitive religion, or elementary form of religion. It may refer to the question of the essential nature of religion or its grounding in human experience. The questions could be approached empirically or analytically, and they were often confused with each other.

Tylor and Frazer

The search for the primitive form of religion was particularly the preoccupation of the anthropologists, whose work at this time cannot be sharply distinguished from that of early sociologists of religion —recall particularly W. Robertson Smith and Emile Durkheim (see chapter 3). E. B. Tylor, often considered the founder of cultural anthropology and certainly of profound influence on religiohistorical study, described the task as one of forming a "minimum definition of religion."[11] Contrary to John Lubbock, Tylor argued that while it

11. E. B. Tylor, *Primitive Culture*, 2 vols. (London, 1871; hereafter cited as *PC*). References are to the 1889 New York edition, from the second English edition of 1873.

was theoretically possible for man to be utterly without religion, no such tribes had ever been discovered.[12] Mankind has always been religious.

On the analogy of natural history, Tylor assumed the principle of development, whereby lines of connection could be uncovered by ethnographic study, and without recourse to theological evaluation, from "the rudest forms [of religion] up to the status of an enlightened Christianity" (*PC*, 1:23). He introduced the term *survivals* to denote processes, customs, and views which have been carried over from their original home into different states of society, and from which the older conditions and views can be known (*PC*, 1:16; see 1:21, 158f., and 2:356). "Progress, degradation, survival, revival, modification, are all modes of the connection that binds together the complex network of civilization," but "the main tendency of culture from primeval up to modern times has been from savagery towards civilization" (*PC*, 1:17, 21). A rational ethnography, for Tylor, also assumed a commonality of the laws of mind (as of nature), whether ancient or modern, and a uniformity of results from uniformity of causes (*PC*, 1:20, 158).

To denote the primitive form of religion, Tylor coined the term *animism*, which, with various meanings, remained unchallenged for many years.[13] For Tylor, it was a conception of souls or spiritual beings resulting from reflection on the differences between waking and sleep, dream and trance, and life and death. There must be an immaterial and invisible double for the physical self, a phantom self which can detach itself from the physical body. The minimum definition of religion is thus the "belief in Spiritual Beings," both the souls of individuals and thence other spiritual beings (up to powerful deities). Such belief appears in "all low races with whom we have at-

12. Lubbock's principal work was *The Origin of Civilization and the Primitive Condition of Man* (London, 1870). In it Lubbock asserted that the earliest level of human culture was atheistic, wholly devoid of religious ideas. Then fetishism, a phase of magic in which some sort of divine powers can be compelled to carry out man's designs, emerged, followed by nature worship or totemism, with veneration of animals, trees, rivers, and stones. At the next level, shamanism elevated the divine powers, which the shaman is alone able to reach, to a distance from the human world. After shamanism anthropomorphism or idolatry appeared, with humanly shaped creator gods who can be approached and persuaded. From this level emerges the worship of one deity as creator and utterly transcendent, and finally morality becomes connected with religion.

13. The theory of animism was shared, with variations, by Albert Réville, C. P. Tiele, and Wilhelm Wundt. Tiele thought that animism was not itself a religion, but a sort of primitive philosophy that controlled the life of natural man. Wundt sought to develop Tylor's idea of souls further; see *Völkerpsychologie 4: Mythus und Religion* (Leipzig, 1909).

tained to thoroughly intimate acquaintance" (*PC*, 1:424–26). Animism in relation to mythology is "the belief in the animation of all nature, rising at its highest level to personification" (*PC*, 1:285). Animism is not only the original form; it is the fundament of all subsequent religion. It not only characterizes tribes "very low in the scale of humanity," but also ascends in unbroken continuity, even though with deep modifications, "into the midst of high modern culture." Animism is, "in fact, the groundwork of the Philosophy of Religion, from that of the savages up to that of civilized man" (*PC*, 1:426). Hence the evolution of ancestor worship, fetishism, totemism, polytheism, and monotheism.

James G. Frazer, Smith's protégé, is probably the most widely known figure in nineteenth-century anthropology. In *Totemism and Exogamy* and *The Golden Bough* he brought together, with great industry and erudition, information about what he referred to as primitive superstitions.[14] Except at one point, where he developed the relation of religion and magic, Frazer did not add much to Tylor's theory of the origin of religion. Throughout most of *Totemism and Exogamy* he seemed concerned rather to show the almost universal prevalence of totemism in "savagery"—though in volume 4 he retrenched the boundaries considerably. According to his final definition, "Totemism is an intimate relation which is supposed to exist between a group of kindred people on the one side and a species of natural or artificial objects on the other side, which objects are called the totems of the human group" (4:3–4).

In the earlier essays, Frazer wavered on the relation between totemism and religion. He could say that totemism was not a factor of primary importance in man's religious and economic development, and that only exogamy has bequeathed anything to the customs of civilization, by fostering social ties (1:xiv). Or he could say that totemism had a real influence on religion, though it has been greatly exaggerated (ibid.). Or he could describe totemism as both a religious and a social system. As religious, it is the "relations of mutual respect and protection between a man and his totem" (1:4; see 5–52); as a system of society, "it comprises the relations in which men

14. *Totemism and Exogamy: A Treatise on Certain Early Forms of Superstition and Society*, 4 vols. (London, 1910). The work begins with an 1887 essay expanding his article on totemism in the ninth edition of the *Britannica*, and concludes in volume 4 with numerous revisions of the earlier statements. *The Golden Bough: A Study in Magic and Religion*, 3d ed., 10 vols. (London, 1900–1915; 1st ed., 2 vols., 1890).

and women of the same totem stand to each other and to the members of other totemic groups" (1:101). He could say (early) that the origins of totemism are not at all religious, but practical, in the interests of securing food supply—the prohibition of eating the totem being a later development (1:117–23)—yet that "as a system of religion it embraces the mystic union of the savage with his totem" (1:101).

In the end, with a less ambiguous view of religion, Frazer concluded that totemism is not religion, for the relation to the totem is friendship and kinship, which is not the relation to a god. "In pure totemism, such as we find it among the Australian aborigines, the totem is never a god and is never worshipped. . . . If religion implies, as it seems to do, an acknowledgement on the part of the worshipper that the object of his worship is superior to himself, then pure totemism cannot properly be called a religion at all, since a man looks upon his totem as his equal and friend, not at all as his superior, still less his god" (4:5). He also concluded that the origin of totemism (a female-originated theory) comes from the savage's complete ignorance of the true causes of conception, the woman imagining (when she feels movement in the womb) that a spirit animal or plant has entered the womb—thus the notion of identity with the totem and the refusal to eat it (4:64).

Frazer's theory of magic and religion, which also appeared in the later portions of *Totemism and Exogamy*, was especially detailed in *The Golden Bough* [GB]. In general, mankind passes through three stages of intellectual development: from magic to religion to science. Sympathetic magic may be homeopathic (imitative), based on "laws" of similarity, the principle that like produces like, or that an effect is like its cause. Or it may be contagious, based on the law of contact, the principle that things which have been in contact with each other can act on each other at a distance (*GB*, 1:52–53). In both forms, magic is false science, based on a mistaken system of natural law, and thus a fallacious guide to conduct (though it is always an art for the primitive, who never theorizes on it). Each form represents a different misapplication of the association of ideas: "Whenever sympathetic magic occurs in its pure unadulterated form, it assumes that in nature one event follows another necessarily and invariably without the intervention of any spiritual or personal agency. Thus its fundamental conception is identical with that of modern science" (*GB*, 1:220). The error is simply in the misconception of laws of nature.

But eventually it is discovered by some savages of "deeper mind" and "shrewder intelligence" that magic does not attain its goals, and the illusion arises that there are spiritual beings who can help. That is the emergence of religion (Frazer demonstrated how frequently rulers were magicians or priests, or magicians who became priests). Religion means "a propitiation or conciliation of powers superior to man which are believed to direct and control the course of nature and of human life" (*GB*, 1:222). The beliefs come first, then the practice. Finally, it is concluded that the gods of religion are false, and the dawn of science arrives; humanity is able to overcome its difficulties by empirical means.

The arguments from ethnological materials that Frazer used to support his claim for the historical relation of magic and religion have proved to be highly vulnerable, and his theory of stages was quickly rejected by ethnologists and anthropologists.[15] But equally problematic was his assumption that magic and science rest alike on a notion of invariable natural laws. Psychologically the magician and the scientist do the same things, except that one is in error about the laws, the other correct. Religion, unlike magic and science, rests on a conception of the world as capricious, open to intervention by spirits.

Lang and Marett

Whereas Tylor was fully committed to the theory of development of higher religion out of primitive forms of animism, as the means of understanding the survival of ancestral relics and explaining the rites and doctrines of civilized religion as evolving from savage religion, his pupil Andrew Lang argued that animism should be viewed as a degeneration from an earlier anthropomorphism,[16] even a sort of primordial theism. Tylor's theory cannot account for the high gods, the supreme and moral beings that have in fact been found in the religions of many primitive tribes. They are rather magnified nonnatural persons than ghosts or spirits. Their origin can be explained by human reflection on the experience of being able to make things. But there are many things, both present and desired, that human beings have not made and could not make; hence the rational conjecture of a Maker of things and the gradual ascent to the idea of the

15. He found in Australian aborigines evidence of magic without religion (in his sense) and hence conjectured that magic was prior in all cases.

16. Lang, *The Making of Religion* (London, 1898; 2d ed., 1900).

great Unseen One. Animism is thus not the first step toward a belief in God. That theory cannot account for the experience of belief in the higher gods. The route is much simpler. Among the lowest savages, the highest conceptions of deity—apart from the Jewish and Christian—are already found. Barbarian, semicivilized, and even civilized deities show a decline. The practical universality of belief in spirits, which must be admitted, is an instance of unhappy corruption and degradation. Lang's idea was, of course, so widely out of keeping with the prevailing animistic theories and evolutionary perspectives that, except for a few quite inadequate rebuttals (such as Tylor's contention that high-god concepts among primitives must have come from missionaries), the theory was largely passed over until revived and pursued by Father Wilhelm Schmidt.[17]

A much more influential line of critique of Tylor emerged in the early writings of another of his pupils, his successor in the chair at Oxford, R. R. Marett (1866–1943).[18] Marett shared the assumption of Tylor and most other anthropologists that the fundamental nature of religion is best discovered in its primitive forms.[19] As a minimum definition, however, animism will not do, widespread as it may have been. It is too narrow and especially too intellectualist a conception. Spirits are only one class of powers; belief is also directed to material objects. Besides, the animism theory neglects religious practice. Like Smith, Marett saw ritual as primary, beliefs and myths as secondary, for it is action that gives rise to ideas. "Savage religion is something not so much thought out as danced out" (*Threshold*, p. xxxi). Moreover, with Durkheim, Marett criticized the psychological interpretations of most British anthropologists as individualistic, calling instead for social-psychological methods, since religion is essentially a social product (*Threshold*, chapter 5).

Initially, in an 1899 lecture (*Threshold*, pp. 1–28), Marett spoke of "Pre-Animistic Religion," a term he did not coin but which caught on immediately; he became widely regarded as the founder of a preani-

17. Schmidt, *Der Ursprung der Gottesidee* (Münster, 1912–55).

18. Among the pre–World War I writings, see esp. the collection of essays, *The Threshold of Religion* (London, 1909; 2d enl. ed., 1914—references are to this edition); the article "Religion (Primitive)" in the eleventh edition of the *Encyclopaedia Britannica*, 22:61–67; and *Anthropology* (London, 1912).

19. Further, "anthropology is the child of Darwin"; its subject is man in evolution, i.e., anthropology is "among the biological sciences and accepts their naturalistic and evolutionary outlook" (*Anthropology*, pp. 7–8).

mistic theory of religion's origins. He did not, however, intend to assert a stage of religion prior to animism, but to "dig deeper into human nature" for the raw material of religion. To denote that deeper level, which belongs much more to feeling than to belief, he adopted the Melanesian term *mana*,[20] whose nearest English equivalent he judged to be *awe* (*Threshold*, p. 13). This is something prior to personification or theorizing. It is supernatural power, for example, of a dead person, but inherently "indefinite and mysterious in its effects" (p. 91). Mana is an occult power in persons and things. The term is "a general category to designate the positive aspect of the supernatural, or sacred, or whatever we are to call that order of miraculous happenings which, for the concrete experience, if not usually for the abstract thought of the savage, is marked off perceptibly from the order of ordinary happenings" (*Threshold*, p. 99). "*Mana* is selected by me for special emphasis merely because it comes nearer than any other available term to the bare designation of that positive emotional value which is the raw material of religion, and needs only to be moralized—to be identified with goodness—to become its essence" (*Threshold*, p. xxxi). The concept of mana also illumines for us the relation of primitive magic to religion. Contrary to Frazer's intellectualist notion of magic as primitive science, only a negative condition of religion, Marett found that rudimentary magic (at least in Melanesia) actually contributed to religion the idea of mana. Mana is the projective power, the spell, of the magic, and the obtaining of mana is the object of religious rites and practices. A type of worship is generated by magic, though religion is a wider and more complex thing than magic. Magic does not arise from mistaking an ideal connection for a real one (as in Tylor), or from confusion about causation (as in Frazer). The savage is well aware of the difference between symbolic and empirical action. Magic arises out of emotional intensity that has to be vented in surrogate activities which become mimetic auxiliaries to empirical activity.

Finally, mana is inseparably connected with taboo, which also belongs wholly to the realm of the magicoreligious (against Frazer's intellectualist conception). Taboo is a mystical affair, bespeaking rela-

20. Relying especially on the reports of R. H. Codrington, in *The Melanesians: Studies in Their Anthropology and Folklore* (Oxford, 1891), much as Durkheim relied heavily on the reports about Australian aborigines by Spencer and Gillen.

tion to a power whose modes of action transcend the ordinary. Taboo is, indeed, the negative aspect of mana. "To break a taboo is to set in motion against oneself *mana*, or supernatural wonder-working power" (*Threshold*, p. 74). The chief is taboo because he has mana. The negative and positive aspects are always together. "Altogether, in *mana* we have what is *par excellence* the primitive religious idea in its positive aspect, taboo representing the negative side, since whatever has *mana* is taboo, and whatever is taboo has *mana*" (*Britannica*, s.v. "religion [primitive]"). Properly speaking it is *tabu-mana* that is the minimum definition of religion (*Threshold*, p. 119).

Although Marett is at important points an exception, the anthropologists surveyed (as well as many others) reveal several common characteristics of this late-nineteenth-century quest for the root of religion. First is the assumption of the evolutionary scheme. The more complex evolves from the simpler. Comparative method can distinguish the complex from the simple and thus the earlier (or earliest) from the later forms of a more developed culture. Tylor affirms this in the opening paragraph of *Primitive Culture*: "On the one hand, the uniformity which so largely pervades civilization may be ascribed, in great measure, to the uniform action of uniform causes; while on the other hand its various grades may be regarded as stages of development or evolution, each the outcome of previous history, and about to do its proper part in shaping the history of the future" (p. 1). Hence the frequent attempts to identify the (chronological) steps through which religion must have developed from totemism-animism to monotheism.[21]

A second assumption was that in the historical origins could be found the essence of religion. The quest was thus a "historical" substitute for the Enlightenment attempt to define a common natural religion lying behind all religions—though the nineteenth-century

21. F. B. Jevons, *An Introduction to the History of Religions* (London, 1896), was a widely read book which exemplified the notion of uniform evolutionary development from totemism to polytheism to monotheism. E. E. Evans-Pritchard, in *Theories of Primitive Religion* (London, 1965), p. 5, cites Jevons' work as "the best example I know for illustrating how erroneous theories about primitive religions can be, for I believe it would be true to say that there is no general, or theoretical, statement about them in it which would pass muster today. It is a collection of absurd reconstructions, unsupportable hypotheses and conjectures, wild speculations, suppositions and assumptions, inappropriate analogies, misunderstandings and misinterpretations, and, especially in what he wrote about totemism, just plain nonsense."

methods of argumentation were often more psychological and philosophical, even conjectural, than historical, given the nature of the ethnological data.

Third, many of the influential anthropologists thought that the origin of religion was also its explanation, and that if primitive religion was shown to be an illusion or an intellectual aberration, higher religions could be discounted on the same grounds. This intention was quite explicit in Frazer:

> The comparative study of the beliefs and institutions of mankind is fitted to be much more than a means of satisfying an enlightened curiosity and of furnishing materials for the researches of the learned. Well handled, it may become a powerful instrument to expedite progress if it lays bare certain weak spots in the foundations on which modern society is built—if it shows that much which we are wont to regard as solid rests on the sands of superstition rather than on the rock of nature.[22]

Fourth, there was a common assumption of a primitive mentality quite different from ours. Though there may be a progression from savagery to barbarism to semicivilization to civilization, the savage mind seems a singular mentality—superstitious, ignorant, "pre-logical" (as Lévy-Bruhl was early to term it). Primitive thought is compared to modern science and appears childlike and lacking a critical dimension.[23]

Fifth, seemingly in contradiction to the previous assumption but probably an explanation of it, the interpretations of primitive mentality were remarkably intellectualist or rationalist (except for Marett). Tylor focused on ideas or beliefs about spirits and gods, animism being a rational inference from experiences of dream and trance, and so forth. Myths become rational attempts to make sense of the environment. For Frazer, both magic and religion were intellectual mistakes. For Lang it was ideas of supreme beings—creator beings inferred from man's own activity of making—that counted. So also Goblet d'Alviella, writing in *ERE* (1:535), asserted that animism "represents an attempt to explain in a rational way all the facts

---

22. *Golden Bough*, 1:xxv–xxvi. See also Edward Clough, *The Childhood of Religions* (London, 1875). And recall David Hume's *Natural History of Religions* and Herbert Spencer's identification of fear as the basis of all religion, in his *Principles of Sociology*.

23. Frazer speaks of "the gulf which divides these savages [of central Australia] from ourselves" (*Totemism and Exogamy*, 1:93; see pp. 93–96).

of the universe. It is the religion and the philosophy of all non-civilized peoples." Inquiry into the cause of phenomena leads to the assumption of acts of will and thus imaginary personalities. In general, primitive explanations were compared with sophisticated explanations, and little account was taken of the elaborate and complex ceremonial life of primitive religion.

Sixth, most of the influential anthropological theorists were armchair anthropologists who had never been near a primitive people. They were entirely dependent on highly selective reports, heaping up vast quantities of materials (almost indiscriminately in the case of Frazer), lumping together items that seemed to be similar but without genuinely analytical comparison or study of terms and practices in their contexts. Only later, after Malinowski, did field experience become a requisite for serious anthropology. They sought exclusively to interpret primitive modes of thought by Western categories; not until Max Weber's later work was there any attempt to interpret Western religious categories by other people's experiences and perspectives.

Söderblom and Otto

Nathan Söderblom (1866–1931), who has been remembered more as an ecumenist than as an important figure in the development of the history of religion, well illustrates a transition from the purely anthropological form of the question of the origin of religion to a question of the roots that would treat the ethnological data about primitive religion as a way of asking about the enduring core element, the sources of the developed belief in God.[24] With the anthropologists, whose work he reviewed extensively, Söderblom was seriously concerned with the earliest form of religion. Appropriately cautious about taking extant primitive forms as original—since existing primitive tribes have as many thousands of years behind them as we do—he held that the science of religion could not give up the hope of finding in these tribes some keys to the beginnings of religion as well as to the psychological presuppositions of belief in God.

24. See esp. *Das Werden des Gottesglaubens; Untersuchungen über die Anfänge der Religion* (Leipzig, 1916), a translation and enlargement of *Gudstrons Uppkimst* (Stockholm, 1914). See also his article "Holiness (General and Primitive)" in *ERE*, 6:731–41. Early a student of Mazdaism, and editor of the 3d ed. of Tiele's *Kompendium*, Söderblom was professor at Uppsala from 1901 and at Leipzig from 1912. In 1914 he was chosen archbishop of Uppsala and became an important leader in the ecumenical movement.

Söderblom's proposal was synthetic. No key will fit all locks. The origin of religion is richer than any of the current theories. Animism has validity as a description of primitive religion and as an element in the development of belief in God. "For belief in God, animism means the same as for the conception of man, that the deity is viewed as will and personality" (*Werden*, p. 31). But animism did not play an exclusive role. He found Lang's work helpful in getting beyond the pure animist theory, although the creator gods in primitive religion are not the only or even the most important starting point for belief in God. Söberblom rejected the idea of primitive monotheism, finding a clear distinction between the high gods of primitive religion and the actual monotheism that appeared in the biblical religion of revelation. For the high gods, he preferred the more modest term *Urheber* (creator, maker).

Codrington and Marett, he thought, provided an even more important corrective, directing us to the role of mana among the Pacific Islanders and its equivalents among other peoples. Mana—a mysterious, usually impersonal power, though closely bound with living natures—goes deepest into the inner being of primitive religion (p. 380). Mana distinguishes which being can be viewed as divine. "The signature of the divine is power," and it is power that decides which things and beings belong to religion (p. 111). The distinction between the holy and the profane, essential for religion, is connected with power. Here Söderblom stood consciously with Durkheim. This indeed is a more fundamental criterion for religion than the idea of God. There can be god-ideas without religion and there can be religion without a definite conception of God (for example, in Buddhism, as well as in primitive religions).[25]

Of the elements found in primitive religion, none can be reduced to or explained by the others. Belief in God develops partly from each, as an irreducible source. These roots need to be explored not only in primitive religions, but also in relation to Shang-Ti and T'ien in Chinese religion, to Brahma in India, to power in the Avesta, and to Israel's conception of God as will, in which holiness and personal-

25. *Werden*, esp. p. 193. See also *ERE*, 6:731: "The only sure test is holiness. From the first, holiness constitutes the most essential feature of the divine in a religious sense. The idea of God without the conception of the holy is not religion. . . . Not the mere existence of the divinity, but its *mana*, its power, its holiness is what religion involves." Initially, this is not a moral distinction; though the holy eventually is identified with the clean, the pure.

ity are joined (see chapters 6–8). Together, the elements of primitive religion are the roots to which the developed spiritual life of mankind are connected, not in a simple and unilinear way but as each culture finds its own path within the world-embracing spiritual process.

Söderblom's emphasis on the holy forms a direct bridge to Rudolph Otto's classic work, *Das Heilige* (Breslau, 1917).[26] Here the empirical interest is fully and explicitly joined to (or taken up in) psychological-philosophical analysis of what is common to experience in all religions. Manifestations in primitive and developed religion are completely interwoven, so that Otto could move with ease from mana to the mystics, from daemon to divination in Christianity, and from the Bible to Luther.[27] That should not be surprising, since Otto was a professor of theology whose first major work was a study of Luther's view of the Holy Spirit; he was deeply influenced by Schleiermacher, and he had written on the religious problematic in Kant and Fries, before his world travels (1911–12) impressed on him more fully the broader religious context.[28]

With Schleiermacher, Otto found the distinctive and enduring element in religion in the affective or feeling-awareness dimension of experience. The holy as "a category of interpretation and valuation peculiar to the sphere of religion" is nonrational, that is, distinct from the rational; it is ineffable "in the sense that it completely eludes apprehension in terms of concepts," and in its original and foremost meaning it transcends the moral.[29] As a name for this sui generis experience, beyond the rational and the good, Otto coined the term *numinous* (from *numen*: God, spirit, or will, as *ominous* from *omen*). The experience of the numinous is the experience of "creature feeling" (not unlike Schleiermacher's feeling of dependence,

26. Eng. trans., *The Idea of the Holy* (London, 1923; page references are to the 1968 Oxford edition). Otto found in both Marett and Söderblom "a welcome confirmation." "It is true that neither of them calls attention quite as precisely as, in this matter, psychologists need to do, to the unique character of the religious 'awe' and its qualitative distinction from all 'natural' feelings. But Marett more particularly comes within a hair's breadth of what I take to be the truth about the matter" (p. 15n.).

27. "No mere inquiry into the genesis of a thing can throw any light upon its essential nature" (pp. 21–22).

28. See *Die Anschauung vom heiligen Geiste bei Luther* (Göttingen, 1898) and *Kantische-Fries'sche Religionsphilosophie* (Tübingen, 1909).

29. See pp. 5–6. Compare Marett, *Threshold*, p. 112: "*Tabu* and *mana* apply to the supernatural in what I should like to call its first, or existential dimension. With its second, or moral dimension they have nothing to do."

though that was an emotion of self-valuation, with God being merely an inference from self-consciousness) before the numen that is objectively present.

Mysterium tremendum is the only appropriate expression for this deepest element in religious emotion, the apprehending of the numinous. As *mysterium*, it is the feeling of awe before the mystery: religious dread (whose antecedent is daemonic dread), the feeling which is "the starting-point for the entire religious development in history," a primary and unique fact of our nature which is "the basic factor and the basic impulse underlying the entire process of religious evolution" (pp. 14, 15). Mysterium tremendum involves the element of "overpoweringness," of majesty, of an urgency or energy of the numinous object. *Tremendum* involves the sense of the wholly other, which is beyond apprehension and comprehension. At the same time, the content of the numinous experience has the aspect of fascination, of the alluring and the entrancing (the Dionysiac element in the numen). Finally, the holy is a category of value; the creature-feeling is paralleled by the feeling of uncleanness, of unworthiness, from which come the consciousness of sin and the need for atonement.

The philosophical and analytical sides of Otto's argument came most explicitly to the fore in his effort to establish the holy as an a priori (recalling Kant's a priori cognitive elements, but also Troeltsch's idea of a religious a priori). For the numinous to be an a priori, it must issue "from the deepest foundation of cognitive apprehension that the soul possesses," arising not out of, but only by means of, sensory data and empirical material (p. 113). By introspection and critical reflection, we conclude that there are psychical predispositions (Anlagen) of the human spirit, "propensities, 'predestining' the individual to religion," or "principles in the mind" enabling religion to be "independently recognized as true," or a priori cognitions which are such as everyone is capable of having; the "universal 'predisposition' is merely a faculty of *receptivity* and a *principle of judgment and acknowledgement*" (pp. 115, 175, 177).

Only on such a basis can one understand the historical origin and the development of religion, which at its threshold appears in magic, in worship of the dead, in conceptions of souls and spirits, in the idea of mana, in the animation of nature, in fairy-stories and myth, in the rise of the daemon, and in association with the notions of the clean and the unclean. None of these "prereligious" elements is the explanation of religion. All of them are possible and explainable only "from a basic religious element, viz., the feeling of the numinous" (p. 124).

Finally, then, an a priori character belongs to the connection between the nonrational and the rational elements in religion, "their inward and necessary union," whereby in the course of history "the numinous feeling becomes charged with progressively rational, moral, and cultural significance" (pp. 136, 134).

RELIGIONSWISSENSCHAFT

In Söderblom and Otto we come much closer to the interests of Religionswissenschaft. Although influenced by the developing anthropological work, as well as by the psychology and sociology of religion, the focus and intent of Religionswissenschaft was much more inclusive, aiming (usually) at nothing less than a general account of all religions and their historical growth. The last decades of the nineteenth century and the first decade of the twentieth saw a steady stream of serious scholarly compendia, general histories, and manuals, as well as a vast literature on particular religions and places, both ancient and modern.[30]

Related to this outpouring of general histories of religion was the establishment of a series of chairs and programs in *Religionsgeschichte*

30. Leaving aside the mere popularizations, we may note among the important general works the following: Albert Réville (of Paris), *Prolégomènes de l'histoire des religions* (Paris, 1881; Eng. trans. with introduction by F. Max Müller, *Prolegomena of the History of Religions*, London, 1884), and *Histoire des religions*, 5 vols. (Paris, 1883–88); Pierre Daniel Chantepie de la Saussaye (of Amsterdam), *Lehrbuch der Religionsgeschichte*, 2 vols. (Freiburg, 1887–89; 2d ed., 1897; 3d ed., 1905; Eng. trans. of vol. 1, 1st ed. [London, 1891], which Louis Jordan, in 1905, called the "standard work in all countries"; the 4th ed. [Tübingen, 1925] was quite a new work, edited by Bertholet and Lehmann); Cornelius Petrus Tiele (of Leiden), *Elements of the Science of Religion*, 2 vols. (his Gifford Lectures; Edinburgh, 1897–99), and *Kompendium der Religionsgeschichte* (Berlin, 1880; rev. ed. by Söderblom under Tiele's supervision, Breslau, 1903; the 1st ed., Amsterdam, 1876, was entitled *Geschiedenis van der Godsdienst tot aan de heerschappij der Wereldgodsdiensten*; Eng. trans., *Outlines of the History of Religion to the Spread of the Universal Religions* [London, 1877]); Christian Tischhauser, *Grundzüge der Religionswissenschaft zur Einleitung in die Religionsgeschichte* (Basel, 1891); Eugène Goblet d'Alviella (of Brussels), *Introduction à l'histoire générale des religions* (Brussels, 1887); Conrad von Orelli (of Basel), *Allgemeine Religionsgeschichte* (Bonn, 1890); George Foot Moore (of Harvard), *History of Religions*, 2 vols. (New York, 1913–19); and F. Max Müller, *Introduction*, and the four series of Gifford Lectures: *Natural Religion* (London, 1889), *Physical Religion* (London, 1891), *Anthropological Religion* (London, 1892), and *Theosophy or Psychological Religion* (London, 1893). For further bibliographical (and biographical) detail on most of these authors, see Jacques Waardenburg, *Classical Approaches to the Study of Religion* (2 vols., The Hague, 1973–74).

(frequently called "history and philosophy of religion").[31] The most striking early development was in the Netherlands, where by governmental decree in 1876 the theological faculties were changed to scientific bodies comparable to those in philosophy, law, and medicine. Old Testament, New Testament, church history, and even dogmatics were to be taught as historical scientific disciplines, which the churches could supplement in nonofficial separate seminaries. To each of the four universities (Amsterdam, Gröningen, Leiden, and Utrecht) was added, in 1877 and 1878, a chair in general and comparative history of religions, whose study was incorporated into the required theological curriculum. Tiele of Leiden and Chantepie de la Saussaye of Amsterdam were the most distinguished of the initial appointees.[32] Earlier, to be sure, some regular lectures on the history of religions given by members of the theological faculties had been offered in Switzerland (at Basel from 1840; at Geneva in 1868, with a chair founded in 1873; at Lausanne in 1871; and at Berne in 1876). Albert Réville was the first incumbent of a new chair at the Collège de France (1880) and lectured also in the Ecole des Hautes Etudes of the University of Paris in the Section des Sciences Religieuses, which was established in 1886 with fourteen special lectureships on the greater and lesser religions. Montauban established a special chair in comparative history of religions, and the subject was required of theological students.

From 1876, comparative religion was combined with Old Testament literature at Mansfield College, Oxford, and in 1904 the first full university chair in comparative religion in Britain was established at Victoria University, Manchester. Elsewhere in Britain the lectureships were generally in special subjects: Oxford had a chair in anthropology, Cambridge a lectureship in ethnology, and London had lectureships in Chinese religion, in Egyptology, and in Buddhism.

Count Goblet d'Alviella was lecturing on history of religions at Brussels from 1884. Copenhagen had a regular lectureship in the history of religions from 1900 in the faculty of philosophy, and an occasional course was offered and required in the theology faculty.

31. Louis H. Jordan, in *Comparative Religion: Its Genesis and Growth* (New York, 1905), pp. 580–604, presents a valuable chart, with dates of establishment, of all the chairs and programs that he could identify throughout the world.

32. See also Jastrow, *Study of Religion*, pp. 47, 367.

At Uppsala, from 1878 half of the appointment in theological propaedeutic and encyclopedia was devoted to history of religions (Söderblom assumed this chair in 1901).

In the United States, regular courses of lectures in the history of religions had been offered in the divinity school at Harvard since 1867 (initially by James Freeman Clarke, after 1891 by George Foot Moore), and the history of particular religions was widely covered in the faculty of arts and sciences. Special courses in the history and philosophy of religion were offered at Boston University from 1867, and in comparative history of religion at Cornell from 1891. At the University of Chicago, by 1892, comparative religion had attained the status of a distinct department offering the Ph.D degree. The Imperial University of Japan, in Kyoto, had a professor of the science of religion in 1903.

In the preceding summary, even though it is intended as indicative rather than exhaustive, the absence of German universities is noteworthy. Resources in Germany for study of the histories of various religions in the faculties of philosphy were extensive—as in faculties of arts and sciences at places like Oxford, Harvard, and Chicago. But the interest in Religionsgeschichte or Religionswissenschaft as a discipline was very slow in developing in Germany. None of the major general works cited above came from Germany. The *Archiv für Religionswissenschaft* was not founded until 1898, eighteen years after the bimonthly *Revue de l'histoire des religions.* Since 1870 there had been a German society for anthropology, ethnology, and primitive history, with a journal, and the *religionsgeschichtliche Schule*, centering in the work of Gunkel, Bousset, and Weiss, emerged in the 1890s. But the first lectureship in general history of religions did not appear until 1904.[33]

Adolf Harnack's famous rectorial address at Berlin in 1901, *Die Aufgabe der theologischen Fakultäten und die allgemeine Religionsgeschichte*, is a critical document for the interpretation of the German scene.[34] The question is, he said, whether the theological faculty should restrict itself to examination and presentation of the Christian religion or become a faculty for general religious study and his-

33. See *RGG*, "*Religionsgeschichte und Religionsgeschichtliche Schule*," by Rade, who compares this late development with Switzerland and the Netherlands.

34. "The Task of the Theological Faculties and the General History of Religion" (Berlin, 1901; cited from 2d ed., Giessen, 1901; reprinted in *Reden und Aufsätze*, 2, Giessen, 1910).

tory, on the grounds that only as all religions are dealt with can one religion actually be understood. Or, as a minimum, should every theological faculty have one or more chairs in the general history of religion?

In the abstract, Harnack admitted the advantages of such an expansion. If religion is a fundamental element in human existence, we need to study the religions of all peoples at all stages. Further, other religions can be studied by the same method essential for study of the Christian religion, namely, the historical method. Finally, the practical life of the church seems to recommend the expansion, as the christianization of the world requires basic knowledge of the religions of foreign peoples.

But Harnack had serious doubts. Religion, after all, cannot be studied in isolation but only with thorough knowledge of the language, literature, and history of a people, including the economic and political institutions. Otherwise the exercise is mere dilettantism. But to do this for many religions and areas in the theological faculty, even if possible, would duplicate the work of the philosophical faculty.

If, then, study is restricted to one religion, which one? Surely the one with the Bible, a religion whose history is known for 3,000 years, and which can be studied now as a living religion. "He who does not know this religion, knows none, and he who knows this one in all its history knows all" (p. 11). The Bible is the book above all. It is inexhaustible. What are Homer, the Vedas, and the Koran beside it? In it there is contact with the whole of the ancient historical world—Babylonia, Assyria, Greece, and Egypt—and with all levels of belief, from the folk cult to the religion of the psalmist. Whoever explains this development fully "does not need to study any multiplicity of religion in order to know the way of religion and religious history" (p. 12). The student of the Bible doesn't need the other historians of religion; they need him! The Old Testament is only the prehistory. There is scarcely any religious doctrine, rite, or mood that is not paralleled in the history of Christianity. There are no greater thinkers in any other religion. In Christianity the richest and most varied forms of religious life stand close together. Indeed, the fullness of possibilities is nearly exhausted in Christian history.

Yet the decisive thing, for Harnack, was that Christianity is not *a* religion but *the* religion. Christ is not *a* master, but *the* master. If the claim to redemption is not an illusion, then there can be no more im-

portant business in the history of man than attention to this religion. That is the task of the theological faculty, which after all has a practical calling, to train for service in the evangelical church. Although Harnack could wish that no theological student leave the university without some knowledge of at least one nonchristian religion, the task of the theological faculty remains one of pure scholarship, carrying on the struggle of the nineteenth century for freedom and truth in teaching, in the service of the church. Perhaps, he concluded (wistfully?), we can some day come to a comparative science of religion, but that day seems farther off now than it did three generations ago, when the University of Berlin was founded.[35]

Most of the general histories of religion that we have noted show a strong interest in the question of the origin of religion, and they draw heavily on anthropological data, but, like Söderblom and Otto, their interest is different from that of Tylor, Lang, Frazer, and Marett. Partly because Religionsgeschichte is directed in principle to the whole of religious phenomena, the question of origins is less about historical beginnings than about that root of religion in human experience which can be identified both in the early forms and in the mature religions. Of course, Tylor said much about animism in developed religions, but with a different interest. Tiele put the point most sharply: "The question whether religion is as old as the human race, or whether it is the growth of a later stage, is as little open to solution by historical research as that of its origin and essence; it can only be answered by psychology, and is a purely philosophical in-destitute of belief in higher beings, we can conclude that "religion in its most general sense [is] a universal phenomenon of humanity" (*Outlines*, p. 6). We may agree that the earliest form of religion

35. Compare with this not only Ernst Troeltsch's formulation of the problem of Christianity and other religions (see chap. 8, below), but also the incorporation of the history of religions into the theological curriculum in the Netherlands and the urgings of Morris Jastrow that study in the history of religions, including special study of another religion —perhaps Judaism, Islam, or Buddhism—should be a requirement in every Christian seminary (Jastrow, *Study of Religion*, pp. 369–75).

36. Tiele, *Outlines*, p. 6. See also *Elements*, 1:71: "The question of the origin of religion is not of a historical or archaeological nature, but is purely psychological, and is quite distinct from the inquiry as to the oldest form of religion." This does not, of course, mean abandoning empirical investigation. In determining the essential nature of religion, what is permanent in the forms, we must start from the facts, "from the solid ground of anthropology and history, the well-ascertained results of which can alone enable us to understand the essence of religion and trace it to its source" (ibid., 2:2).

was animistic. However, this did not mean, for Tiele, that religion
sprang from animism, or that animism was a religion, but only that
the early manifestations were dominated by animism. More important, however, the question of the earliest historical form is no longer
decisive.

Hence the question of the origin of religion is the same as the question of the essence of religion. The problem is identifying that permanent element which is present in both earlier and later stages of
religion.[37] For Max Müller, that element was a "perception of the
infinite"—only vaguely present at the beginning, but genuine. Religion has its origin in "a mental faculty which independent of, nay, in
spite of sense and reason, enables man to apprehend the infinite under different names and under varying guises."[38] For Tiele, the
whence of religion, "its source in man's spiritual life," was not in the
perception of the infinite, but rather "consists in the fact that man *has*
the Infinite within him, even before he is himself conscious of it, and
whether he recognizes it or not." Then one may speak of "man's
original, unconscious, innate sense of infinity that gives rise to his
first stammering utterances of that sense, and to all his beautiful
dreams of the past and the future. . . . The sense of infinity from
which they proceed remains a constant quantity . . . it lies at the root
of man's whole spiritual life. It is revealed in his intellectual, his aes-
thetic and his moral life."[39] More precisely stated, "religion always
begins with an emotion" (a predisposition, an impression or the affection itself and its perception) which is called forth by an object and
transformed into a conception and "a definite sentiment, the direction of the will which impels to action . . . produced by such a conception and awakened by emotion." All three constituents—emotion,
conception, and sentiment—are essential, in equilibrium, to the
mental condition which is religion.[40]

37. See Tiele, *Outlines*, p. x: "My history is one of religion, not of religions. . . . It is the
same history, but considered from a different point of view. The first lies hidden in the
last, but its object is to show how that one great psychological phenomenon which we call
religion has developed and manifested itself in such various shapes among the different
races and peoples of the world. By it we see that all religions, even those of highly civilised
nations, have grown up from the same simple germs, and by it, again, we learn the causes
why these germs have in some cases attained such a rich and admirable development, and
in others scarcely grew at all."

38. Müller, *Lectures on the Origin and Growth of Religion* (London, 1880), p. 23.

39. *Elements*, 2:209, 230, 233.

40. Ibid., 2:15–23.

For Réville, similarly, the root of religion, the permanent and substantial element that underlies all the multicolored development, is in the affective dimension of life. As distinct from science and philosophy, which are intellectual, religion "rests essentially on the awakening, on the calling into activity, of a sentiment *sui generis*, which impells the intellect to imagine the object of it under forms corresponding to its degree of knowledge, but which springs spontaneously in the soul, when placed under certain circumstances." Schleiermacher was right in recognizing the sentiment of dependence as integral to religion, but wrong in failing to see the no less essential "sentiment of union, of reciprocity and of mutuality." Thus the series of feelings "respect, veneration, fear, dismay, and terror" must be joined with the series "admiration, joy, confidence, love and ecstasy," that is, of delight in feeling united with the mystery which dominates the world and the self. So defined, religion "is inherent in the human mind and *natural*."[41]

Obviously, the interest in the origin of religion displayed by these historians of religion was at the same time an equal (or greater) interest in the growth of religion(s), from the early to the highest manifestations. The general pattern was of an evolutionary and progressive development. The "principle of continuity," that all things hold together, when applied to history is, as Réville put it, "the *principle of development*, in virtue of which everything begins in the form of germ, of rudiments full of promise and of marvellous ductility, but as yet very incomplete and very crude, and in a state of rough outline. . . . Continuity in history is not the identity of successive facts; it is their development."[42] In Tiele's terms, the task of the history of

41. Réville, *Prolegomena*, pp. 25, 32, 66, 73. Jastrow, reviewing various definitions of religion, proposed that "religion may be defined as the natural belief in a Power or Powers beyond our control and upon whom we feel ourselves dependent; which belief and feeling of dependence prompt (1) to organization, (2) to specific acts, and (3) to the regulation of conduct, with a view to establishing favorable relations between ourselves and the Power or Powers in question" (*Study of Religion*, pp. 171–72). His notion of the origin of religion was similar to those of Müller and Tiele: "So far as historical study can solve the problem, [the origin] is to be sought in the bringing into play of man's power to obtain a perception of the Infinite through the impression which the multitudinous phenomena of the universe make upon him" (ibid., p. 196).

42. *Prolegomena*, p. 65. Jastrow commented that no theory of modern times has proved more fruitful than evolution: "Scholars are pretty generally agreed on two points—that the religious development of mankind proceeds in accordance with definite laws, and that this development is on the whole an upward movement from crude ideas and primitive forms of worship to a philosophic conception of the universe, accompanied by a ceremo-

religion (not religions) is "to show how religion, considered generally
as the relation between man and the superhuman powers in which
he believes, has developed in the course of ages among different nations and races and, through these, in humanity at large." The hypothesis of development implies that all changes and transformations are results of natural growth. "The history of religion unfolds
the method in which this development is determined by the character of nations and races, as well as by the influence of the circumstances surrounding them, and of special individuals, and it exhibits
the established laws by which this development is controlled."[43] Yet
this is not to be understood as simply unilinear or progressive evolution. For Tiele, religious development was not necessarily (nor probably) from a single historical origin, and the laws of development included both the movement from uniformity to diversity and the
constant striving after unity—a dialectic of unity and partition,
"ever-increasing differentiation, coupled with efforts for reconciliation and unity."[44] Morris Jastrow, perhaps the most important
American contributor of the time to the theory of the study of religion, though heavily dependent on Müller, who had spoken of the
dialectic of growth and decay observable in all religions,[45] on
Réville, and especially on Tiele, emphasized the role of differentiation in the evolution of religion.[46]

A corollary of the attempt to trace the development of religion was
an interest in the morphology or classification of religions—not
through a philosophical scheme, as in Hegel, but on the basis of the
actual historical data. The details of these classifications need not detain us. They ranged from simple distinctions such as Abraham
Kuenen's division of national and universal religions,[47] to Max Müller's distinctions on the basis of linguistic families, to the elaborate
scheme, with twenty-two classifications, of Raoul de la Grasserie.[48]
Réville and Tiele can serve as sufficient examples.

---

nial correspondingly elaborated and refined." This does not entail a low view of the primitive forms, but rather "establishes a close bond between the primitive and the advanced
forms of fatih" (Study of Religion, pp. 63, 64).

43. Outlines, p. 2. Réville spoke of "active causes" of development (Prolegomena, pp. 77–
88).

44. Elements, 1:295.

45. Lectures on the Science of Religion (New York, 1872), p. 122.

46. See Study of Religion, pp. 98–117.

47. National and Universal Religions (London, 1882).

48. Des Religions comparées au point de vue sociologique (Paris, 1899). See also the Hegelian-
oriented conception in Edward Caird, The Evolution of Religion, vol. 1 (London and New
York, 1893).

For Réville the main division was between polytheistic and monotheistic religions. The former include the primitive religion of nature (for him the earliest), then animist and fetishist religions, then national mythologies (in China, Egypt, Babylonia, Germany, Gaul, Italy, Greece, Mexico, Peru), then polytheistic-legalistic religions (Brahmanism, Mazdaism, and the two Chinese philosophical religions of Confucius and Lao-tse), and finally Buddhism, a universalist religion of redemption, in principle opposed to polytheism but in practice blending with local polytheisms. The monotheistic category, of course, includes Judaism (legalistic and national), Islam (legalistic and international), and Christianity (an international religion of redemption).[49]

Tiele's most general distinction was between nature religions and ethical religions. At the lowest of the former is animism, the general form of thought determining all lower nature religions; then spiritism, with fetishism as its reverse side; then the stage of myth formation and polydaemonism, still under the domination of animism; then the higher nature religions with developed mythologies, where polydaemonism has become an ordered polytheism (Vedic, Greek, Mexican, etc.) and the ethical element begins to enter. Among the ethical religions proper are Judaism, Brahmanism, Confucianism (not Taoism), Islam, and Zoroastrianism. Buddhism and Christianity fall outside the morphology, and are to be viewed as distinct, universalist ethical religions.[50]

Explicit in the history of religions approach was the principle that Christianity should be studied by the same methods applied to other religious phenomena. Max Müller put it eloquently:

> Not many years ago great offence was given by an eminent writer who remarked that the time had come when the history of Christianity should be treated in a truly historical spirit, in the same spirit in which we treat the history of other religions, such as Brahmanism, Buddhism, or Mohammedanism. And yet what could be truer? He must be a man of little faith who would fear to subject his own religion to the same critical tests to which the historian subjects all other religions. We need not surely crave a tender or merciful treat-

---

49. *Prolegomena*, pp. 89–101.

50. *Elements*, 1:58–149. Tiele's earlier work is entitled *Outlines of the History of Religion to the Spread of the Universal Religions*. Jastrow's classification proposes a different principle, namely, the relation of religion to the whole of life: thus the religions of savages, the religions of primitive culture, the religions of advanced culture, and the religions "which emphasize as an ideal the coextensiveness of religion with life, and which are at a consistent accord between religious doctrine and religious practice" (*Study of Religion*, p. 117).

ment for that faith which we hold to be the only true one. . . . In the
Science of Religion we can decline no comparisons, nor claim any
immunities for Christianity, as little as the missionary can, when
wrestling with the subtle Brahman, or the fanatical Mussulman, or
the plain-speaking Zulu.[51]

But Christianity was not always set in parallel with other great traditions. In the manuals, only the histories of traditions other than Judaism and Christianity were usually surveyed.[52] Chantepie de la
Saussaye's classic *Lehrbuch*, for example, sought to be inclusive—except for postbiblical Judaism and Christianity. Similarly, Tiele's well-
known *Kompendium der Religionsgeschichte* included Judaism up to the
time of Jesus, who claims a few pages, but there is nothing on later
Judaism or Christianity. Though Jastrow found this kind of restric-
tion a defect, the series of seven handbooks on particular religions
that he edited also failed to include either Judaism or Christianity.

This may be one reason why the history of religions tended to be
identified as the study of primitive religion and of non-Western religions. But the principle of including Christianity in the scientific
study of religion on the same basis as other religious phenomena was
clear. Christianity must be located in the morphology (as in Réville,
Tiele, and Müller) of types of religion. The question of the root of
religion is as much a question about Christianity as about primitive
religion. The patterns or laws or causes of development in religion
are applicable to all traditions. In the comparative examination of
such topics as myth, symbol and rite, doctrine, religious authority,
sacrifice, priesthood, community, worship, and morality, the Christian phenomena have an integral place[53]—even though most of
these writers were convinced that Christianity was the highest form
of religion.[54]

51. *Selected Essays*, pp. 13–14. In his 1870 lectures, Müller noted that he expected to give
offense both to those who think that religion is too sacred to study scientifically and to
those who think it beneath science, on a level with astrology and alchemy.

52. Moore, *History of Religions*, is a particularly important exception. Volume 2 was devoted to Judaism, Christianity, and Mohammedanism.

53. See esp. Réville, *Prolegomena*, pt. 2; Tiele, *Elements*, vol. 2; and Müller, *Theosophy*.
Réville, though a specialist on religion in Mexico and Peru, also wrote *Jesus of Nazareth*
(Paris, 1879).

54. See, e.g., Tiele, *Elements*, 1:148–49: "Even those who, like myself, are convinced that
the Gospel, rightly understood, contains the eternal principle of true religion, may well
conceive that, besides the existing ethical religions, and probably from their bosom, others
will yet be born which will do better and more complete justice to these principles and
which will then perhaps exhibit a somewhat different character from the religions we have
termed ethical or supernaturalistic."

In the literature we have been examining, the term *science of religion* (Müller, Tiele, Tischhauser, Jordan) is for all practical purposes interchangeable with the terms *history of religion* (Réville, Chantepie de la Saussaye, d'Alviella, Tiele, Moore) and *study of religion* (Jastrow). What does the term *science* mean in this context, beyond the free and impartial spirit of inquiry? Plainly, it was intended to suggest the emergence of a discipline of study comparable to the sciences of anthropology and philology (among the *Geisteswissenschaften*) and even to the natural sciences. It means the thoroughgoing application of a principle of criticism to all religion(s) considered as phenomena of human experience (hence Religionswissenschaft rather than wissenschaftliche Theologie). No religious tradition or phenomenon is exempt. As Müller put it, the distinction between natural religion and revealed religion is useless for scientific purposes. For comparative religious studies, if any people consider their religion as revealed, it is revealed.[55] In principle, all the data of religion, the whole territory, must be surveyed—from the most primitive to the most advanced, and with all the information available from archeology, anthropology, sociology, psychology, philology, and history.

The mere collection of data, of course, is by itself unilluminating. To cite Müller again, "As anthropologists, we ought never to forget [that] we gain nothing, or very little, by simply collecting superstitions or similar customs among different and widely distant nations."[56] Critical comparative study is essential. Though only in the case of Louis Jordan[57] was comparative religion separated out as a special science within a science, comparisons are essential in any attempt to identify common features of religion, the common origin of

55. See *Lectures on the Science of Religion*, pp. 44–47.

56. *Theosophy*, p. 60.

57. *Comparative Religion* was an attempt to define comparative religion as a special science within the science of religion parallel to comparative anatomy, philology, psychology, literature, history, geology, zoology, jurisprudence, economics, etc. This was to be distinguished from history of religion, which precedes and provides the data for scientific comparisons of religions with one another and of conceptions within the development of a single religion, and from the philosophy of religion, which is more speculative. "Comparative Religion is that Science which compares the origin, structure, and the characteristics of the various Religions of the world, with the view of determining their genuine agreements and differences, the measure of relation in which they stand one to another, and their relative superiority or inferiority when regarded as types." The philosophy of religion "seeks to determine the relation of all Religions alike to a common fundamental instinct in man" (pp. 63, 65). Jordan's hope for a special science of comparisons of religions was not widely shared, but given the limitation of his preoccupation with specifically comparative studies, his book is a remarkably valuable and inclusive survey of the types of the study of religion, of the principal figures, and of the literature up to 1905.

religion, and related patterns or laws of development. Even one's own religion cannot really be understood apart from the comparative framework. In contrast to Harnack's judgment that one who knows the Christian religion fully knows all religion, Müller had earlier proclaimed the principle of Religionswissenschaft by applying Goethe's statement about language: "He who knows [only] one knows none."[58] Just as in comparative philology, all higher knowledge is gained by comparison.

For Tiele, the method of the science of religion was ultimately philosophical. Anthropology and history can be one-sidedly empirical, hence positivistic and powerless to explain the data. What is needed is a philosophical, deductive (but not speculative) analysis of "the results yielded by induction, by empirical, historical, and comparative methods." The science of religion, as Tiele laid it out in his Gifford Lectures, requires the development of a morphology of religion (more empirical and historical), and then an ontological consideration, "which treats of the permanent elements in what is changing, the unalterable element in transient and ever-altering forms—in a word, the origin and the very nature and essence of religion."[59]

Müller's statement of the principles of Religionswissenschaft was probably most characteristic of the endeavor as a whole. To be sure, his view was distinctive in the weight given to philology. As a student particularly of the Aryan family of languages and of comparative philology for whom the finding of the common Aryan origins of Greek and Indian civilizations was one of the greatest discoveries of our age, he argued that there is "no solid foundation for the study of the religion of savages except the study of their language." In his view, the nature of human language necessitated that when primitive man named the sun, moon, rivers, trees, and so on, he could name them only as agents, without necessarily ascribing life or soul to inanimate objects—thus the error of much animist theory.[60] He viewed the major types of religion as corresponding to the three groups of languages: Aryan or Indo-Germanic, Semitic, and Turanian.[61] And

58. See Müller's introduction to the English translation of Réville's *Prolegomena*, p. viii.
59. *Elements*, 1:18–19. Volume 1 is thus morphological, volume 2 ontological.
60. See *Introduction*, p. 56, and *Anthropological Religion*, pp. 73–74.
61. Though Müller clung to this basic conception to the end, it was quickly recognized as untenable and arbitrary, oversimplifying the relation of languages and races and of language groups (Turanian had to involve a common religious type for peoples as distant as the Chinese and the Lapps).

he was primarily interested in the eight great historical religions which made their claims on the basis of possessing sacred books (see *Sacred Books of the East*; *Last Essays*, p. 331).

More and more, however, Müller tended to stress that the adequate method for the study of religion is the historical method. Recalling Schiller's dictum—"Die Weltgeschichte ist das Weltgericht"—Müller affirmed in his final series of Gifford Lectures that "the true science of religion is . . . the history of religion." This of course involves comparative analysis and philosophical reflection, but at the same time "the only effective way of studying what is called the philosophy of religion, or the philosophical criticism of religion, is to study the history of religion."[62] The study of history enables us to understand the four major kinds of relationships among religions: (1) "the most distant relationship . . . which is simply due to our common humanity"; (2) the relationships due to a common language, which are more important even than blood relationships; (3) "real historical relationship"—resemblances or identities deriving from common political and social history; and (4) relationships of "mere neighbourhood," which may lead to a borrowing of one thing or another.[63] Further, the true route to and the safe foundation for natural religion are found in the history of religion, which (notably in the case of the eight great scriptural religions) shows that there is "an ancient and universal religion" and that "the points on which the great religions differ are far less numerous, and certainly far less important, than are the points on which they all agree."[64]

But the history and comparison of religions provide the strongest confirmation of the truth of the Christian religion by directing us to the common foundation of religion, by teaching us (for example) that belief in miracles "is almost inevitable," that is, by placing us "in a new and real world where all is miraculous" (*Theosophy*, p. 25), and by showing us the distinctiveness of Christianity. "It should never be forgotten that while a comparison of ancient religions will certainly show that some of the most vital articles of faith are the common property of the whole of mankind, at least of all who seek the Lord, if

62. *Theosophy*, pp. 4, 3.

63. Ibid., pp. 59–65. Two or three of these relationships may, of course, often exist at the same time.

64. *Last Essays*, p. 335. In *Physical Religion*, Müller traced the history of Vedic religion at length (especially the history of Agni) to show, as he put it later, "how the human mind was led by a natural revelation, far more convincing than any so-called special revelation, from the conception of agents behind these phenomena" (*Theosophy*, pp. 7–8).

haply they might feel after Him, the same comparison alone can possibly teach us what is peculiar to Christianity, and what has secured to it that pre-eminent position which now it holds in spite of all obloquy."[65]

THE FINALITY (?) OF THE CHRISTIAN RELIGION[66]

The statement just cited from Müller makes clear that for him, as for Tiele and Réville, the scientific study of the history of religions finally supports the claim for the superiority of Christianity. Even the research into primitive religion, which discloses the common root and the continuity of Christianity with the "religion of savages," serves to show—contrary to the views of Tylor and Frazer, and of Freud and Durkheim in their own ways—the truth and not the error of the developed religions. Christianity regularly appears at the apex of the morphology of religious types. This was also true for Söderblom and Otto. The former rejected the idea of a simply continuous development, holding to a sharp distinction between nature religion and prophetic religion, and thus to the uniqueness of biblical religion as shown by comparative studies. Yet in a broader sense Christianity was seen as the central point of the entire history of religion, so that religions could properly be classified according to their relation to Christianity.[67]

For Otto, the steeping and saturation of the holy with rational and ethical elements guarded the nonrational from "sinking into fanaticism or mere mysticality" and the balance of the rational and the nonrational provides a criterion for ranking religions. "Applying this criterion, we find that Christianity, in this as in other respects, stands

65. *Selected Essays* (London, 1881), p. 19. See *Lectures on the Science of Religion*, p. 103.

66. The term *finality* comes from such writers as William Adams Brown, G. B. Foster, Hastings Rashdall, P. T. Forsyth, and A. C. Bouquet, as a way of denoting the supremacy of Christianity without the implication of exclusive truth that *absoluteness* often suggests. Forsyth, for example, said that the crucial question between the church and the world is not whether there is revelation, but "whether that revelation in Christ was final" (see Forsyth, *The Person and Place of Jesus Christ* [London, 1909], p. 84). Egbert Smyth said that "the question of the salvation of the heathen is simply one aspect of the fundamental religious question of our time: the claim of Christianity to be the one perfect and final religion for mankind" (see Smyth et al., *Progressive Orthodoxy: A Contribution to the Christian Interpretation of Christian Doctrine* [Boston, 1885], p. 178). Finality may also be preferred as better English than absoluteness and as a more developmental term that suited the evolutionary image so important in the Anglo-Saxon world. But see also Troeltsch's view of the role of the idea of absoluteness, in chapter 8, below.

67. See Söderblom, *Einführung in die Religionsgeschichte* (Leipzig, 1920).

out in complete superiority over all its sister religions." We recognize
that in Christianity, "placed without prejudice in the comparative
study of religions . . . an element of man's spiritual life . . . has for the
first time come to maturity in a supreme and unparalleled way."[68]

"Placed without prejudice in the comparative study of religions"
was the critical phrase for the historians of religion. Claims for the
exclusive truth of Christianity could no longer be made. Study of the
history of religion shows that the Christian vision is fundamentally
continuous with other religious visions. And while one may hold that
Christianity is supreme, or completely superior, or the fulfillment of
universal religious aspirations (though not necessarily the perfect religion, as for Tiele), every such estimate of the final truth of the
Christian religion must be set in the context of the actual nature of
other religions, sympathetically considered.

So much for the historians of religion. But to what extent did the
new perspective alter the problematic for late-nineteenth-century
theology and philosophy of religion? Apart from Ernst Troeltsch, in
whom the depth of the question was most fully perceived (see below,
chapter 8), the responses to Religionswissenschaft fall generally into
three categories. First, some (though not many) influential thinkers
could simply ignore the problem. Frank, for example, could discuss
at length the certainty and truth of Christianity in four volumes without ever mentioning the relation of Christianity to nonchristian religions. Nor does any hint of the problem of other religions appear in
William G. T. Shedd's dogmatics.[69]

Second, there were those who, without becoming directly involved
in comparative or ethnographic studies, recognized a new problem
and sought in varying ways to specify the sharp distinction between
Christian and other faiths or between theological methods whereby
the uniqueness of Christianity could be maintained. Kaftan thought
it important both to use historical and comparative data for the foundations of dogmatics and to order Christianity within the history of
religion as a whole. He viewed all religion as consisting in judgments
of value (Wertbeurteilungen—adapted from Ritschl's Werturteilung),
but differentiated by their conceptions of the highest good. What
clearly distinguishes the Christian religion from all others, as without

68. *Idea of the Holy*, pp. 141–42.
69. See Frank, *System der christlichen Gewissheit* (Erlangen, 1870; 2d ed., 1884) and *System der christlichen Wahrheit* (Erlangen, 1878; 3d ed., 1894), noted in chap. 2, above, and Shedd, *Dogmatic Theology*, 2d ed. (New York, 1889).

parallel, is that it is a religion of revelation which teaches us to find our highest good in the supernatural kingdom of God.[70]

Augustus Strong was less open. In his big system, heathenism rated a couple of pages as mainly negative preparation for the redemption in Christ. He did not exclude God's working in nonchristian religions and was prepared to see Confucius, Buddha, and Zoroaster as reformers raised up by God, "but the positive element in heathenism was slight."[71]

Martin Kähler, rejecting modern evolutionary theories of religious development, found in the certainty of faith in justification by Christ the direct implication that any other religiosity, however intimate and upright it might be, lacks personal reciprocal relation with God. All other religions are merely earthly, human, and nonhistorical. Guilt and redemption are decisive Christian categories. Even the viewpoint of the so-called modern missions, which sees points of contact in the high culture religions, is to be rejected. Only in a purely formal sense can one speak of a unity of the concept of religion that includes Christianity with nonchristian religions. The ethic of Buddhism has quite a different soul from the ethic of Jesus; the monotheism of Islam excludes the living God; and the pantheism of India has no place for the holy independent God. Here are no foundations for Christian faith, not even comparability, but only antithesis, truth versus falsehood.[72]

For Kähler, the uniqueness of Christianity is not something affirmed on the basis of Religionswissenschaft, which can only deal with human teaching, not with revelation. So theology has no occasion to expand into a general science of religion or to be dependent on any scientific investigation of religion. That judgment was made even more forcibly, if possible, by Herrmann, whose radical disjunction between all judgments of scientific history and the immediacy of the personal encounter with the inner life of Jesus was discussed in chapter 2. Herrmann applied this judgment to the history of religions question briefly, in a reply to Troeltsch's essay on the absolute-

70. See *Das Wesen der christlichen Religion* (Basel, 1881; 2d ed., 1888), esp. pp. 64–81. Interestingly, in *Die Wahrheit der christlichen Religion* (Basel, 1888), Kaftan does not take up the question of other religions.

71. See Augustus H. Strong, *Systematic Theology* (Philadelphia, 1886; issued as 3 vols. in 1, 1912), pp. 665–66.

72. *Die Wissenschaft der christlichen Lehre*, 3d ed. (Leipzig, 1905), esp. pp. 11, 177–87; and *Dogmatische Zeitfragen 2: Angewandte Dogmen*, 2d ed. (Leipzig, 1908), esp. pp. 357–65.

ness of Christianity. Historical research, he said, always leaves us in relativities. That is its nature and nothing else is to be expected. It can neither lead us to the conclusion of the absoluteness of Christianity, nor in any way require us to give up this judgment. The immediacy of faith is its own certainty—and "Christian faith not only possesses but is the conviction of the absoluteness of Christianity"; it makes impossible the idea that there could be a greater than Christ.[73]

Among the German theologians perhaps Ihmels confronted the question most directly, though reaching a conclusion not greatly different from Herrmann's. Ihmels recognizes the question as a modern one. In view of historical research and the recent great religious congresses, isolation is no longer possible; nor can one hold, as in the older dogmatics, that Christianity is the true religion and the others simply false. Christianity belongs with everything called religion, and in a certain sense it is undeniably a religion among others. Yet Christianity stands or falls with the claim to be *the* religion. How then can it be "*a* religion and at the same time *the* religion?" However much other religions may approach a relation to God, Christianity knows that its fellowship with God, the indissoluble belonging with him, is either there or not there. In its fellowship is the absoluteness, the religion that cannot be surpassed. One may recognize that there are high points in other religions (Buddhism, Sufism, Indian mysticism), but also that the dark sides of those religions belong with their essences, whereas the shadows in Christianity contradict the essence. In the end one must reject any attempt to judge the absoluteness of Christianity on the basis of general considerations, of either the history of religions or the history of the origins of Christianity. There can be no scientific proof of the absoluteness of Christianity. We can only show that the Christian claim to absoluteness is not contradicted by the scientifically ascertainable facts. Hence on this question we start (and end) with the apprehension that God in our religious experience forces us immediately to the judgment that revelation in Christ is actuality and truth.[74]

Finally, we may recall Harnack's refusal of the suggestion that the general history of religions be incorporated into the theological task.

73. *Schriften* (Munich, 1966), 1:193–99.
74. *Centralfragen* (Leipzig, 1912), pp. 44–45. See also *Wahrheitsgewissheit*, 3d ed. (Leipzig, 1914), p. 177. Georg Wobbermin was another who took the problem seriously, but his systematic theology belongs to the post-World War I period.

Harnack did in fact seem open to the problem, partly because of his commitment to the historical method in all study of religion, including Christianity. Some of his reasons for not wanting the theological faculty made into a general history of religions faculty were of a practical sort. Yet he too fell back on the assertion simply that Christianity is *the* religion and Christ *the* master. Harnack's view recalls Ritschl's lack of interest in a scientific history of religions. In accord with his radical christocentrism Ritschl, in a passing reference to the status of other religions, not only reaffirmed "the claim of Christianity to occupy the highest place," but asserted that "those qualities in other religions by which they *are* religions are intelligible to us chiefly as measured by the perfection which they assume in Christianity, and by the clearness which distinguishes the perfect religion from the imperfect." Thus "the arrangement of religions in stages . . . amounts to no more than a scientific attempt to promote mutual understanding among Christians" (*Justification and Reconciliation*, p. 197).

The third pattern of theological response was characterized by those who found in the historical and comparative study of religion a positive confirmation of the superiority or finality of Christianity. In a significant way this was a continuation and renewal of the perspective of Schleiermacher and Hegel, according to which the essence of religion finds its fullest realization in Christianity. In Schleiermacher that theme was more explicitly sounded in the fifth of the *Speeches*, where Christianity is the religion of religiousness. But even in the *Glaubenslehre*, Christianity is plainly the highest of the monotheistic and ethical religions, and the appearance of Christ is not something *absolutely* new. For Hegel, of course, Christianity was the absolute religion, gathering up the truth of all preceding stages of religious development into the full realization of the absolute self-consciousness.

Toward the end of the century, the broad emphasis on continuity was more fully informed by the study of the history of religion. It was also dominated by the idea of evolutionary progress, with the superiority of Christianity being shown by its ethics, its universality, and its cultural impact and support.

In a few cases, as in Edward Caird of Glasgow, the evolutionary concept was married to a fundamentally Hegelian analysis. For Caird, conscious life is defined by three ideas: the object (or not-self), the subject (or self), and the unity presupposed in the difference (the idea of God). The broad stages in the evolution of religion are objective religion, subjective religion, and absolute or universal religion.

The data of the history of religion (though Caird did not deal with these in detail) enable us to see in the religious development of mankind the "necessary stages of one process of evolution." The evolutionary idea makes possible the interpretation of the fundamental idea of humanity, of the highest form of man's consciousness of himself in his relation to all other things and beings, even in the lives of the "utterly uncivilized races." It is not that we find essentially common elements in primitive and developed religion, but by reading backward from the most mature forms we can find in primitive religion a "germinative principle," an "obscure beginning" of the religious consciousness of God as a self-revealing Spirit.[75]

An extreme case of the argument for the supremacy of Christianity can be found in James Freeman Clarke. Clarke averred that the factual study of comparative theology would show that "while most of the religions of the world are ethnic, or religions of races, Christianity is catholic, or adapted to become the religion of all races," because "the ethnic religions are one sided, each containing a truth of its own, but being defective, wanting some corresponding truth. Christianity, or the catholic religion, is complete on every side." We have thus a better apologetic. The older apologetics tried to prove the superiority of Christianity; comparative theology shows it from a new class of evidence, whereby Christianity is seen to be capable of development, a religion of progress and universal unity. Others decline and fall, or are arrested and stationary.[76]

Andrew Fairbairn, principal of Mansfield College, Oxford, sounded the themes of continuity and development more impressively.[77] Christianity must be seen among the religions, must be construed through religion, and the justification of its truth requires knowing the point of departure. Primitive man's absorption in religion is no "mere accident" or "mistaken inference." To say so would

---

75. *Evolution of Religion.* See esp. volume 1.

76. *Ten Great Religions,* pp. 15, 21. This work was not of much scholarly importance as a history of religions, but as a theological statement it was enormously popular, going through thirty editions by 1892. With Clarke's work we may also associate Allan Menzies, *History of Religion* (2d ed., London, 1901), a popular work somewhat more restrained than Clarke's but stressing the theme of progress from tribal to national to individual and to universal religion, so that "with growing experience the world becomes more assured that the simplest and broadest religion ever preached upon this earth is also the best and truest, and that in maintaining Christianity as at first preached, and applying it in every needed direction, lies the hope of the future of mankind" (p. 432).

77. *The Philosophy of the Christian Religion* (London, 1902).

be to discredit Christianity as well. The comparative study of primitive religion is something we cannot afford to despise. Here we see
that man is religious by nature, the nascent human mind feeling its
kinship with the divine and groping after it, "and the more it gropes
rises the higher in its manhood" (p. 190). And the history of the development of the religions "studies the organism as it lives and grows
in its own home, affected by all the forces that surround and play
upon it" (p. 208), all the variations from race, place, ethnic relations,
social and political forces, and creative persons. At the highest level
are the "founded religions," which include Buddhism and Islam but
especially Christianity. Part of a universal historical process, Christ is
yet "the keystone of the arch which spans the gulf of time" (p. 567).

Similarly, for William Adams Brown, in his widely used and reprinted textbook, the possession of Christ is the final evidence of the
distinctiveness and finality of the Christian religion.[78] The question
of the relation of Christianity to other religions is "one of fact, to be
determined by the researches of scholars." The facts show that the
new contribution of Christianity comes from its founder's character,
which still stands unsurpassed. "We know no better formula for religious progress than to describe it as the growing conformity of mankind to the spirit and principles of Jesus." The perfectness of
Christianity is not finished, but is a perfection of life, of a process of
growth, and the proof of the divinity of Jesus is that he is the source
of transforming influence. As "the religion of divine sonship and human brotherhood, revealed and realized by Jesus Christ, . . . [Chris-
tianity] is the fulfillment and completion of all earlier forms of religion, and the divinely appointed means for the redemption of
mankind through the establishment of the kingdom of God. . . . The
possession in Christ of the supreme revelation of God's love and
power constitutes the distinctive mark of Christianity, and justifies its
claim to be the final religion."[79]

In Reinhold Seeberg, though he might also be grouped with a
thinker like Kaftan, we find a modest attempt to set Christianity in

78. Brown, *Christian Theology in Outline* (New York, 1906), pp. 32–41. See also *The Essence
of Christianity* (New York, 1902). A similar view had been set forth in W. N. Clarke, *An
Outline of Christian Theology* (New York, 1898).

79. *Outline*, p. 41. Enslin Carpenter's popular small work, *The Place of Christianity among
the Religions of the World* (London, 1904), was more open in its claims. Christianity, because
of its ethical element, is up to the present the highest emergent, but the purging of out-
worn elements in it by the modern spirit will be paralleled by transformation in other religions, so that they too will contribute to the goal of inspiring one faith and one truth.

the context of general religious development and at the same time to affirm its absoluteness.[80] Man's general religious experience expresses the hunger of the soul in many forms. Christianity came in the "fullness of time" as the development of ancient religion. It makes a claim to absoluteness, a demand which belongs to the essence of religion, a claim to be unsurpassable and to judge all religions. In accord with the only measures applicable to systems of religious concepts—logic, history, and the spiritual needs of the soul—the proof of the absoluteness of Christianity is threefold: it is consistent and logical; its supremacy is shown in the history of religious development—other religions fell, Christianity has been inwardly reformed and is ever new; and it satisfies the deepest need of the human spirit for a near and strong spiritual authority and for a distant final goal.

Otto Pfleiderer, in his four-volume *Philosophy of Religion on the Basis of Its History*, dealt much more extensively with the history of religions data and reflected strongly the progressive development motif.[81] In what he called the genetic-speculative philosophy of religion, he traces (volume 3) at length the immanent and continuous development of religious consciousness from primitive forms through Indo-Germanic (Vedic, Persian, Buddhist, Greek, Roman) and Semitic religious consciousness to the Christian consciousness. "As every living thing only unfolds its nature in the whole course of its development," religion must be seen in its entirety in human history, and Christianity must be seen within this total framework. History is at the same time judgment: the description of the rise, growth, and decay of religions "comprises a judgment of them." Thus the science of the history of religion "manifestly furnishes us with the most brilliant and irrefutable apology for the unique superiority of Christianity to all the other religions. And if the past history of Christianity shows so unbounded a capacity of development, it would manifestly be very arbitrary to assume that that capacity is now extinct; on the contrary, everything tends to assure us, that the same law of development which in the past enabled Christianity to adapt itself to new needs as they arose, will not fail in the future to meet with and to satisfy the needs which may yet emerge."[82]

80. *Die Grundwahrheiten der christlichen Religion* (Leipzig, 1902; 7th ed., 1921), esp. pt. I: *Die Wahrheit der christlichen Religion*, pp. 24–31.
81. London, 1886–88; trans. from the 2d German ed.
82. Ibid., 4:310–22.

A final illustration of the evolutionary model for the history of religions, in which Christianity emerges as the highest attainment, can be found in the work of the French Protestant leader Auguste Sabatier.[83] The model is qualified, for Sabatier rejected the idea of a totally unilinear or continuous development. "The idea of religious progress is a great and luminous idea, but it is not possible to apply it to all the details of history" (p. 94). One can see differences of degree in the development of a continuous evolution in the Hebrew tradition, from early Israel through Christianity and Islam. But when it comes to Chinese religion or religion in Mexico, India, Egypt, or Greece, one finds differences of kind. Yet again one can (must) speak of revelation as progressive, of growth in the representations of the divine—from polytheism to monotheism to the revelation of love in Christianity. To speak of progress is especially appropriate in the movement from domestic to tribal to national to universalist forms of religion. The movement toward universalism is seen in Buddhism, Islam, and Christianity. But Islam is not original, deriving from Judaism and Christianity and retaining nationalistic elements. Buddhism has an inner dualism of esoteric (and atheistic) mysticism and popular superstition. Hence Christianity stands as the only truly universalist religion: "The terms 'universal religion' and 'Christian religion' coincide so exactly that if a form of Christianity is not universalist on any side, on that particular side it ceases to be Christian" (p. 95). Here there is absolute freedom of spirit and a higher righteousness; the universal and the truly ethical are joined. "In the religion of Jesus there is nothing religious but that which is authentically moral, and nothing moral in human life that is not truly religious. The perfect religion coincides with the absolute morality, and this naturally extends to and is obligatory on all mankind" (p. 101).

What can we conclude about the theological responses to the late-nineteenth-century study of the history of religions? Surely a new kind of openness to other religious claims was emerging. But even leaving aside the orthodox thinkers who believed it possible still to maintain the exclusive truth of Christianity, we are surprised by the relative ease with which the superiority of the Christian religion was affirmed, both by the liberals and by the historians of religion. Christianity was no longer the only religious truth, but even a sympathetic consideration of the values of other religions seems to have left confi-

83. *Philosophy of Religion* (London, 1902).

dence in the supremacy of Christian faith largely untouched. In this respect, the theological judgment at the end of the century does not seem much different from the position of Schleiermacher at the beginning of it.

Why was this so? One reason is doubtless the dominance of the evolutionary perspective in the late nineteenth century, even though that perspective was not as universal as is sometimes assumed. A second reason is that the liberals, at least, believed in the finality of a Christianity stripped down to its essentials. For many, the supremacy of Christianity lay in its moral character, which made it worthy of export. Again, the Jesus of history/Christ of faith problem seems to have been a more immediate and intense focus of concern for theology than was the diversity of religions. Finally, in spite of forty years' development before World War I, the study of the history of religions was still in its infancy.

In the broadest terms, however, we can describe this theological outcome as a function of the nineteenth-century struggle, from Schleiermacher and Hegel on, to resolve the problem of the ideal and the actual through a view of history as redemptive. God's promises and redeeming action were understood as immanently reflected in cultural development, making the West superior to other cultures and the religion of Jesus superior to other religions. Thus the absoluteness of Christian civilization and the absoluteness of Christianity were defended in terms of each other.

5

History and Faith

THE JESUS OF HISTORY/THE CHRIST OF FAITH

Harnack

In the early mornings of the winter semester of 1899–1900 at the University of Berlin, Adolf Harnack (not yet von Harnack) delivered a course of extemporaneous lectures for hundreds of students of all the faculties. Harnack was then at the midpoint of a career as the greatest church historian of the age—already the author of the most important nineteenth-century history of dogma, founder (and editor since 1881) of the *Theologische Literaturzeitung*, and member of the Prussian Academy of Sciences.[1]

The lectures were published from a student transcript in 1900 as *Das Wesen des Christentums*, and they made an extraordinary impression. Harnack's eminent academic stature, coupled with the issues posed in the lectures, made them an immediate center of controversy, eliciting within two years some eleven books by German Protestants, fourteen Catholic responses, six translations of the lectures themselves, and scores of articles and reviews.[2]

The critical issue in *Das Wesen* was precisely that of the historical Jesus. This posed in reality a multiple question. Can historical research uncover the Jesus of history? What kind of historical study? How does the picture of this Jesus that is discovered stand with the Christ of faith, considered as orthodox Christology? Is this Jesus available, or of use, for modern faith and culture? Is historical research thus a help to faith? And can any security for faith be found in history?[3]

---

1. See pp. 305–07 for fuller data on Harnack's life and works.

2. See Ernst Rolff, *Harnacks Wesen des Christentums und die religiösen Strömungen der Gegenwart* (Leipzig, 1902; originally published in *Die christliche Welt*).

3. In what follows, I deal only with those figures for whom these were real questions, not the Protestant orthodox or Catholic traditionalists, who rejected the historical critical view of the New Testament, and for whom therefore the gospel portrait was essentially unquestioned as a basis for Christological dogma.

Nearly all the changes were rung on these questions in the two decades from 1890 to 1910. Orthodoxy of course evaded or resisted the questions. To the question whether the real Jesus could be discovered through scientific history, many lives of Jesus in the latter nineteenth century said yes, but created a modern Jesus who was read into the gospels. Martin Kähler vigorously said no. Herrmann offered a halfway yes and no. Weiss, Wrede, and Schweitzer (in varying ways) said yes, but doubted whether the Jesus so discovered could be of much help to modern faith. Loisy said yes, but in such a way that the Catholic church was the natural development out of the historical Jesus. Drews said no because it was to be doubted whether there was a Jesus of history.[4]

Harnack's answer to the question whether the Jesus of history could be recovered and found available for modern belief was affirmative and relatively clear-cut. He had not moved far from Ritschl's confidence in the discoverable facts of history as the basis and norm of faith, from the assumption of an easy continuity between the revelation of the first century and contemporary Christian affirmation. The historical Jesus could indeed be known and appealed to as the basis for modern belief and moral imperative. (On Ritschl, see chapter 1, above.)

Harnack was irrevocably committed as a historian to finding the essence of Christianity in "what is of permanent value" (*WC*, p. 13). For him, there had to be a positive relation of Jesus and the Bible to modern culture and morality—and historical study was the way to disclose this. Even though in *Das Wesen* Harnack disclaimed any attempt to take up the question of the modern world systematically (p. 299), the degree of his commitment was strikingly shown in a series of fifteen questions that he later addressed to Karl Barth in *Die christliche Welt* (January 1923). He asked: Can the religion of the Bible be either so clear and unified that historical knowledge and reflection are unnecessary or so opaque that they are useless? If one is to remain in the world, can the experience of God be altogether disparate from other experience? Can one erect barriers between the experience of God and the experience of what is good, true, and beautiful,

---

4. For a wide spectrum of reactions, see the *Hibbert Journal Supplement* (London, 1909), "Jesus or Christ?," in which seventeen authors of almost every theological stance responded to a previous (though not very good) article by R. Roberts entitled "Jesus or Christ? An Appeal for Consistency." The essays are of widely varying worth, but the diversity of the replies is instructive.

instead of relating them by means of historical knowledge and reflection? "If the person of Christ Jesus stands at the center of the gospel, how else can the basis for a reliable and communal knowledge of this person be gained but through critical-historical study so that an imagined Christ is not put in place of the real one?" Finally, "Is there any other theology than that which has strong ties and is in blood relationship with science in general? Should there be one, what persuasiveness and value belong to it?" Harnack was baffled by a theology that appeared to deny these positive relationships. Theology, for him, must be responsible to culture, though it is also concerned to transform culture.

For Harnack the question "What is Christianity?" is to be answered "solely in its historical sense," by employing "the methods of historical science, and the experience of life gained by studying the actual course of history" (WC, p. 6). This method must be distinguished from apologetics in order that historical research not be "brought into complete discredit" (WC, p. 7), though Harnack's whole endeavor in Das Wesen was in another sense an apologetic.[5] Das Wesen abjures any effort, by speculative reasoning about a general notion of religion, at defining a philosophical essence of Christianity, for Christianity is not that but a living reality.

Where does the historian look? The point of departure must simply be "Jesus Christ and his Gospel." But that cannot be restricted to what he said and did, for personalities are known by their effects, and one must "look at the reflection and the effects which he produced in those whose leader and master he became." Hence one must include the first generation of Jesus' disciples and indeed all the later products of this spirit and life. In all of this, the historian's highest duty is "to determine what is of permanent value . . . what is essential." The gospel is not "in all respects identical with its earliest form" but rather "contains something which, under differing historical forms, is of permanent validity," a kernel which is in the husk (WC, pp. 10–15).

One starts therefore with the classical epoch, for Christianity "had a founder who himself was what he taught" (WC, p. 11). Study begins with the message brought by Jesus Christ, as seen in the Synoptic

5. W. A. Brown, in *The Essence of Christianity* (New York, 1902), p. 285, commented that "there is more apology in Harnack's history than in twenty volumes of the Bridgewater treatises."

gospels and distinguished from the accidental elements of miracle, of apocalypticism, and of the sociopolitical condition of the time. The best-known feature of Harnack's *Das Wesen*, though one often taken out of context, has been the summary of Jesus' distinctive teaching under three interpenetrating aspects: the kingdom of God and its coming, God the father and the infinite value of the human soul, and the higher righteousness and the commandment of love (*WC*, p. 51).

In each of these aspects, the whole of the message is contained. The kingdom of God, stripped of the husk of traditional elements, is proclaimed by Jesus as the future and present "rule of the holy God in the hearts of individuals . . . coming to the individual by entering into his soul and laying hold of it" (*WC*, p. 56). "God the Father and the infinite value of the human soul" is the gospel within the gospel, the formulation of the message most accessible "to our modern way of thinking and feeling" (*WC*, p. 63), reminding us of what we already know, yet expressing the paradox that for all humanity to be children of God is both a gift and a task. In the ethical message, Jesus sets righteousness free from legalism, from external forms, and from alien religious connections, focusing on the heart of the matter—disposition and intention—and finding in the moral principle one root and one motive: love.

Harnack has often been accused of locating the reality of Christianity simply in the *teaching* of Jesus. That charge is patently unfair. At the outset he laid down that "a complete answer to the question, What is Christianity, is impossible so long as we are restricted to Jesus Christ's teaching alone" (*WC*, p. 10). To be sure, Harnack had little use for the traditional Christological dogma; that sort of intellectualism could well be described as part of the "heap of rubbish" (*WC*, p. 272) in which real Christianity was later buried. His historical judgment was that Jesus, in his interpretation of the messianic role, "desired no other belief in his person and no other attachment to it than is contained in the keeping of his commandments" (*WC*, p. 125). Again, *"The Gospel as Jesus proclaimed it, has to do with the Father only and not with the Son"* (*WC*, p. 144). But this statement, so often cited without the qualifying clause, is followed on the next page by the complementary assertion that Jesus knew himself as the way to the Father: *"He is the way to the Father, and as he is the appointed of the Father, so he is the judge as well. . . .* It is not as a mere factor that he is connected with the Gospel; *he was its personal realization and its strength, and this he is felt to be still.*"[6]

Such is the reality of Christianity as history discloses its beginnings. Subsequently the gospel was uprooted from the soil of Judaism and planted in the field of Greco-Roman culture. It underwent a transformation into the ecclesiastical and political institution of Catholicism, a church of doctrine and law. Under the influence of Greek philosophy, it was overlaid with a system of dogma. Latin Catholicism produced "an outward and visible Church and a State founded on force and law," which was in fundamental contradiction to the gospel (*WC*, p. 264). Yet the gospel persisted and was renewed in the Reformation as the message and the corresponding religious experience were brought again to the foreground and alien accretions were rejected. *"Protestantism reckons . . . upon the Gospel being something so simple, so divine, and therefore so truly human, as to be most certain of being understood when it is left entirely free, and also as to produce essentially the same experiences and convictions in individual souls"* (*WC*, p. 275; see pp. 268–85). But there was also a dark side to the Reformation; its work was unfinished and Protestantism became re-catholicized. Because of this the gospel needs again to struggle to the surface.

It is often assumed that in the late nineteenth and early twentieth centuries there was general confidence about the discovery of the historical Jesus and his usefulness for modern faith. That might seem to be the case for Ritschl and even for Harnack, though the latter shows some signs of the uneasiness that began to appear in the Ritschlian school. And in many of the lesser lights, both liberal and conservative, the assumption appears to be warranted.

For example, Theodor Haering, the last of the Ritschlians, found no serious obstructions to knowledge of the historical Jesus. Historical knowledge, as provided by scientific historiography, and faith

6. In "Legenden als Geschichtsquellen" (*Reden und Aufsätze*, 1:8–25), Harnack argued that it is in the form of legend (as distinguished from myth and fairy tale) that the work and significance of a person are known historically. True legends offer interpretation and judgment of historical facts. They characterize history by seeing in a single representative event the complete impression of a historical nexus, or by showing the whole significance of a person in a single anecdote, or by creating impressions by selecting and grouping facts. Every historical judgment, by involving the subjective judgment of the historian, based on his own inner experience, has thus the form of legend, though the historian's primary task is to establish the facts. The true kernel about Jesus, as one who concerns me, is in this sense legendary, but the knowledge is certain because the effects of the personality of Christ are clearly evident in the three great sources of historical knowledge: great events, memorials, and institutions. (See also *Christianity and History*, pp. 52–68, esp. p. 61.)

knowledge, as described by the Ritschlians, correlate perfectly.[7] The Scottish theologian H. R. Mackintosh concluded that "while nothing in the past can be so certain for the historian, *purely as an historian*, as that it will bear the weight of personal religion," yet if we take the gospel record as a whole, including both the earthly Jesus and the exalted Lord as aspects of "the historic Christ," then "the ground and content of Christian faith is eventually superior to the shifting results of historic criticism. . . . The final proof of the Gospel . . . lies in the living interrelation and correspondence between the New Testament picture of Christ and our experience of His redeeming energies."[8] The noted British Congregationalist P. T. Forsyth, arguing for a positive and evangelical theology, was confident that the New Testament fully supports an Athanasian rather than a Socinian or an Arian Christology, provided we do not allow criticism to become our master but let it be our friend and servant.[9] For the leading British Unitarian, James Martineau, modern historical study left much less of the traditional picture standing, but he was comforted that the reliable residue, "understood as the personal religion of Jesus, stands clear of all the perishable elements, and realizes the true relation between man and God."[10]

Among American liberal theologians at the turn of the century, Chicago's G. B. Foster seems to have been most sensitive to the questions posed by critical history, perhaps because he was more attuned to the German discussions. He resolved the problem by distinguishing sharply between the object of faith and the object which historical science has the right and duty to explore, and by finding the essence of Christianity in the religion of Jesus, which was to him clearly enough discoverable.[11]

7. Haering, *Der Christlich Glaube: Dogmatik* (Stuttgart, 1906; trans. from the 2d ed., 1912, by John Dickie and George Ferris, *The Christian Faith: A System of Dogmatics* [London, 1913]).

8. Mackintosh, *The Doctrine of the Person of Christ* (Edinburgh, 1913), pp. 306–20.

9. Forsyth, *The Person and Place of Jesus Christ* (London, 1909).

10. Martineau, *The Seat of Authority in Religion* (London, 1891), p. 651; see pp. 573–652. Martineau is not typical, but it may be noted that most English New Testament criticism was incurably conservative. See, for example, the essay "The Historic Christ," by B. H. Streeter, in *Foundations* (London, 1912). Streeter starts with an apparent recognition of the problem as posed by Weiss and Schweitzer, but draws the fangs of the criticism at every point.

11. Foster, *The Finality of the Christian Religion* (Chicago, 1906), pp. 395–518: "The Essence of the Christian Religion: Jesus." In a way not unlike that of Harnack, Foster stressed the prevalent idea that the gospel portrait rests on the overwhelming personal impression

On the other hand, the authors of the two most widely used American liberal theology textbooks of the day, W. N. Clarke and W. A. Brown, felt quite comfortable that the essential features of the historical Jesus, including the fundamental elements of his consciousness, were not really open to doubt on the basis of historical analysis alone. The problems are rather those of Christological interpretation.[12] And A. C. McGiffert's otherwise perceptive study of the rise of modern religious ideas finds no place at all for the Jesus of history/Christ of faith question.[13]

Kähler and Herrmann

The question whether scientific history could support or throw doubt upon faith's judgment about Jesus was much more acutely debated in the 1890s and the early 1900s than one would suppose from reading most of these thinkers. One major focus of the issue emerged in 1892 in an exchange between Martin Kähler and Wilhelm Herrmann, following Kähler's now famous lecture, "The So-Called Jesus of History and the Historic Biblical Christ."[14]

In the introductory essay to the 1896 edition of *SHJ*, Kähler put

---

of Jesus, and he concluded that if there was anything new in the thought of Jesus, it was "faith in the infinite worth of human personality in the sight of God" (p. 481).

12. Brown, *Outline of Christian Theology* (New York, 1906), pp. 326–52. See also *Essence*, where Brown showed thorough familiarity with the late-nineteenth-century discussion by the Ritschlians and their critics. But he still did not see the question of history as decisive, opting for more philosophical sorts of definitions dominated by the problem of the natural and the supernatural. Judgments like those of Kähler about the uncertainties were described by him as "superficial," a "result of too close contact" (p. 298). For William Newton Clarke, see *An Outline of Christian Theology* (New York, 1898).

13. McGiffert, *The Rise of Modern Religious Ideas* (New York, 1915). His nearest approach to the problem is a generalized discussion of the decline in the idea of the authority of the Bible.

14. *Der sogenannte historische Jesus und der geschichtliche, biblische Christus* (Leipzig, 1892). In the 2d ed. (1896), Kähler added three essays, including a reply to Herrmann. The English translation by Carl E. Braaten (Philadelphia, 1964) includes the title essay and the 1896 prefatory essay, but not the response to Herrmann. Except for this response, references in the text (cited as *SHJ*) are to the Braaten translation, which also contains an excellent introduction to Kähler.

A student of Rothe, Julius Müller, and Tholuck (see *Prot. Thought*, 1), Kähler (1835–1912) was for most of his career professor of systematic theology at Halle. (He was a teacher of Paul Tillich.) On the debate between Kähler and Herrmann, see Charles E. Carlston, "Biblicism or Historicism? Some Remarks on the Conflict between Kähler and Herrmann on the Historical Jesus," *Biblical Research* 13 (1968): 26–40. See also Daniel Deegan, "Martin Kähler: Kerygma and Gospel History," *Scottish Journal of Theology*, 16:1 (1963): 50–67; and Georg Wobbermin, *Geschichte und Historie in der Religionswissenschaft* (Tübingen, 1911).

the issue succinctly: "How can Jesus Christ be the authentic object of the faith of all Christians if the questions what and who he really was can be established only by ingenious investigation and if it is solely the scholarship of our time which proves itself equal to this task?" (p. 102). Orthodoxy's appeal to an infallible Bible will no longer do. Christianity must be juxtaposed to scholarship. Yet modern historical research seeks the human Jesus, and the question is how its tentative residue can be invoked as an object of faith. The dual question of the normative status of the Bible and the credibility of its portrait of Christ arises, which is the problem of historical revelation. If orthodoxy's verbal inspiration cannot now be accepted (though the Bible should not simply be put in the same category as other writings), neither can mediating theology's willingness to settle for "a 'minimum' of historically reliable facts whose revelatory value is readily discernible" (*SHJ*, p. 119)—for that leaves the ordinary believer at the mercy of scientifically trained minds.

Kähler attempted to deal with the problem by drawing a sharp (and arbitrary) distinction between the usually interchangeable adjectives for "historical," historisch and geschichtlich—and the nouns *Historie* and *Geschichte*—as different modalities of historical apprehension. By historisch he referred to the process and results of scientific or critical historical analysis, which abstracts at the outset from presuppositions of faith and operates on principles of causality and psychological analogy in human experience. By geschichtlich he meant a historical reason shaped from the beginning by the confession that Jesus is Lord, by the recognition that the divine cannot be separated from the human in the gospel story of Jesus.

The entire historisch life-of-Jesus movement Kähler called a blind alley. In its quest for the historical Jesus behind the primitive Christian reports, it started from the worthy motive of distinguishing the biblical Christ from the dogmatic Christ. But its attempt to produce a real life of Jesus was quite impossible, for "we have no sources for a biography of Jesus of Nazareth which measure up to the standards of contemporary historical science." We have only "a vast field strewn with the fragments of various traditions," out of which no sure account of the development of Jesus' life can come. Therefore the biographers, on the basis of psychological analogies and preconceived religious and ethical views, had to create a so-called historisch Jesus, which was not a product of scientific biography but a fantasy. By doing this they simply substituted another dogma for the traditional one, and this "modern example of human creativity . . . [is] not an iota better than the notorious Christ of Byzantine christology." Both are "isms," historicism and gnosticism (*SHJ*, pp. 48, 49, 43).

The real Christ, whom we set out to find not because he is like us but because he is unlike us, because we have faith, because he is revealed God and our savior, is not to be found in scientific reconstructions by source criticism and historical analogy, but in the faith of his disciples. The truly historisch element in any great figure is in the influence on later generations. The *geschichtliche Christus* is the Christ of the whole New Testament, of the apostolic preaching which includes the resurrection as part of the datum.

It is important, of course, that Jesus was a human being, and this is found on every page of the gospels, but in such testimony the historical and the suprahistorical are inseparable. We want to know this Jesus, and in every smallest detail possible—yet in a different way from the life-of-Jesus movement, for we want to know him because he is the revelation, the picture of the invisible God, the Word made flesh. Throughout the New Testament, the reports of Christ are proclamation. For Geschichte, the person and the witness are inseparable. According to the total biblical proclamation, Christ is not known, and *is* not, apart from his abiding effectiveness in the community. We believe not because of any authority, even biblical authority, but because *"Christ himself is the orginator of the biblical picture of the Christ"* (*SHJ*, p. 87). Jesus proclaimed himself in his preaching, and he remains the subject of the gospel proclamation.[15] For Geschichte, in which the gospel history and the apostolic kerygma, pre-Easter and post-Easter, belong together, there is no dichotomy between Jesus of history and Christ of faith.

Wilhelm Herrmann replied immediately in the *Zeitschrift für Theologie und Kirche* with an essay entitled "Der geschichtliche Christus der Grund unseres Glaubens."[16] He agreed that Kähler was right in distinguishing sharply between historisch and geschichtlich. The historisch cannot attain Christ as the ground of faith for us because its results are only uncertain and probable. Kähler was also right in recognizing that the gospels as much as the epistles are witness, that the new life originates in the Christ laid hold of in faith and pro-

15. See Kähler's 1901 response to Harnack, "Gëhort Jesus in das Evangelium?" in *Dogmatische Zeitfragen* (Leipzig, 1908), 2:51–78.
16. *ZTK* 2:3 (1892): 232–73. Reprinted in *Schriften zur Grundlegung der Theologie* (Munich, 1966), 1:149–85. References in the text are to the *Schriften*. On Herrmann, see also chap. 2, above.

claimed out of faith. Faith indeed originates in the witness (pp. 166, 162). But Kähler was wrong in identifying the Christ of faith in its fullness, Christ as resurrected and ascended, as the ground and final resting place (Halt) of faith. He failed to distinguish, as Herrmann says we must, between Christ as the ground of faith and Christ as the content of faith (that is, between the *Halt* and the *Inhalt* of faith, between the *Entstehen* and the *Bestehen* of faith). The Christ of glory is the content of faith, not the ground out of which that content arises —and to identify the whole of the witness as the ground is to move back in the direction of a false and external conception of the Bible as a series of authoritative assertions.

Kähler was right, of course, in insisting that the ground of faith is not something behind the New Testament proclamation that is discovered by historisch research, for what that research can find is only probability. Yet Kähler undervalued Historie, which, though it cannot threaten faith (p. 176), can nevertheless assist by eliminating false props for faith and by producing results to which faith cannot be unattentive, for example, corrections of misunderstanding by the evangelists or their sources (p. 167). The ground of faith, properly understood, is not the testimony but the historical (geschichtlich) person of Jesus, the fact of the life of Jesus that the New Testament tradition allows us to recognize in its geschichtlich reality as a person convincing us. The inner life of Jesus is the indubitable fact, geschichtlich known, which we ourselves encounter as the authority for our inner life, the ground of our communion with God (pp. 172–73).

In this exchange between Herrmann and Kähler several levels of encounter can be distinguished that illuminate the entire Jesus of history/Christ of faith debate. Herrmann and Kähler were agreed on the need for certainty in faith, and they were both concerned for the right of the ordinary believer not to have to depend for the validity of faith on the research of the experts. They agreed on the importance of the historisch/geschichtlich distinction, insisting that faith could not be made to depend on the results of Historie.[17] They sought an alternative both to positivistic historical orientation (whether of Historie or of orthodoxy, which alike claimed to be based on verifiable past events) and to speculative reliance on general truths indifferent to historical process (as in Lessing).

17. In contrast, for example, to Harnack, for whom the scientific historical conclusion that Jesus was a thoroughgoing apocalypticist would have fundamentally altered the nature of Christianity. See *Christianity and History*, p. 56.

But in their employment of the same distinction, differences quickly appeared. First, we may say that for both thinkers Historie designated critical or scientific historical scholarship whose methods were objective, detached from faith presuppositions, and whose conclusions could be drawn with only relative confidence. Geschichte, on the other hand, denoted a historical method and knowledge in which the historian is vitally concerned and in which the geschichtlich refers to "past events that influence the present whether or not they are recoverable in detail by the historian."[18] In the use of the distinction, however, Herrmann seemed more firmly committed to the neutral or presuppositionless character of Historie—even though he wavered in the consistency with which he employed the distinction, for the "objective fact" of the inner life of Jesus seems often to depend on the historisch reliability of the main features of the gospel portrait of Jesus.[19] Kähler, on the other hand, saw the supposed presuppositionless nature of Historie as simply a myth. The critical historian, for Kähler, is fully committed to his dogmas about analogy and psychology and natural process, about what can and cannot be accepted as historical fact. Historie is as much controlled by belief as is the fundamentalist idea that scripture is in no way subject to the canons that apply to other writings.

Second, in respect to Geschichte, another level of difference between Kähler and Herrmann emerged, which involves both the nature and the object of faith. For Kähler, the object and ground of faith, the real geschichtlich Jesus Christ, is the earthly and resurrected Jesus, the whole Christ. For Herrmann, in more Ritschlian fashion, the ground of faith and the geschichtlich object is the earthly Jesus—the indubitable fact of his inner life, which lays hold of our inner life and compels us to learn for the first time what is the true reality of personal life. This ground of faith must be distinguished from the content of faith—Christ risen and victorious —which arises in faith's maturity.

A fundamental issue between Herrmann and Kähler, then, is

18. George Rupp, *Culture Protestantism: German Liberal Theology at the Turn of the Twentieth Century* (Missoula, Mont., 1977), p. 25. See pp. 25–32 for an excellent statement of aspects of the Jesus of history/Christ of faith issue.

19. This is noted by Wobbermin, among others, in *Geschichte und Historie*, pp. 29–47. Wobbermin's effort was to develop a more adequate distinction in which Historie is a secondary level of investigation, namely, the submission of Geschichte or experienced history to disciplined inquiry. See p. 51.

whether we are looking for a Jesus Christ essentially like us or essentially unlike us. For Herrmann the likeness constitutes the ground. It is the Jesus given in the New Testament portrait as the reflection and disclosure of our humanity at its best and fullest which enables us to respond to him and to remain free (though this encounter is also a purely miraculous event in that Jesus as the ground of faith bears in himself a claim that transcends all the rest of humanity, and thus is a compelling revelation of God). But such a view, for Kähler, is merely a continuation of the nineteenth-century prejudice for viewing the humanity of Jesus as the point of departure and making the divinity into the problem. On the principle of analogy, likeness is all that historical method can give us, and this is utterly contrary to the point of the gospel witness. To be sure, Christ is wholly like us. But we are interested in him because of the unlikeness. From the beginning, Christians have confessed Jesus to be unlike us in his sinlessness, in his total commitment to God. As long as we are truly in the tradition of the church—in contrast to those whose devotion to Christ has all but ceased—we are seeking Christ as our savior, as revealed God, as our opposite and our fulfillment. In this his work we find the real Jesus Christ.[20]

Thus we come full circle to the question of security in faith, for which both Kähler and Herrmann were concerned. But is our faith sure because we find in the inner life of the geschichtlich Jesus something that compels our inner life? Or does our surety lie in the fundamental difference, in the redeeming character of the whole Christ?[21]

Loisy

The questions at the heart of the debate between Kähler and Herrmann were approached in a different way by Alfred Loisy (1857–1940), the Catholic modernist who replied to Harnack's Wesen in L'Evangile et l'église.[22] Among the diverse collection of indi-

20. See SHJ, esp. pp. 58–68. It is not unrelated to this point that Kähler was unwilling to put the Bible simply in the same category as other literary productions, though he was also unwilling to exempt it from the canons of historical study. See pp. 110–12.

21. Kähler's judgment on the issue was strongly echoed in Forsyth, Jesus Christ, esp. pp. 59–60.

22. Paris, 1902; trans. Christopher Home as The Gospel and the Church [London, 1903; reprinted Philadelphia, 1976]; hereafter cited as GC. Bernard B. Scott's introduction to the 1976 edition is helpful. For a balanced general interpretation of Loisy, see also Alec Vidler, A Variety of Catholic Modernists (Cambridge, 1970). Loisy was already under suspicion by the

viduals called modernists, whose general desire was to adapt Catholicism to modern intellectual, moral, and social needs, Loisy was the best representative of the growing historical consciousness that the modernists had more or less in common. What he sought to do was rebut Harnack on his own ground by offering a strictly historical refutation. But that required a reconsideration of Harnack's historical principles. It is poor history, for example, to take as essential only what we can today judge acceptable—and Loisy questioned whether Harnack was not in fact acting as a theologian rather than as a historian, taking only what suited his theology (GC, pp. 4, 8). It is equally poor history to regard as essential only that which differentiates, for monotheism would not be essential to Christianity, which shares it with Judaism and Islam. Thus when we describe the essence of the gospel of Jesus, the importance of the historical elements does not depend either on their antiquity or on their novelty, "but on the place they fill in the teaching of Jesus, and on the value Jesus himself attached to them," as determined by a critical examination of the most sure and clearly expressed texts, rather than by building on a "small number of texts of moderate authority" (GC, pp. 9–11).

Further, in contrast to Harnack, Loisy argued for the recognition that Christ is known only by and across the tradition, that he is inseparable from his work, and that no breach need be admitted either between Jesus and Judaism or between Jesus and the early church or the continuing life of the church. If there is no continuity, there is no preservation of the gospel. Instead of Harnack's image of the kernel and the husk, which implies an identity persisting through change (or the one Geist which manifests itself in different epochs), Loisy prefers the image of the seed, whose nature is seen in the fullness and totality of its growth. Change is necessary for preservation, and the essence of Christianity is seen in the fullness of its life, its features being recognized throughout development.[23]

When we look at Jesus' gospel, it is clear that at its center is the proclamation of the kingdom of God. But sound historical analysis will not allow us to restrict this by Harnack's mystical and individual-

---

authorities, having been removed from his position at the Institut Catholique in 1893 because of the controversy over the biblical question.

23. Loisy thought his own idea an extension of John Henry Newman's theory of development, though Newman had a totally premodern view of scripture, so one must go beyond him.

istic notion of God and the soul as the entire content of the gospel. The kingdom is something to come. It is at hand, therefore "Repent!" This does not contradict the idea of its already being present, yet the *hope* holds the most prominent place in the teaching of Jesus. Moreover, the kingdom is not a rule of God simply in the life of individuals, but is collective, destined to be enjoyed in common. It is objective, implying all the external and internal conditions of life, a completion of history. This hope regards the future as the renewal of the world (*GC*, pp. 53–72).

So, too, as the kingdom is essentially future, the office of the Messiah is essentially eschatological. Jesus is the agent of the kingdom, both now the Messiah and presently to become the Messiah (*GC*, pp. 102–03). Jesus' proclamation necessarily leads to the apostolic preaching of the kingdom, through the faith in the resurrection which called the church into being. Thus the oft-quoted statement of Loisy, "Jesus foretold the kingdom, and it was the Church that came" (*GC*, p. 166), expresses the necessity of the church to the gospel. She was essential to the preservation of the gospel, only enlarging its form, for continuance simply in its primitive state was impossible because of new conditions. Allowing for the easily recognizable transformations, "it is easy to see in the Catholic church what stands today for the idea of the Heavenly kingdom, for the idea of the Messiah, the maker of the kingdom, and for the idea of the apostolate, or the preaching of the kingdom," which were the essential elements in the activity of Jesus (*GC*, pp. 166–67).

In similar vein, Loisy counters Harnack's attack on the development of Christology, of the church as an institution, of dogma, and of worship (though not in ways calculated to please the traditionalist). Throughout, the Jesus of history and the Christ of faith are held together. The institution of the church by the risen Christ, which faith affirms, is not a datum for the historian, but the continuity of the church's life with the preaching and activity of Jesus can be shown by proper historical method.

Loisy was sharply attacked, not only by the Catholic traditionalists, who rejected his entire historicocritical view of the New Testament, but also by the Catholic philosopher Maurice Blondel, who is thought by some to have contributed to the Jesus of history/Christ of faith question. Though not mentioning Loisy by name, Blondel sought in his essay "History and Dogma" to overcome the "false

antithesis" between historicism (Loisy) and what he called "extrinsicism" (as in Abbé H. Gayraud), or between modernism and
veterism.[24]

Neither extrinsicism nor historicism, Blondel argued, offers an adequate answer to the question of the relation of facts and ideas. Both
views are incomplete and equally dangerous to faith. For extrinsicism, historical facts are considered only in their accidental, extrinsic,
and generic character; they are merely a vehicle for apologetic use in
support of dogma. "The Bible is guaranteed *en bloc*, not by its content, but by the external seal of the divine" (p. 229). Historicism, on
the other hand, assumes that historical study is independent and self-
sufficient. But it is not. As applied to Catholicism, it does not even
prepare the passage from facts to faith. "The truth of Christianity is
not to be found in an idea extracted from a fact analysed in isolation,
nor in the fragmentary interpretation of the successive moments of
history, but in a view and appreciation of the whole, in the concrete
realities, in the person of Christ and the Church which prolongs it"
(p. 242). As the vital intermediary between history and dogma,
Blondel proposes tradition—tradition not in the old sense of a transmission of facts, received truths, and so on, but as a (humanly discoverable) process that preserves the living reality of the past, which in
the depths of faith recovers what it discovers in the mediation of the
collective life. Tradition thus discovers the real Christ.

Whether Blondel rightly interpreted Loisy is not a matter for our
present concern. But it would appear that insofar as he really differed from Loisy, he did so by finally evading the historical question.
Unlike von Hügel, who criticized him sharply on the point, Blondel
never submitted to the discipline of historical method in the precise
examination of historical documents, and he did not finally accept
the principle of the historical consciousness—that the biblical critic
uses the same procedures that are employed in the study of secular
documents, free from the determination of results by dogma. Tradition, for Blondel, could positively supplement the findings of the
critical historian. He was wholly comfortable with the authority of
the church and the validity of dogma (see p. 222). He found it a corollary of his view—though one may ask if it was not rather a presupposition—that "the Church is a proof of itself: *index sui est*; for it sup-

24. See "Histoire et dogma: Les Lacunes philosophiques de l'exégèse moderne," *La
Quinzaine* (1904), pp. 145–67, 349–73, 433–58; trans. Alexander Dru and Illtyd Treth-
owan, in *The Letter on Apologetics and History and Dogma* (New York, 1964), pp. 219–87.

plies the verification of what it believes and teaches in its age-old experience and its continuous practice." "The infallible *Magisterium* is the higher and really supernatural guarantee of a function which has its natural foundation in the concert of all the powers of each Christian and of all Christianity" (pp. 269, 278). In this way facts and faith support each other. Blondel admitted that this is a circle, but he did not consider it a vicious one.

Weiss and Schweitzer

Another element of the problem, not overlooked by Loisy, though much controverted or simply avoided by many, was vigorously set forth, also in 1892, in a brief essay by Johannes Weiss (1863–1914), "The Preaching of Jesus concerning the Kingdom of God."[25] Weiss most vividly opened up the possibility that the historical Jesus is sufficiently recoverable to make clear that he is not at all an easy ground for modern faith. In particular, Jesus is different from the Ritschlian picture of him. With Kähler, and later Heinrich Holtzmann and others, Weiss was thoroughly skeptical of the possibility of writing a real life of Jesus. But more important, he grasped fully the thoroughly eschatological conception of the kingdom in Jesus' message. It was a conception from which all modern ideas must be eliminated, a kingdom that was wholly future, at present purely supramundane, which Jesus did not establish but only proclaimed. Even the disciples began to weaken this thoroughly eschatological view.

Thus arrived what Albert Schweitzer in 1906 called the third great alternative that the study of the life of Jesus had to consider. The first had been laid down by Strauss: "*either* purely historical *or* purely supernatural." The second had been set out by the Tübingen school and by Holtzmann: "*either* Synoptic *or* Johannine." The alternative now presented by Weiss was "*either* eschatological *or* non-eschatological."[26]

25. *Die Predigt Jesu vom Reich Gottes* (Göttingen, 1892), 67 pp. (2d enl. ed., 1900). The 2d ed. (with selections from the 1st ed. omitted in the 1900 version) was reissued at Göttingen in 1964 under the editorship of Ferdinand Hahn, with a foreword by Rudolf Bultmann. Although Weiss was well known to the English-speaking world through a translation of *Das Urchristentum* (Göttingen, 1914; trans. and ed. F. C. Grant, *The History of Primitive Christianity* [New York, 1937; reprinted under the title *Earliest Christianity: A History of the Period A.D. 30–150*, New York, 1959]), *Predigt Jesu* was largely neglected by British and American scholars. An English translation (of the 1st ed.) was published at Philadelphia in 1971 (ed. R. H. Hiers and D. L. Holland).

26. Albert Schweitzer, *Von Reimarus zu Wrede* (Tübingen, 1906). Cited from the 1968 New York ed. of the translation by W. Montgomery, *The Quest of the Historical Jesus*, p. 238.

Schweitzer claimed that a new epoch had begun. Weiss was the first to achieve a consistent and inclusive understanding of the eschatological character of the person and message of Jesus, an understanding that was decisive for much subsequent interpretation, including that of the dialectical theology of the twentieth century. And it was a most disturbing understanding. As the conservative Ritschlian Julius Kaftan put it: "If the kingdom of God is an eschatological matter, it is a concept unusable for dogmatics."[27]

Weiss's argument became the basis for Schweitzer's famous summation of the outcome of the entire nineteenth-century quest for the historical Jesus:

> There is nothing more negative than the result of the critical study of the life of Jesus.
>
> The Jesus of Nazareth who came forward publicly as the Messiah, who preached the ethic of the Kingdom of God, who founded the Kingdom of heaven upon earth, and died to give His work its final consecration, never had any existence. He is a figure designed by rationalism, endowed with life by liberalism, and clothed by modern theology in an historical garb.
>
> This image has not been destroyed from without, it has fallen to pieces, cleft and disintegrated by the concrete historical problems which came to the surface one after another, and in spite of all the artifice, art, artificiality, and violence which was applied to them, refused to be planed down to fit the design on which the Jesus of the theology of the last hundred and thirty years had been constructed, and were no sooner covered over than they appeared again in a new form. . . .
>
> The study of the life of Jesus has had a curious history. It set out in quest of the historical Jesus, believing that when it had found Him it could bring Him straight into our time as a Teacher and Saviour. It loosed the bands by which He had been riveted for centuries to the stony rocks of ecclesiastical doctrine, and rejoiced to see life and movement coming into the figure once more, and the historical Jesus advancing, as it seemed, to meet it. But he does not stay: he passes by our time and returns to His own. What surprised and dismayed the theology of the last forty years was that, despite all forced and arbitrary interpretations, it could not keep Him in our time, but had to let Him go. He returned to His own time, not owing to the application of any historical ingenuity, but by the same

27. Quoted by Bultmann in his foreword to the 1964 ed. of Weiss, *Predigt Jesu.*

inevitable necessity by which the liberated pendulum returns to its original position.[28]

Schweitzer's own way of dealing with the problem—in a quasi-mystical idea of "the real immovable historical foundation which is independent of any historical confirmation or justification," whereby Jesus "means something to our world because a mighty spiritual force streams forth from Him and flows through our time also" —can be passed over. More important is the way in which his summation of the quest reveals a new kind of intense distress in the late nineteenth century over the question of the Jesus of history and the Christ of faith.

Schweitzer saw clearly that this distress involved the moral imperative of Christianity, for the demands of Jesus upon his disciples could not be separated from his eschatology. They are not universally valid moral principles, to be applied anywhere and anytime. They are, in Schweitzer's view, *interims Ethik*, demands on the followers for the interim before the coming establishment of God's kingdom. They are therefore also strange to us. The kingdom is not something purely inward (Harnack), or a kingdom of ends for the progressive moral organization of humankind (Ritschl). Nor does the ethic of the kingdom lend itself as a guide for the transformation of the political and economic order of the ancient or the modern world (the social gospel).

For modern humans, the ethic of obedience to the will of God cannot derive directly from the injunctions of Jesus. The human figure we know as Jesus stands in painful contrast to both the traditional and the modern Christ of faith. The certainties of faith in the God of Jesus Christ have become the most troubling uncertainties. And the inner connections of the struggle for faith, the attachment to Jesus, and the relation of both to the moral life have been shattered.

Drews

Except for the popular excitement it generated—and the fact that it became the occasion for an important essay by Ernst Troeltsch on the significance of the historicality of Jesus—the Karlsruhe philosopher Arthur Drews's book *The Christ Myth* was really an anticlimax in

28. Schweitzer, *Quest*, pp. 398–99.

the Jesus of history/Christ of faith debate.[29] Drawing on the work of
the religionsgeschichtliche Schule, on the growing body of research
into ancient Near Eastern religion, and on such historians of religion
as Frazer, Drews argued that primitive Christianity was a syncretistic
creation of previously existing religious ideas drawn from diverse
sources, which were attached by early Christianity to a historical figure who may or may not have existed. There was, he held, a preexisting Jesus cult, probably going back to Joshua, which took up Jewish
apocalypticism and Hellenistic motifs of a dying and rising redeemer
and shaped them into a Jesus myth. When this material is put together with the modern historians' admitted uncertainty about all
the details of the life of Jesus, Drews contended, we have to conclude
that we know nothing of a Jesus figure behind the myth. As he put it
in one of his more moderate statements: "The denial of a historical
Jesus, according to the advanced history of religions insight of our
time, can rest on such good grounds that it may claim for itself at
least the same degree of probablity as the form in which the beginnings of Christianity are commonly presented from the theological
side" (p. xii).

All the religiously significant features of the picture of the historical Jesus can be seen as purely mythological; hence not only is there
no possibility of finding a historical person behind the myth, but
none is needed to explain the emergence of Christianity. "We know
nothing of Jesus, of an historical personality by this name, to which
the events and words recorded in the gospels refer." "A historical Jesus, as the gospels describe him and as he lives in the heads of today's liberal theologians, did not exist at all; nor did he even found
the wholly insignificant little messianic community in Jerusalem.
Rather, the Christ-faith arose quite independently of any kind of
known historical personality and was in this sense doubtless a creation of the religious 'mass spirit,' set by Paul, with appropriate interpretation and development, in the center of the communities he
founded" (pp. 138, 178).

But this conclusion, for Drews, was not religiously negative. Except for the liberals, the historical Jesus is not religiously important.
He is only of antiquarian interest. What is important is the idea of

29. Drews, *Die Christusmythe* (Jena, 1909; Eng. trans. from the 3d German ed., C. D.
Burns, *The Christ Myth* [London, 1910]). Page references in the text are to the 1st German
ed.

God-manhood, of the divine nature of humanity, in which Drews (in line with the idealistic monism of von Hartmann) saw the struggle of an immanent deity to overcome finitude within the human consciousness.

Drews's conclusion was largely scorned by the historical specialists (Troeltsch called it absurd), despite the flurry of popular debate. And rightly so, for the arguments (which Drews readily admitted were not new, but simply drawn from others) were open to serious criticism. Yet the importance of the contention was that it posed the most extreme form of the Jesus of history/Christ of faith problem: Is Jesus necessary at all to Christian faith? And there were some, perhaps most notably D. C. Macintosh of Yale, for whom the answer could be, "Not altogether." Belief in the historicity of Jesus, Macintosh averred, is "not indispensable, though very valuable" to faith. Christianity has found in Jesus the supreme historic example of the filial relationship with God which is its essential character, and the loss of the example would be serious, but not irreparable.[30]

EXCURSUS: CRITICISM AND THE BIBLE

The question of the historical Jesus was without doubt at the center of the issues of faith and history as these were posed for late-nineteenth-century Protestant thought. In this discussion the broader problems of biblical authority were both implicit and explicit, with nearly all the positions well represented. We can therefore glance briefly at the general state of the biblical question before turning to a reassessment of the history of the church.

In the time with which we are concerned, the debates over the application of historicocritical methods to the Bible were sharpest in the United States. On the European continent the main positions were those already worked out earlier in the century in the aftermath of the controversy over David Friedrich Strauss. In Britain biblical

---

30. Macintosh, "Is Belief in the Historicity of Jesus Indispensable to Christian Faith?" *American Journal of Theology* 16:1 (1912): 108. The Princeton orthodox Presbyterian, B. B. Warfield, found such a view the natural outcome of the whole liberal view (in contrast to his own view that unbiased history yields a supernatural Christ). See Warfield, "Christless Christianity," *Harvard Theological Review* 5:4 (1912): 423–73. The whole debate over Drews is well summarized in B. A. Gerrish, "Jesus, Myth, and History: Troeltsch's Stand in the 'Christ-Myth' Debate," *Journal of Religion* 55 (1975): 13–35. Otto Pfleiderer, in *The Early Christian Conception of Christ* (London, 1905), had taken a more restrained view than Macintosh, though strongly insisting on the mythical character of the early Christian stories and on setting them in the context of other religions' myths and legends.

scholarship took generally conservative lines. But in America polarization was acute, leading to a series of heresy trials and ultimately to the formalization of a fundamentalist movement in which the inerrancy of scripture was a principal bastion to be held against liberal onslaughts.

American liberal theology, deeply influenced in the latter part of the century by German scholarship, as well as, in some cases, by Bushnell and Maurice, was confident of its advances and secure in its conviction that the program of adaptation of the tradition to modern needs and thought would triumph. The day of heresy trials was over, or so thought David Swing, for example, in the years immediately preceding his own trial in 1874.[31] The biblical question was only one of many points (too many and too vague, as it turned out) on which Swing was charged with deviation from the standards of the Westminster Confession. But prominent among the charges was that "he did not believe in the plenary inspiration of the scriptures."

The subsequent controversies were marked by the prevention of pastoral appointments and by the exclusion of suspect faculty from seminary teaching posts, as well as by widely publicized heresy trials. The installation of James F. Merriam as a pastor was blocked by Congregational conservatives in Massachusetts in 1877; R. L. Cave was expelled from the ministry of the Disciples of Christ in 1889; and the consecration of Phillips Brooks as Episcopal bishop of Massachusetts was challenged in the early 1890s (R. Heber Newton was more directly involved in the Episcopal debates over biblical views). In 1879 Crawford Toy was forced to resign from the faculty of Southern Baptist Theological Seminary in Louisville, in a dispute over higher criticism; Newman Smyth was refused appointment to the Abbot chair by the Andover Seminary board of visitors.

Most prominent in the biblical controversy from the time of David Swing was the Presbyterian tradition. The doctrine of Princeton's Charles Hodge and his successor Benjamin B. Warfield—that the "inspired Word, as it came from God [in the "original autograph"] is without error"—was formally adopted by the General Assembly in 1892 and reaffirmed in 1893, 1894, 1899, and 1910. Thus in the most famous heresy trial of the century, Charles A. Briggs of Union Seminary was suspended from the Presbyterian ministry in 1893 after two years of controversy over his inaugural address as Robinson

31. Swing was a leading precursor of the New Theology. See chap. 7, below.

Professor of Biblical Theology. His fellow Old Testament scholar at Lane Seminary in Chicago, Henry Preserved Smith, was dismissed in the following year, and Arthur C. McGiffert, the church historian at Union who dealt with New Testament literature, resigned from the Presbyterian ministry in 1900.[32]

A peculiarity of the American scene, its almost freewheeling pluralism, meant that the biblical views of the liberals were by no means suppressed by such measures, but were if anything given broader dissemination. Swing, for example, though reluctantly resigning from the denomination instead of enduring an appeal by the opposition against the favorable decision of his presbytery, was able to establish an independent church at Central Music Hall, where he was a more popular preacher than ever. Union Seminary in New York, largely as a result of the Briggs case, freed itself from Presbyterian control in 1892, with a subsequent heightening of its national stature.

As noted in volume 1 of this work (pp. 167–69), the biblical criticism question broke into the open in Britain with the publication of *Essays and Reviews* in 1860. And there was controversy. John William Colenso, bishop of Natal, as a result of the furor over his 1862 book, *Introduction to the Pentateuch and the Book of Joshua*, was deposed in the following year (though he was later reinstated). In the 1870s W. Robertson Smith was forced to resign his post at the Free Church Divinity School in Aberdeen because of protests against some of his early biblical essays. At the end of the 1860s, Samuel Davidson had resigned his position at Lancashire Independent College in the interest of freedom to pursue his critical biblical studies.

But biblical criticism in Britain seems not to have been attended by quite the fireworks that were set off in the United States. British scholarship—eminently represented by the famous Cambridge tri-

---

32. For a useful general survey of the controversies from the time of Swing, see William R. Hutchinson, *The Modernist Impulse in American Protestantism* (Cambridge, Mass., 1976), chaps. 2, 3. More detailed accounts may be found in George H. Shriver, ed., *American Religious Heretics: Formal and Informal Trials* (Nashville, 1966); Daniel Day Williams, *The Andover Liberals* (New York, 1941; reprinted 1970); Lefferts A. Loetscher, *The Broadening Church: A Study of Theological Issues in the Presbyterian Church since 1869* (Philadelphia, 1958); and Carl E. Hatch, *The Charles A. Briggs Heresy Trial: Prologue to Twentieth-Century Liberal Protestantism* (New York, 1969).

For a statement of the conservative Lutheran view in America, see Charles Porterfield Krauth, *The Conservative Reformation and Its Theology* (New York, 1871; reprinted Minneapolis, 1963), e.g., p. 186: the "original alone, just as the sacred penman left it, is absolutely in every jot and tittle God's word."

umvirate, the biblical students B. F. Westcott and J. B. Lightfoot and the historian F. J. A. Hort, who were influenced by Maurice—inclined to a moderation, conservatism, and gentility, particularly in New Testament studies, that rarely left faith threatened by history. In *Lux Mundi*, for example, the founding document of liberal Catholicism in the Church of England, the essay by Charles Gore, "The Holy Spirit and Inspiration," is characteristic.[33] Gore fully maintains the inspiration of prophets and apostles. Yet it is an inspiration that does not supersede but intensifies human faculties. It is "an endowment which enables men of all ages to take [the Apostles'] teaching as representing and not misrepresenting" Christ and his teaching (p. 290). For the Old Testament (and this acknowledgment has been viewed by some as the sensational element in *Lux Mundi*) this means recognizing that inspiration does not necessarily guarantee the historical accuracy of the earliest records. Though the biblical record from Abraham on is substantially historical in the strict sense, the fact that revelation was made in a historical process implies the possibility of later idealization, of dramatic embodiment of ideas, and even of a "mythical stage of mental evolution" as the earliest mode of apprehending truth. Of course, the New Testament record has none of this ambiguity; what "can be admitted in the Old Testament, could not, without results disastrous to the Christian Creed, be admitted in the New" (pp. 297, 296). For Gore, while theology should

> leave the field open for free discussion of [the] questions which Biblical criticism has recently been raising, we shall probably be bidden to "remember Tübingen," and not be over-trustful of a criticism which at least exhibits in some of its most prominent representatives a great deal of arbitrariness, of love of "new views" for their own sake, and a great lack of that reverence and spiritual insight which is at least as much needed for understanding the books of the Bible, as accurate knowledge and fair investigation. (p. 301)

Despite the generally less confident tone of the Oxford essays published under the title *Foundations* two decades later,[34] the attitude toward criticism is not radically different from that of *Lux Mundi*. In his essay "The Historic Christ," to be sure, Streeter does not rely on

33. Charles Gore, ed., *Lux Mundi: A Series of Studies in the Religion of the Incarnation* (London, 1889; cited from the 5th English ed., 1890).

34. B. H. Streeter et al., *Foundations: A Statement of Christian Belief in Terms of Modern Thought* (London, 1912).

the Gospel of John, as Gore had been able to do, but only on the Synoptics, and he is willing to consider interpretations of the resurrection event that would have been unthinkable for Gore. Criticism has a much freer rein, and a considerable distance has been traveled in the details of interpretation from the time of *Lux Mundi.* Yet finally Streeter blunts the edge of the eschatological view of Weiss and Schweitzer, represented in England by F. C. Burkitt of Cambridge, and in general reflects the caution and care for the tradition characteristic of the Anglican ethos (see note 10, above).

Nor was this conservatism limited to scholars in the Church of England. As we have seen, the Scot H. R. Mackintosh and the Congregationalist P. T. Forsyth both managed to keep criticism in the role of servant rather than master. A bit earlier A. M. Fairbairn, principal of Mansfield College, seemed more openly to recognize the problem of reconciling the "old theology" and the "new criticism" in Germany, yet he also took comfort in the "more assured results" of historical study, in which field "the services of English scholarship have been conspicuous and meritorious, and happily complementary to the more audacious and brilliant inquiries of continental scholars."[35] The Unitarian Martineau counts as a theologian for whom the results of the commitment of historical biblical criticism were more radical, though not at all unsatisfying. And one may think of the provocative New Testament scholarship of the Anglican Kirsopp Lake, in his early writings as professor of New Testament exegesis at Leiden (1904–14). Yet it is a fair judgment that biblical scholarship in Britain, while becoming committed to the historical method, was generally restrained in its conclusions.[36]

A. E. Garvie, after reviewing current Continental theories of the origin of Christianity in the *Encyclopedia of Religion and Ethics*, stated a position acceptable to many:

> The present writer cannot, then, accept the theories of the origin of Christianity which have been sketched as characteristic of modern thought. That the Synoptic Gospels present the common Christian

35. Fairbairn, *The Place of Christ in Modern Theology* (New York, 1893), pp. 291–92. See pp. 230–97.

36. Old Testament studies were more venturesome, as shown by such scholars as W. Robertson Smith and S. R. Driver (who was convinced by Wellhausen, and whose *Introduction to the Literature of the Old Testament* [Edinburgh, 1897; 8th ed., 1909] was a landmark in Britain). Because Old Testament critical studies were less conservative, they were also more the focus of controversy in Britain.

tradition from the distinctive standpoints of their respective authors; that the Fourth Gospel contains historical reminiscences still more highly coloured by doctrinal reflexions set in a metaphysical Hellenistic framework; that St. Paul, in interpreting a real experience of the saving power of the living Christ, uses categories of Jewish and even Greek thought; that the fact of the virgin birth and the doctrine of the preexistence of Christ are not so well attested historically as the moral and religious teaching and the miracles of Jesus (as contained in the common Christian tradition in the Synoptics) or the Resurrection (as borne witness to by the leaders of the Apostolic Church and notably by St. Paul, whatever difficulties still attach to the Gospel records of the appearances of Jesus)—these are conclusions of criticism which we may fully accept without in any way lowering the general reliability of the NT as the literary source of the history of the beginnings of Christianity.[37]

For the Continental scene, in addition to what has earlier been said, some special note should be given to the so-called religionsgeschichtliche Schule, among whose early leaders were Albert Eichhorn, Hermann Gunkel, Wilhelm Wrede, Wilhelm Bousset, Johannes Weiss, W. Heitmüller, Paul Wernle, and Ernst Troeltsch (reputedly the systematician of the school). The interests of these writers were not primarily in literary criticism (Gunkel was, of course, a founder of form criticism). The results of that work were largely accepted: the Graf-Wellhausen theory of the literary composition of the Hexateuch (from the J, E, D, and P sources) and the consequent reconstruction of the history of Israel, with a postexilic dating of the priestly code and a new and formative place for the prophets; the division of the book of Isaiah into at least two sources; and the two-source theory of the composition of the Synoptic gospels.[38]

37. *ERE*, 3:585. James Orr may be cited as one of the ablest of the opponents of criticism. See, for example, his book *The Bible under Trial* (London, 1907). A lively survey of the British scene may be found in L. E. Elliott-Binns, *English Thought, 1860–1900: The Theological Aspect* (Greenwich, Conn., 1956), chaps. 5–7.

38. Although directly anticipated by Karl H. Graf, in *Die geschichtliche Bücher des alten Testaments* (Leipzig, 1866), by the Dutch scholar Abraham Kuenen, in *Godsdienst van Israel* (Haarlem, 1869–70), and by August Kayser, in *Das vorexilische Buch der Urgeschichte Israels und seine Erweiterungen* (Strassburg, 1874), as well as rooted in a tradition going back as far as Hobbes (1651), Simon (1678), and Astruc (1753), Julius Wellhausen's statement of the Hexateuch's literary origin and development became the classic one. See his 1876–77 articles in *Jahrbücher für deutsche Theologie*, published in book form as *Die Composition des Hexateuchs* (Berlin, 1885), and *Geschichte Israels* (Berlin, 1878). Pfleiderer commented in his history that Wellhausen's "arguments for the new hypothesis, derived from the parallel

The new element in the work of the religionsgeschichtliche Schule sprang out of the fundamental conviction that Christianity is a historical reality and can only be understood as such. Thus biblical religion has to be seen as fully a part of religious history, intimately related to its socio-religious surroundings and influenced by them. For example, the creation stories of Genesis have to be understood in relation to Babylonian creation myths; the psalms need to be compared with the cultic poems of Egypt and Mesopotamia; late Jewish apocalypticism, including the messianic expectation, must be seen to have involved a strain of Persian influence (Bousset); parallels in other religions to the stories of virgin birth and temptation need to be taken into account; the death and resurrection of Jesus must be viewed in the light of the myths of the ancient dying gods, of Adonis, Osiris, and Attis; the ascription of the title Kyrios is to be understood against the background of general ascriptions of dignity in late antiquity (Bousset, especially); early Christian baptism and the Eucharist must be seen in the context of the practices of the Hellenistic mystery religions (Heitmüller); and so forth. It could even be concluded (by Gunkel) that, in Paul and John, Christianity emerged out of a syncretistic Judaism as itself essentially a syncretism. But the main thrust of the religionsgeschichtlich movement was to make clear in a new way that, in its origins and antecedents, Christianity cannot be viewed as an isolated and nonhistorical event, but only as one enmeshed from the outset in a broad and complex religious and cultural history that can be illuminated by comparative religious studies. Outside that context, it cannot be understood.[39]

---

development of law, ritual, and literature, were exhibited with such cogency that the impression produced on German theologians (especially of the younger generation) was almost irresistible; thenceforth 'Graf's hypothesis,' the resuscitation of the long-ignored theory of Vatke, was universally regarded as a question deserving most serious consideration, and by many as an ascertained fact. It was a special merit in Wellhausen's book to have excited interest in these questions outside the narrow circle of specialists by its skillful handling of the materials and its almost perfect combination of wide historical considerations with the careful investigation of details, and to have thus removed Old Testament criticism from the rank of a subordinate question to the center of theological discussion" (*The Development of Theology in Germany since Kant and Its Progress in Great Britain since 1825* [London, 1893], p. 259). One may add that by the end of the century Wellhausen's view had also won the day in Britain and the United States.

39. Among the works illustrative of the school, see Eichhorn, *Das Abendmahl im Neuen Testament* (Leipzig, 1898); Bousset, *Kyrios Christos* (Göttingen, 1913), and *Die Religion des Judentums im neutestamentlichen Zeitalter* (Berlin, 1902; 2d ed., 1906); Gunkel, *Genesis übersetzt und erklärt* (Göttingen, 1901), and *Zum religionsgeschichtlichen Verständnis des Neuen Tes-*

Reassessing Christian History

A full-scale application of a religionsgeschichtlich method to the history of the church and its theology did not come until Troeltsch's great social history of the Christian churches (see chapter 8). Until that time the problems posed for Protestant thought by critical historical method largely centered in biblical studies, especially of the New Testament. This was a consequence of the traditional Protestant principle of *sola scriptura*. Because of the primary and sometimes exclusive appeal to biblical authority and the Reformation call for renewal in the church, Protestantism could easily adjust to the application of general historical principles of development in understanding church history and theology, as well as to the idea that Christianity should be adapting to its cultural environment. Protestants were accustomed to thinking of one or another kind of fall in the course of Christian history after the New Testament period.

Thus while John Henry Newman's *Essay on the Development of Christian Doctrine* (1878) was a daring work for a Roman Catholic theologian, and while its conclusions might be anathema to Protestant thinkers, the notion that doctrine in the church had developed and changed could only be "old hat" to the Protestant mind. The issues were what kind of change and growth, whether improvement or retrogression, how this development was to be accounted for, and (for some) whether definitive interpretations of biblical doctrine had been achieved. Even for those who believed the last point, the authority of ecclesiastical formulations remained secondary. The Reformed and Lutheran confessions were always in principle subject to the norm of scripture. And for theology in the tradition of Schleiermacher, and especially of Maurice and Bushnell, wholly normative and nonhistorically conditioned dogmatic statements were no longer conceivable.[40]

---

taments (Göttingen, 1903; 2d ed., 1910); Heitmüller, *Im Namen Jesu* (Göttingen, 1903), and *Taufe und Abendmahl bei Paulus* (Göttingen, 1905). For related literature, see Richard Reitzenstein, *Die hellenistischen Mysterienreligionen* (Leipzig, 1910), and *Poimandres* (Leipzig, 1904); A. Dieterich, *Eine Mithras-Liturgie*, 2d ed. (Leipzig, 1910); Franz Cumont, *Les Religions orientales dans le paganisme romain* (Paris, 1907); and James Frazer, *The Golden Bough*: pt. 3, *The Dying God*, and pt. 4, *Adonis Attis Osiris* (London, 1911, 1914).

40. The biblical question, though it surfaced in Catholicism in the late nineteenth century (notably in Loisy, as well as in Leo's 1893 encyclical *Providentissimus Deus* and the appointment of the Biblical Commission in 1901), was at that time far less important for Catholic thought than for Protestantism. The full force of Catholic authority, from the *Syllabus of Errors* (1864) through the condemnation of Modernism in 1907, was directed much

Yet the historical critical method also had consequences for the Protestant understanding of the history of the church and its theology. The chief architects of the new perspectives, prior to Troeltsch, were Ferdinand Christian Baur and Adolf Harnack, in whose work historical theology came of age as a discipline.

Baur

Baur first and most fully developed the idea of a historical theology. His role in the truly historical investigation of the New Testament and primitive Christianity was discussed in volume 1 (pp. 155–60). Here we are interested in Baur's reflections on the writing of church history and dogma from the standpoint of critical study, as these were articulated especially in *The Epochs of Church Historiography* and his massive studies in the history of dogma.[41]

For Baur, the application of historical critical method to church history meant several things. First, it meant self-consciousness of a new sort in historiography, serious reflection on the *how* of the study, the method. Since church history and the history of theology themselves have histories, Baur reviewed previous writings extensively in the *Epochs* (from Hegesippus and Eusebius down to his own time) and in the introduction to his lectures on the history of dogma. From the days of Eusebius, by whom dogma was identified as the substance of Christian history—and in dogma nothing changes—the task for Catholic historiography had been to identify pure doctrine and trace its struggle with error, whether heresy or paganism. In contrast to this old Catholic view of inwardly undisturbed unity and unrestricted forward movement, the Protestant view of history, which was massively expressed in Flacius and the *Magdeburg Centuries* (1559–74), had to justify the reformation principles by returning to history. "If

---

more against the idea that the church might have to adapt its structure and thinking to a modern world, and in defense of the old view that the doctrines and essential institutions of the Catholic church have been always and identically the same (or, in the newer orthodoxy, that the later defined dogmas and institutions were logically implicit in the earlier).

41. *Die Epochen der kirchlichen Geschichtschreibung* (Tübingen, 1852), republished in *Ausgewählte Werke*, vol. 2 (Stuttgart, 1963); *Die christliche Lehre von der Versöhnung in ihrer geschichtlichen Entwicklung von der ältesten Zeit bis auf die neueste* (Tübingen, 1838); *Die christliche Lehre von der Dreieinigkeit und Menschwerdung Gottes in ihrer geschichtlichen Entwicklung*, 3 vols. (Tübingen, 1841–43); and *Vorlesungen über die christliche Dogmengeschichte*, ed. F. Baur, 3 vols. (Leipzig, 1865–67). *The Epochs of Church Historiography* and the introduction to the *Lectures on the History of Christian Dogma* are translated in Peter Hodgson, *Ferdinand Christian Baur* (New York, 1968). See also Hodgson's fine study of Baur, *The Formation of Historical Theology* (New York, 1966).

the church in reality is not what it ought to be intrinsically, then it must at one time have become what it is now, since it is unthinkable that its original condition could not have been inadequate to its Idea; and the problem now is to explain from history how in the course of time so great a change ensued."[42] In other words, where and how did Catholicism go wrong? Yet for the *Centuries*, as in the old Catholic view, dogma was still the substantive content of church history.

Second, a proper method meant that historical theology and church history cannot be separated from universal history but are understood as parts of it, as delimited fields with relatively homogeneous phenomena. Mosheim's great church history[43] was a methodological landmark in asking what church history is and how it is conceived, abandoning narrowly ecclesiastical and particularist interests in a movement toward unbiased study, and treating the church as a society like the state. (Mosheim, though, made the church too much like a society and failed to understand the organic continuity and inward relation of church developments.) For Baur, no exclusive disjunction is to be drawn between secular history and *Heilsgeschichte*. The principles of historical interpretation in the one are no different from those in the other. No sharp distinction between Geschichte and Historie would be allowable. Any simple appeal to the supernatural as the adequate explanatory principle for ecclesiastical manifestations must be abandoned, as well as the mythology of a redemption scheme in which church history is the sphere of divine activity and secular history is largely controlled by Satan and demons.

Third, however, a proper method does not mean that faith and scientific research are radically disjoined. Church history is a theological discipline. Study of the church and its dogmas is both critical and theological. In Baur's idealistic understanding of the relation of Spirit to the historical process, all history is a factual manifestation of an Idea which is its content, and any comprehensive church history involves the subordination of the particular to the universal. Everything individual is related to the Idea that is the basis of the whole. The basis is the nature of Christianity, whose center is the reconciliation of God and man, whose point of origin is Christ, and whose subsequent historical manifestation is the historicity of the church. (Baur at one time used more Hegelian language about the inner movement

---

42. *Epochs* (Hodgson's translation), p. 79.

43. Johann Lorenz Mosheim, *Institutionum historiae ecclesiasticae et recentioris*, 4 vols. (Helmstädt, 1755).

of the concept in history; later, in the *Epochs*, he spoke of Idea and its manifestation.) Thus Baur could see a conjoining of faith and critical historical knowledge.

A view of history, for Baur, inevitably manifests the theological vantage point of the author, and so Protestant historiography differs from Catholic. Catholics judge the idea and the reality to coincide completely. For Protestants, these are not so immediately one, and the goal of a Protestant history is to exhibit the pattern of relations of the Idea to its manifestations in the concrete and objectively ascertainable historical development. Protestant historiography is able to incorporate the empirical discovery that history tends to develop through opposing tendencies (for example, in the Petrine-Pauline antithesis, for which the Tübingen school became famous, or in the growth of trinitarian and soteriological doctrine). Baur has often been unfairly charged with imposing Hegelian categories of thesis/ antithesis on historical interpretation. But he had already formed his conclusions about the conflict of Jewish and Gentile Christianity before he came under the influence of Hegel, and throughout it was his understanding that speculation did not mean imposing rationality but eliciting meaning from history. Truth is mediated by the historically real.

Harnack

Adolf Harnack's *History of Dogma* (1886–90) is without doubt the landmark of late-nineteenth-century reconsideration of the development of Christian doctrine. This is not to make light of the work of others such as Friedrich Loofs, Reinhold Seeberg, Otto Pfleiderer, Philip Schaff, and G. B. Fisher (in church history), Karl Holl (in the reinterpretation of Luther), and even A. V. G. Allen and James Orr. It should also be remembered that Harnack's interests were equally in the development of institutions, and that there was scarcely any question of early church history that he left untouched. However, our concern is chiefly with the development of thought, and Harnack's *Dogmengeschichte*, with its incomparable mastery of the sources, is plainly the classic, which became an essential point of reference and measuring rod for all subsequent histories of Christian thought.[44]

44. Thus Jaroslav Pelikan, in the first volume of *The Christian Tradition: A History of the Development of Doctrine* (Chicago, 1971), p. 359, writes: "Superseded but never surpassed, Harnack's work remains, after more than eighty years, the one interpretation of early Christian doctrine with which every other scholar in the field must contend."

Harnack picked up the thread of historical theology directly from Baur. The Reformation, he thought, had opened the way to a critical treatment of the history of dogma, but this at first remained in the service of polemics, carried on from the standpoint of confessional doctrine. In Mosheim and in the English deists he found the beginnings of nonpartisan and unbiased critical consideration of the history of the Christian religion and its doctrines. C. W. F. Walch provided the impetus for viewing Dogmengeschichte as a special discipline. Johann Semler first contributed the insight that dogmas originate in particular historical circumstances and gradually develop. Early in the nineteenth century, under the influence of Herder, Schleiermacher, and the Romantics on one side and Hegel and Schelling on the other, the rationalism of the eighteenth century dissolved and the way was prepared for an inner understanding of the process of the development of dogma. This led to the epoch-making writings of Baur, which for the first time attempted to give an inclusive conception of the dogmaticohistoric process without relinquishing the critical accomplishments of the eighteenth century.[45]

Yet Baur's work was too much dominated by an abstract philosophical scheme, and if supernaturalism and rationalism are to be rejected, so also is philosophical dependence. Harnack thought that the second edition of Ritschl's *Die Entstehung der altkatholischen Kirche* (1875) had emancipated the proper study of Christian origins from bondage to philosophical systems. The Tübingen school had rightly begun with Paul and Paulinism and correctly seen the chief problem as the rise of Catholicism. But Baur's view of the two opposite tendencies, Jewish Christianity and Gentile Christianity, was both oversimple and dubiously interpreted by the idealistic philosophical notions of idea, image, reality, and consciousness. Ritschl's critical work had shown a far richer and more complex historical reality and development, freed from speculative categories of interpretation. Harnack's concern, therefore, was not with an immanent unfolding of a central Christian idea but with a detailed investigation of the circumstances of the origins of theology and dogma.

45. See Harnack's introductory review of the history of dogma in *Dogmengeschichte*, 1:20–35. Harnack noted that in casting out rationalism, we need to be careful not to throw the baby out with the bath. From the rationalist historians of doctrine we can learn that the development of dogma is to be understood in the closest connection with the total history of the church.

But for Harnack, as much as for Baur, Dogmengeschichte is a theological discipline which cannot be undertaken by turning away from present-day convictions. Indeed, Harnack could describe his own fundamental task as a historian thus:

> We study history in order to intervene in the course of history, and it is our right and duty that we do this, for if we lack historical insight we either permit ourselves to be mere objects put in the historical process or we shall have the tendency to lead people down the wrong way. To intervene in history—this means that we must reject the past when it reaches into the present only in order to block us. It means also that we must do the right thing in the present, that is, anticipate the future and be prepared for it in a circumspect manner. There is no doubt that, with respect to the past, the historian assumes the royal function of a judge, for in order to decide what of the past shall continue to be in effect and what must be done away with or transformed, the historian must judge like a king. Everything must be designed to furnish a preparation for the future, for only that discipline of learning has a right to exist which lays the foundation for what is to be.[46]

More specifically, dogma must be purified by history. "The history of dogma, in that it sets forth the process of the origin and development of the dogma, offers the very best means and methods of freeing the church from dogmatic Christianity, and of hastening the inevitable process of emancipation, which began with Augustine"—though "the history of dogma testifies also to the *unity* and continuity of the Christian faith in the progress of its history, in so far as it proves that certain fundamental ideas of the Gospel have never been lost and have defied all attacks."[47] As a tool for theological critique and reconstruction, historical theology can complete what the Reformation left unfinished.

Harnack's standpoint obviously was deeply influenced by Ritschl in its antimetaphysical bias; in the conviction that the norm or essence of Christianity will be found by going back to the origins (by way of the Reformation); and in the judgment that the heart of Christianity is not an idea but a new form of life and human society —the centrality of the ethical. But his historical vision was also shaped by his favorite poet, Goethe, who is most often quoted by

46. *Reden und Aufsätze*, 4:7.
47. *Outlines of the History of Dogma*, pp. 7–8.

Harnack and one of whose sayings stands as a motto for *Dogmenge-geschichte*.[48] There is a Geist that prevails in history. It is to be located especially in those individuals who have changed history. And it must be assumed that this spirit is one in all history if it is to have any dynamic relation to the present.[49]

In summing up the task of the historian of dogma, Harnack held that all further progress in the discipline depended on viewing the history of dogmatic development in the closest connection with the general history of the church, in its cultural milieu, and on properly understanding what the Christian religion was originally. Thence the impartial historian has two standards by which he can judge the history of dogma: either he measures the history, insofar as possible, by the gospel, or he judges it according to the circumstances of its time or its results. As long as one does not confuse them, the two modes of judgment can coexist.[50]

It was natural, therefore, that in the *History of Dogma* Harnack should be particularly concerned with the question of the origin of dogma. The three big volumes *Dogmengeschichte* constitute a masterful account of the unfolding of early church doctrine and its threefold outcome in Catholicism, antitrinitarianism, and Protestantism (Luther). Yet the critical problem for the history of dogma, as Harnack poses it in the prolegomena, is how dogma came into being. He stated his central thesis bluntly: "Dogma, in its conception and its construction, is a work of the Greek spirit on the soil of the gospel."[51]

Thus Harnack devoted the first of the two parts of his history (the nearly seven hundred pages of volume 1) to the question of the origins of ecclesiastical dogma. This required at the outset a detailed examination of the *presuppositions*, in the gospel preached by Jesus Christ himself and in the proclamation of Christ in the first generation of his followers, set in the context of current interpretations of the Old Testament (particularly of the apocalyptic literature), of the

48. From *Conversation with Eckermann*: "The Christian religion has nothing to do with philosophy. It is by itself a powerful entity at which fallen and suffering mankind has from time to time raised itself up again; insofar as one concedes that it has exercised this influence, it is superior to all philosophy and does not need to seek its support."

49. See Harnack, *Christianity and History*, and Troeltsch's essay in honor of Harnack's seventieth birthday, in *Festgabe für Adolf von Harnack*, ed. Karl Holl (Tübingen, 1921), pp. 282–91 (trans. in Pauck, *Harnack and Troeltsch*, pp. 97–115).

50. See *Dogmengeschichte*, 1:34–35.

51. Ibid., p. 16.

religious conceptions and philosophy of religion of Hellenistic Judaism, and of Greco-Roman religious dispositions and philosophy of religion in the first two centuries. Against this background Harnack could analyze the beginnings of apostolic-Catholic doctrine and the first ecclesiastical doctrinal systems.

Harnack explicated the foundation of dogma as a twofold process: the establishment and gradual secularization of Christianity as a church; and the establishment and gradual Hellenization of Christianity as doctrine in the apostolic age. The first process involved the recasting of the baptismal confession into a rule of faith, the recognition of certain writings as apostolic scriptures, and the transformation of the bishop's office in the church into an apostolic office. The second process began with theological explication and revision of the rule of faith, in opposition to gnosticism, on the basis of the New Testament and the Apologists' Christian philosophy (especially in Irenaeus, Tertullian, and Hippolytus). It continued as the transformation, notably in Clement and Origen, of the Christian tradition into a philosophy of religion. In the struggle with gnosticism the personnel were defeated, but the church adopted an intellectualism or frame of dogma that had been the crucial element in the gnostic program. This was the origin of a scientific ecclesiastical theology or dogmatics, and the result was the defining of the church's doctrinal norm through adoption of the Logos Christology as the counter to gnostic dualism. So the rule of faith was transformed into a compendium of Greek philosophical systems, and Neoplatonic speculation was legitimized within the church. Not that the process was avoidable. Historical circumstances require historical decisions. Christianity had to contend with Greek culture and make the faith intelligible, and while we may regret the combining of Jesus' religion with metaphysics as a besmirching of the gospel, we can understand how it happened.

In the second part of the work (volumes 2 and 3) Harnack traced the *development* of church dogma: first as the articulation of the doctrine of the God-man, and redemption through him, down through the sixth ecumenical council and John of Damascus (concentrating on the East); then (chiefly in the West) as the expansion and recasting of the dogma into anthropological and soteriological doctrines of sin, grace, and the means of grace in the Roman Catholic church. In this process, which Harnack traced through the medieval scholastics, Augustine claims a special place, not only as a fresh theological departure but also as representing (to Harnack) the finest expression of Christian piety between Paul and Luther, the man who rediscovered religion and rescued it from communal and cultic form, and who bound together religion and morality.

The conclusion of the entire development was described by Harnack as threefold: the outcome in the Roman Catholic codification at Trent, in opposition to Protestantism, and the subsequent events through the first Vatican Council; the outcome in antitrinitarianism and Socinianism; and the outcome in Protestantism (by which Harnack meant essentially Luther, hardly mentioning Calvin or the Lutheran confessions). It was Luther who really did away with dogmatic Christianity in principle and put a new (or renewed) evangelical conception in its place, though he made only a partial beginning, and Protestantism subsequently relapsed into a quasi-Catholicism.[52]

The outline of Harnack's work gives scarcely any indication of why it was so important. Harnack obviously had axes to grind. There was his Ritschlian antimetaphysical attitude—though Harnack examined the philosophical currents with enormous industry. There was an anti-Catholic polemic—though certainly not, in contrast to his contemporary Rudolf Sohm, an anti-institutional bias. The church, for Harnack, must have earthly form; if there is a tension between spiritual things and social institutions or law, it is a tension inescapable in all of human history. Harnack expended great energy in analyzing institutional development.[53] He even had a kind of grudging admiration for the massive development of Catholicism, judging it to have encompassed nearly all the religious possibilities, so that one who knows this religion in the whole of its history knows all religion.

Harnack's thesis might also be viewed as a new variant on the old Protestant theme of a fall in the history of the church. Others had located the fall in the emergence of coercion and the alliance with the state, or in the emergence of law in contrast to spirit. Harnack identified the fall with the displacement of religious life by philosophy and creed.

It might further be argued that Harnack merely replaced the old supernaturalism with the idea of a special perception of faith (as Herrmann more obviously did). After all, for Harnack, Christianity

52. Ibid., 3:759–64, esp. 763–64, for the concluding reflection.
53. See not only *Dogmengeschichte* but also Harnack's work on the early expansion of Christianity and on the development of constitution and law in Christianity in the first two centuries. See also his comments on Jesus and the law in *WC*, pp. 105–12.

was historical, but the gospel was in a sense without history, unchanging and capable of breaking free from its encumbrances. Though the principles of historical interpretation, in the attention to individual phenomena and to patterns, relations, and laws of development, were common to all historical study, church history and Dogmengeschichte were still theological disciplines. Church history was still faith's history, and it is important that Harnack did not question the final truth of Christianity. He had a clear idea of what was essential Christianity and he used it as a tool of interpretation.

Yet just because of the majesty of his scholarship—in the care for the investigation of the sources, in the richness of the account of the interplay of social, political, and intellectual influences—Harnack took a long step toward the kind of social history that later appeared in Troeltsch, even toward the eventual displacement of "church history" by "history of Christianity" or "religion in Western culture." He saw that the church is not isolable from its surrounding culture, but is a genuinely historical and social phenomenon (or pattern of phenomena). More clearly than Baur, he saw the contingencies and irrationalities in the play of historical forces, whose movement is not a matter of logical or dialectical necessity but of historical decisions that might have gone differently. The history of dogma could not provide, as it had for Newman and even for Baur, the predictability of further progress, but an opportunity and necessity for decision.

The decisions required are precisely decisions about the truth and value of dogma and doctrine. This is why history overcomes dogma. We see that once a historical decision has been made (e.g., dogma) it changes the elements that led to it and has a power in the future. Doctrine acquires a life of its own. But as soon as the historical process is understood, the decisions are open to reconsideration. Dogma is radically relativized. Not only can the developed doctrines of the ecumenical councils be rendered dubious because of Greek philosophical influences; even the Apostles' Creed can be called into question—and Harnack created a furor by suggesting in 1892 that the acceptance of this creed in its literal sense is not the test of Christian and theological maturity, saying that it might better be replaced (or paralleled) by a brief confession more clearly expressing the understanding of the gospel achieved by the Reformation.[54] In a similar

54. See the account of the controversy in Agnes von Zahn-Harnack, *Adolf von Harnack*, pp. 144–60. Harnack's detailed history of the development of the creed, *Das apostolische Glaubensbekenntnis* (Berlin, 1892), appeared in twenty-five editions within the year.

vein, Harnack later concluded that history opens up the question whether Protestantism should retain the Old Testament in its canon, since we see that it does not manifest Christ. Given the historical circumstances, it would have been an error for the church to reject the Old Testament in the second century, and we can understand why the sixteenth-century reformers could not break with the tradition. But modern Protestantism can and should make a different decision, holding only to the New Testament as Holy Scripture.[55]

The point here is not the rightness of *Harnack's* decisions, but that decisions must once more be made, and now against the background of an immensely fuller understanding of the history of doctrinal development. Harnack was highly persuasive for many as to the generally unsatisfactory character (for modern believers) of the ancient formulations. More important was the historical destruction of any easy assumption that Christian faith was adequately expressed for posterity in the Greco-Roman intellectual forms. This claim could indeed continue to be made, and other theologians and historians of doctrine were ready to make it. But Harnack's work, we may say, decisively shifted the burden of proof to the shoulders of those who argued for the necessity of the ancient dogmas or their value in the modern world.

The story of Christianity as a whole, like that of Jesus and of scripture, was brought fully within the orbit of historical understanding. And with respect to the history of theology, Harnack's work became a point of reference for all subsequent studies.

55. See *Marcion: Das Evangelium vom fremden Gott.*

6

Evolution and Theology:

Détente or Evasion?

Phrases like "the greatest book of the century," "the convulsions of the national mind," "the warfare of science and religion," and "Darwin's century" have commonly swirled around the discussion of Charles Darwin's impact. And not wholly without reason. From one perspective, of course, Darwin's work was a culmination of a history of advance in natural science that made the old world views obsolete. Yet because it was a biological theory, Darwinism dealt with the origins and nature of the human species in a way that astronomy, physics, and geology had not. It raised directly the question of humanity's place in the world and the viability of the biblical and traditional view of man and woman as specially created and fallen.

Darwin's revolution may thus be compared with Isaac Newton's. But Newton's machine universe had been tamed theologically by William Paley (and others) as a world perfectly ordered by divine act, whereas Darwin's conception of evolution—a mechanistic process without implications of design, with random variations and natural selection, presupposing conflict and not harmony—demanded an unfinished rather than a perfected world.

For three or four decades after 1859, *The Origin of Species* was both a special focus for the problem of relating the religious and scientific world views and a symbol of the changing relations of theology and culture in general. By the end of the century, except for incipient Protestant fundamentalism and Roman Catholicism, the controversy over biological evolution seemed largely resolved. Evolution even became a master image for new ways of viewing all things religious and cultural.

Yet this is far too simplistic a rendering of the story. The popular notion of Darwin as the principal cause of a conflict between science and religion badly needs to be demythologized. Indeed, much of the mass of material on the Darwinism debate has involved misinterpretation, even nonsense, regarding what Darwin actually proposed, the responses of scientists and theologians, and the actual issues. We must therefore seek to sort out the issues more properly and to avoid confusing those questions that have all too often been blurred: the social versus either the scientific or the theological reasons for accepting or rejecting Darwinism; the acceptance of Darwin versus the embracing of evolutionary ideas or principles in general; the changes in scientific theory that Darwin's view involved; "design" and "evolution" versus "design" and "natural selection"; debate about Darwin among the scientists versus debate among religionists; Darwin as a cause versus Darwin as an occasion of controversy; and the evolution question versus the question of the scientific method and mood as a pervasive problem for religious thought. We shall then be in a better position to assess the "resolution" of the debate which had taken place by the end of the century.[1]

INITIAL DEBATE (1860–63)

In a joint paper with Alfred Russell Wallace, who had independently arrived at many of the same conclusions, Darwin presented a brief sketch of his theory in July 1858. But it was *The Origin of Species*, published in November 1859 and sold out in the first edition in a day, that precipitated the public and prolonged debate. Darwin was at once supported, among the scientists, by Thomas Huxley and the botanist Joseph Dalton Hooker, both of whom had already been won to his view, and encouraged by the renowned geologist Charles Lyell, who nonetheless had some reservations. He was roundly attacked in *The Spectator* (March 1860) by his former geology teacher, the Reverend Adam Sedgwick.

But no event did more to dramatize the debate than the sessions at Oxford of the British Association for the Advancement of Science in June 1860. There Sir Richard Owen, the great anatomist, and the American John William Draper soberly challenged aspects of Darwin's account. But the sensation was occasioned by a foolish and tasteless attempt on the part of the Oxford Bishop Samuel Wilberforce, a man of considerable gifts of oratory but with no scientific training or competence and no understanding of what Darwin had really said, to discredit Darwinism by making fun of it. This provided the opportunity for Huxley to respond with devastating force, ex-

1. See Bibliographical Notes: Chapter 6.

posing Wilberforce's ignorance, explaining Darwin's ideas, and concluding that while he would not be at all ashamed to have an ape for an ancestor, he would be ashamed to be connected with a man who used "eloquent digressions and skilled appeals to religious prejudice" to obscure the truth.

That exchange served to fix in the public mind a distorted view of the response of theologians to evolutionary theory. It suggested that the religionists were not only confused and obscurantist (as many were, in fact) but also devious, whereas Huxley was able to take the high road (as he mostly did) of virtue, honesty, and devotion to truth. In general, Darwin's supporters were able to maintain a coherent strategy and an esprit de corps quite lacking among their opponents. The encounter also marked a big step toward what was to become Huxley's career as the champion of Darwin and the apostle of scientific freedom and the capability of science to clarify every human question—an apostleship that was prosecuted with great skill through constant lecturing and writing, both popular and technical, so that Huxley was a powerful force in the intellectual struggles throughout Europe and America. He was as much concerned to convert the scientists as to combat the church (especially Roman Catholicism).[2]

Wilberforce's was not the only kind of theological response, though probably the majority of clerics shared his hostility. For example, the Anglican Charles Kingsley, already committed to an evolutionary conception, found Darwin and Huxley no threat. The immediate response of Roman Catholic thinkers was restrained, as in the 1860 reviews of Darwin by Richard Simpson and Canon John Morris.[3] But we will return later to the varieties of theological response.

In America the scientific issue was immediately taken up in early 1860 at Harvard between the foremost American botanist, Asa Gray, and the geologist Louis Agassiz. Gray strongly supported his friend Darwin, though not uncritically, arguing (to Darwin's discomfiture)

2. Huxley's own *Evidence as to Man's Place in Nature* (London, 1863) was no mean scientific contribution—through embryology, paleontology, and comparative anatomy—to the establishment of man's anthropoid origin.

3. Catholic thought had some preparation for developmental theory in Nicholas Wiseman's *Twelve Lectures on the Connexion between Science and Revealed Religion* (London, 1836), and Roman Catholicism was less troubled than Protestantism by the problem of reinterpretation of scripture and by the commitment to natural theology. Later, there was a shift to stronger opposition. See John D. Root, "Catholics and Science in Mid-Victorian England" (Ph.D. diss., Indiana University, 1974).

that *Origin* need not be in conflict with a teleological and theistic view. Agassiz was vigorously on the attack, condemning Darwin for presenting "marvelous bear, cuckoo, and other stories" instead of facts. His argument, however, needs to be seen against the background of his own recent "Essay on Classification" (Boston, 1857), in which he had intended to set the guidelines for future scientific work, assuming the immutability of species. Further in the background, though not so far as to prevent it from being confused with *Origin* in the popular mind, was Robert Chambers' *Vestiges of the Natural History of Creation* (London, 1844; tenth edition, 1853), which aroused a furor by its peculiar (semi-Lamarckian) doctrines, which excluded God from the process and alienated both scientists (including Agassiz) and theologians. The failure of *Vestiges* prepared the American soil for criticism of *Origin*. After the publication of *Origin*, much of the debate with Agassiz was carried on by William Barton Rogers, later president of the Massachusetts Institute of Technology. Together, Gray and Rogers made sure that Darwin would not go down with *Vestiges*.[4]

Among other nations, it was only in Germany that the initial impact of Darwin could be compared with that in Britain and the United States. Translated in 1860, *Origin* at once called forth a lively discussion among biologists, philosophers, and clergy. The translation of Huxley's *Evidence as to Man's Place in Nature* in 1863 also made a deep impression, second only to that of *Origin*. (Much of Huxley was translated into German, as were works by Wallace, Gray, and Agassiz.) Among the early champions of Darwin was the young zoologist Ernst Haeckel, who became a close friend of Huxley and played a role on the Continent comparable to that of Huxley in England, though with a kind of violence that horrified the English supporters.

In France, Darwin's book was met with little more than silence. French attitudes were still under the spell of Cuvier's denunciation of Lamarckian evolutionary views in 1830, and Flourens had continued the attack on both *transformisme* and spontaneous generation. It took two years for Darwin to find a French translator (Clemence Royer), who then provided an introduction that fundamentally mis-

4. See esp. the chapter by Edward J. Pfeifer, "United States," in Glick, *Comparative Reception*, pp. 168–206. See also Gray's *Darwiniana*, ed. A. Hunter Dupree (Cambridge, Mass., 1963; first published as a collection of papers in 1876), and the selections from Agassiz and Gray in R. J. Wilson, ed., *Darwinism and the American Intellectual* (Homewood, Ill., 1967).

interpreted the work. Though a few favorable reviews appeared, most French scientists were opposed. There was no Darwinian revolution in France.

The reception of Darwin in the Netherlands was generally favorable, with the exception of two older scientists near the end of their careers, Jan van der Hoeven (Leiden) and Willem Vrolik (Amsterdam). Pieter Harting (Utrecht) was perhaps the most important supporter and interpreter. Ilse Bulhof has made a persuasive case that the profound changes taking place in Dutch society were supportive of the alteration in scientific theory.[5]

WHY THE EXCITEMENT?

One cannot easily avoid the question why *The Origin of Species* should have come as a shock, in view of what seems to have been extensive preparation for Darwin's ideas, both in the development of science and in philosophical religious thought. The nature of that preparation, quite apart from any specific anticipations of Darwin's theory, has bearing both on the initial reception of Darwin and on later responses to his theories in the scientific and religious communities.

Much earlier, the progress of geology had brought into question the short time scale for the world that had been popularized by Bishop Ussher's calculation of the date of creation as 4004 B.C. It was widely accepted in the early nineteenth century that geological time had to be very long, and this massive extension of the age of the earth posed no serious problem for many theologians. Even among conservatives it could be recognized, as early Christian thinkers had also said, that the Genesis account of the days of creation was allegorical, and that a day in the Creator's work might be of great duration.

Well before the mid-nineteenth century, the idea of the death or disappearance of whole species was already current, as fossil remains came to be seen as records of creatures once living but long extinct. There were, of course, many who believed that God would not permit any of his creatures to be annihilated and who devised ingenious explanations for the troubling fossils. The apparent waste implied by the idea of extinction was not so easy to deal with in the traditional Christian view. But the idea of the death of species, an indispensable

5. Bulhof, "The Netherlands," in Glick, *Comparative Reception*, pp. 279–306.

presupposition for Darwin's theory, gained unmistakable dominance in the scientific community.

The early favored explanation for the disappearance and appearance of species was the theory of catastrophism (a notion so attractive to the romanticism of the human mind that it has reemerged in the twentieth century in the popularity of Velikovsky's *Worlds in Collision*). Catastrophism was the view, formulated particularly by Baron Georges Cuvier, that the observed changes in fossil content were the result of a series of cataclysmic destructions, which were followed by new creations, so that the world had been successively depopulated and repopulated without any genealogical connection. Obviously this was a nice theory to relate to the biblical flood story. Such was the view taught by Darwin's geology professors before his voyage on the *Beagle*, and it was still argued against Darwin by Agassiz.

Catastrophism, however, was decisively overthrown by Sir Charles Lyell's *Principles of Geology* (London, 1830–33; tenth edition, 1867–68), which on the basis of an additional half-century of geological evidence was able to reassert the earlier uniformitarian principle of Hutton and Playfair: that the geological past is to be interpreted by presently known and observable processes, which take place slowly and continuously. Thus a further scientific step prerequisite for Darwin's theory was taken. The earth's geological history formed an essential unity, and the extinction of individual species had to be understood as part of a single related changing world rather than as a series of stops and starts.

Another scientific proposal that was important in the discussions before Darwin and continued to play a role later in the century was the evolutionary theory of Jean Baptiste Lamarck. The farfetched evolutionary speculations of Chambers, in *Vestiges of Creation*, were not of much lasting significance, except here and there to confuse the popular debate. But Lamarck was another matter. Though never clear about extinction, Lamarck had offered (in *Recherches sur l'organisation des corps vivants* [Paris, 1802], and *Philosophie zoologique* [Paris, 1809]) a model for evolutionary organic process. According to this model, although species were fixed, they had immanent within them, as created, the possibilities of progressive improvement, of transformation through adaptation to their environments and through the inheritance of acquired characteristics. Thus a mechanism was proposed, without appeal to special divine act but in reference to use and disuse of organs, whereby changes in the species could occur.

On the philosophical and religious side as well, by the mid-nineteenth century there was nothing novel about the idea of a general evolutionary world process. Indeed, it was a commonplace, even though not often applied specifically to the origin of humanity. It was written large in the German idealist tradition. There were preparations in Lessing, Herder, and Kant, and it was above all in Hegel's grand vision that the development of the world was seen as the unfolding, according to the dialectical principle, of the life of Spirit. Schelling affirmed in another way the basic coherence of nature and the gradual development of the sequence of organic being. At the end of the century, in his lectures on the history of Protestant dogmatics, Kähler claimed that it was easy for German theologians to become Darwinians because "we were already Hegelians and Hegel anticipated the whole of Darwin."[6]

Among theologians, for example, we may recall the evolutionary themes in Richard Rothe's *Theologische Ethik* (Wittenberg, 1845–48; see *Prot. Thought*, 1:287). S. T. Coleridge had referred in his philosophical lectures of 1818–19 to the belief as being "quite common even among Christian people, that the human race arose from a state of savagery and then gradually from a monkey came in through various states to be man." The Oxford professor of geometry Baden Powell may well have been the first English divine of note formally to bless evolution. Some form of it, he had argued in *The Connexion of Natural and Divine Truth* (London, 1838), is the only solution to the scientific problem; evolution, furthermore, provides an argument for design. In *Essays and Reviews* (London, 1860) he hailed Darwin's work as now substantiating the principle of the origination of new species by natural causes. But Baden Powell's views did not make any great impact on the world at large, any more than did Nicholas Wiseman's in Roman Catholic thought.

Even the American Taylor Lewis, professor of Greek at Union College and a biblical literalist who believed that Genesis was a divinely inspired account of creation to be placed above science as a source for knowledge of the beginnings of the world, could in 1855 not only affirm the long day view of creation but (surprisingly) allow for the possibility that man's body had evolved over a long period of

6. *Geschichte der protestantischen Dogmatik im 19. Jahrhundert* (Munich, 1962; published from notes of lectures between 1896 and 1912), p. 100. The statement is both overdrawn and confused; it poses a question we shall deal with later.

time from some form of lower animal. Evolutionary theories that denied a divine origin could not be accepted, of course, but evolution could be understood to allow for multiple divine interventions and thus be an acceptable description of God's manner of creativity.[7]

For those many thinkers influenced by Schleiermacher, the importance of the historical accuracy of the Genesis creation accounts had long since been rejected, so that the seeming conflict between evolutionary theory and biblical history was no real problem. In short, there are good reasons for suggesting that, at least in Britain and Germany, the theological as well as the scientific world was ripe for *The Origin of Species*.

But in another sense the climate was unfavorable. This had to do, on the religious side particularly, with the prevailing conservatism that had become even stronger in Germany, Britain, and America around mid-century (see *Prot. Thought*, 1, chapter 9). It was also in part because of the common prior interplay of scientific and theological assertion. William Irvine put it vividly for the British scene: "As the Bible itself had long been taken for a biological and geological treatise, so the *Origin* became a treatise on religion and ethics, eventually on politics and sociology. Scientists themselves didn't know whether to reply to it with science or theology, and often maintained the most incoherent and contradictory opinions with the utmost vehemence. Seldom has scientific detachment met so severe a trial or come off so badly."[8]

WHAT DARWIN REALLY PROPOSED

The heart of Darwin's proposal was succinctly expressed in a concluding statement of chapter 4 of *Origin*, a passage that remained essentially unchanged in the six editions of the work:

> If under changing conditions of life organic beings present individual differences in almost every part of their structure, and this cannot be disputed; if there be, owing to their geometrical rate of increase, a severe struggle for life at some age, season, or year, and this certainly cannot be disputed; then considering the infinite complexity of the relations of all organic beings to each other and to their conditions of life, causing an infinite diversity in structure, constitution, and habits, to be advantageous to them, it would be a most extraordinary fact if no variations had ever occurred useful to

7. Taylor Lewis, *The Six Days of Creation* (Schenectady, 1855).
8. *Apes, Angels, and Victorians*, p. 107.

each being's own welfare, in the same manner as so many variations have occurred useful to man. But if variations useful to any organic being ever do occur, assuredly individuals thus characterised will have the best chance of being preserved in the struggle for life; and from the strong principle of inheritance, these will tend to produce offspring similarly characterised. This principle of preservation, or survival of the fittest, I have called Natural Selection. It leads to the improvement of each creature in relation to its organic and inorganic conditions of life; and consequently, in most cases, to what must be regarded as an advance in organism. Nevertheless, low and simple forms will long endure if well fitted for their simple conditions of life.

Natural selection, on the principle of qualities being inherited at corresponding ages, can modify the egg, seed, or young, as easily as the adult. Amongst many animals, sexual selection will have given its aid to ordinary selection, by assuring to the most vigorous and best adapted males the greatest number of offspring. Sexual selection will also give characters useful to the male alone, in their struggles or rivalry with other males; and these characters will be transmitted to one sex or to both sexes, according to the form of inheritance which prevails.

Whether natural selection has really thus acted in adapting the various forms of life to their several conditions and stations, must be judged by the general tenor and balance of evidence given in the following chapters. But we have already seen how it entails extinction; and how largely extinction has acted in the world's history, geology plainly declares. Natural selection also leads to divergence of character; for the more organic beings diverge in structure, habits, and constitution, by so much the more can a large number be supported on the area—of which we see proof by looking to the inhabitants of any small spot, and to the productions naturalised in foreign lands. Therefore, during the modification of the descendants of any one species, and during the incessant struggle of all species to increase in numbers, the more diversified the descendants become, the better will be their chance of success in the battle for life. Thus the small differences distinguishing varieties of the same species, steadily tend to increase, till they equal the greater differences between species of the same genus, or even of distinct genera.[9]

9. *The Origin of Species,* 6th ed. (1872; cited from the P. F. Collier ed. [New York, 1909]), pp. 141–42. Anthony Leeds, in Glick, *Comparative Reception,* pp. 437–38, offers a useful and somewhat more technical summary of Darwin's model: "A living population of animals is designated a 'species' when it is marked off from other populations rather similar to itself if the first population cannot or can only poorly and under highly specific circum-

The distinctive feature of Darwin's work was not the idea of evolution, which we have seen to be a widely current notion. It should also be said that natural selection per se does not imply evolution; "it only implies that when evolution does occur it will proceed according to certain rules"[10]—though it should be said that apart from Darwin's massive array of data and his biogeographical synthesis, evolution was largely a speculative idea and not part of a compelling system of explanatory theory. The notion of struggle for existence was not the basic element; rather it was presupposed as the condition under which natural selection occurs. Even the idea of competition as the means of selecting variations was common in Victorian thought.

What was decisive in Darwin's contribution, so that it led to a reorientation of our idea of the world, was the way in which the principle of natural selection, in conformity with the "law of common descent," was developed into a powerful, coherent, and inclusive model to account for the origin of species, interlocked with a vast body of data. That was further supported by Darwin's elaboration of sexual selection in *The Descent of Man, and Selection in Relation to Sex* (London, 1871), particularly in the second and larger portion of the book, in which he was not talking about man.

Whether Darwin's theory was anticipated by others is a matter of some dispute among historians of science. But that is unimportant for us. It is important that his idea was of natural selection "without balance," the concept that new species come into being from preexisting varieties by an irregularly adaptive divergence, in which the main agent in the conversion of varieties into species is natural selection. It is also important, as Leeds puts it, that Darwin's model "accounted for a wider array of facts than any other conception except Christian creationism; dealt with certain aspects of reality—fossils,

---

stances interbreed with the second. Changes observed in such a population do not occur within an unchanging, ever-repeating range, fixed forever by the nature of the species itself (the fixity-of-species notion), nor are they immanently determined by the essence of the species even if these changes occur in an unfolding, nonrepetitive sequence (the Lamarckian version of the fixity of species). Changes observed are (a) events inherent in natural processes; (b) phenomena which are nondirectional, i.e., random, in origin, even if, cumulatively, directional in retrospective view; (c) the basis of the appearance of new species; (d) statistical results of the reproductive activity of the population of individuals; (e) statistical results of the elimination of individuals less suited and the survival of those more suited to external environmental conditions by 'natural selection.' The mechanism of sexual reproduction accounts for both the continuity of the species characteristics *and their changes* through natural selection."

10. Ghiselin, *Darwinian Method*, p. 66.

for example—much more simply than any other theory, including Christian creationism; and even permitted dealing with man-directed action—e.g., stockbreeding."[11]

Darwin's scheme needed no god or principle of teleology or design. Whether Darwin himself was a kind of theist is not relevant. The process as he described it did not leave a place for divine action or design. Even though he could write vaguely about "improvement," the process was ruled basically by chance and natural selection. Whether Darwin's model could be made, or viewed as, compatible with some idea of design or divine activity is of course a different question, one that was much debated in both scientific and theological circles.

Finally, it needs to be noted both that Darwin underestimated the magnitude of variation and that, as he admitted, his theory lacked an adequate account of the cause and the laws of variation, having to appeal to unknown hereditary factors. This lack could not be remedied until after the rediscovery of Mendel around 1900 and the development of modern genetics.[12]

VARIETIES OF RESPONSE: SCIENTIFIC

In the first decades after the publication of *Origin*, and for much longer in some places, the reactions to Darwin's proposals in the scientific community ranged from vigorous rejection to enthusiastic embrace. Among the opponents in Britain were not only Richard Owen, who finally came to accept evolution but not natural selection, and Adam Sedgwick, but also Sir William Thompson (later Lord Kelvin), whose calculations of the cooling time of the earth, based on thermodynamic principles, could not allow for the millions of years that the uniformitarians and evolutionists required—an objection that Darwin thought serious indeed. With Owen and Sedgwick, Thompson also insisted that biology needed design as an explanatory principle. John Edward Gray, vice president of the Zoological Society of London, insisted on the fixity of species.

In the United States, the early opposition was led by Agassiz and

11. In Glick, *Comparative Reception*, p. 439.

12. Ghiselin, *Darwinian Method*, pp. 7–8, argues that the difficulties in the scientific problem were not resolved until the publication in 1930 of R. A. Fisher, *The Genetical Theory of Natural Selection*, which "gave natural selection so firm a mathematical basis that within a few years a 'synthetic theory' had emerged. Natural selection, Darwin's fundamental contribution, is now as well established as any hypothesis in all the natural sciences."

James Dwight Dana. In Germany, the opponents were generally among the more established scientists in prestigious universities, such as Heinrich Bronn of Heidelberg, Rudolf Virchow and Adolf Bastian of Berlin, and Albert Wigand of Marburg.[13] We have already noted the cool reception that Darwin received in France. Not until 1878, after having been voted down on several previous nominations, was Darwin elected a corresponding member of the French Academy of Sciences, and then on grounds other than acceptance of his theory of evolution. In the Netherlands, as we have noted, scientific opposition was largely restricted to two of the older scholars.

At the other extreme, the enthusiastic supporters in Britain included Darwin's principal early associates, Huxley, Hooker, and Wallace—though Wallace's 1868 paper "Limits of Natural Selection as Applied to Man," by its assertion that natural selection could not account for human intelligence, gave pause to the proponents of natural selection and comfort to theistic interpretations. (See Wallace, *Contributions to the Theory of Natural Selection* [London, 1870].) Among German biologists, the leaders of the Darwinist party included Carl Vogt (at Geneva, following the loss of his zoology post at Giessen after the revolution of 1848), Ludwig Büchner (a physician in Darmstadt), and of course the very young Ernst Haeckel (at Jena), along with a dozen or so others. In the United States, besides Asa Gray, only the Philadelphia entomologist Benjamin D. Walsh was consistently in support of Darwin through the mid-1860s (the Civil War being, naturally, a serious interruption of the debate). In the Netherlands, a relatively small group of freethinkers eagerly welcomed *Origin*—for example, the Leiden zoologist H. H. Heys, who translated much of Darwin's later writing (he had failed to secure appointment to the professorship at Leiden because of conservative opposition).

Between these extremes were many who were supportive but cautious, or willing to accept Darwin's evolutionary theory with modifications or conditions. Among the leading scientists, even Asa Gray might be counted as a cautious defender because of his continuing insistence that natural selection could and should be understood teleologically and indeed as an argument for design, "at least while the physical cause of variation is utterly unknown and mysterious. . . .

---

13. For a detailed discussion, see William M. Montgomery, "Germany," in Glick, *Comparative Reception*, pp. 81–116.

The Darwinian system, as we understand it, coincides well with the theistic view of Nature. It not only acknowledges purpose . . . but builds upon it; and if purpose in this sense does not of itself imply design, it is certainly compatible with it and suggestive of it."[14]

Charles Lyell, who had contributed much to Darwin and strongly encouraged him, was nevertheless a reluctant convert. The tenth edition of his *Principles of Geology* (London, 1867–68) did help powerfully to demolish opposition to common descent, but Lyell was never able to make up his mind about natural selection. Pieter Harting, though described as Darwin's "most convinced defender in the Dutch academic world," nonetheless in his final statement on the "generally accepted" elements of evolutionary theory did not include "natural selection" or "struggle for life."[15] The geologist T. C. Winkler, while embracing natural selection, was typical of the Dutch modernists or mediators (where much of Darwin's support was located) in seeking rapprochement between science and religion and in interpreting the whole evolutionary process as ordered to the growing dominance of spirit over matter. The German scientific inheritors of the idealist tradition were inclined to opt for an internal developmental principle instead of natural selection.

In view of these divergent reactions, what does it mean to say, as is frequently affirmed, that the scientific debate was largely over by 1870?[16] It means that some kind of biological evolutionary theory was widely accepted, usually including the notion of common descent. It does not mean an adoption of Darwin's theory, especially the mechanism of natural selection. In describing the nature of Darwin's theory, we have seen an internal reason why natural selection could not be accepted prior to the development of modern genetics.

14. Gray, *Darwiniana*, pp. 121, 311. Since Gray was especially responsible for the early introduction of Darwin in America, this teleological interpretation moderated the initial theological response. It was Charles Hodge, fearful of what had happened in German materialism, who fostered a much more hostile response, which subsequently was reinforced by the theme of conflict with the Bible.

15. See Bulhof, in Glick, *Comparative Reception*, pp. 280, 263.

16. Ellegård, *Darwin and the General Reader*, certainly has grounds for saying that as early as 1870 the general idea of biological evolution was widely accepted among the educated in Britain. His study also confirms that evolutionary theory received the widest discussion in the newer scientific journals and the popular press. Frederick Burkhardt, in a detailed examination of the proceedings of the learned societies in England and Scotland, makes the interesting point that Darwin's *theory* was little discussed in those forums, largely because it was felt inappropriate to deal with speculative theory rather than facts (see Glick, *Comparative Reception*, pp. 32–79).

In fact, a considerable wave of scientific opposition to natural selection, abetted by Wallace's paper, emerged in England, and this was
strong enough so that in the United States Darwin's *Descent of Man*
caused much less stir than might otherwise have been the case. Evolution was certainly winning favor, but the nature of the cause of evolution was an open question. Edward Pfeifer, in reviewing the history
of Darwin's reception in the United States, concludes that "by the
end of the century there were probably more Neo-Lamarckians than
Darwinians in American science."[17]

In France, by 1900 transformism had won the day, but Darwin's
theory was certainly not dominant as the explanation. In Germany,
as we saw, natural selection (or external factors) had to compete with
internal developmental principles as the mechanism for changes in
species.

Obviously, the mixed reactions in the scientific community to various components of Darwin's theory had an important bearing on the
varieties of theological reception. Insofar as *The Origin of Species* became a focus or an impetus in what has pejoratively and mistakenly
been called by some a warfare between science and theology,[18] this
was the result not only of the defensiveness of some theologians but
also of the policy and program of some of Darwin's supporters. In
Germany, for example, well before they encountered Darwin, Büch-

17. Glick, *Comparative Reception*, p. 199. See also Pfeifer's earlier article, "The Genesis of
American Neo-Lamarckianism," *Isis* 56 (1965): 156–67. And see the important essay by
Leeds, "Darwinian and 'Darwinian' Evolutionism in the Study of Society and Culture," in
Glick, pp. 437–77.

18. John William Draper, *History of the Conflict between Religion and Science* (London,
1874), and Andrew Dickson White, *A History of the Warfare of Science with Theology in Christendom*, 2 vols. (London, 1896; see also his earlier *Warfare of Science* [London, 1876]), have
been important symbols of this general mythology. Draper's *History* went through fifty
printings in the U.S. in fifty years, twenty-one editions in Britain in fifteen years, and
translations in French, German, Italian, Dutch, Spanish, Polish, Japanese, Russian, Portu-
guese, and Serbian. Yet both Draper and White were theists, and they dealt very little with
Darwin (Draper's *History* says nothing about evolution, and White gives only twenty of nine
hundred pages to this debate). Draper's argument was almost entirely with Roman Catholicism, as the largest, most pretentious church, with the most claims to civil power—a church
whose hostility to modern progress was symbolized by the papal *Syllabus Errorum* (1864).

The military metaphor of these books was widely taken up, even by many who should
have known better. Moore, in *The Post-Darwinian Controversies*, shows conclusively how inappropriate this metaphor was to the actual serious discussion in the late nineteenth century, though also how influential the image was in subsequent histories. From the side of
the religionists, the notion of warfare did not become appropriate until the fundamentalist
antievolution crusade of the 1920s. See also F. M. Szasz, *The Divided Mind of Protestant
America, 1880–1930* (University, Ala., 1982).

ner and Vogt had rejected religious views in favor of forms of materialistic monism.[19] They found in Darwin ammunition for a battle they were already heartily waging. Even more harshly antagonistic to Christianity, and enormously influential in popularizing the idea of conflict, was Ernst Haeckel, who in the early 1860s undertook to convert Germany to Darwinism.[20]

In contrast to Haeckel, Huxley was more urbane and persuasive, very much in the style of the Victorian preacher, in his use of Darwin to champion the claims of science against the claims of Christianity (especially Roman Catholic theology). He repudiated materialism, and he had no adulation of scientists as persons. But for himself, he had already found in Carlyle a substitute for the faith of the church. Clemence Royer introduced her translation of *Origin* with antireligious polemic; the preface to the French translation of *The Descent of Man* included an 1869 speech by Vogt. Heys, in the Netherlands, was a freethinker as a student and, after his professional appointment at Leiden had been blocked, partly by conservative Protestants, became a vigorous opponent of the church and religion. Darwin was welcomed by freethinkers as a proclaimer of atheism and materialism and as a weapon against the mediators.

To make these observations is not at all to cast aspersions on the integrity of the authors' scientific work or their commitment to evolutionary views. Rather, we need to understand that Darwin could and did become a focus for an agenda already well established. On an even broader scale, Darwinism could become a symbol of antireligion for reasons that had little to do with the theory of evolution, as it did among the Social Democrats in Germany who hailed Haeckel and

19. See Ludwig Büchner, *Kraft und Stoff* (Frankfurt, 1855; Eng. trans., 1870), which went through many editions and was widely translated; and Carl Vogt, *Köhlerglaube und Wissenschaft* (Backwoods faith and science; Giessen, 1854). Vogt had also translated Chambers' *Vestiges* as *Natürliche Schöpfungsgeschichte* (2d ed., Brunswick, 1858). Already a thoroughgoing materialist (and a despiser of the clergy), Vogt was an eloquent and popular lecturer and, after the publication of *Origin*, he seized upon Darwin as the subject for European lecture tours.

20. Haeckel was a serious scientist, but had only the most superficial knowledge of Christian history. See his *Natürliche Schöpfungsgeschichte* (Berlin, 1868; Eng. trans., *The History of Creation* [London, 1876]), a rather popular work; *Anthropogenie* (Leipzig, 1874; Eng. trans., *The Evolution of Man* [New York, 1874]); and above all *Die Welträtsel* (Bonn, 1899; Eng. trans., *The Riddle of the Universe* [London, 1900]). The *Riddle* in particular was widely read, with 100,000 copies in print in German in the first year, and by 1914 over half a million copies in fourteen languages. Haeckel himself became a symbol almost as important as Darwin.

Büchner and claimed to find in Darwin the scientific justification of materialism and socialism. The logic was simple. Religion was opposed to the aspirations of the workers. "Darwinism" disproved religion. Therefore "Darwinism" supported socialism. But we should not forget the larger body of scientists who did not want to enter into public and popular debate about theology and science, whatever their scientific or religious conclusions.

VARIETIES OF RESPONSE: THEOLOGICAL

The variety of positions taken within the religious communities about the theological import of Darwinism in particular and of evolution in general may be sorted out along lines rather similar to the debate among scientists. Barring an exhaustive account of the significant theologians, a reasonable sample suggests a division among three typical patterns of response: (a) a judgment that a real conflict existed and that Darwinism, and to a lesser extent evolution, had to be rejected; (b) a cautious openness and mediation or accommodation; and (c) enthusiasm for evolutionary theory (of some sort) as a great step forward in the understanding of God and the world.

First, the vigorous opposition. Probably the best statement of this view by an Anglo-Saxon Protestant, and certainly the most influential, was that of Princeton Seminary's Charles Hodge. Hodge understood what Darwin was saying better than most theological commentators, and he took Agassiz as his scientific authority for Darwin's errors. On the theological side, Hodge's opposition was rooted especially in Darwinism's conflict with the teaching of scripture concerning the origin of man, and with the idea of design.[21]

Hodge was not a believer in mechanical inspiration of scripture, but in a plenary inspiration of what is taught in the whole Bible. The emphasis on what is taught allowed for a distinction between teaching and what might have been thought by biblical writers, permitting recognition of errors in scripture. But no error in teaching of fact in the Bible could be allowed. The teachings of biblical writers acting as spokesmen of God were infallible. Biblical authors might have believed the earth to be the center of the universe, but they didn't teach it. Isaiah was infallible in his predictions, but not in his cosmology.

---

21. See esp. Hodge, *What is Darwinism?* (New York, 1874); also *Systematic Theology*, vol. 2 (New York, 1872). For a brief general discussion of Hodge's theological stance, see *Prot. Thought*, 1:200–204.

Paul was infallible in his teaching, though he might not have remembered how many persons he baptized in Corinth.[22] The distinction between fact and biblical teaching on the one hand, and fallible human theory and interpretation on the other, made it possible for Hodge to come to terms with astronomy and geology. However, he counseled caution about too easy acceptance or rejection of any scientific theory.

But Darwinism, both in the principle of natural selection and in the idea of development from lower forms of life, was another matter. Darwinism ran counter both to the direct creative act of God (as distinct from secondary causation) in the making of man and to the reality of design or teleology in the world. It was thus atheistic, even though Darwin was no atheist:

> It is the distinctive doctrine of Mr. Darwin, that species owe their origin, not to the original intention of the divine mind; not to special acts of creation calling new forms into existence at certain epochs; not to the constant and everywhere operative efficiency of God, guiding physical causes in the production of intended effects; but to the gradual accumulation of unintended variations of structure and instinct, securing some advantage to their subjects. . . . All the innumerable varieties of plants, all the countless forms of animals, with all their instincts and faculties, all the varieties of men with their intellectual endowments, and their moral and religious nature, have, according to Darwin, been evolved by the agency of the blind, unconscious laws of nature. . . . The grand and fatal objection to Darwinism is this exclusion of design in the origin of species, or the production of living organisms. . . . The conclusion of the whole matter is, that the denial of design in nature is virtually the denial of god. . . . What is Darwinism? It is Atheism.[23]

The whole Darwinian hypothesis was thus directly contrary to the total Christian view of things. In this kind of judgment, and in the merging of the question of evolution with that of biblical inspiration, Hodge provided some of the substance and set the tone for much of the subsequent Protestant fundamentalist opposition to evolution. This was particularly the case in the American scene, with its bizarre Scopes trial in the 1920s and the restrictions even in the 1970s and

22. See Hodge, *Systematic Theology*, 1:165–70.
23. Hodge, *What is Darwinism?*, pp. 173–74.

1980s on the teaching of evolution in elementary school science courses.[24]

Conservative thinkers elsewhere expressed similar reactions. Near the end of his career, in a sermon preached at Oxford in 1878, the English Tractarian leader Edward Bouverie Pusey indicated a willingness to make concessions regarding the details of the Mosaic cosmogony, even including the possibility of evolution in orders of life below man. But since there was no proof of the evolution of man from lower forms (the "missing link"), he found it easier to believe in an immediate special creation of man, with an original perfection and fall. The British Methodist W. B. Pope could count the "days" of Genesis as epochs, but otherwise insisted that the story of Adam should not be tampered with. For him, the Darwinian theory had one fatal defect in not showing a link between the organic and the inorganic, and a second in the gap at the point of the appearance of man.[25]

On the other hand, the influential Dutch Calvinist theologian Abraham Kuyper (founder of the Free University of Amsterdam and later prime minister) found an ingenious way of looking at evolution "from a Christian point of view." Evolutionism had to be rejected as contrary to the teachings of the Bible, but evolution could be seen as a possible scientific hypothesis tentatively generated by human beings, not to be taken as factual statement or doctrine about reality. With a view to the disagreements among the evolutionists, he was hopeful for the disappearance of evolutionism as a world view. On this point, Kuyper represented a common position of the anti-Darwinists. They often relied heavily on scientists' objections to Darwin. They pointed to the incompleteness of the fossil record (admitted by Darwin), and they made much of the scientific questioning

24. Other Christian anti-Darwinists in North America included Enoch F. Burr, Congregational minister and for some years lecturer at Amherst College (*Pater Mundi* [two series, Boston, 1869 and 1873] and *Ecce Terra* [Philadelphia, 1883]); Luther T. Townsend, Methodist teacher of biblical languages at Boston Theological Seminary (see esp. *Biblical Theology and Modern Thought* [Boston, 1883]); the lawyer George T. Curtis (*Creation or Evolution? A Philosophical Inquiry* [New York, 1887]); and the McGill University naturalist John William Dawson (*Modern Ideas of Evolution as Related to Revelation and Science* [London, 1890]). The argument of these authors are summarized in Moore, *The Post-Darwinian Controversies*, pp. 197–204.

25. *Compendium of Christian Theology*, 3 vols. (London, 1875). See also the many pamphlets of the British rector Francis Morris, e.g., *The Demands of Darwin on Credulity* (London, 1890).

of natural selection and the lack of knowledge about the cause of variation.

Roman Catholic theological reactions were generally more negative than the Protestant responses through the late nineteenth century, even though the conflict was not as severe—Roman Catholicism was initially less threatened by the need to reinterpret scripture and less committed to natural theology of the Paley variety. As in the case of Protestantism, there was no single Catholic response, but multiple responses. The initial reaction to *Origin* in England was restrained and liberal. During the 1860s and 1870s, with some significant exceptions (such as St. George Jackson Mivart), opposition to Darwinism tended to harden. This tendency was represented by W. G. Ward and Edward Cardinal Manning, who were in regular combat with Huxley in the Metaphysical Society. Moreover, liberal hopes regarding the compatibility of Catholicism and science in general, which also involved a conflict over the freedom of thought, were dashed by the "Munich Brief" of Pope Pius IX in 1863, by his encyclical *Quanta Cura* (1864) and the accompanying *Syllabus Errorum*, and by the first Vatican Council (1869–70). The question of compatibility was later merged with the question of biblical criticism. On the whole, Karl Rahner has said, until the early twentieth century Roman Catholic theologians rejected the theory of evolution in favor of a literal interpretation of Genesis.[26]

Second, cautious mediation. In contrast to those who found Darwinism antithetical to Christianity, there were numerous and diverse thinkers who were ready to take up much of general evolutionary theory, including at least parts of Darwin's scheme. In England, for example, the Cambridge historian F. J. A. Hart wrote in 1860 that, in spite of the difficulties, he thought the *Origin* unanswerable. F. D. Maurice, on the principle that every genuine scientific discovery, insofar as it is true, is a revelation from God, found the spirit of Darwin's investigations a model and lesson for churchmen. Maurice's associate Charles Kingsley, who had sent thanks to Darwin for a prepublication copy of *Origin*, wrote to Maurice in 1863: "Darwin is conquering everywhere, and rushing in like a flood, by the mere force of truth and fact. The one or two who hold out are forced to try all sorts of subterfuges as to fact, or else by invoking the *odium theologicum.* . . . But they find that now they have got rid of an interfering

26. Root, "Catholics and Science," admirably traces the complexities of the British scene.

God—a master magician, as I call it—they have to choose between the absolute empire of accident, and a living, immanent, ever-working God."[27]

Charles Hodge's near neighbor and fellow Presbyterian James Mc-Cosh, a Scot who taught logic and metaphysics at Queens College, Belfast, before becoming president of Princeton University in 1868, was initially cautious about natural selection as the mechanism of evolution. But having earlier argued, in *The Method of Divine Government, Physical and Moral* (Edinburgh, 1850), that God works his will by law and spontaneous adaptations, he was able to conclude that natural selection and variation could be understood, on Calvinist grounds, as the operation of supernatural design. Progression from the inanimate to the animate and from the lower animate to the higher is clearly indicated. Science describes this process. Religion simply insists "that we trace all things up to God, whether acting by immediate or by mediate agency." One can believe in evolution, with the possible exception of the human soul and certain psychological phenomena, and remain a Christian because the works of God can be seen in evolution.[28]

Two other Princeton men, Joseph S. Van Dyke, a Presbyterian pastor and lecturer at the university (then the College of New Jersey), and Archibald Alexander Hodge, son of Charles Hodge and his successor in systematic theology at Princeton Seminary, were willing to come close to Darwin. Van Dyke published a volume called *Theism and Evolution* (London, 1886; with an introduction by Hodge) which was cautious, even timid, in its approach to Darwin, but far more favorable than Charles Hodge's work had been. Van Dyke was open to evolution as a biological theory which might one day be scientifically established, and he argued that Darwinism is not necessarily atheistic or in conflict with any statement in scripture. Variation and selection could be understood as occurring under the guidance of divine providence. The immutability of species is not a doctrine needed for defense of the scriptures. Plainly, Darwinism was not something to be

27. Kingsley, *Letters and Memories* (London, 1914), p. 253. See also *Scientific Lectures and Essays* (London, 1880).

28. See McCosh, *Christianity and Positivism: A Series of Lectures to the Times on Natural Theology and Apologetics* (New York, 1871), p. 63; and *The Religious Aspect of Evolution* (New York, 1890), pp. vii–x. McCosh was also influenced by Spencer, but in his later writings became more and more consistently Darwinian in his stress on natural selection as the mechanism of supernatural design, except for human origins.

enthusiastically welcomed, and A. A. Hodge thought it unable to account for man's spiritual nature (reason, conscience, and free will). But neither could it be rejected as absurd or simply incompatible with theism, providence, and scripture.

Even the twelve volumes of *The Fundamentals* (Chicago, 1910–15), from which the aggressive fundamentalism of the 1920s was to take its name, were not basically antievolutionist, though they did contain two antievolutionary essays. They also included works by authors who accepted evolution: Benjamin B. Warfield of Princeton Seminary, who thought evolution might be a tenable theory of providential working; James Orr of Glasgow, who had earlier supported the probability of the hypothesis of evolution as applied to the organic world and was even able to say that evolution might be recognized as only a new name for creation; and the Oberlin College geologist George F. Wright, who in the mid-1870s joined with Asa Gray in defense of Darwinism.

Albert Barnes of Philadelphia was another judicious conservative. In his Ely Lectures on *The Evidence of Christianity in the Nineteenth Century* (New York, 1868), he articulated a common theme, namely, that science and religion cannot be in conflict. Not everything in the Bible is revelation, and nothing significant in scripture will ever be denied by science. Thus science can help us in purifying religion of false and nonessential myths.

Frederick Temple, bishop of Exeter and later archbishop of Canterbury, sounded an especially frequent note. He recalled in his 1884 Bampton Lectures that many great Christian thinkers from early times had regarded the creation accounts as allegories. He was open to the notion that man, over a long period of time, developed in an evolutionary manner like animals, though perhaps along distinctive lines. God then provided a soul by a creative act, or transformed the animating principle into the image of God. That is, man was physically prepared, then spiritually endowed by direct divine action (a kind of adoptionist view). Such a view could not be invalidated by science.[29]

Rudolf Schmid of Stuttgart may serve as an illustration of the

---

29. Temple, *The Relation between Religion and Science* (London, 1885), esp. pp. 176–85. In 1860, on the day after the confrontation between Wilberforce and Huxley, Temple had preached a sermon at Oxford, urging a deep identity between the Book of God and the Book of Nature and proposing to find the finger of God in all the laws the scientists could discover in the universe.

moderate position in Germany. In his discussion of Darwin's theories, he distinguished between Darwin and his materialistic interpreters Büchner and Haeckel. He was puzzled by Darwin's praise of them, for he did not see anything in Darwin himself that was hostile to theism or teleology. Darwinism could even be, for many, a confirmation of the religious view of the world. "Even those occurrences and phenomena, the natural causes of which he has learned to know through science, are not excluded from [the religious person's] standpoint by the knowledge of their causes and laws of their actions."[30] The conservative Ritschlian Julius Kaftan similarly distinguished between Darwin and Darwinism—though Ritschl and the group most influenced by him (an example is Herrmann) seldom referred directly to Darwin, their concern being with the broader problem of a scientific world view and with distinguishing between the judgments of science and those of faith.

We may link the work of the English Roman Catholic biologist St. George Jackson Mivart with these moderating Protestant views. Even after his abandonment of Darwinism in 1869, Mivart did much to propagate the view that evolution and Catholic theology need not be in conflict. Though critical of difficulties in Darwin's theory, particularly the notions of natural selection as the sole mechanism and the elimination of any difference in kind between the mental faculties of man and the higher animals, he found the idea of the organic evolution of the human body reconcilable with theology. The conflict came rather from the metaphysical antitheistic biases so often associated with Darwinism.[31]

Third, the exaltation of evolution. The enthusiasm with which evolutionary theory could be adopted as a support rather than an obstacle to Christianity is vividly illustrated in the contributions of two of the authors of *Lux Mundi*, the 1889 manifesto of liberal Anglo-Catholicism. Aubrey Moore, writing on "The Christian Doctrine of God," proclaimed:

> The one absolutely impossible conception of God, in the present day, is that which represents Him as an occasional Visitor. Science had pushed the deist's God farther and farther away, and at the mo-

30. Schmid, *The Scientific Creed of a Theologian* (Stuttgart, 1906; Eng. trans., New York, 1906), p. 8. See also *The Theories of Darwin and Their Relation to Philosophy, Religion, and Morality* (Stuttgart, 1876; Eng. trans., Chicago, 1883).

31. See esp. Mivart, *On the Genesis of Species*, 2d ed. (London, 1871); *Man and Apes* (London, 1873); *Lessons from Nature as Manifested in Mind and Nature* (London, 1876).

ment when it seemed as if He would be thrust out altogether, Darwinism appeared, and, under the disguise of a foe, did the work of a friend. It has conferred upon philosophy and religion an inestimable benefit, by showing us that we must choose between alternatives. Either God is everywhere present in nature, or He is nowhere. He cannot be here, and not there. He cannot delegate His power to demigods called "second causes." In nature everything must be His work or nothing. We must frankly return to the Christian view of direct divine agency, the immanence of divine power in nature from end to end, the belief in a God in Whom not only we, but all things have their being, or we must banish Him altogether. It seems as if, in the providence of God, the mission of modern science was to bring home to our unmetaphysical ways of thinking the great truth of the Divine immanence in creation, which is not less essential to the Christian idea of God than to a philosophical view of nature.[32]

Even apart from the scientific evidence, Moore found evolution infinitely more Christian as a theory than the theory of special creation, because a notion of occasional intervention implies a theory of ordinary absence (here Moore opposed Frederick Temple, whose book he had reviewed in 1885, finding it essentially deistic).

Similarly, though a bit more cautiously, in his *Lux Mundi* essay on "The Incarnation in Relation to Development," J. R. Illingworth insisted that there is nothing whatever to fear from closing the present chasms in evolutionary theory: "If the remaining barriers between unreason and reason, or between lifelessness and life should . . . one day vanish [as have many of those between species], we shall need to readjust the focus of our spiritual eye to the enlarged vision, but nothing more. Our Creator will be known to have worked otherwise indeed than we had thought, but in a way quite as conceivable, and to the imagination more magnificent." Illingworth argued that an organic teleology furnishes "a far worthier and grander view of teleology than the mechanical theory of earlier days." And we must affirm the "element of truth in that higher Pantheism which is so common in the present day . . . we need not fear to transgress the limits of the

32. *Lux Mundi: A Series of Studies in the Religion of the Incarnation*, ed. Charles Gore (London, 1889; cited from the 5th English ed., 1890), p. 82. Aubrey Lackington Moore (1843 –90) was then tutor at Magdalen and Keble colleges, Oxford. He was widely read in contemporary science; he understood Darwin; and he did as much as any single person to break down the opposition to evolution in the English church. See also his *Science and Faith: Essays on Apologetic Subjects* (London, 1889), and *Essays Scientific and Philosophical* (London, 1890).

Christian tradition in saying that the physical immanence of God the Word in His creation can hardly be overstated, as long as His moral transcendence of it is also kept in view."[33]

Not unlike Aubrey Moore, James Iverach of the Free Church College, Aberdeen (where he taught from 1887 to 1907), argued for a Christian Darwinism—and he strongly criticized Spencerian notions of evolution. Iverach had studied Darwin and was persuaded that natural selection actually strengthens the argument for design, so that it becomes more cogent than in Paley's time. Together with variation, whose laws have not yet been discovered, natural selection provides a proximate explanation of the purposeful guidance by the will of God. Human existence is not an exception to the total process. Though human rationality and self-consciousness are unique, they cannot be attributed to a difference in origin, for there is only one origin, the creative and continuous power of God who is immanent in the world. It is simply not possible to think of God as sometimes absent from his creation—else he is always absent—and acting only at a crisis. He is always present and ever at work in the process.[34]

George Frederick Wright, for twenty years a New England pastor, then professor of New Testament language and literature at Oberlin (from 1881) and editor of *Bibliotheca Sacra*, as well as an authority on glacial geology, represented a striking attempt to combine Calvinist theology with the cause of Darwinism. An early associate of Asa Gray, he was in large part responsible for the publication of Gray's *Darwiniana* in 1876 and went on to extend Gray's view. In his own writings, the *Logic of Christian Evidences* (1880) and *Studies in Science and Religion* (1882), he argued vigorously for a close analogy between Darwinism and Calvinist theology. Though not uncritical of Darwin, especially in his later writings, Wright continued to hold to the compatibility of Calvinism and Darwinism. Both assume the genetic unity of mankind; both are hypotheses based on probable or moral evidence; both assert the sovereign rule of law in nature; both reject the notion of invariable and progressive development; and Darwinism poses no new problems for an inclusive final causation. Further, Wright contended that the best science, as represented by the modesty of Darwin's theory, was on the side of Christian orthodoxy

33. See *Lux Mundi*, pp. 159–62.

34. See esp. Iverach, *Christianity and Evolution* (London, 1894), and *Theism in the Light of Present Science and Philosophy* (London, 1899).

rather than liberalism. Darwinism could indeed be described as the Calvinistic interpretation of nature. In Wright's view, Calvinism can encompass any reasonable system of evolution, including natural selection, and evolution needs only to embrace the Calvinist view of divine sovereignty.[35]

However, most of the enthusiasts for evolution, and certainly the best known, were not Darwinians. The foremost American preacher of the late nineteenth century, Henry Ward Beecher of Plymouth Church, Boston, was much more Spencerian in his idea of evolution. Recognizing that evolution was not only accepted as the working theory everywhere in physical science but was also held by men of profound Christian faith, he judged that despite the need for theological reconstruction, true religion had nothing to fear. "Design by wholesale is grander than design by retail." Beecher's successor in Boston, Lyman Abbott, had no qualms about joining the theistic evolutionists, and he spoke and wrote widely for the acceptability of evolution (chiefly in the vein of the neo-Lamarckian naturalist Joseph Le Conte), even coming to call himself a "radical evolutionist."[36]

Probably no one (with the possible exception of the lay philosopher and historian John Fiske [1842–1901], the chief American interpreter of Spencer) promoted the cause of evolution among the clergy of England and America with more enthusiasm than the Scottish writer and revivalist Henry Drummond. Like Moore and Illingworth, he found that "the idea of an immanent God, which is the God of evolution, is infinitely grander than the occasional miracle-worker, which is the God of the old theology." And he added a further dimension: evolution is throughout a moral process, not only a struggle for life (which the biologists recognized) but also a struggle for the life of others. Thus he could rhapsodize:

> What is Evolution? A method of creation. What is its object? To make more perfect living beings. What is Christianity? A method of

35. See Wright, *The Logic of Christian Evidences* (London, 1880); *Studies in Science and Religion* (Andover, Mass., 1882); *Scientific Aspects of Christian Evidences* (New York, 1898); and *The Origin and Antiquity of Man* (London, 1912). Moore, *The Post-Darwinian Controversies*, pp. 280–98, gives a full account of Wright's work. He argues that Darwinism as an evolutionary theory was appropriated more readily by orthodox theology, especially Calvinism, than by theological liberalism, which took up other ideas of evolution.

36. Beecher, *Evolution and Religion* (New York, 1885); see esp. pp. 113, 115; Abbott, *The Theology of an Evolutionist* (Boston, 1897). Newman Smyth was a similar popularizer of evolutionary ideas in biology and theology, suggesting that the new theologians be trained biologists, to see what the hand of God had wrought in nature.

creation. What is its object? To make more perfect living beings. Through what does Evolution work? Through love. Through what does Christianity work? Through love. Evolution and Christianity have the same author, the same end, the same spirit. Christianity . . . adopted man's body, mind, and soul at the exact level where Organic Evolution was at work upon them; and through processes governed by rational laws, it put the finishing touches to the Ascent of Man.[37]

To such witnesses one might add the prime formulator of the "New Theology," R. J. Campbell, for an extreme immanentist view, as well as the British Unitarian spokesman James Martineau, and Auguste Sabatier in Paris, though Martineau and Sabatier were at least equally concerned with the evolution of culture and religion. But the list need not be extended. These samples already make clear that the idea of evolution was being powerfully coupled with the theme of divine immanence and was becoming a dominant motif for the interpretation of religious history.

BUT WHAT HAPPENED TO DARWIN?

Ernst Troeltsch remarked in 1903, surveying the current theological situation, that the earlier enthusiasm for Darwin "now seems like a fleeting intoxication."[38] The controversy over evolution, except in the case of extreme Protestant conservatism and, for other reasons, Roman Catholicism, did indeed seem to have been resolved. Evolution was accepted as not being in conflict with theology but even supportive of new and truer theological insight.

But not often was it Darwinian theory that had been so baptized. In Germany, as Troeltsch went on to say, the Darwinian hypothesis was replaced by a much more general idea of development. In America, where in biology neo-Lamarckianism was as important as Darwinism in 1900, elements of Darwin were taken up (or confused) with vaguer concepts of evolution that owed at least as much to the "synthetic philosophy" of Herbert Spencer. Spencer was widely considered the philosopher of British Darwinism, but his vogue is better accounted for by the way in which his "law of evolution" was combined with the cause of individual rights, free enterprise, laissez-

---

37. See *The Ascent of Man* (New York, 1894), pp. 45–46, 428, 438–39; also *The Natural Law in the Spiritual World* (London, 1883; 8th ed., 1884).

38. *Gesammelte Schriften* (Tübingen, 1913; Aalen, 1962), 2:6.

faire, voluntary association, and progress, a combination singularly suited to appeal to elements of the late-nineteenth-century American mind.[39]

The popularity of Spencer was also partly due to promotion by his principal American champion, John Fiske. Fiske was an avowed defender of Darwin, though with a theistic interpretation that rejected natural selection as the explanation for the distinguishing features of the human species. But he was actually much closer to Spencer, believing that in his own *Cosmic Philosophy* he had gone beyond Spencer in showing how the evolutionary idea could serve religion. Fiske's blend of evolution and idealism was developed into a view not only of the marvelous moral power at work in the past but also of the glorious future that lies ahead. His philosophical vision had little to do with classical Christian theology, but it was influential among unitarians and liberal trinitarians, and it too was a doctrine well suited to the optimism and spirit of progress of the late nineteenth century.[40]

By the turn of the century the evolutionary principle was broadly accepted, even hailed, among Protestant liberal and moderate thinkers. Some, like Aubrey Moore and James Iverach, were genuinely familiar with Darwin and were prepared to take up his theory in theological reconstruction. Most, however, in their acceptance of evolution, were dealing with much more generalized notions. These included the principle of common descent, though there were occasional reservations with respect to the origin of the soul or the spiritual in man, and the ideas were often more Lamarckian than Darwinian. The general idea of evolution was also widely adopted as the key to the history of mankind and religion, both in the transition from primitive to higher forms of religion and in the growth of the Judeo-Christian tradition. The acceptance of biological and cultural evolution was seen as providing massive support for optimism about the future course of human history.

Social Darwinism, an attempt to justify competition and give a rationale for laissez-faire capitalism, is sometimes referred to as a per-

39. At the same time, the frequent association of Spencer with the positivism of Comte helped to reinforce the hostility to Darwin among some conservative Reformed thinkers. See the useful account by Charles D. Cashdollar, "Auguste Comte and the American Reformed Theologians," *Journal of the History of Ideas*, 39:1 (1978): 61–79.

40. See esp. *Outlines of Cosmic Philosophy* (Boston, 1875); *The Destiny of Man Viewed in the Light of His Origin* (Boston, 1892), a work much reprinted; and *Through Nature to God* (Boston, 1899).

vasive American movement. But it was a relatively minor theme, depending more on Spencer's ambiguous competitive individualism than on Darwin. The commitment to economic struggle, with merited success and deserved failure, was only rarely justified by appeal to biological principles of struggle and survival. Among the important intellectuals in America, probably only the Yale social scientist William Graham Sumner could properly be called a Social Darwinist.[41]

But it is equally evident that if the debate with Darwinian theory had largely ended by 1900, it had not quite taken place. Many of the evolutionary enthusiasts (such as Lyman Abbott and Henry Drummond) had little familiarity with Darwin, and their idea of evolution was usually not his, just as their theology was hardly traditional. (And recall again that the questions of variation and natural selection were still much debated among scientists.) Most of the discussion of theology and evolution was carried on by religionists with simplistic ideas of design and teleology, as well as of Darwin and Spencer, and by scientists with simplistic ideas of theology, which took no account of the major theological revisions already under way. Hence the story of the debate is often dreary.[42]

In a basic sense the issue with Darwin was hardly joined. The debate waned in part because other issues crowded it out: historical questions associated with the quest for the historical Jesus and with the relation of faith and historical judgments; questions raised by the new research in anthropology and comparative religion regarding the origin of religion and the supremacy of Christianity; and questions about the derivative or distinctive nature of early Christianity in the Near Eastern world (see chapters 4 and 5, above).

For some thinkers, a kind of détente had been achieved through the mutual self-limitation of scientific and theological assertions. Particularly in the Ritschlian tradition theologians wanted to define genuine religious judgments as utterly distinct from all theoretical or scientific judgments (whether of natural or historical science) in such

41. See, e.g, Wilson, *Darwinism*, chap. 3, "Darwinism and Social Ethics"; also Robert C. Bannister, *Social Darwinism: Science and Myth in Anglo-American Social Thought* (Philadelphia, 1979).

42. Another major exception among the theologians (along with Moore, Wright, and Iverach) was F. R. Tennant, who in *The Origin and Propagation of Sin* (Cambridge, 1902) made a serious and sustained attempt to restate the account of the origin of mankind and of human evil. But Tennant had little following.

fashion that science could never threaten religion. They were developing in extreme form Schleiermacher's (in contrast to Hegel's) option for understanding the relation of religious truth to the rest of human experience (see *Prot. Thought*, 1:106–07). At the same time, a principle of scientific restraint led numerous scientists to insist that scientific conclusions were methodologically limited to natural causes. Science, qua science, could make no pronouncements at all regarding ultimate causes or philosophical explanations or interpretations arising from other perspectives. Thus, for some, both scientists and theologians, the problem could be considered resolved in this other way.

Confused and unfinished as it was, the debate over Darwinism was nevertheless productive and of profound consequence for religious thinking. Darwin's influence must not be underestimated. Under the impact of his revolution, the whole metaphysical view of things had to be reoriented, as it was in the views of process taken by Henri Bergson, William James, and John Dewey. Where metaphysics could continue, it could not be the older idealism. Mechanical or essence models had to be exchanged for organic and processive models. Mankind's place in the world process had to be reconsidered. For theological reflection, the change in world view required fundamental reconsideration of the nature of God and God's relation to the world (which, to be sure, had already been going on since the beginning of the century). Other ways had to be found in the twentieth century for understanding the relation of science and theology, ways that did not involve relying on scripture as science-like description or on the confusion of scientific data and theory with metaphysical (materialistic or atheistic) dogma.

The outcome of the real debate was thus neither simple evasion nor simple détente, but some of each; it was also an impulse to theological reconstruction. On the popular level, the course of the discussion both symbolized and contributed to the growing secularization of the Western mind in the nineteenth century. In this context, what was significant was not the specific problem of theological ideas and evolutionary theories, but the way the discussion of evolution symbolized changing social attitudes. Never mind whether religion and science were really in conflict; they were increasingly *thought* to be in conflict.

7

Ethics, Church, and Culture

In volume 1 of this study I suggested that the principal question for Protestant thought in the last third of the nineteenth century was Christianity and culture, whereas in the earlier periods of the century the chief problems had been the possibility of theology and the possibility of Christology (*Prot. Thought*, 1:4–7). But is this true? So far, in looking at the late-nineteenth-century scene, we have said little directly about the topic of church and society, approaching the period from somewhat different angles of vision: the views of faith, of faith and history, of religion and the religions, and of religion and science.

Yet it is also true that the question of Christianity and culture has been present in all the dimensions of the latter part of the century that we have so far surveyed, from the work of Ritschl on: in the question of the certainty of faith, viewed in relation to other modes of knowing, and the attempt to justify religious experience in its own terms (chapter 2); in the question of the relation of faith, as seen from within, to objective ways of viewing religious experience (chapter 3); in the question of faith and modern historical science (chapter 5); in the question of Christianity and other religions (chapter 4); and in the question of religion and natural science, as focused by the discussion of evolution (chapter 6).

We now approach the question of Christianity and culture more directly from the standpoint of the concern for ethics, the third principal late-nineteenth-century focus of Protestant thought, along with faith and history. But in doing this, we need to recognize that the question of church and society is essentially related to the question of authority and freedom, of continuity and reform, within the church. Indeed, these are not, finally, two different questions but two ways of describing a single problem. Viewed as an internal problem for the church, it may be called the question of freedom and authority or criticism and tradition. Viewed as an external problem, it may be called the question of church and society or Christ and culture.

Hence, the theological response to the nineteenth-century critique of Christianity needs to be treated both in terms of the tension between freedom and authority and in terms of a new Christian ethical approach to society.

THE SOCIAL CRITIQUE OF CHRISTIANITY

What was the really new element in nineteenth-century criticism of the Christian view of things? Surely not the vigor of the intellectual objections to theological formulations, for it would be hard to surpass the intensity of the Enlightenment attacks that had been made by the radical deists, by the French philosophes, by Hume, and by Kant. The forms of the critique, however, were often new, as in Feuerbach, Marx, Nietzsche, and Freud, and in sociological and psychological reductionism generally. These kinds of criticisms may well have had a more pervasive impact just because their bases were more internal to religious experience than the typical Enlightenment attacks had been. They had special power because they stimulated and were surrounded by larger changes in social consciousness.

Most broadly stated, what was new by the close of the nineteenth century was the extent to which the religious (Christian) view of life had begun to be displaced from the center of Western consciousness. The dominant religious views of the past still largely obtained, at least at the level of conscious belief. People who were no longer church-going were still "Christian." European culture still retained its Christian substance and form, even where it was a post-Enlightenment Christendom, proud to be open, liberal, scientific, civilized, and modern. Victorian doubt (see *Prot. Thought*, 1:184–85), however pervasive it may have been, was still doubt within a generally accepted cultural and religious structure. Conservatism was still the rule rather than the exception even among the intelligentsia of the church—recall the mid-nineteenth-century upwelling of conservatism in both Protestant and Catholic quarters, as well as the revivals in Germany and the United States. The academic theological rebels against Christianity were not within the establishment, but were actually rebels *against* academic and social-political establishments. The new biblical-critical and scientific ideas had to surmount religious controversy in order to be culturally accepted. And in 1900, except in America, the idea of a unity of church and state still prevailed among non-Catholics as well as Catholics.

Yet the religious view had truly begun to be displaced from the center of the cultural consciousness by the secularization of the European mind. Western society at the end of the nineteenth century was not yet a post-Christian society, but the path already pointed clearly in that direction. To describe this process adequately would require a full social history, but we can at least sketch in broad strokes some of the elements in the change.

In the realm of the social critique of Christianity, nothing was more powerful than the impact of Marxism. Karl Marx was no militant atheist, as compared with Feuerbach or Bruno Bauer or the later German philosophical materialists, although he was an uncompromising one in the sense that denial of the existence of a divine being was fundamental to his outlook.[1] For Marx, both Bauer and Feuerbach had unmasked religion by showing its real truth as an epiphenomenon, a reflection of human nature, and he could declare in the introduction to his 1844 *Contribution to the Critique of Hegel's Philosophy of Right* that "criticism of religion is the premise of all criticism."[2] Yet that criticism had in Germany been largely completed, Marx said. He did not have an interest in the kind of antireligious fight that came to characterize later communists. The real enemy was the perverted social order, of which religion was a consequence. Christianity was, if not dead, at least in extremis. And one could not hasten its death by direct attack but only by putting the world straight. Then religion would simply vanish. As Marx put it in the fourth of the *Theses on Feuerbach* (1845): "Feuerbach starts out from the fact of religious self-alienation, the duplication of the world into a religious, imaginary world and a real one. His work consists in the dissolution of the religious world into its secular basis. He overlooks the fact that after this work is completed the chief thing still remains to be done." That chief thing, Marx went on to say in the concluding

1. He was a materialist only in a loose sense of the word. His "historical materialism" was not an ontological materialism, a theory of being in which only matter is real. For Marx, historical materialism was a theory of action, in contrast to those materialisms that are contemplative theories of being reducing humanity to nature rather than dialectically relating consciousness and nature. Marx's materialism was directed to reflecting on praxis in order to further it. (See, e.g., the *Theses on Feuerbach*.)

2. See *Karl Marx and Friedrich Engels on Religion* (New York, 1964), p. 41. This is a convenient and useful selection from the major writings. See also T. B. Bottomore, ed. and trans., *Karl Marx: Early Writings* (New York, 1964) and T. B. Bottomore and Maximilien Ruben, *Karl Marx: Selected Writings in Sociology and Social Philosophy* (London, 1956). The standard editions of Marx's works are Karl Marx and Friedrich Engels, *Historisch-Kritische Gesamtausgabe* (Berlin and Frankfurt, 1927–35); *Werke* (Berlin, 1956–   ); and *Collected Works*, trans. Richard Dixon et al. (London, 1975–).

thesis, is not to interpret the world, as the philosophers have done, but to change it. The call to abandon the illusory happiness of men, which is religion, in favor of a demand for real happiness, is the call to abandon a social condition that requires illusion.

Here then is one side of Marx's critique. Religion is no longer an enemy worth fighting, since it is already done for. To fight against the divine is to take it too seriously. Social action eliminates the need to think about religion any more.

But on another side, particularly when it was recognized that religion was not dying as rapidly as expected, Marx's analysis could be a basis for the kind of militancy that led workers in the German Social Democratic Party to hail Ernst Haeckel's campaign for Darwinism with wild enthusiasm, inasmuch as it was a campaign against religion. Religious alienation, for Marx, is one of the several self-estrangements or alienations that private property and modern industry produce in humanity. It gives a sacred halo to the ideology and to the political and economic power of the ruling class. Religion is thus antirevolutionary. It is the opiate of the people. It could be seen by Marx's followers as a brake slowing history from taking its predicted course. Christianity and the Christian churches could become a genuine enemy, with oppressive social and political doctrines and with organizations that opposed the interests of the proletariat. So, in an interesting qualification, if not a reversal, of Marx's idea that the transformation of society would make religion superfluous, a struggle against religion could be a precondition, or at least an essential element, in the transformation of the social condition.

In the latter nineteenth century, virulence in socialist hostility to Christianity was more characteristic of the Continental situation than of the British or American scene.[3] Germany was more powerfully in-

---

3. An exception to this generalization is the English Marxist Ernest Belfort Bax who, writing almost at the time of the decline of aggressive secularism in Britain, could charge that Christianity as a moral force had largely failed, that "the old theological questions" had "no more ethical or religious importance than . . . the origin of the irregular Greek verbs," that the worship of "a semi-mythical Syrian of the first century" had produced only "a morbid, eternally-revolving-in-upon-itself transcendent morality," and that the Christian "ethic" had tried to impose "an impossible standard of 'personal holiness' which, when realized, has seldom resulted in anything but (1) an apotheosized priggism (e.g., the Puritan type), or (2) an epileptic hysteria (e.g., the Catholic saint type)" (*The Religion of Socialism*, 3d ed. [London, 1891], pp. xi, 96–98; cited by Peter d'A. Jones in *The Christian Socialist Revival, 1877–1914: Religion, Class, and Social Conscience in Late-Victorian England* [Princeton, 1968], p. 3.)

fluenced by atheist-materialist strains of thought; Britain suffered under doubt and anxiety, and the United States was affected more by optimism (and less by open departure from the churches than by the proliferation of sects). Yet plainly in England, the site of the first wave of the industrial revolution, the church was an immediate focus for alienation, an evident part of the unjust established order in its alliance with the economically and politically powerful. The socialism that gained strength among the working class in England, especially during the depression of 1884–87, grew more and more distant from religion. To be sure, the Independent Labour Party, the Labour Church movement, and the Socialist Sunday Schools (which all emerged in the 1890s and gave mass organizational form to the socialist movement) drew strength away from the Marxism of the Social Democratic Federation and sought to maintain a friendliness, or at least neutrality, toward religion. But the Labour Churches, begun explicitly as an attempt to develop the religious life of the labor movement, declined and became more an effort to see the labor movement as itself a religious reality, more Ethical Culture than Christianity. Even the Socialist Sunday School movement of the early 1900s began sharply to distinguish politics as a separate activity from Christianity. Basically, the working-class movement in the cities came to have an irreligious character, and even in places where Marxism was not strong, the feeling grew among workers that socialism and atheism were related.

In the United States, the situation was still more complex. It is generally agreed that there was alienation of the urban workers from institutional religion. Yet industrialization came later in America than in Britain. It is difficult to separate a historic "working class" from the widely varying groups of immigrants. The revival tradition was strong at the grass-roots level, and the most oppressed group, the blacks, remained deeply religious for many reasons. Further, in the pluralistic tradition of America, dispossessed groups often tended to found their own sects, which were frequently apolitical and not at all radical in economic or political views, though a widespread populism could support various social gospels. The British and German working classes had greater homogeneity and concentration, which nurtured class consciousness.

It would be a mistake, of course, to treat estrangement from the church as wholly a function of working-class feelings of oppression or to give a purely economic explanation for the movement of established religion to the periphery of interest. One may note, for example, the formation in England in the 1850s of the Secular Societies, from which the term *secularism* comes, and the various Halls of Science that were established for regular lectures and meetings. The Secular Societies were not simply antireligious, and they were committed to maintenance of the prevailing codes of social behavior. There were strong differences in the movement between those who favored cooperation with Christian liberals in social reform and those who reflected a more militant desire to maintain purity in the antireligious dimension, consistently identifying secularism and atheism. The secularism of these societies was originally defined as a devotion to this world, whose issues could be tested in this life, and the term *secular* was originally chosen to avoid the immediate connotations of atheism and infidelity (the standard terms for any sort of religious deviance). Yet the goal of disentangling morality from theology and developing a scientific morality was not in doubt.[4]

The Secular Societies were never very large, and their attendance declined in the mid-1880s at the same time as the marked decline in church attendance, which suggests both the extent to which the Secular Societies had become a sect and the fact that the decline in church attendance may testify more to changes in social custom than to alterations in belief. Similarly modest numbers populated the Secularists' cognate and successor groups founded in the 1890s, the Ethical Union and the Rationalist Press Association. The latter promoted the kind of enthronement of reason represented by Thomas Paine's *Age of Reason*, a work regularly reprinted by the association, and joined this to the mythology of the warfare of religion and science.[5]

Yet such movements were symbolic of much broader phenomena in their objection to the requirement of submission to authority, especially ecclesiastical authority, in contrast to the right of individual judgment, and in a growing tendency to do without religion. Here, perhaps, connections can be drawn to the wider social and political liberalism of the century. How to define that liberalism is a puzzle,

---

4. Comte was of no small importance here, as also in the German scene, where the term *Säkularisation* emerged in the 1880s in the "moral" context, as a secularization of morality, to free it from its basis in theology. Comte was important in cultivating the idea of a different basis for morality, strictly "scientific," freeing morality from religion, though by founding a new religion of humanity.

5. On the British movements, see esp. Susan Budd, *Varieties of Unbelief: Atheists and Agnostics in English Society, 1850–1960* (London, 1977).

for the word could mean almost anything the user chose it to mean. One might say, only half in jest, that it meant whatever Pope Pius IX had in mind when in the last proposition of the Syllabus of Errors he condemned the view that the Pope should reconcile himself "with progress, with liberalism, and with modern civilization." For whatever liberalism was, it was rightly seen as an onrushing force of the age. One can better associate the word with John Stuart Mill's essay *On Liberty*, published in the same year as Darwin's *Origin of Species*. Though Mill was concerned particularly to stress liberty of the individual and of groups against the new tyranny of the elected majority (old tyrannies being quite familiar), the ideas that hover around the word *liberalism* are manifold: liberty and freedom of individual conscience as a good in itself, justice as equality before the law, tolerance, an open society (open to irreligious as well as to religious opinion—a secular state), liberty as the way to human development, responsibility, and morality. And whatever else liberalism meant, it was associated with criticism of authority and establishment. It was a quality of life, a good in itself.

With the emergence of the modern sense of the term *secularization* we may also connect the rise of modern anticlericalism. The words *clericalism* and *anticlericalism* first appeared in French and English dictionaries in the early 1860s. The meaning was no longer antagonism to the priestly profession, for that sort of suspicion and antipathy had existed as long as the profession itself. What was now meant by anticlericalism, as it came to express the bitterness in modern mass society, was opposition to ecclesiastical power. This hostility was of course directed especially toward Roman Catholic church power, and it flourished in France, since Catholicism was so much a part of the life of that country. Yet anticlericalism was geographically much more widespread and could be directed not only toward Catholic authoritarian regimes or papal power, but also toward Catholic parties, even liberal parties, in relatively democratic situations. As Owen Chadwick notes, "In Belgium the Catholic party accepted all the principles of 1789. They played the political game according to liberal principles and won their spectacular triumph immediately after the introduction of universal suffrage. When in power they were a Catholic social party—developing the welfare state for the worker. Yet their power fostered the rise of anticlerical opinion."[6]

---

6. Owen Chadwick, *The Secularization of the European Mind in the Nineteenth Century* (Cambridge, Eng., 1975), p. 116.

Anticlericalism in Lutheran or Anglican or Presbyterian countries expressed resentment of churchly power allied (or identical) with the power of the establishment. That the church should have been identified with conservative forces, whether explicitly in the Throne and Altar motif of mid-nineteenth-century German Lutheranism or more vaguely in the consciousness that Anglicanism and Presbyterianism were essential elements in the continuities of English and Scottish life and thus integral to the establishment, is not surprising. The religious sense involves a high degree of loyalty to the past and to perpetuation of the past order in the present. The growing estrangement of the working class from the church was due in no small part to the feeling that the church was on the side of authority and privilege, insensitive to the plight of the urbanized and industrialized worker. It is worth recalling that, until the advent of the welfare state in Europe, access by the poor to medical care, housing, and employment was to a great extent under the control of the clergy.[7]

In addition to the growth of anticlericalism, wide-ranging changes in religious belief were occurring at the popular as well as at more sophisticated levels. It is impossible to speak with confidence of such changes because of the notorious lack of reliable detailed information on shifts in popular belief. Yet a few generalizations may be hazarded. Belief in the infallibility of scripture was being deeply eroded in the latter half of the century. One source of evidence for this is the very intensity of the insistence on biblical infallibility that characterized proto-fundamentalism in America, both in the orthodox Princeton school (see chapter 5, above) and in the Bible school movement that took root in the 1890s. The only really comprehensive analysis of popular press response to the Darwinian theory makes it clear that Darwin was used mainly as a weapon in ideological

7. It must be remembered that religious conservatism (and, later, fundamentalism) also got strong support from the working class, often as a function of lower-class status and lack of education. Religious liberals tended to be from the middle and upper classes, as in the *Freie Theologie* in Germany and in the freethinkers and the unitarians (and perhaps the Quakers) in Britain and America.

In relation to the church, we may also recall the emergence of the idea of *Kulturkampf*, a term invented to denote the struggle for civilization against ecclesiastical obscurantism—though Bismarck's Kulturkampf was directed against Roman Catholicism, was ostensibly conducted in the name of evangelical freedom, and was certainly not a liberal movement. In respect to matters of belief, we may think of the tone of the 1912 Oxford volume, *Foundations*. That was hardly a document of popular religion, but as Knox and Vidler once remarked, it gave the impression that it was very hard to believe anything at all anymore. (See W. L. Knox and A. Vidler, *The Development of Modern Catholicism* [London, 1933], pp. 231–32.)

and political warfare. His theory was hardly referred to except in relation to religion and as a stick with which to beat the Bible.[8]

The fear of hell, and even the idea of hell, was greatly weakened.
By the 1850s many working-class as well as middle-class people were
beginning to turn to spiritualism and other vague conceptions of an
afterlife in rejection of the barbarous idea of a God who punished by
eternal condemnation. From early in the century, the Christian doctrines most objectionable to the secularists, as to unitarians and uni-
versalists and liberals generally, had been the ideas of eternal punishment, hell and damnation for unbelievers, and substitutionary
atonement. By the late nineteenth century, the question could be
whether there was any future life at all.

Finally, one can observe a pervasive decline in the sense of providence, except possibly in the American idea of manifest destiny.
Chadwick nicely illustrates the change by noting the difference in
tone between the reactions to the sinking of the *Titanic* in 1912 and
H. P. Liddon's sermon of 1870 following the destruction by storm of
the British warship HMS *Captain*. Liddon's response was a theodicy
which, while unable to state the particular meaning of the tragedy
within the purposes of a God who made the laws of nature and numbers the hairs of every man's head, still focused on affirming that the
event was within the scope of eternal providence. In the reactions to
the *Titanic* disaster, the religious atmosphere and theological language were still there, but the focus had shifted to a judgment on human pride in its exaltation of science and materialism, and God was
set at a distance from the detail of a catastrophe which should be
blamed on human error in design.[9]

We may mark the decline in the sense of providence in another
way. Despite the valiant efforts of some of the more Calvinistic theologians to harness Darwinian theory to total divine causality, and
despite the enthusiasm for the evolutionary image (see chapter 6,
above), the dominant impact of Darwin's revolution was not to support the view of divine controlling agency but to leave it aside. Insofar as Darwinian (or Spencerian) evolutionary ideas supported
the notion of grand law and design, it was not divine law that they
upheld.

    8. Alvar Ellegård, *Darwin and the General Reader: The Reception of Darwin's Theory of Evo-
lution in the British Periodical Press, 1859–72* (Göteborg, 1958).
    9. Chadwick, *Secularization*, pp. 259–63, and chap. 10.

By the late nineteenth century theological reflection had to take place in a social context in which the role of institutional religion was widely becoming suspect and in which major shifts in popular as well as sophisticated belief structures were under way. The church was under attack as a tool, or at least a supporter, of the power elite, the political and economic establishment. Loyalty to the church as the source and sustainer of morality, as the traditional center and main-stay of the cultural ethos, was evidently weakening; the church just didn't matter as much any more, or it was an obstacle to social prog-ress. And prime elements in the received belief patterns of ordinary existence were being seriously undermined: the authority of the Bi-ble as a guide for daily life, the belief in miracles, the confidence in providence, and the assurance of life after death. What a sociologist's survey research study, were one available, might tell us about the quantitative configurations of these changes in religious sensibility is not for us of primary importance. That they were taking place is powerfully reflected in the theological responses of the late nine-teenth century.

AUTHORITY, FREEDOM, AND TRADITION: VARIETIES OF THEOLOGICAL ACCOMMODATION

Many names have been used to denote the late-nineteenth-century theological movements which were responses to the new situation of Christianity in Western culture. These movements were stimulated by both the general changes in religious sensibility just noted and the specific sorts of problems treated in the preceding chapters. Some of the terms used are: liberalism and liberal theology, modernism, evangelical liberalism and modernistic liberalism, empirical modern-ism, the New Theology, liberal Catholicism, Progressive Orthodoxy, fundamentalism, *positive Theologie* and *modern-positive Theologie*, neo-Protestantism, Ritschlianism (or the Ritschlian school), critical ortho-doxy, the Chicago School, biblical realism, *Kulturprotestantismus*, and *religionsgeschichtliche Theologie*.

Of what value are such labels? Some, certainly, were names delib-erately adopted by groups of thinkers to describe their theological programs: for example, Progressive Orthodoxy among the Andover liberals, the New Theology of London's R. J. Campbell (and also some New England thinkers), fundamentalism from the publication of *The Fundamentals*, and the positive Theologie of Reinhold Seeberg. But while a few of the terms have quite specific reference, they are mostly of severely limited value, at best more or less (and often less than more) convenient devices for classification. Any effort to use these labels to range movements specifically on a scale of greater or lesser accommodation or adjustment and freedom from tradition must be suspect.[10] The ambiguities of the term *liberalism* (or *liberal theology*) and its cognates are well known. Does liberalism refer to a spirit of inquiry and affirmation? To a program? To a complex of ideas (immanentism, religious experience, revelation as discovery, evolutionary models and optimism, the primacy of the moral)? Some interpreters have argued for the term *modernism* as preferable to liberalism. This might have value in suggesting the commonality of Roman Catholic modernism with features of Protestant liberalism. *Modernist* seems to have been a preferred term for many in England. But it is impossible to give satisfactory reasons for choosing one term over the other as an inclusive category. In a general way we know what these terms mean, and we cannot avoid using both of them, even though we find it hard to fix on any clear differentiation.[11]

Leaving aside for the present the special concerns for ethical and social reform, we can still identify several kinds of interests and attitudes that were prominent, though in fluid and shifting forms, in the theological stances relating to liberal/modernist theology. Any reading of the late nineteenth century must mark the pervasive sense of modernity, of a new world of thought. Whether perceived as a threat

10. See my comments in *Prot. Thought*, 1:18–21; also my essay "On Theological Typology," *Theology Today* 22:2 (1965): 176–93.

11. In particular, I am now disposed to agree with W. R. Hutchison's criticism of the distinction between "evangelical liberalism" and "modernistic liberalism," which was developed extensively by Kenneth Cauthen in *The Impact of American Religious Liberalism* (New York, 1962). See Hutchison's excellent study, *The Modernist Impulse in American Protestantism* (Cambridge, Mass., 1976), pp. 7–8. The theme of adjustment to modern culture was so pervasive that the attempt to distinguish clearly by primacy of starting point, whether in modernity or in the tradition, now seems to me dubious and of limited heuristic value. Hutchison holds that the modernist impulse was a definable tendency within liberalism (pp. 2–4), but even this distinction does not seem wholly persuasive.

Ahlstrom's comment on the American scene is equally appropriate to British and Continental Protestantism. Describing the impact of liberalism as difficult to estimate "because its legacy was all-pervasive," he goes on to say that "it is impossible to determine whether the people it influenced were called back to the faith, or whether they were merely assured that their minimal beliefs constituted the essence of Christianity" (Sydney E. Ahlstrom, *A Religious History of the American People* [New Haven, 1972], p. 783). The line between conforming to culture and wanting to transform it is exceedingly hard to draw with respect to specific individuals; both impulses were usually present.

or a boon, a new zeitgeist was present in society and in the churches. For the most part, it brought a new feeling of freedom and openness to change. This was certainly the case in the theological circles influenced by Ritschl. It was true, though perhaps more modestly, in the liberal Catholicism of *Lux Mundi*. It was named "a devout Zeitgeist" by George Harris, of the Andover liberals.

The same experience can be described in another way as a sense of the loss of tradition, even of the irrelevance of antiquated costumes in a new situation. Yet for many, instead of a loss to be regretted, we should speak of a sharp critique of the tradition, a powerful antidogmatic and antiauthoritarian impulse and a correlated sense of emancipation (from Ritschl through Harnack and Herrmann and all the Anglo-Saxons influenced by Ritschl, and from Maurice and Bushnell through Swing and the Andover liberals). Coupled with that sense are a reforming impulse (from Ritschl onward) and a quest to identify the essential in Christianity which had been overlaid or corrupted in the past but which could now be brought to new relevance.

In still different terms, the new mood reflected a drive (in Sabatier's language) for a religion of freedom and of the Spirit, for authority found in history and experience rather than given to or imposed on history. To see religion as life, not doctrine, gives a different locus for authority.

Through all these ways of marking change there is the thread of the need for accommodation and adjustment, especially to a new kind of scientific world view but also to new politics, new economics, new sociology and psychology, and new art and literature. In a sense, of course, this is a continuation of the older apologetics and the more recent mediation theology, but it was distinguished from them by the nature of the demand for compromise or, better, for inner reform and renewal, and by the heightened sense of discontinuity with the past. And this demand was surely intimately connected with the concern to frame a gospel intelligible and relevant to the ordinary believer, one that would speak to the apparent growing indifference.

If we take the theme of adjustment and accommodation as the most inclusive category for the late-nineteenth-century efforts to relate Christianity to modern culture, we can distinguish at least four attitudes of response. These represent what in volume 1 I have called the levels of theological stance or strategy. Although those are vague terms, they can suggest a higher level of approach to the Christ and culture problem than that of the theological school or program and one which may usefully complement discussions of individual thinkers and problems.[12]

Our treatment here must be highly condensed, almost to catalog form, in the interest of inclusiveness. Many of the major characters have already made several entrances in earlier scenes of this script and need not be viewed in detail again. But this also means that we shall often be looking (in this section) at thinkers and ideas that have proved to be more ephemeral than those treated elsewhere.

No Compromise

Outright rejection of compromise could come from opposite directions. It was most broadly represented by the forces leading to the fundamentalist movement, which must be distinguished from the simple continuation of conservative or orthodox theology. Some conservative and orthodox thinkers were sufficiently isolated from the acids of modernity as not to feel any threat to the tradition. What may meaningfully be called the fundamentalist impulse, especially vivid in the United States, was acutely responsive to a perceived danger from the late-nineteenth-century growth of liberalism. (Its no-compromise attitude had a parallel in Catholicism in the mentality of Pius IX and Pius X, and in what Blondel called the "extrinsicists.") For the late nineteenth century, this might well be dubbed *proto-fundamentalism*, since the term *fundamentalist* derives from the series of tracts *The Fundamentals*, sponsored by Lyman and Milton Stewart and widely distributed between 1910 and 1915. Yet the shibboleths of fundamentalism had emerged much earlier: the inerrancy of scripture, the virgin birth, substitutionary atonement, and the physical resurrection and future bodily return of Christ—as formulated, for example, at the Niagara Bible Conference of 1895. These were all wrapped in a suspicion of science, especially "evolution," of urbanism, and of the growing complexity of modern thought generally. This kind of self-conscious conservatism had its roots not only in the sophisticated orthodoxy of, say, the late-nineteenth-century Princeton school (and its Lutheran parallels), but also in the more popular level of reaction represented by the Bible conference and Bible school movement (for example, Moody Bible Institute, founded in

---

12. See *Prot. Thought*, 1:20, 141–46, where I indicated the difficulties of applying this approach to the mid-nineteenth-century scene.

1886).[13] In the nineteenth century proto-fundamentalism was essentially a guerrilla action, which was to mount a general institutional offensive after World War I. The question of accommodation to modern culture was viewed as an either/or. One could either say yes to the new scientism and go all the way with it or maintain without qualification the faith as once and for all delivered.[14]

In a more isolated way, and from quite another direction, the no-compromise response was represented by the lonely figure of Franz Overbeck (1837–1905), a close friend to Nietzsche and a teacher at Basel from 1870. One who would have liked to be religious, he vigorously protested in *Ueber die Christlichkeit unserer heutigen Theologie* (Leipzig, 1873) against all attempts to combine Christianity and modern culture, giving as his reason the eschatological character of primitive Christianity, and turned for the rest of his career to historicocritical studies, mainly of early Christianity. In an afterword to the 1903 reissuing of *Ueber die Christlichkeit*, Overbeck identified Harnack as the high priest of the unchristian modern theology.[15]

Ventures along the Periphery

At another location, though still within the Christian orbit, were those who self-consciously sought radically new beginnings. This stance might be viewed as a more radical Christ of culture than H. R. Niebuhr had in mind in his classic *Christ and Culture*, though I do not want to suggest that we are dealing with lines of thought that come together at the left end of the spectrum. They might better be viewed

13. Ernest R. Sandeen, *The Roots of Fundamentalism: British and American Millennarianism, 1800–1930* (Chicago, 1970), makes a strong argument that fundamentalism was not simply congruent with a culturally conservative reaction but had special roots in the premillennial movement that began in England in the early nineteenth century.

14. The "faith once and for all" often turned out to be a post-Grotian Christology and soteriology, a post-sixteenth-century understanding of revelation, and in general a Protestant scholastic theology, with a corollary in the form of laissez-faire economics. This was at least as much a form of Kulturprotestantismus as any liberal Protestantism. The ostensible Christ against culture can turn out to be a Christ of culture, though of a different culture.

15. *Christentum und Kultur: Gedanken und Anmerkungen zur modernen Theologie* (Basel, 1919), which Karl Barth subsequently made famous, was put together from Overbeck's papers by his student Carl A. Bernoulli, but in such an indiscriminate way, and with such rewriting and sewing together of Overbeck's notes, as to be largely Bernoulli's interpretation of Overbeck. See esp. the 1975 Claremont dissertation by John Elbert Wilson, "Continuity and Difference in the Course of Franz Overbeck's Thought: An Analysis of Overbeck's Concept of the Relation between History and Religion," which makes intensive use of the Overbeck *Nachlass*.

as different modes of adjustment near the circumference of a circle. Such styles of thought are not as easy to find as one might suppose because so much of the progressive impetus, like that of earlier unitarianism, was co-opted by liberalism in general.

In Britain, this radical mood was well represented by the New Theology and the Progressive League of R. J. Campbell, the great preacher of London's City Temple from 1903. In connection with the social gospel, which was in one sense its substance, the New Theology was marked by a thoroughgoing, almost exclusive, doctrine of divine immanence in the universe and in mankind. Supernaturalism was to be removed from Christianity. The God of the ordinary churchgoer was "an antiquated theologian who made His universe so badly that it went wrong in spite of Him." The New Theology was to be a religion of science, abandoning the dangerous and dualistic doctrine of transcendence. God is the uncaused cause of existence, "the unitary principle implied in all multiplicity," expressed entirely through his world. The starting point of the New Theology was "a re-emphasis of the Christian belief in the divine Immanence in the Universe and in Mankind." Everyone is a potential Christ or a manifestation of the eternal Christ. And thus the corollary, for Campbell, that the New Theology was the articulation of the social movement; indeed, it was spiritual socialism.[16]

Something of the theological mood of a new start may be seen in the ebullient optimism that here and there characterized American liberal theology. William Hutchison aptly calls this "the optative mood" and "exultant progressivism."[17] It was not the work of a person or a definable group, because it was so widespread. But we may note the Scottish-born George A. Gordon, who became a famous Boston preacher and leader of the American New Theology, as perhaps the theologically most articulate (though not the most extreme) spokesman for the operative mood. He was influenced by F. D. Maurice, particularly in the direction of universalism, and also by his Harvard teacher William James's "will to believe" that could improve circumstances. Gordon's was an explicitly religious optimism,

16. See esp. Campbell, *The New Theology* (London, 1909), and *Christianity and the Social Order* (London, 1907). Campbell was initially denounced by other Congregationalists, though later the theological controversy (e.g., with P. T. Forsyth) came to an end as Campbell moved back toward more traditional positions, eventually reentering the Church of England.

17. See *Modernist Impulse*, esp. pp. 186–93.

founded "on the divine intention." It was a moral obligation. While not denying the realities of evil, or the possibilities of doubt and despair, he insisted on the necessity of optimistic and affirmative attitudes, which had their justification both in the divine intention for perfection and in the history of humankind, especially in the unquestionable evidence of progress in the nineteenth century. Moral evil is temporary. "Injustice and inhumanity are not here to stay." Human culture is, after all, suffused with divinity.[18]

Another kind of new departure can be seen in the Chicago School, which took its lead especially from Shailer Mathews, who was appointed to the new divinity school at the University of Chicago in 1894 and was its dean from 1908 to 1933. Here the interest was not in the maintenance of traditional values—even though in his later response to fundamentalist critiques of liberalism, Mathews could say that "modernists are evangelical Christians . . . [whose] religious starting point is the inherited orthodoxy."[19] Nor was the chief concern at first for the creation of alternatives. The distinctive impulse was a sociohistorical approach to the development of doctrines as functional (therefore changeable, not normative) expressions of cultural patterns. Doctrines were viewed as products of the dominant social mind-sets of their times—a view with obvious resemblances to Ernst Troeltsch's understanding of the development of Christian social teachings. G. B. Foster represented the more systematic theological side of the faculty. Though in his major work, *The Finality of the Christian Religion*, he was not really far to the left, his writing often gave an impression of negativity and doubt. Hence he formed a transition to the later development in the 1920s when, under the influence of John Dewey and G. H. Mead, the Chicago School moved toward theological naturalism.[20]

A still different, and quite novel, venture can be found in Douglas Clyde Macintosh of Yale, who tried to develop theology in rigorously scientific fashion. Though his work was also characterized by thor-

18. See esp. Gordon, *The Christ of Today* (Boston, 1898), and *Ultimate Conceptions of Faith* (Boston, 1907); also *Immortality and the New Theodicy* (Boston, 1897), and *The New Epoch for Faith* (Boston, 1901).

19. *The Faith of Modernism* (New York, 1924), pp. 34–35.

20. On Mathews as the spokesman for the Chicago School, see Francis S. Fiorenza, "American Culture and Modernism: Shailer Mathews's Interpretation of American Christianity," in T. M. McFadden, ed., *America in Theological Perspective* (New York, 1976), pp. 163–86. See also Charles Harvey Arnold, *Near the Edge of the Battle: A Short History of the Divinity School and the "Chicago School of Theology," 1866–1966* (Chicago, 1966).

oughly informed and highly sophisticated analyses of the course of
modern philosophy and by the attempt to create a more adequate
"critical realistic epistemological monism," the most intriguing aspect
of Macintosh's thought was his proposal for a theological method
strictly parallel to the methods of the natural sciences. Beginning
with the verifiable object of religious experience, which has as much
right to be affirmed as the objects of sensory experience, even if as
yet largely undefined, one could move to demonstrable laws of religious experience describing the (fundamentally moral) results of
changes in the subject's religious adjustment and come eventually to
justifiable theological theory. Macintosh never had any disciples who
took up this proposal in a large way. When reduced to the formulas
that Macintosh devised, it could seem either sterile or comical, an
unappealing vehicle for the profound Baptist piety out of which it
sprang. But it stands as a remarkable illustration of one way of attempting to be strictly scientific in theology.[21]

Parallels to these Anglo-Saxon self-conscious new directions are
not easy to find in the German-speaking theological community.
Some interpreters would think, in the present connection, of the religionsgeschichtliche Schule, with Troeltsch as its systematician. But
that would be a mistake. The historical work of Gunkel, Bousset,
Heitmüller, and others had a different significance (see chapter 5,
above). And Troeltsch can hardly be adequately identified as the
dogmatician of a school (see chapter 8, below).

As a possible exemplar of an attempt at a really new direction for
the church, I would suggest Ritschl's Göttingen colleague and critic,
Paul de Lagarde, whose proposals for reform were of a quite different (and foreboding) sort. Though most important as a learned phil-
ologian and orientalist, whose goal was to produce a critical edition
of the Septuagint, Lagarde was also convinced that Protestantism as
it had developed was without cultural power. His answer was to emphasize its potential as a German national religion. Since the community that most deeply grasps humanity is that of folk and fatherland,
religion has to stand in connection with national life. The universal
gospel must have a German edition. The state and the nation lack Je-

---

21. See Macintosh, *Theology as an Empirical Science* (New York, 1919). We have earlier
(chap. 5) noted Macintosh's willingness to give up the absolute necessity of a historical Jesus
to Christianity.

sus as the bearer of the gospel, but the evangelical church can make up this deficiency through the growth of a national evangelical piety, which will be the most sacred task of the German people and of theology. Of course, life, the state, the fatherland, science, and art are not ends in themselves, but means for the growth of the relationship to God by individual human beings.[22]

Liberalisms

Most liberal theology sought to be authentically Christian, yet open in change and adjustment. Continuity with the past was vital, through the maintenance of essential life and truth. Hence the title of A. V. C. Allen's remarkable little history, *The Continuity of Christian Thought: A Study of Modern Theology in the Light of Its History* (Boston, 1884). But it was a continuity newly understood, freed from dogma considered as unchangeable formulas for belief. One did not need unshakable allegiance to the ancient language of Cyrillian Christology, or the trinitarian dialectic of the Athanasian Creed, or the medieval and Calvinist doctrines of substitutionary atonement and vicarious satisfaction in order to be authentically Christian. Those formulas may in their time have been valid, even necessary, ways of articulating elements of the Christian experience, but the vitalities of religious life lie elsewhere. Thus one must be open to the reconsideration of all doctrinal formulations, to newer statements of the meaning of faith in the light of scientific investigation, to new philosophies and modern ways of thinking generally. Scripture must be freed from interpretations of infallibility that inhibit its power as truly personal communication. As such, liberal theology in the late nineteenth century seemed to be sweeping everything before it, so that we are justified in speaking of that period as the age of theological liberalism.

Yet this was an internally complex and varied movement. The German variety was most prominently expressed in the work of Adolf Harnack and Wilhelm Herrmann, whom we have already treated extensively, and who can serve as sufficient representation of

22. See Lagarde, *Verhältnis des deutschen Staates zu Theologie, Kirche und Religion* (Göttingen, 1873), and *Deutsche Schriften* (Göttingen, 1878, 1886). Significantly, Lagarde's writings were extensively reissued in the National Socialist period, e.g., in *Schriften für Deutschland*, ed. A. Messer (Stuttgart, 1933); *Schriften für das deutsche Volk*, 2 vols., ed. K. A. and P. Fischer (Munich, 1934–37); and *National Religion*, ed. G. Dost (Jena, 1934, 1941).

whatever is meant by the Ritschlian school in Germany (though The-odor Haering is also often counted as a systematician of that school, along with Julius Kaftan in a more conservative vein).

In America, liberalism came to early self-conscious focus in the work of the Andover liberals, so called because of their association with the Andover (Massachusetts) school of theology and their con-tributions to the *Andover Review* from 1884 to 1893. The movement was also given the name of the New Theology and, in a book pub-lished from editorials in the *Review*, Progressive Orthodoxy.[23]

David Swing was a precursor of themes of the New Theology in his ideas of God's presence in the world and culture, of the imperfection of human utterances and the cultural conditioning of creeds and scripture, of the emphasis on life and on doing what Christ taught as more important than rectitude in doctrine, and of adaptation as es-sential to the regeneration of the church and to the spread of Chris-tian life and civilization. Horace Bushnell (see *Prot. Thought*, 1, chap-ter 11) was highly influential (for example, in his idea of the relativity of creeds), notably through his disciple and biographer, the New Ha-ven pastor Theodore Munger. And Isaak Dorner, the best known of the German mediating thinkers in America, was of special impor-tance because he taught the possibility of a second chance after death.[24]

Along with the Andover professors Egbert Smyth, George Harris, and William Jewett Tucker—all of whom were charged in 1886 with violation of the creed of the school, though only Smyth was convicted and deprived of his chair—other thinkers who can be counted in the New Theology group are Egbert's brother Newman (who had been refused appointment to Andover), Theodore Munger, the historian A. V. G. Allen of Episcopal Theological School, the biblical scholar Charles A. Briggs, the social gospel's Washington Gladden, and the famous preachers Phillips Brooks, Henry Ward Beecher, and G. A. Gordon.

Munger's *Freedom of Faith* (Boston, 1883) was something of a mani-

23. Egbert C. Smyth et al., *Progressive Orthodoxy: A Contribution to the Christian Interpreta-tion of Christian Doctrines* (Boston, 1885). This group of thinkers has been much studied. Among the best interpretations are Daniel D. Williams, *The Andover Liberals* (New York, 1941), and Hutchison, *Modernist Impulse*, esp. chap. 3.

24. See esp. Newman Smyth, *Dorner on the Future State: Being a Translation of the Section of His System of Christian Doctrine Comprising the Doctrine of the Last Things, with an Introduction and Notes* (New York, 1883). On Dorner generally, see *Prot. Thought*, 1, chap. 12.

festo of the movement, though its major themes had already been laid out in Newman Smyth's three volumes: *The Religious Feeling, Old Faiths in New Light,* and *The Orthodox Theology of Today* (New York, 1877, 1879, and 1881). This New Theology considered itself not at all a radical break from the Christian tradition, but rather as thoroughly christocentric. It was not iconoclastic, and indeed the attempt to define the movement in *Progressive Orthodoxy* asserts that "theological progress does not involve or require any break with the faith of the church catholic, any recasting of the primitive ecumenical creeds, any departure from the fundamental principles of the Reformation" (p. 5). What was wanted, as Munger put it, was a "broader and larger" use of reason in theology, a "more natural" (historical) interpretation of the Bible, a more solidaristic in place of an excessively individualistic view of human nature, an attention to real human nature rather than abstractions, a restatement of eschatology that would be more moral, stressing God's love in seeking and saving, and a recognition of "a divine revelation and process" within the "composition and ongoing of human society." No unnatural and unscriptural line need be drawn between the sacred and the secular, because such a line "by its distinction ignores the very process by which the kingdoms of this world are becoming the kingdom of our Lord Jesus Christ."[25]

After the 1880s the story of liberal theology in America was largely one of its rapid spread. The conservatives were still doubtless the majority, and controversy continued. But the early fundamentalist forces sensed rightly that liberalism was about to overwhelm them. Liberal views were widely popularized in the 1890s by such works as Washington Gladden's *Who Wrote the Bible? A Book for the People* (Boston, 1891) and the half dozen volumes by Lyman Abbott, who also edited the rapidly expanding *Christian Outlook.* Their growing dominance in the theological centers is indicated by an almost wholesale changing of the theological guard. For example: Charles A. Briggs, already at Union Theological Seminary, was appointed to the new chair of biblical theology in 1891, and the controversy over his inaugural address led Union out of conservative Presbyterian control. He was shortly joined at Union by A. C. McGiffert, Henry Preserved Smith, and William Adams Brown. Borden Parker Bowne had come

---

25. See Munger, *Freedom of Faith,* pp. 7–44. F. H. Foster thought the Andover liberals incurably conservative in relation to the historic creeds.

to Boston University in 1876, but became dean of the graduate
school in 1888 and produced his most influential works in the 1890s
and after. H. C. Sheldon also came to Boston in the 1890s. William
Newton Clarke went to Colgate University as Professor of Theology,
Ethics, and Apologetics in 1890. G. B. Stevens at Yale transferred to
theology in 1895, succeeding Samuel Harris, who had already been
moving in liberal directions, and he was followed in 1909 by D. C.
Macintosh. Milton Terry replaced Miner Raymond at Garrett in
1895, and O. A. Curtis replaced John Miley at Drew in the same year.
Henry Churchill King went to the Oberlin theological professorship
in 1897. F. H. Foster was at Pacific Theological Seminary from 1892
to 1902 and subsequently at Oberlin. G. B. Foster joined Shailer
Mathews in the new faculty at Chicago in 1895.

Attempts at synoptic presentation of liberal theology appeared in
H. C. King, *Reconstruction in Theology* (New York, 1901), and especially in the widely used textbooks by W. N. Clarke, *An Outline of
Christian Theology* (New York, 1898), and W. A. Brown, *Christian Theology in Outline* (New York, 1906). In the works of Clarke and Brown,
liberalism took an almost scholastic form. In Brown, and also in
King, we see the marked influence of German theology, especially of
the Ritschlian variety.[26] In these texts all the characteristic elements
of the mainstream of liberal theology were present: the emphasis on
divine immanence as a corrective to the Latin overemphasis on transcendence (particularly in Clarke), thus a different view of God's relation to the natural and historical process and an evolutionary perspective; the understanding of revelation not as an intrusion but as
correlative to human discovery, as a process of God disclosing himself through genuine human means in a never-ending process of
criticism and experiment; religious experience as a verifiable datum
comparable to scientific data; the Bible as a document of religious experience and thus a different sort of authority; the distinction between the essential and the accidental in historic Christianity; the
person of Christ as the center of Christianity and as its special claim
to distinctiveness (and finality); salvation through Christ as a process

26. Briggs, of course, had long been prominent in mediating the work of German biblical scholars. Along with Briggs, the Smyths, and Bowne, Americans who had studied in
Germany included Brown, George A. Coe, King, Mathews, McGiffert, and Walter Rauschenbusch. Among the German teachers, Harnack and Herrmann were of special
importance.

and especially as moral regeneration; and a theology of the kingdom of God and therefore of social criticism and action.

The formulation of the problem of Christianity and culture as a question of freedom and authority, while endemic in liberalism, was nowhere more pronounced than in the work of the leading French Protestant theologian Auguste Sabatier, whose works were speedily translated in America and who was also close to the German liberals (especially Herrmann).[27] In *Religions of Authority*, Sabatier proposed that the proper aim of authority is "to render itself useless," the true education of mankind being "the passage from faith in authority to personal conviction, and to the sustained practice of the intellectual duty to consent to no idea except by virtue of its recognized truth" (p. xxi). Free inquiry is a duty. Authority can justify itself only by becoming moral and interdependent with autonomy. Proper respect for authority requires its criticism. Sabatier criticized both Roman Catholic and Protestant authoritarianism (in books 1 and 2) as survivals of ancient religion, whether paganism or legalistic Judaism. In Protestantism, of course, external authority has been assigned to the Bible, but this is no better than Catholic institutionalism. The question is whether Christianity does not exclude every rule of authority. The religion of the Spirit escapes even the external authority of metaphysical Christology (p. 330) in favor of a moral and spiritual relation to Jesus and his gospel. The metaphysics of trinitarian dogma leads to mythology and tritheism—idolatry—for it has a root of paganism (ibid.). What is required is a reconstruction of the whole theological edifice in the style of the present, by way of scripture (though not as dogmatic authority), the scientific spirit, and religious experience (pp. 359–61).

The extent to which late-nineteenth-century liberalism could be churchly in character is illustrated by the liberal Catholicism of the *Lux Mundi* group. We have already encountered important emphases of these Anglican writers: Scott Holland on the nature of faith (chapter 2), Charles Gore on biblical criticism (chapter 5), and Aub-

27. See Sabatier, *Esquisse d'une philosophie de la religion d'après la psychologie et l'histoire* (Paris, 1897; Eng. trans., *Outlines of a Philosophy of Religion Based on Psychology and History* [New York, 1902]), and esp. *Les Religions d'autorité et la religion de l'esprit* (Paris, 1904; Eng. trans., *Religions of Authority and the Religion of the Spirit* [New York, 1904]). Sabatier's view of the self-certifying nature of religious experience, as developed particularly in the *Philosophy of Religion*, has been noted in chap. 2, above.

rey Moore on evolution (chapter 6). To these we may add the characteristic stress of J. R. Illingworth (who was the regular host for meetings of the group) on immanence as well as transcendence in the Christian doctrines of incarnation and trinity.[28] As one might expect, the tone of *Lux Mundi* was more traditionalist than some of the liberalisms we have noted, and the theology of the group was strongly incarnation-oriented. It generated excitement in late-Victorian England (for a learned work it was widely distributed—ten printings within a year) especially because of Gore's essay on the inspiration of scripture. While this was very conservative by German standards, it did include the suggestion that even Jesus' quotation did not guarantee the historical validity of the Old Testament, implying that Jesus was not omniscient and foreshadowing the mild kenoticism which Gore and others popularized in England (without apparent awareness of the German kenotic controversy of the middle of the century—see *Prot. Thought*, 1:233–40). Yet the purpose of the volume as a whole was explicitly one of adjustment, "to put the Catholic Faith in its right relation to modern intellectual and moral problems." Disencumbering, explaining, and reinterpreting were needed because

> the epoch in which we live is one of profound transformation, intellectual and social, abounding in new needs, new points of view, new questions; and certain therefore to involve great changes in the outlying departments of theology, where it is linked onto the sciences, and to necessitate some general reinstatement of its claim and meaning [so that the Church can show] again and again her power of witnessing under changed conditions to the Catholic capacity of her faith and life.[29]

Most response to the volume was positive, a sense of relief and emancipation.

Critical Orthodoxy

The critique of liberal theology in the late nineteenth century was most interestingly represented, not by incipient fundamentalism or

28. Illingworth was one of the more important representatives of the influence of philosophical idealism in late-nineteenth-century British theology. See esp. *Personality, Human and Divine* (London, 1894), *Divine Immanence* (London, 1898), and later, to balance the emphasis, *Divine Transcendence and Its Reflection in Religious Authority* (London, 1911). Most of the essayists in *Lux Mundi* were influenced by T. H. Green's philosophy, with its assurance of the essential spirituality of the universe.

29. *Lux Mundi*, 10th ed. (London, 1890), pp. vii–ix.

the thundering orthodoxy of the Princeton school and its German and Anglo-Saxon cognates, but by those thinkers whom we can call critically orthodox, who felt the claims of modernity keenly but who judged that liberalism, despite its intentions, had abandoned or at least badly compromised central elements of the Christian faith.

In the German tradition, critical orthodoxy is best represented by Martin Kähler, whose work we have dealt with at length in chapters 2 and 5 above. Here we shall call attention to the *moderne-positive Theologie* of Reinhold Seeberg.[30] By *modern* he meant openness to contemporary life in a high degree, a new critical appreciation of German idealism, and an incorporation of evolutionary thought. By *positive* he meant to emphasize that the development of the history of religion is not solely an immanent process but one conditioned by the transcendent. Christianity is not merely a psychological phenomenon in history, but a work of almighty God. To be modern requires entering fully into the problems, questions, interests, and methods of the present day. To be positive requires stress on the facts and realities of Christian spiritual life. As modern, we have to recognize that the evolutionary idea (and psychologism) changes the shape of the problem of revelation. Dogmas must be seen in their historical contexts. Hence the task of theology is to show, by the measures of logic, history, and the needs of the soul, that Christianity is the religion for all, the absolute religion—not a subjective delusion but actuality, founded in the personality of Jesus Christ and in the power of his life, and bringing certainty of God's rule and his kingdom. In the last point, Seeberg picked up the Ritschlian emphasis on the ethical, though overall he was closer to the earlier nineteenth-century mediating theologians.[31]

30. Seeberg (1859–1935), professor at Dorpat, Erlangen, and Berlin, is best known, and rightly so, for his massive *Lehrbuch der Dogmengeschichte*, which first appeared in 1895–98 and was eventually expanded to five large volumes (3d ed., 1913–23). But he ought also to be remembered for his systematic works, e.g., *Die Kirche Deutschlands im 19. Jahrhundert* (Leipzig, 1904; 3d ed., 1910), *Die Grundwahrheiten der christlichen Religion* (Leipzig, 1902; 7th ed., 1921), *System der Ethik* (Leipzig, 1911; 2d ed., 1920), and *Christliche Dogmatik*, 2 vols. (Leipzig, 1924–25). See also Richard Grützmacher, *Modern-positive Vorträge* (Leipzig, 1906).

31. The "biblical realism" of Hermann Cremer, Adolf Schlatter, and Erich Schaeder might also be thought of here as continuing the line of Martin Kähler. But on the whole, these thinkers are better associated with the more patently conservative tradition. Cremer is interesting for his *Das Wesen des Christentums* (Gütersloh, 1901), a rebuttal to Harnack; Schlatter for the way he dealt with a historicocritical view of the Bible and dogmas; and Schaeder for his pointed call for a "theocentric theology."

A more lively kindred spirit to Kähler was the British Congregationalist P. T. Forsyth, who became principal of Hackney College in
1901. He was recognized in his time as a major thinker who gave new
life to nonconformist theology, though he was neglected for some
time after his death in 1921.[32]

Forsyth was significantly influenced by F. D. Maurice, and in the
direction of kenotic Christology by Gore and A. M. Fairbairn (who
led him to an appreciation of Hegel). In his early thought Forsyth
was very close to Ritschl, using an elliptical model of the Cross and
the Kingdom, but he moved sharply away from Ritschl except in the
basic approach to Christianity through moral categories. He was sympathetic to Kähler and to Schlatter. He was one of the few late-nineteenth-century Anglo-Saxons who knew something of Kierkegaard.
And he could speak (1907) of W. A. Brown's outline of theology as
"the most able . . . which we now possess in English" (*Preaching*, p. 267), a comment that shows us how hazy the lines of demarca-
tion are between types of theology. Forsyth's particular criticism of
liberalism was aimed at Harnack, Herrmann, and R. J. Campbell.
Contrary to Harnack, the gospel is not simple, but involves dialectic
and paradox; with Kähler and fellow Englishman James Denny, Forsyth argued that the gospel records are primarily evangelical testimony. Herrmann's theology, among all the liberals, is most bound
up with personal religion, but his subjectivism does not enable him to
get to the core of evangelical faith as a revolutionary power. Campbell's New Theology is a vague kind of near-pantheistic humanism
tinged with evangelical sentiment.

The modern principles that Forsyth heartily approved (he liked
the term *modern* much better than *liberal*) included the freedom of

---

32. See *Positive Preaching and the Modern Mind* (London, 1907), *The Person and Place of Jesus Christ* (London, 1909), *The Principles of Authority in Relation to Certainty, Sanctity and Society*
(London, 1913), *The Cruciality of the Cross* (London, 1909), and *The Work of Christ* (London,
1910). Several of Forsyth's works were reprinted in the late 1940s.

With Forsyth one might want to associate his teacher, Andrew M. Fairbairn, the first
principal of Mansfield College, who was a moderate liberal with strong philosophical interests and social concern. See *Religion in History and in Modern Life* (London, 1894), *The Place
of Christ in Modern Theology* (London, 1893), and *The Philosophy of the Christian Religion* (London, 1902).

One may also think of the Scot Hugh Ross Mackintosh, who was involved in the translations of both Ritschl (1900) and Schleiermacher (1928), but whose major works, except for
The Doctrine of the Person of Jesus Christ (Edinburgh, 1912), belong to the post–World War I
period. From a twentieth-century vantage point, Mackintosh appears less interesting and
creative than Forsyth.

the individual from external authority, the social idea of organic salvation and the socialized conception of personality, the distinction between theoretical and practical knowledge (stressing the ethical dimension), the idea of historic evolution, and the passion for reality (see *Preaching*, pp. 258–70). But against liberalism's misuse of these principles, Forsyth wanted to insist on the objectivity and authority of the gospel. Liberation from a too speculative and overdefined Christianity is needed. But freedom is not without content, and it is not experience, not even moral experience, that is authoritative, but something given to experience in history. The real court of morals is not conscience but history centered in Christ, whose Cross is the final seat of authority.

The decisive point in Forsyth's differentiation of his view from that of liberalism was the holiness of God and the reality of sin. Against Ritschl's idea of a divine love stripped of holiness and wrath, it must be insisted that God is not just Father, but holy Father. Holiness is God's being himself, not a contradiction of love but an indispensable quality of love that will not permit him to ignore or countenance the unholy; he must destroy it or redeem it. "Holiness is love morally perfect; love is holiness brimming and overflowing." "The love of God is not more real than the wrath of God. For He can be really angry with those He loves. . . . If God's love were not essentially holy love, in the course of time mankind would cease to respect it, and consequently to trust it" (*Preaching*, p. 145; *Work*, pp. 242, 113). The corollary of God's holiness is the reality of sin, which liberalism has ignored with all its ideas of inevitable progress and of the particularity and isolation of sins. The human race, for Forsyth, is not simply in arrears, but is infected by disease. The train of history is not merely late but has been involved in a terrible accident due to malice and crime. Sin is total, in that no aspect of life is untainted, and is "racial," a solidary act: "In so far as it is real, it affects and vitiates the whole conscience, the whole man, that is, and the whole race in its moral aspect and reliability. That follows from the unity of personality and the race, from our solidarity" (*Authority*, p. 404). Therefore we must regain a sense of guilt, not just a sense of sin, for the sake of the soul and the kingdom.

And so to the cruciality of the Cross. That means atonement—not the simple gospel of Jesus, but the New Testament message of a final settlement of the issue between a holy God and the guilt of man. God's forgiveness is not something to be taken for granted, but is wrought out in a satisfaction of God's holy love by a solidary (in the solidarity of the race) reparation in the obedience of Christ unto death. This is the covering of sin which God has performed, the self-justification of God and the justification of the sinner. The cruciality of the Cross also means the "super-historical finality of Christ." Against all evolutionism, Christ is the redeemer. We do not believe with him, but in him. In language close to Kähler's, Forsyth insisted that we do not find the center of gravity in what Christ has in common with us, but in his difference from us (see *Preaching*, p. 237). If the gospel is not just what Jesus preached in his earthly life, but what he preaches through his Spirit, then "the essence of Christianity is not in the bare fact, but in the fact and its interpretation . . . not in a mere historic Jesus, evidentially irresistible, but in a Christ evangelically irresistible" (*Person and Place*, p. 168).

To these central themes for Forsyth we should add his high view of the church (and ministry) as an organic reality, created to actualize the reconciliation Christ has effected for the race as a whole. (Against liberalism; compare W. N. Clarke's *Outline*, which had no section on the church at all.) As a nonconformist, Forsyth wanted to emphasize the organic and universal character of the church: against the individualism that had cost nonconformity its sense of churchmanship; against Catholicism, for displacing Paul from primacy among the apostles and for sacrificing the freedom of the spirit; and against the established Church of England, for sacrificing the autonomy of the church and losing the true continuity of evangelical succession. Finally, for Forsyth, all this had to issue in the social struggle, in which Christianity might seek a reordering of the social machine to give all the blessings and none of the dangers of socialism.[33]

SOCIAL GOSPELS

The term *social gospel* came into common usage in the early 1900s, particularly, though not uniquely, in the American scene. It must be set in the context of much broader movements of social Christianity,

---

33. It has been suggested that in America, which was generally more polarized between liberal and conservative than was Britain, Augustus H. Strong might be counted among the critically orthodox. But Strong seems an only slightly chastened conservative, willing to make some adjustments to biblical criticism and evolution, but mainly concerned to defend the faith as delivered (see, e.g., the preface to the 1907 edition of his *Systematic Theology*, 1st ed. [Rochester, N.Y., 1886]). Strong must be credited with having brought Rauschenbusch to Rochester, but his own theology was highly scholastic in form and substance.

which were as varied and as international as the theological liberalisms with which they were often associated. But *social gospel* can serve
as a happy symbol for the late-nineteenth-century moral response to
the social crises and the estrangement from the church, a response
which at its deepest level could mean the reshaping of the whole of
theology, especially the relation of faith and ethics, in a new vision of
the connection of church and society.

We can distinguish three major levels or stages in the responses of
social Christianity. One was the level of charitable or philanthropic
works, efforts to alleviate the suffering of the poor and the unfortunate—which we might dub the Band-Aid or aspirin approach, an attempt to bind up the wounds and ease the pains. The second was the
level of specific reforms such as support for the rights of workers
and unions, concern for pay and hours of work (particularly regarding women and children), support of cooperatives and social security
measures, and so on. This approach tried to change the rules of the
struggle or adopt health measures that would help to avoid the more
serious wounds and diseases of society—and it could take either a
monarchist or a republican form. The third level involved a call for
sweeping reconstruction of social and economic institutions and of
the understanding of the Christian message as it related to society, in
the interest of eliminating the social warfare or disease entirely. This
was the mode of reform that emerged in the various sorts of religious
socialism, or Christian socialism, or social gospel.

Christian Social Reform in Germany

The story of the Protestant church's involvement in social reform
in late-nineteenth-century Germany is on the whole sad, and at some
points dismaying. The roots of the attempts at a new relation of
church and society go back to the pioneering work of J. H. Wichern
(1808–81) of Hamburg, following the failure of the revolutions of
1848, in establishing the Kirchentag (church congress, which met an-
nually in various cities from 1848 to 1871) and the Innere Mission.
While the chief consequence of the revolutions for German Protestantism was an even greater identification of the church with political
and economic conservatism, and thus estrangement from labor and
political liberalism, the Kirchentag and Innere Mission were promis-
ing attempts to give a social dimension to the work of the church.
They aimed at a spiritual regeneration of the German people and
at arousing lay discussion of practical social problems. Wichern in-

tended Christian-Socialism to mean a positive answer to communism (which he distinguished from socialism). Christianity was to be applied to social and industrial life and particularly to the problems of the cities. Activity, however, was mainly directed to the provision of social services—the building of nurseries, schools for infants, reformatories, asylums, hospitals, and the direct relief of poverty —rather than to any kind of political or economic reordering. German Protestantism's concern for the plight of the poor, the laboring class, and the urban masses (industrialization came rather late in Germany) rarely moved beyond this perspective. The traditional Lutheran dualism of the two kingdoms and the Pauline principle of obedience to the authorities were still strong.

Even though by the time of the tenth Evangelical Social Congress (1899) it could be felt that considerable progress in social reform had been made, and some genuine support for the workers was expressed, the main thrust of social Christianity in the late nineteenth century was twofold. First, there was a continuation of Ritschlian emphases. Despite Ritschl's attempts to restore the idea of the kingdom of God and the ethical demand to their proper places in the Christian message, and despite his language about the corporate nature of the kingdom and the church, he remained fundamentally conservative and even individualistic in his application of the ethical perspective. Moral reform was to develop within the structure of the vocations. While he probably had no conscious intention of supporting the Prussian social-economic-political system, Ritschl took that system for granted as the framework within which Christians would courageously exercise their free self-determination and contribute to the universal moral community. Thus he opposed the enemies of the system and had the impact of supporting it.

A good illustration of that sort of social Christianity can be found in the three addresses by Adolf Harnack and Wilhelm Herrmann at the Evangelical Social Congresses of 1894, 1902, and 1903, which were chosen for translation in a volume called *Essays on the Social Gospel*.[34] Much as he later said in *Das Wesen des Christentums*, Harnack

34. Trans. G. M. Craik and ed. M. A. Canney (London and New York, 1907). Harnack's papers on "The Evangelical Social Mission in the Light of the History of the Church" and "The Moral and Social Significance of Modern Education" were read at the Frankfurt, 1894, and the Dortmund, 1902, sessions. See his *Reden und Aufsätze*, 2 (Giessen, 1904). Herrmann's paper on "The Moral Teachings of Jesus" was given at the Darmstadt Congress of 1903 and published separately in an enlarged form, *Die sittlichen Weisungen Jesu*

made clear that while the gospel of the New Testament had no definite social or economic program, the commandment of love involved Christian concern for any social condition that was a source of distress to one's neighbor. This required the arousing of individual consciences and the binding together of congregations of individuals into communities of brotherly love and active charity. It also involved, in the course of Christian history, arrangements with the temporal order. And in the present (nineteenth-century) scene, because it was a progressive age, the social mission of the church had become more urgent. Concretely, this meant renewed preaching of the gospel, the combination of worship with active charity, and protest against social and moral evils, including such things as prostitution, dueling, and bad penal conditions—and (especially in the essay on education) Harnack made some gestures in the direction of improving the lot of women.

But the church's activities were to take place within limits. Economic questions could not be included. The church should have nothing to do with matters such as the nationalization of property, legislation of hours of work, taxation, and land-tenure reform, all of which require technical information beyond the competence of the church. Though he recognized that the church had generally been on the wrong side of social questions in the first two-thirds of the century and still needed to intensify its philanthropic work to avoid the danger of conservatism and indolence, Harnack could see nothing appropriate in promoting major economic or political reform. Even if it were true that Christianity had never taken the lead in economic reform, that would be no genuine reproach. "It is enough if religion prepares men's minds for great economic changes and revolutions; if it foresees the new moral duties which these impose; if it knows how to adapt itself to them, and perceives the right moment at which to step in with its forces, and do its work. A religion which aims at saving the soul and transforming the inner man, and which regards a change in outward circumstance as but a small matter in comparison with the power of evil, can only follow in the wake of earthly

---

(Göttingen, 1904). It may be worth mentioning that Harnack had written a foreword in 1893 for a German translation of sermons by the British preacher Frederick W. Robertson (1816–53), several of whose works were published in German in the 1890s. Robertson had some connection with the British Christian socialists of the mid-century, though he was not in the center of the movement, and he was to be of much influence (through his theological liberalism) on the American social gospeler Washington Gladden.

changes and experience an after-influence; it is not qualified to lead the way in economic development" (*Essays*, pp. 18–19).

In particular, though a certain kind of communitarian ideal has (unfortunately) clung to the church like a shadow, communism in economic matters is a fantastic idea, and social democracy is at least in part "merely a modified and disguised form of eighteenth century individualism, and knows no higher ideal than the temporal well-being of the individual, and no forces superior to the instinct of self-preservation and the universal right of suffrage" (p. 64).

Herrmann's essay, though touching little on current social issues, emphasized the givenness of the actual circumstances of life, within which there is little scope for change. The apparent conflict between Jesus' seeming repudiation of all concern for material needs and for the state and the social duties to which we want to cling is a problem for us. The special danger lies in taking Jesus' injunctions as laws to be followed; that is the worst misuse of his teaching. But if we understand the particular teachings as due to Jesus' outlook (including his eschatological expectation), and attend to his person and his moral earnestness, to the morality that goes beyond justice to love, then it is possible for us to be moral within the structures, under the conditions of real and effective life. Even the pursuit of power and possessions, as protected by law, is a moral obligation except in particular circumstances where love requires sacrifice of them. In short, Herrmann hardly approached questions of social reform. He made a few references to philanthropic sorts of activities, but his concern was almost entirely for the inner moral renewal that remains even after we recognize the relation of Jesus' sayings to his world view.

The second, and more dismaying, line of development is seen in the story of Adolf Stoecker (1835–1909) and Friedrich Naumann (1860–1919), though in spite of their own final directions they were stimuli to other and more fruitful ventures. Stoecker, Prussian court preacher until forced out of the post by Kaiser Wilhelm in 1890, was originally inspired by Wichern and for twenty-five years promoted a social Christianity on the basis of evangelical orthodoxy. He was deeply concerned about the material misery of the urban proletariat and the increasing abandonment of the church by the workers, as well as the church's neglect of them. In 1871, after the Paris Commune, he called for the christianization of the great cities. In 1873 he was promoting a presentation of the social-political thought of the New Testament. In 1878 he entered the political arena with the formation of an association in Berlin for "Social Reform on Christian and Constitutional Principles," for a healthy socialism and a validation of the Christian world view in public life.

But the word *constitutional* was of special importance, for Stoecker was a thoroughgoing conservative and monarchist, who wanted to bring back the godless and socialist masses to the old evangelical Christianity. The true help of the people was to be found in love and obedience to the church and the fatherland, God and the Kaiser. The Social Democrats were for him the enemy, impractical, unpatriotic, and unchristian; and they had contempt for him. What was planned as a Christian-social workers party became a small party of the middle class. Stoecker was distrusted by a paternalistic government, was used by Bismarck to divide the socialist forces (most of the specific proposals of 1878 having been incorporated in Bismarck's program of 1881), and was eventually openly attacked by Wilhelm II for meddling in politics, though even then he maintained his loyalty to the monarchy. By this time, he had been infected by anti-Semitism, and his opposition to liberalism and socialism had also become opposition to Judaism.

Naumann, who as a pastor in industrial Saxony came to know firsthand the problems of the workers, also started from within the Innere Mission movement. He became convinced that the charitable work of this movement was not enough to deal with the social problems, and he took a different attitude toward the Social Democrats than did Stoecker (with whom he broke publicly in 1894). Whereas for Stoecker the Social Democrats were simply enemies, for Naumann they represented a modern heresy, deeply bound to Christianity yet presenting a question and a challenge to it. In 1889 he published a workers' catechism with a program for social reform of the existing orders. The details of the program—restrictions on the accumulation of capital, extension of social security, the right to work, limitation of women's work, protection of sabbath rest, and so forth—were not dramatically different from Stoecker's proposals of 1878. Naumann too thought imperial Germany the best friend of the worker, within which church and Bible could serve the laborer.

But the ethos was different. Naumann envisaged a new social Christianity that would bring reforms into economic and political life, based on his view of Jesus as a man of the people and friend of the poor with a religiosity open to the world. A new form of social relationships should emerge out of the power of Christianity. Thus

Naumann became a major leader in the Evangelical Social Congresses of the 1890s. Gradually, however, the national component became stronger in Naumann's thinking. Unlike Stoecker, Naumann did not favor the old patriarchal state but the new dynamic German imperialism. Social and national aspirations joined, and the Christian-social program fell into the background with Naumann's formation of the National-Social Party in 1896 and his relinquishing of the pastorate in the following year. Under the influence of his close friend, Rudolf Sohm, the famous jurist, Naumann moved in the direction of a purely inward, anti-institutional conception of Christianity, which could also reinforce the old dualism of the two kingdoms. Power politics, organization, technology, and legal structures are left to the "world." We do not seek Jesus' advice on matters of state administration or political economy. No rules for these can be found in the Sermon on the Mount. "I give my vote and I canvass for the German fleet, not because I am a Christian, but because I am a citizen" and have given up hope of dealing with all questions by reference to Jesus' sayings (*Briefe*, p. 49).[35]

The withdrawal of Stoecker from the Evangelical Social Congress in favor of a new, exclusively orthodox Church Social Conference, Naumann's founding of the National-Social Party, and Kaiser Wilhelm II's telegram declaring "Christian-social is nonsense"—all in 1896—mark the end of the early Protestant-social(ist) movement in Germany. The Social Congresses continued and were not without influence as a stimulus to some (for example, Ragaz) who moved in more creative directions, but they were less a national movement than a forum for the liberal-academic segment and were preoccupied with particular questions of praxis and reform measures rather than new modes of social outlook. Essentially, an incipient social gospel had vanished in the smoke of national religion.

Yet we cannot leave the story of German Protestantism's response to the Social Democrats without at least mentioning two rather lonely exceptions. The first was Rudolf Todt, who, just at the time of

35. Among Naumann's writings, see esp. *Arbeiter-Katechismus, oder der wahre Socialismus, seinen arbeitenden Brüdern dargebracht* (Calw, 1889), *Jesus der Volksmann* (Göttingen, 1894), and *Briefe über Religion* (Berlin, 1903). For Stoecker, see esp. *Christlich-Sozial: Reden und Aufsätze*, 2d ed. (Berlin, 1890). The story of Stoecker and Naumann is briefly summarized in Andreas Lindt, *Leonhard Ragaz: Eine Studie zur Geschichte und Theologie des religiösen Sozialismus* (Zollikon, 1957), pp. 205–16. (See also Andrew L. Drummond, *German Protestantism since Luther* [London, 1951].) Lindt's book is particularly useful for the account of Swiss social Christianity, and I have relied on it heavily in the subsequent discussion.

Stoecker's formation of a Christian-social workers' association in opposition to the Social Democrats, published a work in which he was led (to his surprise) to argue that the program of the Social Democrats, apart from their atheistic world view, was not at all contradictory to the message of the New Testament.[36] But Todt's ponderous work was of little influence even in Germany. The second (later) exception, much more important particularly because of his influence on the Swiss scene, was Christoph Blumhardt (1842–1919), who startled his friends by declaring publicly for the Social Democrats in 1899 and becoming their delegate to the Württemberg Diet from 1900 to 1906 before withdrawing from public life into a time of silence. Blumhardt's grounds for his action were distinctive. He discovered a biblical promise of the kingdom of God being realized in a reshaped and newly created world, coming on the very streets where the poor, the suffering, and the transgressors were found. Faith in the power of the living God and the coming of his kingdom was not to be expressed in new Christian parties (as for the young Naumann), or in Christian social reforms, or in opposition to the "godlessness" of the Social Democrats (as for Stoecker), or even in the sociopolitical program of the Social Democrats, but precisely in their faith in the future and their standing on the side of the proletariat. There is the mark of Christ's presence. God's coming kingdom means change in the world, and he is now active in history. He wills peace, freedom, and justice. The Social Democrats are fighting for these goals; therefore Blumhardt must be on their side.[37]

Religious Socialism in Switzerland

Protestant social Christianity in Switzerland, led mostly by pastors, took a course quite different from that in Germany. Freedom from the heavy burden (and excitement) of the new German nationalism made an enormous difference. Two strands need to be distinguished in the Swiss groups, the evangelical or conservative (*Positiven*) and the liberal. The former were deeply influenced by the Innere Mission and the Christian social activists of Germany, including the early Stoecker and Naumann. The Swiss Evangelical Church Union (the

36. *Der radikale deutsche Sozialismus und die christliche Gesellschaft* (Wittenberg, 1877; 2d ed., 1878).

37. See Christoph Blumhardt, *Eine Auswahl aus seinen Predigten, Andachten und Schriften*, ed. R. Lejeune, 4 vols. (Erlenbach-Zurich, 1925). On Blumhardt see esp. Gerhard Sauter, *Die Theologie des Reiches Gottes beim älteren und jüngeren Blumhardt* (Zurich, 1962).

conservative group) and its cognate workers' unions and social congresses in the cantons were hardly radical, tending to follow the line of antipathy to "atheistic," "materialistic," and "collectivist" socialism, and being modeled much after the early German image of social reforms. Yet even within this circle, Jakob Probst (1848–1910) could express openness to the affirmative positions of the Social Democrats and criticize the capitalist system.[38]

Among the liberal Swiss Protestants (the *freie Christentum* or *freisinnige Protestantismus*), other influences were at work that led in more radical directions. This was the tradition of Alois Biedermann (see *Prot. Thought*, 1:160–67), whose speculative theology was no longer appealing, but whose representation of the spirit of a free and flexible Christianity was. Also, Richard Rothe's influence was significant, particularly his idea of the church as a merely transitory phenomenon whose destiny was to be dissolved in a broader moral community, the liberal state (see *Prot. Thought*, 1:282–91).

The pioneer of social Christianity in the freie Christentum group was Albert Bitzius (1835–82), a leader in the Swiss reform party in Berne. For him, the kingdom of God was a thoroughly this-worldly moral concept, and the state a powerful means of serving the kingdom (in a more practical sense than Rothe's speculative idea). Hence the Swiss factory law of 1877 could be seen as a concrete means to the actualization of the kingdom of God. For Zwingli Wirth (1818–1905), "religion" and "humanity" were two names for the same thing. Rothe's idea of the dissolution of the church in a genuine Christianity of the world was combined with the thesis that modern individualism must be complemented by an ideal socialism. Hence the call to social responsibility. Step-by-step social reform was the right way, trusting to the activity of God in world history to take care of the utopia of the Social Democrats. Conrad Kambli (1829–1914) was more penetrating in analysis of the complexity of social questions and in study of the theoretical foundations of Social Democracy, as well as of the contemporary parties and movements. Social conservatism had to be rejected because the teaching of Jesus consists of a "new social idea" which joins the idea of the infinite value of personality with the idea of the kingdom of God being realized on earth. On

38. See Probst's speech, *Die soziale Arbeit des Pfarrers* (Bern, 1894). The other chief figure in the evangelical-social movement was Gustav Benz (1866–1937). See Lindt, *Ragaz*, pp. 223–28.

the economic side of the social question, the Social Democrats were right, though their collectivism had to be rejected as a threat to the freedom of personal life and their polemic against Christianity did not apply to free Protestantism. Bismarckian state socialism was not the way, nor was Stoecker's Christian party movement. Kambli had much appreciation for the British Christian Socialists and opted for a "scientific socialism" that involved continuing reform within the existing social orders, where possible by cooperative associations rather than state action, and without any supposition that Christianity has a monopoly on sociopolitical programs.[39]

None of these Swiss voices represented extreme or revolutionary programs. But they offered progressive, if gradualist, proposals for genuine social reforms, on a theological foundation, that moved beyond the level of palliative and charitable relief of suffering to the level of attack on the abuses of the system which caused the misery. For them the Christian imperative was not only to bandage the wounds but to change the conditions of fighting responsible for them. These earlier voices formed the background for the more dramatic religious socialism of Hermann Kutter (1863–1931) and Leonhard Ragaz (1868–1945), which can be looked upon as a parallel or analogy to the social gospel of Rauschenbusch and his associates, given the differences in social, economic, and political setting, and in particular the optimism of American culture. The kinds of reshaping proposed were not the same, but both movements held that theology and the stance of the church must be thoroughly reorganized.

Kutter and Ragaz, especially the latter, belong as much to the twentieth century as to the late nineteenth. Yet Ragaz began to publish in 1890, and much of Kutter's decisive work was completed before World War I (notably *The Immediate*, 1902; *They Must!* 1903; *Justice*, 1905; *We Pastors*, 1907; and *The Revolution of Christianity*, 1908).[40] *Das Unmittelbare* was a call back to the concreteness of life and the world, in contrast to intellectual abstraction. Will, not thought, truly constitutes life, which is in movement rather than being static. Here Fichte (as well as Kant's moral philosophy) was

39. Bitzius, Wirth, and Kambli are all represented in the social essays in *Stimmen des Freien Christentums aus der Schweiz* (Zurich, 1898).

40. Kutter, *Das Unmittelbare. Eine Menschheitsfrage*, 3d ed. (Basel, 1921); *Sie Müssen! Ein offenes Wort an die christliche Gesellschaft* (Jena, 1903); *Gerechtigkeit (Römerbrief Kap. I–VIII): Ein altes Wort an die moderne Christenheit* (Berlin, 1905); *Wir Pfarrer* (Leipzig, 1907); and *Die Revolution des Christentums* (Leipzig, 1908).

clearly in the background. But more important was Kutter's judgment that Social Democracy was the actual inaugurator of the return
to the immediacy of the world and of will. In Marx and Engels, Kutter saw the deepest concern for the dignity of humanity. Marxism
represented the revolution of man against the tyranny of things.

In *Sie Müssen!* Kutter declared passionately that the Social Democrats have a Must that the church does not have because it has no
God. The church ought to be opposing its Must to that of the Social
Democrats rather than attacking their socialist theories. At present,
by their enthusiasm and mission to work for the renovation of social
life, their energy for righteousness, Social Democrats are bringing
about the fulfillment of God's promises. True, they have no genuine
notion of sin, but while Christians are always talking about sin, for-
getful that Christ has conquered sin, the Social Democrats are actually fighting against evil. A divine force is compelling them to do the
work for which Christianity was called into existence; hence they
must go forward. The standard complaints of the Christians against
the Social Democrats all finally boomerang. They are charged with
atheism, but it is really the church that worships a dead God and
turns the message of Jesus into a harmless inwardness. The church
complains of the revolutionary character of Social Democracy, but
the New Testament announces a great revolution in the world. The
Social Democrats are charged with materialism, but the church is
practicing the worship of mammon. The Socialists have no national
loyalties, but their internationalism corresponds to the Christian
hope for peace among the peoples. The future, in fact, belongs
to the Social Democrats, not to the social reform proposals of the
church parties. "The Social Democrats are revolutionary because
God is revolutionary. They must go forward because God's kingdom
must go forward. They are men of disturbance because God is the
great disturber" (*Sie Müssen!* p. 93). Though Kutter did not himself
join the Social Democratic party (compare Blumhardt) or engage in
political activity, his protest in *Sie Müssen!* was one of the most important statements in the history of Christianity and socialism in Europe.

Social issues became central in Ragaz's preaching, particularly during his years as pastor of the Basel Münster (1902–08).[41] The social

---

41. Ragaz had studied at Basel, Jena (with Lipsius), and Berlin (with Otto Pfleiderer).
His move away from speculative theology was influenced by Ritschl, though he was never a
Ritschlian. Prior to the Basel pastorate, he had been the preacher at Heinzenberg (1890

question was now the great God question, the social movement the breaking in of a new world, a new time of God. Coming out of the tradition of social responsibility of Bitzius and Kambli, Ragaz was also influenced by the English social thought of Carlyle and Robertson, by the early Naumann (even including Naumann's *Briefe über Religion* of 1903), by Herrmann's moral passion, by Weiss's eschatological view of Jesus' preaching of the kingdom, by Kierkegaard's antithesis between Christianity and bourgeois liberalism, and (much later) by Blumhardt. He was of course fully in touch with current German social thought and movements. But at least equally important were such matters as the Boer War (1899–1902), which shattered world-historical optimism; the concrete economic struggles; and the stagnation of the church's response. Thence came his conviction that the church must be on the side of the weak and therefore socialist in the deepest sense.

In particular, the bricklayers' strike of 1903, together with the impact of Kutter's *Sie Müssen!* and *Das Unmittelbare*, drove him beyond the level of charitable palliatives and reform measures. He saw the strike not as just an economic or political occurrence, but as an event in Heilsgeschichte, the vanguard of a new world. He drew closer to the Social Democrats: the church and the Social Democrats need each other; a new reformation is at hand, in which the workers must help. All this led to the manifesto of his address at the 1906 annual meeting of the Swiss pastors' association, "The Gospel and the Social Struggle of the Present," and the founding in the same year of the journal *Neue Wege*, of which Ragaz was an editor for thirty-nine years until his death in 1945.[42]

The new lines developed in the 1906 address were Ragaz's programmatic statement of his religious socialism. The struggle of the present is between socialism, whose principle is economic solidarity, and an unjust capitalism which has replaced the handcraft economy with mechanization and industrialization and whose principle is

---

–93) and Chur (1893–1902). In 1908 he was appointed professor at Zurich and held this post until 1921, when he resigned to devote himself fully (especially as writer and publisher) to the religious-socialist movement. The career of Ragaz is examined in detail in Lindt, *Ragaz*.

42. See Ragaz, *Das Evangelium und der soziale Kampf der Gegenwart* (Basel, 1906), and his sermons from the 1904–08 Basel years, *Dein Reich Komme*, 2 vols. (Basel, 1909); his address to the 1908 Aarau Christian Student Conference, *Der Christ im sozialen Kampf unseres Tages* (Bern, 1908); *Die Neue Schweiz* (Olten, 1917); and *Neue Wege, Blätter für religiöse Arbeit* (1906–), to which Ragaz contributed nearly a thousand items.

profit. The social ethic of conservative Christianity belongs to the patriarchal thinking of a precapitalist era. In relation to the new mechanistic thought and lifestyle of capitalism, socialism presents a humane way of thinking, oriented to freedom and justice. How does
the gospel of Jesus apply to this struggle? Historically, Christianity
has moved between quiescent and forward-thrusting forms of faith.
The former looks backward to a salvation that has occurred in
Christ, and it is concerned with individualistic piety, pure doctrine,
and the ecclesiastical institution (as in Lutheranism). The latter,
which stresses discipleship to Christ rather than belief in him, looks
forward in hope to the redemption of humanity. It places the coming
kingdom of God in the center rather than the church as the institution of salvation. It is an active, radical, social kind of religion. For
Ragaz this is clearly the authentic tradition. To serve God is to serve
humanity, human freedom, and brotherhood. The capitalistic economy contradicts that gospel; it cannot be defended in the name of Jesus. We must again praise God by looking forward in hope for the
kingdom of God. Hence Ragaz declared for socialism (though on an
ethical idealist rather than a crumbling Marxist basis) in the struggle
for freedom from the captivity into which capitalism has brought humanity. The task in the present struggle is to work for an ethical and
religious foundation of the new order. What is needed is not only
personal involvement in the social struggle, but the understanding of
that struggle as a criterion for God's way in history, for allowing the
gospel to come alive again and to burst all the ecclesiastical static-
conservative bonds in the interest of the formation of a new social
order.

Such was the task of *Neue Wege* and the circle of religious socialists
that began to meet in 1906 and to organize religious-socialist conferences. Kutter also belonged to that circle, though personal and ideological differences emerged between Ragaz and Kutter, with Ragaz
being more strongly for solidarity with the workers and more concerned with practical steps in the political struggle for the realization
of socialism. In the years before the war, there were also contacts
with the British Christian Socialists, both Anglican and nonconformist, and with the modest circle of French Protestant social Christians.

The hopes for a new order, especially an order of peace, were dramatically dashed by the outbreak of World War I, which pressed
Ragaz to see the world's hostility to God not only in capitalism but
also in the spirit of power and militarism and to devote himself to the

task of rebuilding Swiss life in its entirety (see *Die Neue Schweiz*, 1917). The story of the renewal of hope for religious socialism after 1918 belongs to another account.

British Social Christianity

Compared to the German Protestant church's struggle with the weed of Social Democracy, British Christianity in the late nineteenth century seemed ready to cultivate a whole garden of Christian socialist or socialist Christian movements (that is, those who were socialist because they were Christian and those who were socialist and also Christian). Three Anglican groups could qualify for such designation: the Guild of St. Matthew, 1877 (quite Anglo-Catholic); the Christian Social Union, 1889; and the Church Socialist League, 1906. In addition, there were the largely nonconformist Christian Socialist Society, 1886, and the Christian Socialist League, 1894 (later the Christian Social Brotherhood); the New Church (Swedenborgian) Socialist Society, 1896; the Socialist Quaker Society, 1898 (after 1924, the Society of Socialist Christians); the short-lived Free Church Socialist League, 1909; and R. J. Campbell's League of Progressive Thought and Social Service, 1908.[43] And from 1909 there was a British section of the American Christian Socialist Fellowship (largely Congregationalist).

The reasons for this difference are various. Surely the inspiration of the mid-century Christian socialism of Maurice, Kingsley, and Ludlow had its impact, especially among the Anglicans, even though that movement did not last and its leaders were thoroughly middle-class in orientation. Certainly it was significant that socialism as it developed in Britain was much less heavily Marxist in ideology and less antireligious. Few British socialists were aggressively hostile to Christianity, and activist secularism declined in the 1890s, though the labor movement offered a convenient vehicle for the expression of the religious fervor of the masses, once that was detached from the middle-class religious establishment. The multiplicity of religious socialist groups had something to do with denominationalism, which led to the formation of independent, even competitive, societies with little overlapping in membership. The extreme vagueness of the idea of

43. The story of these groups, and indeed of the whole non-Catholic Christian socialist movement in Britain, is admirably told in Jones, *Christian Socialist Revival*. For the Roman Catholic development, see A. P. McEntree, *The Social Catholic Movement in Great Britain* (New York, 1927).

socialism also made its contribution, in that socialism could mean anything from support of cooperatives to thoroughgoing collectivism or nationalization.[44] Add to this the developing liberalism in theology, which in Britain as in the United States was coupled generally with a deepened concern for social and economic conditions, especially in the urban centers, and with recognition of the need to come to terms with the emergence of the labor movement and socialism, as well as with the apparent alienation of the working class.

Another important influence on the British scene was Henry George's *Progress and Poverty*, published in the United States in 1870 but widely read in Britain, where it had special impact because of the fiery indictment of present society and the dramatic proposal of the Single Tax on land rent, which spoke to the English concern with the land question. George's proposal was widely taken up by the Christian socialists. And the literature of exposure, from popular tracts (such as *The Bitter Cry of Outcast London*, 1882) to detailed studies of slum conditions, played a large role in the latter part of the century.[45]

After the time of Maurice, the first important Christian socialist society was the Guild of St. Matthew, founded in 1877 by Stewart Headlam (1847–1924). Relatively small, exclusively Anglican, high church and sacramentalist in its understanding of the responsibility of the church to society, the Guild became increasingly radical in its reform proposals (from Henry George's Single Tax to the progressive income tax, limitation of workers' hours, reform of public secular education and of the church) and pioneered the way for other broader-based and much more influential groups. Among these (still Anglican) societies was the Christian Social Union, which sprang largely out of the same Oxford group that published *Lux Mundi* and was organized in the same year (1889).

---

44. Jones remarks that "most Christian socialists stopped short, on the collectivist track, at municipal 'gas-and-water' socialism coupled with various types of welfare and factory-control legislation or consumer action of a respectable variety" (*Christian Socialist Revival*, p. 9). It would seem that the Fabian Society, which was to be so important in the British socialist development, almost deliberately cultivated vagueness about the relation between its collectivism and other sorts of social action.

45. See esp. Charles Booth, *Life and Labour of the People in London*, 3d ser., vol. 16: *Religious Influence* (London, 1902). For an earlier influence, see Sir John Seeley, *Ecce Homo: A Survey of the Life and Work of Jesus Christ* (Boston, 1866; published anonymously in both England and America), which emphasized the social side of the ethics of Jesus and made popular the phrase "enthusiasm for humanity."

The initiating spirit of the Union was Henry Scott Holland (1847 –1918), who was joined by Charles Gore and Cambridge's B. F. Westcott, among others.[46] The declared aims of the Union were "to claim for Christian law the ultimate authority to rule social practice," "to study in common how to apply the moral truths and principles of Christianity to the social and economic difficulties of the present time," and "to present Christ in practical life as . . . the enemy of wrong and selfishness, the power of righteousness and love." Much less given to particular platforms of action than was the Guild of St. Matthew, the Union was formed mainly as a fellowship to study and publicize problems, educating members to social reform. Yet it publicly encouraged selective buying from businesses that had acceptable trade-union wage scales and petitioned Commons for revision of the factory laws. Although largely an elitist group, the Union nonetheless had a powerful effect on the Anglican communion and established a branch in the United States. Scott Holland, as preacher at St. Paul's in London (1884–1910) and subsequently Regius Professor at Oxford, and Charles Gore (1855–1932), the first principal at Pusey House and later a leading bishop, were the chief spokesmen. Gore thundered prophetically against the guilt of the church, against economic selfishness, against the failure of the church to be a society of the moral law of God's kingdom, organized to express moral opinion in such areas as economics and the relations of the social classes. Holland, witty and confident, was more appreciative of the role of the state as an agent of social change, and looked toward a Christian welfare state. Westcott was the most optimistic of the group, and less typical in this respect of the English social Christians. He could say to a young generation in 1887: "All things are ready. . . . The issue will . . . be decided in your generation" (see Social Aspects, pp. 95–96).

The CSU did not have a really "socialist" economic policy and generally stayed at a distance from the Independent Labour party. It was progressive, humanitarian, Henry-Georgeist, mildly feminist, and proworker. As Jones aptly puts it, "most Social Unionists were more *anticapitalist* than pro-socialist" (*Christian Socialist Revival*, p.

46. See Scott Holland, in the Union's *Ground of Our Appeal* (1890), *Labour Movement* (London, 1897), and *Our Neighbors* (London, 1911). For Gore, see *The Social Doctrine of the Sermon on the Mount* (London, 1893) and *Christianity and Socialism* (London, 1908). For Westcott (who was explicitly not a member of the *Lux Mundi* group), see *Social Aspects of Christianity* (London, 1887), *Socialism* (London, 1890), and *Christian Social Union* (Bristol, 1897; includes addresses by Westcott, Holland, and Gore).

197). Their socialism focused on cooperative, rather than competitive, organization of industry and on rectifying the abuses of capitalist society through reforms based in Christian ethical ideals. (See Gore's paper on *Christianity and Socialism*, delivered at the important 1908 Lambeth conference.) The more extreme Anglican society was the Church Socialist League, founded in 1906 and rooted in Yorkshire radicalism, which protested the timidity of the CSU's Mauriceanism and opted for "real" economic and social change, with, for example, community ownership of land and capital, and for much closer association with the Independent Labour Party and the Social Democratic Federation.

Yet the Christian Social Union, because of its broad clergy membership, had much to do with altering the official stance of the Anglican church in relation to economic questions. And it should be noted that the CSU leaders were vigorously opposed to the Boer War and the economic colonialism they saw in it (much more so than the Fabian Society, for example).

The Christian socialism of the Anglican societies and spokesmen was generally incarnational or sacramental in its theological basis. In the Mauricean tradition, the incarnation was understood to mean the consecration of the human body and the whole of daily life, which implied that Christianity had to be as much concerned with the material as with the spiritual. The sacraments, especially baptism and the Eucharist, reassert and express the incarnation and the sacrifice of Christ for all humankind, and thus the brotherhood of man and the equality of all before God.

The socialism of the non-Anglican Christian groups, in contrast, was based more on the idea of divine immanence (when it was doctrinally oriented; many of the social reformers among the nonconformists were not). The most vivid example of the immanentist view was doubtless the New Theology of the great Congregationalist preacher R. J. Campbell, who drew enormous crowds (over seven thousand) to the London City Temple (1903–15) at a time when other congregations were shrinking. The heyday of the movement, and the climax of Congregational social Christianity in the prewar period, was in the years 1907–10, beginning with Campbell's announcement of the New Theology and the formation of the Progressive League, of which he became president. In a sermon on "Christianity and Collectivism" (1906), he announced his new socialist faith, which meant common cause with the labor churches, trade unions, the Fabians, and the Independent Labour Party. The theological side of the New Theology, as noted earlier, was a thoroughgoing emphasis on divine immanence in the universe and in mankind, on human divinity as a manifestation of the eternal Christ. But the New Theology was also equally and essentially the social gospel, understood as the revival of the impulse of primitive Christianity. It was, he said, simply "spiritual socialism," the proper theology of the labor movement, whether that movement knew it or not. The proposals of Campbell and the Progressive League went far beyond such half-measures of reform as profit-sharing, land reform, Henry Georgeanism, and cooperatives, to real changes such as socialization of capital, national ownership of natural resources, railroads, and basic industries, and freedom for women—in short, a genuine collectivist socialism.[47]

The Social Gospel in America

If social Christianity in Britain included a wide variety of views on social reform and of relations to socialism, as well as of theological foundations, the same is equally true of the movement in the United States. We shall focus on the social gospel as it emerged in the liberal theological tradition because in it the social concern posed the most significant theological questions, and because of its prominence in the American Protestant scene as well as its continuing influence after World War I. But we should not suppose that the impulse to social reform was limited to liberal Christianity. On the contrary, there was deep concern among conservative Protestants for the plight of the poor and the conditions of the worker, though on a largely individualistic basis and with attention devoted chiefly to relief measures. A similar perspective was dominant in such independent groups as the Salvation Army and the various rescue missions. At the other extreme were the radical voices that called for even more extensive social reconstruction than was characteristic of the main line of the

---

47. See Campbell, *New Theology*; also *Christianity and the Social Order, The New Theology and the Social Movement* (London, 1907), *The New Theology and the Socialist Movement* (Stockport, 1908), and *Primitive Christianity and Modern Socialism* (London, n.d.). As noted earlier, Campbell was initially opposed by his Congregationalist brothers, but later reconciled with them, including P. T. Forsyth, who was also a strong proponent of social theology (rejecting mere philanthropy and attacking the social theory of capitalism). By the end of the war, Campbell had returned to his original Anglican connection, and he served a number of parishes, eventually becoming chancellor of Chichester Cathedral (1930–46). Full accounts of other nonconformist social activists and groups, as well as the Anglicans', can be found in Jones, *Christian Socialist Revival*.

social gospel, for example, thoroughgoing Christian socialists like George D. Herron, who eventually left the church for political action, and W. D. P. Bliss, who founded several socialist societies in the United States, including the American Fabian Society.[48]

Although the social gospel came to have distinctive American features, and may not unjustiy be thought of as an important American contribution to modern Protestant thought, it was not, as should by now be evident, either original or unique to the United States. Impulses to social Christianity, rooted in Maurice and his associates, were earlier in Great Britain, and through the latter part of the century (especially between 1900 and 1910) there was significant interchange across the Atlantic. Gladden was influenced by the Brighton preacher Robertson. Henry George's ideas were taken up by both Britons and Americans. The Christian Social Union had branches in America, and the American Christian Socialist Fellowship had a section in England. Ely's book on socialism was hailed by Scott Holland in 1895, and Ely praised Fremantle's Bampton lectures on "The World as the Subject of Redemption" as giving a religious basis for reform. The American socialist evangelist J. Stitt Wilson (a disciple of Herron) was involved with R. J. Campbell's League and made four lecture campaigns in England along with his extensive work in the United States (which included running as socialist candidate for the governorship of California in 1910).

Yet there were important differences between British and American developments. For one thing, the violent labor conflicts in the United States' railroad and steel industries which took place in 1877,

48. From the extensive literature on American social Christianity, the following works are of particular value. Henry F. May, *Protestant Churches and Industrial America* (New York, 1949), remains the classic study of the various forms of social Christianity against their historical background. Charles H. Hopkins, *The Rise of the Social Gospel in American Protestantism, 1865–1915* (New Haven, 1940), is a pioneering and detailed account of the main line, though overstating the uniquely American character of the movement. For the conservative stream, see Norris Magnuson, *Salvation in the Slums: Evangelical Social Work, 1865–1920* (Metuchen, N.J., 1977), and George M. Marsden, *Fundamentalism and American Culture: The Shaping of Twentieth-Century Evangelicalism, 1870–1925* (Oxford, 1982). For the rescue missions and the Salvation Army, among others, see Aaron I. Abell, *The Urban Impact on American Protestantism, 1865–1900* (Cambridge, Mass., 1943); see also, for Roman Catholic trends, Abell, *American Catholicism and Social Action: A Search for Social Justice, 1865–1950* (Garden City, N.Y., 1960). Ahlstrom, *Religious History*, and Hutchison, *Modernist Impulse*, provide good summaries. Robert T. Handy, *The Social Gospel in America, 1870–1920* (New York, 1966), presents an excellent selection, with brief introductions, from the work of Gladden, Ely, and Rauschenbusch. See also James B. Gilbert, *Work without Salvation: America's Intellectuals and Industrial Alienation, 1880–1910* (Baltimore, 1977).

1886, and 1892−94 (May calls them the "three earthquakes") were of particularly dramatic impact and probably contributed more than any other single cause, even the general conditions of the urban poor, to the rise of the Christian social movement in America. Second, American religious pluralism (or at least denominationalism) and the absence of the idea of a state church that was always present in Britain and Europe meant different understandings of how socialist programs might be developed.

Third, with the exception of a few thinkers like Westcott, Fremantle, and Campbell, the mood in Britain was marked more by anguish and even doubt about progress than by the optimism and cultural confidence that generally characterized the American social movement. There were gloomy views, and certainly perceptions of crisis, in the United States movements, but ebullient hopes and feelings of liberation were more prevalent. A characteristically American idea of the early 1900s was that, given a renewed high point in revivalism, the world could be evangelized "in this generation." Yet it should not be thought that the social movement was given to the baptizing of "American destiny." On the contrary, at least among the liberals, the confidence was in a stripped-down Christianity, a deculturalized gospel that was worthy of export. Imperialism was criticized as compromising the true goal of missions.

Did the social gospel triumph in America? On balance, it would be difficult to argue that the American social gospel had a greater impact on religious, social, or political life than did the British social Christian movements. Both had a broadly leavening influence. The social gospel was a minority movement. Certainly not all theological liberals were social liberals, and indeed the late nineteenth century in general was the time of the closest identification of American Protestantism with bourgeois society and the free-enterprise system. The social gospel was much stronger among clergy and in seminaries than among the laity (and what theological movement hasn't been?). It affected some denominations more than others. The First World War dashed much of the optimism that had powered the movement—though the impact of the war was much less shattering in the United States than across the Atlantic—and after the war the movement persisted in a chastened form and with less contagious enthusiasm. Yet from its origins in the 1870s and 1880s the social gospel did reach a kind of prominence in the years from 1900 to 1914 that has led this period rightly to be described as the "era of the social gospel"

in American Protestantism. In several of the liberal denominations—Congregational, Episcopal, and the Northern segments of
the Methodist, Baptist, and Presbyterian churches—the leaders of
the movement were particularly articulate and conspicuous. Social
creeds were adopted. The major Southern white denominations also
underwent significant changes in social consciousness and programs
to effect social justice. The high point of influence was marked by the
formation of the Federal Council of the Churches of Christ in the
United States of America (1908), which was almost as much a chan-
nel for the social gospel as for church cooperation, and the "Men
and Religion Forward Movement" of 1911–12, which did much to
spread the social gospel. The classic statement of social gospel theology was Walter Rauschenbusch's *Theology for the Social Gospel* (New
York, 1917).

Along with Rauschenbusch (1861–1918), Washington Gladden
(1836–1918) and Richard T. Ely (1854–1943) can most usefully
serve as representatives of the movement. Gladden and Ely both
came out of strict Presbyterian backgrounds, Gladden becoming a
Congregationalist, Ely moving into the Episcopal church; Rauschenbusch was a Baptist. They represented both the Northeast and the
Midwest.

Gladden has often been called the father of the social gospel, not
only because he was among the first of its exponents, but also because of the way he exhibited the characteristic elements of the
American movement, and because he was a strong stimulus to others
through his editorial work and his more than thirty volumes (largely
sermons). He was more a popularizer than an original thinker. After
a brief time as a public school teacher, he was ordained a Congregational minister (1860) and served pastorates near New York City and
in New England, where he became immersed in the problems of
industrial labor. He spent the final thirty-two years of his career as
pastor in Columbus, Ohio. For four years (1871–75) he was religion
editor of the formerly Congregational New York weekly, *The Independent*, where he became famous both for his support of the New
Theology (backing David Swing in the early heresy trial—see chapter 5, above) and for his attacks on the corruption of the notorious
Tweed Ring.[49]

49. See Gladden's editorial, "What We Are Going to Do about It," in *The Independent*, August 31, 1871, a reply to Tweed's cynical response to the campaigns by *The New York Times*
and *Harper's Weekly*, "What Are You Going to Do about It?"

Having been liberated theologically by the works of Frederick W. Robertson and Horace Bushnell (especially Bushnell's "Preliminary Dissertation on Language"; see *Prot. Thought*, 1:258–63), Gladden was one of the prime interpreters of the New Theology. In particular, he was instrumental in popularizing the new historical approach to the Bible and the positive relation of evolution and theology.[50] He was influenced by, among others, Theodore Munger, Newman Smyth, W. N. Clarke, W. A. Brown, H. C. King, A. M. Fairbairn, R. J. Campbell, and Richard Ely.

Gladden's representation of the social gospel first came to major published expression in *Working People and Their Employers* (Boston, 1876), which grew out of his Springfield, Massachusetts, experience and focused on the theme of the relations of labor and capital. Though he later judged that in this work he had been less sympathetic to labor unions than he ought to have been, the early themes of the social gospel were there. The Christian principle requires that competition be replaced by cooperation. The "war" occasioned by the wages system will end only when the system "is abolished or greatly modified." Christianity must cease to be the ally of despotism. Now that the crisis of slavery has been resolved, primary attention must be turned to the problem of the workers. Later on, Gladden joined the struggle against monopolies and could argue for government ownership of natural monopolies as an element in what he called "applied Christianity." If there is to be war between employer and laborer, then "we must grant to labor belligerent rights," but what we most need is the peace of cooperation that will serve the interests of both capital and labor. This is not a socialist program. We are not ready yet for a revolution in which private enterprise should be abolished and capital belong to the state. But major changes are possible. The principle of cooperation is what we are coming to by and by.

In the last point, Gladden shared the optimistic progressivism of many of the social gospelers. The complete Christianization of life —which is what the kingdom of God means—is not only "what we pray for and work for," but is a goal that can be achieved. It is cer-

---

50. See esp. the lectures and subsequent book, *Who Wrote the Bible? A Book for the People* (Boston, 1891); also *Burning Questions of the Life that Now Is, and of that Which Is to Come* (New York, 1889); *How Much Is Left of the Old Doctrines? A Book for the People* (Boston, 1899); and *Present Day Theology*, 3d ed. (Columbus, 1913).

tainly not inevitable, but it is possible for the United States some day to be a fully Christian land. Here Gladden exemplifies the combination of deep optimism with a powerful critique of culture, notably of the system of competition, and an equally strong call for reform of the church. His optimism was not so much about what is, but about what might be, under God.[51]

Richard T. Ely was the academic advocate of the social gospel. A noted teacher of economics and cofounder (1885) of the American Economic Association, he was deeply immersed, through speaking and writing, in the social gospel during the decade following the mid-1880s and did as much to shape its economic thinking as any other single figure. Like Gladden, his origins were in rural New York state. After attending Williams and Columbia colleges, he spent four years (1876–80) studying economics in Germany at Halle, Heidelberg, and Berlin, returning to teach at Johns Hopkins University for eleven years and then at the University of Wisconsin for more than three and a half decades.

More than any other figure in the social gospel movement, Ely was a careful student of European socialism, drawing on his research abroad. He published an important work, *French and German Socialism in Modern Times* (New York, 1883), which reflected his training and interest in historical economic development rather than economic theory.[52] He took socialism seriously and was sympathetic to a Christian mild and evolutionary development in that direction, though he held that "socialism and communism are not practicable theories for modern industrial society."

Ely's theology was clear and uncomplicated, what he could call "the simple gospel of Christ," summarized in the dual commandment of love for God and neighbor. The heart of the problem is the neglect of this teaching and the failure to apply it in the past. He concluded, after "years of observation and reflection," not only that there was a "clear alienation of the thinking wage-workers from the church,

51. Among Gladden's social writings, see *Applied Christianity: Moral Aspects of Social Questions* (Boston, 1886); *Tools and the Man: Property and Industry Under the Christian Law* (Boston, 1893); *Social Salvation* (Boston, 1902); *Christianity and Socialism* (New York, 1905); *The Church and the Kingdom* (New York, 1894); and *The Church and Modern Life* (Boston, 1911).

52. See also *The Past and the Present of Political Economy* (Baltimore, 1884), and *The Labor Movement in America* (New York, 1886). For Ely's other contributions to social gospel thinking, see *Social Aspects of Christianity and other Essays* (New York, 1889), and *The Social Law of Service* (New York, 1896).

which, on the whole is growing" and which "sometimes amounts to positive hostility, as I think is quite generally the case in New York and Chicago," but also that this was due to the church's indifference to the wage-earner. The church has failed to rebuke corruption in high places and has seemed to have a negative attitude "with respect to every proposed reform" (see *Social Aspects*, pp. 1–48). Christianity has failed both to maintain and to apply the gospel of Christian love and self-sacrifice, which is the condition of social service. There is thus need for renewal of the gospel of Christ in the church, and also for more thorough social-scientific research, which the church has sadly neglected. Both were tasks which Ely set himself.

Ely's proposals for economic reform were restrained and cautious. As early as 1884 he was attacking laissez-faire economics and the competitive warfare principle in contrast to the cooperative principle. He was strongly pro-union and spent much energy interpreting the labor movement to the public, but he thought there were better means of achieving labor's ends than strikes (a necessary evil in a conflict situation) and defended himself vigorously at the time of the disastrous Pullman strike of 1894 against charges of inciting violence (anarchy being for him the sum and substance of evil). He saw that the role of the state was bound to grow, and he was prepared to support the "socialization" of natural monopolies either by government ownership or, depending on the historical and social circumstances, by firm government control. He wanted to emphasize the idea of "social solidarity," which he saw as a central biblical and Christian view that was independently confirmed by science, literature, politics, and economics (see *The Social Law*, chapter 6). Here, as elsewhere for Ely, religion and social science supported each other. Social science, like all science, was a progressive unfolding of truth and formed a unified whole with one's commitment to the most perfect system of ethics, the teaching of Jesus. This understanding continued in Ely's later extensive involvement in municipal reform, land economics, and church unity.

Walter Rauschenbusch was the most theologically able among the exponents of the main-line American social gospel and was recognized as its leading prophet in the decade after 1907. His opinions were widely accepted apart from his opposition to American participation in World War I. He was also the social gospel's most international figure in the influences that played upon him and the connections he made in his writings. With a background of Lutheran

pastors in Germany, he was brought up in a strict pietist German
Baptist family in Rochester, New York (where his father was a professor in the German department of the seminary, having been persuaded of Baptist views after coming to the United States as a Lutheran missionary). Some of his early schooling was in Germany
(Gütersloh and Berlin), and he was in Germany again in 1891
studying New Testament and in 1907–08. Ritschl (and the liberal
historical Jesus movement, for example, Harnack) was doubtless of
greatest importance for him, but he was acquainted with the social
movement in Germany, including the work of Todt, and with Kutter
and Ragaz in Switzerland. He was also influenced by Maurice and
Kingsley and had studied current social movements in England during his 1891 trip. He was close to American liberal theology from
Bushnell through Clarke and Brown.

The book that brought Rauschenbusch to national attention was
Christianity and the Social Crisis (New York, 1907), which appeared a
decade after he had become a professor at Rochester Theological
Seminary. The ultimate source for the work, however, was the dozen
years of his pastorate to a poor immigrant group, ground under by
the urban industrial situation, in the Second German Baptist Church
of New York (1885–97), located in one of the most depressed slum
sections of the West Side, Hell's Kitchen. There he had become
a leader in the emerging social gospel, and he was influenced by
Henry George and associated with other ministers in the publication
of a short-lived periodical *For the Right*, in a group called the Brotherhood of the Kingdom, and in the annual Baptist Congress.

As the title proclaims, the mood of the book was one of crisis—a
crisis of injustice and an immoral order brought on by industrialism
and especially by capitalism (gross inequality, land monopoly, the triumph of commercial values, meaningless work under inhuman conditions, and so on). This was a historical moment out of which collapse might indeed come. There are, he said, no guarantees of
progress or even survival. The continents are strewn with the ruins
of nations and civilizations. The crisis cannot be dealt with by the old
evangelicalism, with its merely individualistic personal regeneration,
even though no amount of outward social reform would ever eliminate the need for inner personal transformation. We are confronted
by a plain alternative: the deluge, or revitalization through a genuinely social Christianity. The choice is a real one. Collapse is not inev-

itable. Renewal can be accomplished, and the process is not impossible to find.

Rauschenbusch's closest approach to reflecting the culture of the day, especially its optimism, as well as that vision of social reconstruction which took him furthest along the line of his practical or pragmatic socialism (as distinct from the scientific or doctrinaire socialism that he found theoretically as well as practically defective), appeared in *Christianizing the Social Order* (New York, 1912).[53] There he was willing to speak of "our semi-Christian social order." In large domains of social life, Christianity has been tried and it has succeeded. Not that they have become top-to-bottom Christian, but they have been brought "under the sway of Christ's law in their spirit and in their fundamental structure" (p. 123). In that sense, the family, the church, education, and even political life have become Christian in modern times. The great unchristianized domain that remains is the economic system.

All the great themes of Rauschenbusch, and the characteristic notes of the social gospel generally, were summed up in his classic statement, *A Theology for the Social Gospel*.[54] The work is rooted explicitly in the judgment that the church requires an enlarged theology—a systematic theology large enough to match and vital enough to motivate the social gospel. The social gospel has recovered the authentic message of the Hebrew prophets' demand for justice and Jesus' proclamation of the kingdom of God as a call to a new righteousness under the law of love. Rauschenbusch had no time for the

53. In a 1901 address, Rauschenbusch carefully set out his distinction between dogmatic and practical socialism and his reasons for rejecting the former. Practical socialism he described as involving such measures as appropriation of economic rent by taxation of ground values, municipal ownership of natural monopolies, postal office control of express and telegraph business, steeply graduated income tax to break up great capital accumulations, trade organization for possible eventual management of industry, labor laws relating to hours and working conditions and to restrict female labor and prevent child labor, and the use of increased government income for the general welfare. The address is reprinted in Handy, *Social Gospel*, pp. 308–22. In *Christianizing the Social Order*, Rauschenbusch could speak of socialism as "far and away the most powerful force for justice, democracy, and organized fraternity in the modern world." Like most of the others in the social gospel movement, he saw labor and capital as the great problems; race and women's suffrage were only touched upon.

54. New York, 1917. The substance of the book was delivered as the Taylor Lectures at Yale, just before the entry of the United States into the war and a few months before his own terminal illness.

eschatological interpretations of Weiss and Schweitzer, which he put down partly to the professional German theologians' kinship to bourgeois society and their constitutional incapacity to understand revolutionary ideas. Jesus was not of course a social reformer in the modern sense, but his teaching does speak directly to social problems.[55]

We note here the extent to which, in an enlarged theology, Rauschenbusch sounded themes typical of liberal theology: not only the confidence in the availability of the Synoptic Jesus for modern life, but also the revision of the ideas of revelation and inspiration to restore the spirit of prophecy to the center; the definition of sin as selfishness and rejection of the righteousness of the kingdom and the best interests of humanity; the redeeming work of Christ as centering in his battle against religious bigotry and the sinful corruptions that conspired to kill him (his death revealing both the power of sin and the love of God); the inherent worth of human nature; and the immanence of God, his "all-pervading life" as the ground of the "spiritual oneness of the race and our hope for its closer fellowship." The conception of God has to be freed of all despotic and monarchical elements, "democratized" by reappropriation of Jesus' teaching of the fatherhood of God—in one of Rauschenbusch's many vivid expressions, "the worst thing that could happen to God would be to remain an autocrat while the world is moving toward democracy" (*Theology* [New York, 1945 ed.], p. 178). Like most of the social gospelers, Rauschenbusch had an instrumentalist view of the church, which should not be an institution for itself, but, renewed and cleansed, will be a means to prepare for the realizations of the kingdom.

Yet these themes were balanced by others. The kingdom of God is unequivocally divine in origin, in its progress, and in its consummation. It is eternal in the midst of time, both present and future. We do not build it, but can only share in it or retard its realization as the moral organization of humanity according to the will of God. The idea of the kingdom is judgment as well as promise. The social gospel and the individual gospel are inseparably linked. Here, as at so many

55. It is instructive to contrast Rauschenbusch's popular and most widely circulated work, *The Social Principles of Jesus* (New York, 1916), with Herrmann, *Die sittlichen Weisungen Jesu* (see above).

points, Rauschenbusch's polarity reminds us of Ritschl's ellipse with two foci, the religious and the ethical.

Rauschenbusch's most creative contribution in the *Theology* was his interpretation of the idea of human solidarity in sin and salvation. He thought he found this solidaristic conception in Schleiermacher and Ritschl, and in principle he could have. But in his own articulation, particularly in his sociopsychological understanding of the transmission and universality of sin, he was closer to Horace Bushnell. The idea of the kingdom of God, for him, had to be correlated with the idea of a real, superpersonal kingdom of evil. Traditionally, evil had been viewed as a satanic kingdom and related to the idea of the hereditary transmission of original sin. Those ideas did point, Rauschenbusch thought, to a fundamental reality, really corporate sin and evil. But that reality may now be better understood as a natural historical process of the transmission and perpetuation of evils through the channels of social tradition. Here we can see real superpersonal (that is, superindividual) forces of evil, social idealizations and institutionalizations of evil, which can be recognized by contrast to the kingdom of God and its righteousness, and this kingdom of evil must be overcome in genuine social salvation.

In his use of psychological and sociological ideas of the self and society to interpret the organic unity of humanity in sin, Rauschenbusch went quite beyond what Schleiermacher and Ritschl had been able to say. In his application of the idea of the kingdom of God to social reconstruction, he moved in a direction that Ritschl could hardly have imagined. He shared with Ritschl the confidence in a relatively easy harmony of faith, history, and ethics, but he injected the new principle of a critical relation to social structures.

A Theology for the Social Gospel was not intended to be a theological summa, but rather a pointed proposal for a new kind of contextualization of theology. In his tendencies to acculturation and his critique of culture, Rauschenbusch exemplified the distinctively American version of the social gospel, which can be set alongside the thoroughgoing Christian socialism in Britain and the Swiss religious socialism of Ragaz and Kutter as prophetic announcements of a genuinely new view of the church's relation to social structures.

8

Ernst Troeltsch: Faith, History,

and Ethics in Tension

Any reader of the preceding chapters will be keenly aware of the absence of extended examination of Ernst Troeltsch at many points where he was deeply involved with the issues being considered. Indeed, discussion of any of the problem areas we have dealt with is incomplete without taking account of Troeltsch's contribution. The reason for deferring a full treatment of Troeltsch is simple: more than any other single figure, he stands at the end of nineteenth-century Protestant thought as the one in whom the central issues converge in sharp focus. As Albrecht Ritschl opens the period from 1870 to World War I with a concentration on the dominant concerns of the theology of the time, so Troeltsch most clearly reflects the results of the consideration of faith, history, ethics, and their interrelations at the end of the century. He did not "solve" the problems, but he most acutely showed the state of the discussion, in which the harmony of faith judgments, historical investigation, and moral impulse that seemed so comfortable in the thought of Ritschl were replaced by sharp inner tension. In this sense, Troeltsch may rightly be looked upon as the outcome of Protestant thought in the nineteenth century, the one who most effectively posed the problems facing twentieth-century theology.

Such a judgment is reflected in the renaissance of interest in Troeltsch in recent decades and in the rapidly growing body of literature dealing with his thought. But the reappraisal of Troeltsch is far from complete; much of his work needs further analysis. In this chapter I do not attempt to give a full account of all aspects of his work or development. Instead I suggest a perspective in relation to the general view of late-nineteenth-century Protestant thought proposed in the preceding chapters from which the importance of Troeltsch can be estimated. In particular, I join the increasing number of interpreters who reject the once common view that somehow

Troeltsch's theology failed, or collapsed, or even that in his later career he abandoned theological concerns for philosophy of history and social philosophy. In fact, Troeltsch posed the problems of Christian religious reflection in their acutest form and laid out certain directions of thought that cannot be evaded by subsequent generations. In this sense he is like Kant: one cannot go around him in the attempt to recover a prior state of theological reflection; one must rather go through the critical perspective that he embodied. Troeltsch did not find fully satisfying answers to his questions but he put the questions in an inescapable way.

Ernst Troeltsch (1865–1923) was born near Augsburg, the eldest son of a physician, into a family characterized (according to Troeltsch) by a mild religious rationalism. He opted for the study of theology at Erlangen, beginning in the winter of 1884–85, where he could study both historical problems and metaphysics.[1] But Erlangen proved unexciting because it was dominated theologically by a neopietist, mild Lutheran confessionalism (see *Prot. Thought*, 1:218–27). The faculty was not strong in philosophy, and Troeltsch's interests in social and political problems, as well as in exploring the natural scientific world view, were unsatisfied. So Troeltsch (along with his friend Wilhelm Bousset) moved shortly to Göttingen, where he was among the last of Ritschl's pupils. While there he was also influenced by the great philologist Paul de Lagarde, to whom Troeltsch dedicated the second volume of his collected writings, and the Old Testament scholar Bernhard Duhm, from both of whom he absorbed a commitment to historical integrity, as well as by Ritschl's philosophical colleague and mentor, Hermann Lotze (though later Troeltsch shifted his interest in contemporary philosophers from Lotze and Dilthey to the Baden neo-Kantians Windelband and Rickert).

After completion of his doctoral dissertation, *Vernunft und Offenbarung bei Johann Gerhard und Melanchthon*, which was expanded into his *Habilitationsschrift* (Göttingen, 1891), Troeltsch lectured briefly at Göttingen, then was Extraordinarius at Bonn for two years, and in 1894 became Professor of Systematic Theology at Heidelberg for

---

1. See the autobiographical statement in "Meine Bücher," *Gesammelte Schriften* (Tübingen, 1925), 4:3–18 (hereafter cited as *GS*), a sketch originally published in *Die Philosophie der Gegenwart in Selbstdarstellungen*, vol. 2, ed R. Schmidt (Leipzig, 1922). The *Deutsches Biographisches Jahrbuch V. Das Jahr 1923* (Stuttgart, 1930), p. 350, gives the date of Troeltsch's entrance at Erlangen as 1883.

twenty-one years. In 1915 he accepted a call to a chair in philosophy at Berlin, where he taught until his early death in 1923. He also served for two years, 1919–21, as a member of the Prussian Landtag and undersecretary of state in the ministry of public worship. The move from Heidelberg to Berlin has sometimes been interpreted as Troeltsch's abandonment of theology for philosophy. But although he said in his autobiographical sketch (*GS*, 4:12) that he had "somewhat outgrown the theological faculty," that is, the specific task of educating clergy, such an interpretation is highly dubious. It overlooks the fact that for Troeltsch the borderline between philosophy of religion and theology was fluid, and that he went to the chair of the famous philosopher of religion Otto Pfleiderer, and it conveniently omits to mention that the conservative ecclesiastical authorities in Berlin opposed his participation in the theological faculty. Troeltsch's view was that the fundamental problem of the normative in theology, from the perspective of the historical consciousness, was not essentially different from the questions of the normative and of value in the philosophy of history and in culture generally. He had a keen sense of the intellectual's responsibility and a great concern for the whole life of the nation, of which Berlin was so obviously the center. It seems fairer to hold that the writings of the Berlin period represent a continuation, with an enlarged scope, of the interests and commitments that characterized Troeltsch from the beginning. He may have been content to leave the specific tasks of clergy-training, but that did not mean loss of his theological interests.[2]

A QUESTION OF APPROACH

Any one of several points of departure might be adopted for an overall account and assessment of Troeltsch's massive efforts.

First, one might seek to interpret him as the systematician or dogmatician of the religionsgeschichtliche Schule. After all, he was a professor of systematic theology at Heidelberg for twenty-one years, and earlier he had been closely associated with Bousset (especially), Wrede, Gunkel, and Eichhorn, who came to be popularly known as the "little faculty" at Göttingen and who (along with Weiss, Heitmüller, and Wernle) constituted the history of religions school in biblical studies. Troeltsch did not himself pursue biblical scholarship extensively, but, from the tutelage of Lagarde and Duhm, he shared

2. See Bibliographic Notes, pp. 307–08.

the school's understanding of historical method and was frequently thought of as its systematician. He wrote an essay entitled "The Dogmatics of the 'religionsgeschichtliche Schule'" and contributed fifteen doctrinal articles to *RGG*. He lectured on systematic theology, and careful transcripts of his lectures from 1911–12 (which he had reviewed and approved) were published posthumously in *Glaubenslehre von Ernst Troeltsch* (Munich, 1925).

Troeltsch defined the task of theology fundamentally along lines that had been laid down in Schleiermacher's *Brief Outline of the Study of Theology* (see *Prot. Thought*, 1:69–71), saying that the *Brief Outline* "simply needs to be carried out consistently." Yet Schleiermacher's program had to be adapted to subsequent developments in historical understanding and in the study of the history of religions, and finally Troeltsch could say that of Schleiermacher's own teaching (in *The Christian Faith*) "scarcely one stone can remain standing on another."[3] Accordingly, Troeltsch proposed a threefold task: first, to show from a historical-philosophical consideration of comparative religions that Christianity has fundamentally and generally the highest value for our culture and sphere of life (though not that it is the absolute religion); second, to define what Christianity really is for the present epoch, again through religiohistorical consideration; and third (dogmatics in the narrow sense), to develop this understanding of essential Christianity in the concepts of God, world, man, redemption or enhancement, community or the kingdom of God, and hope or eternal life. A fourth element, not a specific task of dogmatics but something that must permeate the whole enterprise, was the necessity to draw out the consequences for the guidance of preaching and teaching.[4]

It was Troeltsch's contribution to the third of the tasks, dogmatics proper, that is primarily in question when viewing him as the systematician of the history of religions school. What he said or did not say in the articles in *RGG* and in the *Glaubenslehre* was a factor in

3. In the essay on a half-century of theology, *GS*, 2:225–26; M&P, p. 20.

4. See *GS*, 2:509–15; *AJT*, pp. 10–17. Compare Schleiermacher's division in the *Brief Outline* into philosophical, historical (including contemporary), and practical theology. It is clear from Troeltsch's fourth point that he shared Schleiermacher's conception of the goal of the dogmatic enterprise as service of the church, though Troeltsch's outlook was throughout much less church-oriented than Schleiermacher's in the *Brief Outline* and (especially) in the *Christian Faith*. The question of the normative in dogmatics was for Troeltsch finally an element in the question of the normative in religion and culture generally.

the charge that his theology had failed. But that charge involves a basic misunderstanding and an application of criteria wholly external to Troeltsch's point of view. He understood the task of theology as the presentation of a normative Christian-religious view of totality, and in dogmatics proper it was essential to develop both historical-religious theses, which set forth the religious significance of the historical foundations (the prophets, the person of Jesus, and the unfolding of the Christian spirit in history), and metaphysical-religious theses relating to God, the world, and the soul. Theoretically, a clear distinction was to be made between the historical and the metaphysical assertions in dogmatics proper, with the latter free of any historical admixture and shaped entirely as decisions relating to experience in the present. Schleiermacher, Troeltsch judged, had mixed up the historical with the present-day assertions.

But in Troeltsch's view the dogmatic enterprise was in fact much more historically conditioned than even Schleiermacher's notion of dogmatics as the articulation of contemporary religious consciousness (and thus ever ephemeral). Theological formulations must be set in the context of the entire history of religions study. And the ever-renewed decisions of Christian faith for the experience of the present are made in light of the whole development of Christianity, not just the Bible or Jesus, for present experience gets its life from the cumulative conditioning of history. *Glaubenslehre* is thus not a science in the sense that it can provide permanently valid doctrinal norms, any more than it can be based on unique, supernatural events in an objective salvation history. It is free, creative activity proceeding from confession (decision) of faith and intended for the guidance of preaching and teaching.

To expect from Troeltsch a set of normative Christian dogmas (even revised dogmas) in the old sense is to expect something he believed Schleiermacher had in principle shown to be impossible. What Troeltsch could do, and sought to do in the doctrinal articles in *RGG* (on dogmatics, salvation, eschatology, justice of God, faith, faith and history, grace of God, means of grace, church, revelation, predestination, and theodicy) and in the lectures on the topics of God, world, man, redemption, church, and consummation (which he did not think it necessary to publish because of the *RGG* articles), was to indicate how, from the standpoint of a thoroughgoing historical consciousness, the various areas of Christian affirmation might be approached in the present situation. Troeltsch did sketch out how the questions had to be reformulated and what the central doctrines might look like far more completely than he has often been given credit for. The great reality of God, which Troeltsch never ceases to affirm (even though for Troeltsch, as for Schleiermacher and Rothe, it is our idea of God rather than revelation that is the immediate object of theology), is that of the God of the whole, of the vast cosmos of the post-Copernican world (and why not of other worlds?), whose apprehension involves mystery, immensity, and even terror and namelessness. That we are dependent on subjective apprehension is no bar to the conviction that faith refers to the actuality of God's being and that our idea refers to a revelatory impulse. God is also the God who deals with us personally and into whose life we are called to grow. The image of trinity is the affirmation that the disclosure of God in history is grounded in his being; it is not a doctrine of inner divine relations. Christology is less concerned with questions of a metaphysical relation of Jesus to God than with the question of faith's connection with Jesus. The meaning of redemption is to be interpreted in terms of the problem of the value of life (the infinite worth of the soul) in the face of modern life's mechanization and our cosmic anxiety. Faith arises and is sustained in community—an important qualification of the individualism with which Troeltsch has often, and not altogether wrongly, been charged. The final destiny of man, which may include further moral growth in communion with God beyond death, may well mean an absorption into God, a sinking of the separate consciousness into the divine life, a return of the creation into the creator (the element of truth in pantheism).[5]

Proposals of this sort were not of course happily received by Troeltsch's conservative contemporaries or by the post–World War I dialectical theology. The lack of receptivity has much to do with the notion that Troeltsch's theology failed, as also did his lack of reverence for Luther as the great genius of modern religion.[6] But such

5. See B. A. Gerrish, "The Possibility of a Historical Theology," in Clayton, *Ernst Troeltsch*, for the most perceptive account that I know of the dogmatics of Troeltsch. Two other articles by Gerrish, "Theology and the Historical Consciousness," *McCormick Quarterly* 21:2 (1968): 198–213, and "Jesus, Myth, and History: Troeltsch's Stand in the Christ-Myth Debate," *Journal of Religion* 55(1975): 13–35, mark him as one of the most fruitful interpreters of Troeltsch in the recent literature in English.

6. The latter seems to be a crucial sticking point for W. Bodenstein, *Neige des Historismus: Ernst Troeltschs Entwicklung* (Gütersloh, 1959), who was one of the chief exponents in the German literature of the view that Troeltsch failed because he had no real systematic theology. Troeltsch's sense of isolation from his Protestant ecclesiastical contemporaries is

criticisms are quite beside the point. They only signal disagreement
with Troeltsch. To suppose that Troeltsch ought to have produced a
work like Schleiermacher's *Christian Faith* is completely to misunder-
stand his intentions. Troeltsch had no desire to be a dogmatician in
the classical (or even mid-nineteenth-century) sense. He wanted to
examine the fundamental principles, the perspective of a real historical consciousness, from which modern theologizing must proceed.
Hence it does not seem most useful, finally, to approach Troeltsch
primarily as the dogmatician of the religionsgeschichtliche Schule.
The great substantive problems for him were not the content of religious thoughts but the nature of religious thinking in the modern situation, the question of the absoluteness of Christianity, and the possibility of being a Christian in the present world.

Second, one might seek to interpret Troeltsch mainly as a philosopher of religion, focusing particularly on his idea of the religious a
priori. Apart from the fact that Troeltsch was schooled in the whole
tradition of German idealism and continually dealt with its representatives in his writings, the basis for his insistence on the importance of a philosophy of religion was his constant concern for the
normative in religion rather than mere historical description. This
he saw as a problem for all contemporary thought and culture generally, and theology stood at the center of it.[7] Philosophy of religion,
while necessarily related to history and presupposing religious experience, is concerned with the metaphysical grounding of religion, its
validity and necessity. Thus theology and philosophy have an inner
connection (pace Ritschl).

The point is vividly made in an essay in memory of William James
written for the *Harvard Theological Review*.[8] Troeltsch had a high appreciation for James's empirical account of the varieties of religious
experience, and he would never have abandoned the empirical approach. But the empirical and psychological level, or even the pragmatic estimate of the worth of religion, does not deal with the question of validity, or reality content, or inner necessity of religion. That
is a philosophical, epistemological question of rational validity.

---

vividly seen in his correspondence with his friend Baron von Hügel. See *Ernst Troeltsch:
Briefe an Friedrich von Hügel, 1901–1923*, ed. K.-E. Apfelbacher and P. Neuner (Paderborn, 1974).

    7. See "Moderne Geschichtsphilosophie" (1903), *GS*, 2:673–728, esp. pp. 675–76.

    8. "Empiricism and Platonism in the Philosophy of Religion," *HTR* 5 (1912): 401–22;
"Empirismus und Platonismus in der Religionsphilosophie," *GS*, 2:364–85.

James's view is ultimately no different from positivism. Earlier, in "Religion and the Science of Religion," Troeltsch had made a similar point.[9] There he distinguished two basic positions, the position of idealism and the position of positivism, between which a decision has to be made at the outset. The psychology of religion, which is a characterization of the primary phenomenon in its various forms and levels, must be followed by epistemological investigation into the validity and truth of the psychological events and by the philosophical history of religion and the philosophical treatment of the idea of God. Troeltsch's principal contention was to reject the positivistic presupposition in favor of a critical idealism in the tradition of Kant and Schleiermacher, an idealism that does not determine the interpretation of religion in advance or import philosophical postulates of a metaphysical kind, but only implies "the possibility of seeing in religion a qualitatively individual and creative power of life" (M&P, p. 86; see pp. 82–89, 114–120).

Here is the point of the "religious a priori," for which Troeltsch is (unhappily) best remembered by some. Partly under the influence of the Baden neo-Kantian Rickert, who reawakened his interest in Kant, Troeltsch seems to have first used the phrase in 1904.[10] In a modification of Kant's critical philosophy, Troeltsch intended to show, as an a priori element in consciousness, the grounding of religious ideas in the structure of reason—that is, the formal necessity of the religious, though not of course the truth content of the phenomena. Religious life has an autonomous self-sufficient character deriving from its inner necessity. It cannot be reduced to other factors of experience; religious judgments are possible as much as moral or esthetic judgments. The religious a priori is empty and has to be filled with actual religious sensibility and intuition. But it is the ground of the validity of religious intuition and, further, it means that religion is an essential ingredient in human existence, even though not actualized in everyone's experience. Schleiermacher had

9. See M&P, pp. 82–123; "Wesen der Religion und der religionswissenschaft" (1906), GS, 2:452–99.

10. See the St. Louis lecture "Psychology and Epistemology in the Science of Religion," in *Psychologie und Erkenntnistheorie in der Religionswissenschaft* (Tübingen, 1905); "Religionsphilosophie," in *Die Philosophie im Beginn des zwanzigsten Jahrhunderts: Festschrift für Kuno Fischer* (Heidelberg, 1904); especially "Das religiöse Apriori" (1909), GS, 2:754–68; and also the brief statement in the essay "Religion and the Science of Religion" (M&P, p. 116; GS, 2:494–95).

also argued for the universality of the religious, though in another way. In the idea of the religious a priori, Troeltsch was seeking to show the rational character of the necessity of religion.[11]

But Troeltsch did not in fact use the language of the religious a priori very much, and he soon stopped altogether. The problem of the historical and the normative, of psychology and epistemology, of the empirical and the essential, continued in other ways in his explorations of the philosophy of history generally. In *Der Historismus* he developed a quite different, non-Kantian, concept of apriority as a synthesis of culture. Hence it is not profitable to make the idea of the religious a priori the center for understanding Troeltsch. It was a temporary form of his thought but essentially a detour in his attempt to show the independence of religion and to establish a basis for determining the norm within the flux of history. This kind of philosophical analysis was plainly more dated than Troeltsch's contribution to the understanding of history and faith, and he turned to more directly historical (and sociological) concerns.

Third, one might approach Troeltsch primarily from the standpoint of *Der Historismus*, as the attempt to deal with the problems of history and the philosophy of history on the grand scale. This viewpoint has much to commend it, for Troeltsch looked upon *Der Historismus* as the culmination of his work, which shows even more clearly that for him, finally, religious and cultural history are inseparable. Given the "interwovenness of all human events," the real correlation of things, "it is impossible to ascribe to the religious element a different mode of formation and realization than that which is ascribed to the life of the spirit with which it is endlessly entwined" (*GS*, 3:754). No full study of Troeltsch would be adequate which did not deal in detail with *Der Historismus*. But even apart from the bulk and complexity of the argument there and the impossibility of treating it briefly—as well as the fact that Troeltsch was able to complete before his death only the first volume, on historicism and its problems, which was to have been followed by a volume on the overcoming of historicism—it seems more appropriate for our purposes to take a less cumbersome line of approach which should equally well tie together Troeltsch's lifelong concerns and exhibit his importance

---

11. Troeltsch seems also to suggest that mysticism, as the primary phenomenon of all religion, can be regarded as the actualization of the religious a priori. See *Psychologie und Erkenntnistheorie*, p. 47, and the discussion of mysticism and the philosophy of religion in *Social Teaching*, pp. 734–38 (hereafter cited as *ST*).

in representing the outcome of Protestant theological reflection at the end of the nineteenth century.

In no sense did Troeltsch's concern for the general philosophy of culture mean an abandonment of the problem of how one can speak of the truth of Christianity in a world that must have a historical outlook. Earlier, in a preface specially written for the English translation of his monograph on the significance of Protestantism for the origin of the modern world, he had said:

> In the aim which has guided my studies, two main interests may be distinguished. The first is that of gaining an insight into the intellectual and religious situation of the present day, from which the significance and the possibilities of development possessed by Christianity might be deduced. That has led me to engage in historical investigations regarding the spirit of the modern world, for this can only be understood in the light of its relation to the earlier epochs of Christian civilization in Europe. As Adolf Harnack has described the genesis and the disintegration of Christian dogma, so I should like to examine the present situation and its significance for the fate of Christianity in the modern world.[12]

In the autobiographical statement "Meine Bücher," written at the time of publication of *Der Historismus*, the year before his death, Troeltsch declared:

> If life and strength remain, I would then like finally to return to the religious sphere and bring my philosophy of religion to completion. That is my first love, and the religious element remains at the center even of the present cultural synthesis which has to be drawn by the philosophy of history. Without this there is no naiveté and no freshness.[13]

THE HISTORICAL CONSCIOUSNESS

In approaching Troeltsch as a historian concerned with the questions of validity and norm, I want to emphasize the problem that emerged for him almost at the beginning of his work and continued in one form or another throughout his career to his very last writings: the question of the absoluteness of Christianity (and thus of the

---

12. *Protestantism and Progress* (Beacon paperback ed., Boston, 1958), pp. v–vi; hereafter cited as *PP*. The translation was of the second edition (1911) of *Die Bedeutung des Protestantismus*. See also *ST*, p. 19.

13. *GS*, 4:14.

normative within Christianity). This was for him a decisive focus of the general problem of the normative in history and was reflected in his concern with history of religions, his great work on the social and ethical history of Christianity, his treatment of the problem of the historicity of Jesus, and his concern for the possibility and meaning of faith. In all this, Troeltsch was a systematic thinker who sought to come from every side at the question of the validity of religion in a world of historical consciousness.

At the beginning of the final work of his life, lectures prepared for delivery in England (but read by others because of his death), Troeltsch said that because of the significance he attached to the invitation to Oxford,

> I could not select any other subject than the one which contains the center and starting-point of my academic work. This central theme is most clearly, I think, set forth in my little book on *The Absolute Validity of Christianity*, which forms the conclusion of a series of earlier studies and the beginning of new investigations of a more comprehensive kind in the philosophy of history. Moreover, this subject is for me the point at which my own original interests and the problems presented by the modern religious situation have met together.[14]

The importance of these lectures, particularly the first one on "The Place of Christianity among the World Religions," should not be underestimated. To be sure, they do not constitute, as the title given to the German edition (*Der Historismus und seine Ueberwindung*) might suggest, a substitute for the second, unwritten volume of *Der Historismus*. But they were not casual utterances. They give indications of the outcome of Troeltsch's thought that must be taken with the utmost seriousness.

As Troeltsch mentioned in the passage just quoted, his 1902 volume *Die Absolutheit des Christentums und die Religionsgeschichte* grew out of several prior studies.[15] In those essays on the autonomy of reli-

---

14. *Christian Thought*, p. 35; hereafter cited as *CT*. Page references are to the Living Age Edition (New York, 1957).

15. Notably "Die christliche Weltanschauung und ihre Gegenströmungen" (1894; *GS*, 2:227–327); "Die Selbständigkeit der Religion," *Zeitschrift für Theologie und Kirche* (*ZTK*) 5 (1895): 316–436, and 6 (1896): 71–110, 167–218; "Religion und Kirche" (1895; *GS*, 2:146–82); "Christentum und Religionsgeschichte" (1897; *GS*, 2:328–63); "Historische und dogmatische Methode in der Theologie" (1898; *GS*, 2:729–53); "Geschichte und Metaphysik," *ZTK* 8 (1898): 1–69; and *Die Wissenschaftliche Lage und ihre Anforderungen an die Theologie* (Tübingen, 1900).

gion, on the Christian world view (and the church) and the counter-currents to it, and on method, Troeltsch developed certain convictions or guiding principles that he never deserted and that also established his distance from Ritschl's perspective. We can summarize these convictions in three related categories.

First, it was not the Reformation but the Enlightenment that was the great watershed in modern history. Hence the antipathy to Troeltsch of both the Ritschlians and the conservative Lutherans. In an 1897 article on the Enlightenment for the third edition of the *Realencyklopädie für protestantische Theologie und Kirche*, he put it succinctly: "The Enlightenment is the beginning and foundation of the intrinsically modern period of European culture and history, in contrast to the hitherto regnant ecclesiastically and theologically determined culture." At the end of his life, in "Meine Bücher," he insisted that the autonomous and worldly formation of culture, which is characteristic of the whole modern intellectual situation, really emerged at the time of the Enlightenment.[16]

This was a theme that Troeltsch constantly sounded, from early writings through *Social Teaching* and *Der Historismus*. It was spelled out, as clearly as anywhere in brief compass, in his book on the significance of Protestantism for the origin of the modern world (*PP*). There he contrasts the character of modern civilization with the idea of church civilization that was brought to fruition in the Middle Ages. For the church's civilization of authority, which depreciated the earthly sensuous world and opted for a fundamental asceticism in the theory and shaping of life, though reconciling this with natural life in the idea of the *Lex Naturae*, modern civilization has substituted ideals "independently arrived at, the authority of which depends on their inherent and immediate capacity to produce conviction." "Divine infallibility and ecclesiastical intolerance necessarily give place to human relativity and toleration." Scientific thought reigns in place of revelation, autonomous individualism in place of ecclesiastical control. The interests of life tend to be limited to the present world. And the modern spirit is characterized by "self-confident optimism and belief in progress" (see *PP*, chapter 1, especially pp. 17–25).

Now these changes are not to be attributed fundamentally to the rise of Protestantism, though it "had no inconsiderable influence in producing the modern world" (*PP*, p. 40). Luther in particular was still a medieval figure. His reform was "simply a modification of Ca-

16. *GS*, 4:338–39, 7.

tholicism" (p. 59).[17] Modern Protestantism is significantly different. It has had to come to terms with the possibility of multiple religious convictions and denominations existing beside one another, with a nonsectarian religiously indifferent state, and with an emancipated secular life. Tracing the influence of Protestantism historically in family, law, state, economics, and society, science and art, Troeltsch concluded: "While Protestantism has furthered the rise of the modern world, often largely and decisively, in none of these departments does it appear as its actual creator. What it has done is simply to secure for it greater freedom of development . . . in various ways, . . . to favor, strengthen, color and modify the course of development" (PP, pp. 171–72). Protestantism is primarily a religious force and at best secondarily a civilizing power. The question, then, concerns the relation of Protestantism's religious energy and principle to the "religious character of the modern spirit," which is far broader than ecclesiastical religion, even though the religion of the modern world is determined by Protestantism, and modern Protestantism has been suffused by the new outlook.[18] In sum, the Enlightenment marks the fundamental change in outlook of the modern world in which the theologian exists.

Second, the contemporary religious thinker must live in the modern world. This is not to say that the theologian must kneel before every passing fashion of thought. On the contrary, one of the tasks is to "test the spirits." There is a tension between religion and culture. Troeltsch could even say that "the greatness of religion consists precisely in its opposition to culture, . . . its proclaiming supramundane and suprahuman powers, its unfolding of the imagination and point-

17. In his estimate of Luther, Troeltsch had already begun to move away from Ritschl's view in his dissertation on Gerhard and Melanchthon. The continuity of the Reformation ethos and church conception with the medieval outlook was worked out at length in ST. In Troeltsch's argument in PP that Protestantism has been only secondarily a civilizing power, we may perhaps see a relation to Paul Lagarde's view of Protestantism's lack of cultural power (see chap. 7, above), though Troeltsch's view was hardly identical with that of Lagarde.

18. See PP, chap. 6. Troeltsch could also say, in "Protestantisches Christentum und Kirche in der Neuzeit" (in Die Kultur der Gegenwart, 2d ed. [Berlin, 1909], p. 397), that "the real life of Protestantism is to be found outside the church, even though the church itself is acknowledged to be valuable and indispensable." See also GS, 2:21. Yet Protestantism, which has given "to the whole fabric a goodly portion of its strength—the religious metaphysic of freedom and of a faith based on personal conviction; . . . faith in God as the power whence freedom and personality come to us," is the "stand-by for the coming days of the oppression and decline of freedom" (PP, pp. 206–07).

ing to what lies beyond the world of sense. A religion reconciled with culture is usually nothing but bad science and superficial morals; it has lost its salt."[19] But live in this world the theologian must, and he ought to do it self-consciously if his thinking is to be of any value, both because his being is shaped by this structure of modern thought and because only here can one deal intelligently with questions of integrity and norm in religion. The old principles of the ecclesiastical culture—revelations of divine truth in unique disclosure, of a single, supernatural incursion into a natural world, and of an original sin that corrupted the appeal to universal truths of reason—have been undermined by the naturalizing and historicizing of thought. Benjamin Reist puts the point in a singularly happy way by describing Troeltsch's thought as "a theology of involvement," drawing on the statement in *Social Teaching* that the systematic task is "to think through and formulate independently the Christian world of ideas and life *with unreserved involvement in the modern world*."[20]

Third, the dominant element in the modern structure of thought with which Troeltsch was concerned all his life was the historical consciousness, which he did more than anyone else to explore. This was not only a question of proper historical method, but also a matter of recognizing the inescapable historical nature of all thinking, and thus a matter of our entire world view. As Troeltsch put it succinctly in defining the essential task of *Der Historismus*, which necessitated a review of almost the whole of modern thinking, "the problem of the significance and essence of historicism generally . . . [is] the fundamental historicizing of all our thought about man, his culture and his values."[21]

Troeltsch has here gone a long way beyond Ritschl's insistence on a historical point of departure (see chapter 1, above). The nature of Christianity is determined not merely by looking at its origins but by viewing its entire historical development. In no sense can Christianity be exempted from the same kind of historical examination that is applied to any other religion or cultural phenomenon, whether by appeal to an external, supernatural miracle of divine incursion into

19. "Die Kirche im Leben der Gegenwart" (1911), *GS*, 2:100.

20. *GS*, 1:viii; see *ST*, p. 19. The translation and italics are Reist's; see *Toward a Theology of Involvement*, p. 17. We may profitably contrast this idea of involvement with Schleiermacher's idea of an eternal covenant between theology and science. (See *Prot. Thought*, 1:63.)

21. *GS*, 3:102.

history or by appeal (as in Herrmann) to an internal miracle by which the uniqueness of Christianity is protected. From the first Troeltsch insisted that Christianity must be treated like any other religion. One cannot defend the autonomy and integrity of religion against Feuerbach by viewing Christianity as a special case.[22] Troeltsch's attitude toward the comparative study of religion was radically different from Ritschl's and Harnack's.

The general features of a historical outlook, as Troeltsch understood it, can be only briefly indicated here.[23] Central to the historical view are the basic concepts of individuality and development, with which *Der Historismus* deals at length. These are inseparably related. All events are singular and nonrecurrent. Yet every individuality with which history has to deal is a totality, not a simple isolable element but a cluster of psychic occurrences, in natural conditions, that already comprise significant totalities of life. And they are in a process of continual becoming. That process of development cannot be represented (after the fashion of natural science) as a purely causal sequence; this would deny the originality and uniqueness of the historical event. Nor does development mean "progress" or "evolution." The notion of evolution imports the natural sciences, idea of causality, and the idea of progress is a secularization of Christian eschatology that is different from the basic concept of historical movement and fluidity. Both individuality and laws or types relating to historical change must be observed. Recognition of this kind of becoming lies at the heart of the historical sense.

Further, the historical situation of the interpreter is inextricably involved. Historical presentation is symbolic; it requires supplementary imagination and decision in its explanations and interpretations. This is always an ethical task. Historical reflection necessarily seeks norms, or standards of judgment, which arise out of the historical development (pace Harnack, who imported his norms into the historical analysis), yet not without the active engagement of the interpreter. Historical understanding is not a merely contemplative activity, nor a positivistic review of data. It is creative, springing from a "particular living context. . . . As every calculation of motion in the natural sciences is dependent on the position of the reckoner, so also

22. See "Die Selbständigkeit der Religion" (1895–96).
23. A full account would require an interpretation of Troeltsch's relation to Wilhelm Dilthey and Wilhelm Windelband (to whom jointly he dedicated *Der Historismus*), as well as to Max Weber.

in history is every standard indelibly determined by the position out of which it arises." This implies that the purpose of a philosophy of history is for the guidance of the present and the future. Standards in relation to historical matters arise "in living connection with the shaping of the future," and the task of the material philosophy of history is "primarily nothing other than the production of a standard, an ideal, an idea of the actual present—seen on the whole as a total situation and a result of thousands of years—for creating a new unity of culture."[24]

In the same way, it is the task of the historian of Christianity to help determine the course of theology and ethics for the future. In the foreword to *Social Teaching*, Troeltsch affirmed that "all this research . . . was only intended to serve the purpose of solving the systematic problem, in order to think through and formulate the world of Christian thought and life in frank relation to the modern world." Specifically, in view of his growing awareness of the importance of the socially ethical in the history of the church, "I was confronted with this further question: what, then, would be the relation of such a new and formative conception of the Christian attitude to life to its own ancient organizations, the churches? Further, could such a new conception, indeed, in any way be grafted on to the old organizations at all and, if this were not possible, what kind of social adhesion or relation with a fellowship would be possible in harmony with this new view of life?"[25]

In a relatively brief essay on historical and dogmatic method in theology (1900) following his articles on the autonomy of religion and criticisms of them, Troeltsch succinctly identified three essential elements of critical historical method,[26] which he held must inform modern theology. These have been dubbed the principles of criticism, of analogy, and of correlation. The first means that all tradition is to be placed under critical scrutiny, on the basis of the independence and autonomy of the historian, though of course the data

---

24. See *GS*, 3:169, 112. I have drawn here on Reist's translations (see *Toward a Theology of Involvement*, pp. 63, 66). These statements by Troeltsch on the directive purpose of historical reflection may be compared with Harnack's similar words about the purpose of the historian (see chap. 5, above).

25. *GS*, 1:vii–viii. Unfortunately, the English translation by Wyon omits the crucial word "not" in the last sentence of the statements quoted (see *ST*, pp. 19–20).

26. *GS*, 2:729–53, esp. pp. 731–34. See also his article "Historiography" in *ERE*, and the essay on the essence of Christianity.

must be approached with empathy. It further means that in the historical realm only judgments of probability can be made, and with widely varying degrees of likelihood. The second principle indicates the means by which criticism is possible, namely, the ability of the historical critic to discern analogy between events in the past and what happens in the present. This is the key to criticism. One interprets the unknown of the past by the known of present experience. The historian must assume a homogeneity of the human mind, not in the Enlightenment sense of a universal humanity, but in the sense of similarity in the historical activities of human beings. The third principle, correlation, refers to the interplay of all happenings in historical life. No alteration can at one point take place without consequences for what precedes and follows. Every distinctive and autonomous event has a context, so that all historical happening is knit together in embracing correlation. An event is singular and nonrecurrent, yet is related to all others.

The consequence of this historical method is the destruction of the dogmatic method in theology. No single historical happening can stand out from the rest of history as resulting from some exclusive divine causality. All is made relative. Yet historical method seeks universality; it does not allow any happening to isolate itself from relationship to the entire development.

The Absoluteness of Christianity

As we have already emphasized, the question of the absoluteness of Christianity (or its "absolute validity," as von Hügel later happily translated the term *Absolutheit*) was a lifelong concern of Troeltsch, a theme with many variations. In *Die Absolutheit* he took up the theme explicitly in relation to comparative religions study, as well as to the demands of historical method in general.[27]

Again in this work we encounter Troeltsch's commitment to the historical method and his judgment that the historical consciousness is the foundation of modern thought: "The modern idea of history is no longer merely one aspect of a way of looking at things or a partial satisfaction of the impetus to knowledge. It is, rather, the foundation

27. Page references in the text are to the English translation by Reid, from the 2d ed. (1912), in which Troeltsch said he made mostly stylistic changes—though in fact there were at least two significant substantive alterations, which we shall note. In relation to the following discussion, see the treatment of the development of the history of religions, particularly the review of other contemporary theological judgments on the finality of Christianity, in chap. 4, above.

of all thinking concerning values and norms. It is the medium for the self-reflection of the species upon its nature, origins, and hopes" (p. 47). An integral part of this consciousness is the question of normative value.

The question of absolute validity is Troeltsch's way, or one of his ways, of stating the problem of certainty in faith, which we have earlier seen to be a pervasive concern of late-nineteenth-century theology (see chapter 2, above, especially the discussion of Ihmels, with whom Troeltsch deals at some length). But for Troeltsch there can no longer be any supernatural certainty. That kind of certainty "seems unattainable to me because the relative, historical, and limited character of the history of Christian development has been established, in my view, by proofs whose validity cannot be diminished either by the abstract impossibility of the denial of miracle or by the postulates of a religious orientation" (p. 34). The certainty of faith cannot be affirmed on a theory of gaps in the causal sequence into which divine activity intrudes. Nor can we be satisfied with a mere assertion of the superiority of Christianity (pace Harnack?). Neither external nor internal miracle can serve as the court of appeal. Faith gives a certainty, but it must be understood and established in a different way.

The statement of the problem as one of "absoluteness," Troeltsch noted, is a modern formulation deriving from the Hegelian notion of Christianity as the absolute religion. This is a substitute for the orthodox, supernatural apologetic, which affirmed the unique position of Christianity on the basis of "the *form* in which religious truths arise." Christianity is based on a miraculous revelation which "transcends and nullifies all likeness to human events." Consequently, Christianity is held to be exclusively true. But the evolutionary apologetic that grew on Schleiermacherian and Hegelian soil sought to demonstrate "by reference to *content and essence* . . . that the idea of Christianity is to be recognized, in accordance with the requirements of theory, as the realization of the idea of religion itself." Christianity is the highest and ultimate stage and is shown to be so by its fulfillment of the laws of evolutionary development. The expression "absoluteness" is thus the "philosophical substitute for the dogmatic supernaturalism of the church" (pp. 52–55). The term

> derives from the modern evolutionary apologetic and has a precise meaning only under its presuppositions. It has this precise meaning to the extent that it includes the horizons of the history of religion

generally, the acknowledgement of all non-Christian religions as relative truths, and the interpretation of Christianity in relation to
these relative truths as the absolute and completed form of religion.
The term, its presuppositions, and its content are thus modern academic concepts through and through, conditioned by a levelling
process in which all human events are drawn into the modern understanding of history. (p. 51)

But neither of these apologetics, which in their different forms are
closely related in motive and goal, is adequate to the problem. That
problem is essentially one of normative value, which is "something
distinct from exclusively *supernatural revelation* and likewise from *absolute fulfillment of the principle of religion*" (p. 57). Or, as Troeltsch put
it in the final chapter, "Two Types of Absoluteness," the question is
how to give some kind of theoretical basis and justification for the naive sense of absoluteness, the spontaneous and immediate claim to
validity that characterizes genuine religious life, without falling into
the problems of the artificial apologetic that has characterized the
ideas of supernatural, rational, and evolutionary absoluteness.

So understood, the question of absoluteness must be asked in the
light of comparative religious study, or Religionswissenschaft, whose
task is to pinpoint the basic religious content and ideas (the *Grund-
konzeptionen* and *Grundanschauungen*) that have emerged in history,
with the goal of arriving at a norm of evaluation indicated by the development of these basic views. This is a matter of a posteriori discovery, not a Hegelian a priori. Troeltsch asserted in the foreword to the
first edition of *Die Absolutheit* that he was "in complete agreement"
with the main thesis of Harnack's rectorial address on the task of
theological faculties and the general history of religions (see chapter
4, above). But we would be seriously misled if we stopped simply with
this general assertion. Troeltsch agreed that theology must be concerned with normative knowledge and not just a general (empirical)
review of the history of religion. He was certainly concerned with the
practical problems of what a theological faculty could do. And he
judged that, finally, the questions of comparison of religions' material content (such as ideas of God, or Heaven versus nirvana) were
not as decisive as the problems posed by the historical consciousness
and method as a whole.

But Troeltsch plainly took comparative religious studies far more
seriously than did Harnack. He said in the same foreword that it is

important to derive the normative "from the history of religion instead of from scholastic theories of revelation or apologetics against philosophical systems," and that a theory of the normative validity of Christianity "must, in my opinion, go into the general history of religion more thoroughly than Harnack appears inclined to allow," even though as a discipline presuppositional to theology. Twenty years later, in the lecture at Oxford, Troeltsch commented that comparative studies had been especially the work of the English and the Dutch, the great colonizing nations, whereas German attention had been primarily focused on European civilization. But the same problem arises in both kinds of study, namely, "the relativity and transitoriness of all things." Thus, for Troeltsch, while his departure from the Ritschlian point of view was significantly directed by ideas from the history of religions, the problem of the plurality of religions does not finally depend on the quantity of comparative data. It is a matter of basic perspective, of our historical consciousness, and any recognition of religious pluralism raises the essential question.[28]

In his views of the results of *religionswissenschaftlich* investigations, Troeltsch went through significant development. In the early essays, he seems to have thought it beyond dispute that Christianity was the highest religion, though even then he considered it impossible to show more than a relative superiority for Christianity, a relatively absolute position. (See especially the essays on the autonomy of religion and on history and metaphysics.) In *Die Absolutheit*, the yield of the comparative historical method has become more negative. Troeltsch found it easy to distinguish—in opposition to a complete relativism—between the various religions of uncivilized peoples and "the religions of ethical and spiritual greatness." There are only a few great religious orientations (Kräfte). The field narrows to a consideration on the one hand of Judaism, Christianity, and Islam, and on the other hand of the great religions of the East, Hinduism and Buddhism, in all cases including philosophical connections. "Indeed, it is not too much to say that essentially we have to do with the rivalry between the prophetic, Christian, Platonic, and Stoic world of ideas on the one hand, and the Buddhist or Eastern world of ideas on the other" (pp. 92, 93).

The relativity of historical phenomena does not require us to sup-

28. See *CT*, pp. 38–39. Troeltsch did not mention the Scandinavian and French work in comparative studies.

pose that these great forces are only ephemeral in their influence. Nor are we forbidden to compare and rank these main orientations "in accordance with a criterion of value" and to subsume them "under the idea of a common goal" (pp. 94–95). Any criterion that emerges will be "a matter of personal conviction and . . . in the last analysis admittedly subjective." The principle of normativeness and universal validity will always remain a goal "out in front" (pp. 96, 99) which transcends history and can be known only in individual and historically conditioned—relative—ways. The absolute cannot be possessed in an absolute way.

This having been said, and recognizing that Christianity is a relative phenomenon, Troeltsch thought Christianity could be characterized as "in actuality the strongest and most concentrated revelation of personalistic religious apprehension," and thus "not only as the culmination point but also the convergence point of all the developmental tendencies and suggestions into one common goal." It is at least "the highest religious truth that has relevance for us" (pp. 111–12, 114, 107; see chapter 4).

In the second edition of *Die Absolutheit* (1912), Troeltsch seems to have drawn back from the idea of Christianity as the culmination or convergence point, an idea which was really inconsistent with his rejection of evolutionary apologetic, toward a more consistent relativism. He added the assertion that

> The problem faced by the modern approach to history is not that of making an either/or choice between relativism and absolutism but that of how to combine the two. . . . how to discern, in the relative, tendencies toward the absolute goal. Or, to state the problem more accurately: How does one work out a fresh, durable, and creative synthesis that will give the absolute the form possible to it at a particular moment and yet remain true to its inherent limitation as a mere approximation of true, ultimate, and universally valid values? (p. 90)

In the second edition he also added the suggestion that in view of the possibility of the collapse of Western civilization, Christianity in its present form might cease to exist, though this would not eliminate the truth and value of its personalistic understanding of redemption (p. 115). He dropped a conclusion from the first edition that "the scholarly deliberations of the history of religions may appropriate, in a sense expanded by the history of religions, the naive Pauline confession: the surest and strongest foundation of salvation is Jesus Christ," and by this confession "lead a generation . . . back to simplicity, freedom, clarity, and vitality" (1st ed., p. 129). This statement was replaced by the following paragraph: "We need not fret over unknown thousands of centuries of human history. It is enough if we can throw light on the next stretch of the path and if we know now what we want to be and should be. What is called for at this moment of history is to resist the religious chaos and religious devastation that threaten us from every side" (p. 162).[29]

In an important article of about the same time on the future possibilities of Christianity in relation to modern philosophy, Troeltsch had written similarly about the uncertainty of the immediate future (which has to be determined by our decisions), about the seeming conflict with the present world, and about the reconstruction of a Christianity that could be the vitalizing core of the future.[30] There he argued that the monistic tendencies of modern thought had no power over the irrational realities of life, but that there was room and even necessity for the prophetic and Christian idea of a transcendent absolute personalistic unity of truth, beauty, and goodness. He affirmed the superiority of Christian ethics, with its dialectic of affirmation and denial of this world, over modern secular ethics, in which the tension of the *Jenseits* and the *Diesseits* was dissolved. Against the threats of modern individualism to the communitarian nature of the church, and of modern socialism to the individualistic personalism of

29. In connection with these modifications in *Die Absolutheit*, we may note Troeltsch's comment in the 1911 essay on the significance of the historicity of Jesus that, while Christianity will in all probability endure as long as our civilization endures, our culture may not last forever or extend to the whole world and therefore it is "impossible either to affirm or to deny that Christianity will last for ever and community and cult remain bound to the historical personality of Jesus" (see the trans. in M&P, p. 205).

We may also see in the brief statement of the first task of a history of religions-oriented dogmatics (in "The Dogmatics of the 'religionsgeschichtliche Schule,'" 1913) a comparable restraint concerning the possibility of establishing the superiority of Christianity. The task is to show the highest value of Christianity *for our culture and sphere of life*. Troeltsch denies that one can construe Christianity as fulfilling and forever realizing the concept of religion (or, in Hegel's terms, as being absolute), though we have no occasion to abandon the Christian foundations of the European-American world or to look for our religious future elsewhere. He seems to emphasize more strongly than in *Die Absolutheit* the role of decision in the choice for prophetic-Christian theism over the quietism and pessimism of Eastern religions (see *GS*, 2:509–10).

30. "Die Zukunftsmöglichkeiten des Christentums im Verhältnis zur modernen Philosophie" (1910), *GS*, 2:837–62. See also "Religiöser Individualismus und Kirche" (1910), *GS*, 2:109–33.

Christianity, he sought the possibility in Christianity of an ideal for modern society through a harmony and dialectical tension between individualism and socialism.

Troeltsch's final position was stated in the 1923 lecture on the place of Christianity among the world religions, where he summarized the argument of *Die Absolutheit* and explicitly modified the conclusion. First, as a result of his further investigations, notably for *Social Teaching* and *Der Historismus*, he reported that he had become even more strongly impressed by the importance of the concept of individuality, which he no longer believes "to be so easily reconcilable with that of supreme validity." Christianity is thoroughly individual, "a purely historical, individual, relative phenomenon, which could . . . only have arisen in the territory of the classical culture, and among the Latin and Germanic races." It is inseparably bound up with European culture, and it is not a historically uniform development, but contains great diversity. Second, further study of non-Christians "convinced me more and more that their naive claims to absolute validity are also genuinely such." Buddhism and Brahmanism, in particular, are undeniably humane and spiritual religions, and in their historical individuality they appeal to "the inner certitude and devotion of their followers" just as Christianity appeals to its adherents (pp. 51, 52).

The consequence is that the idea of supreme validity falls into the background. No reason can be given for denying that other religions are also products of "the impulse towards absolute objective truth" (p. 61). This is an impulse and a tendency. In every epoch and situation, there is access to God, but only in special historical forms. No historical religion has attained the final synthesis. All lie between the two poles: the divine source and the divine goal. They have a common ground and a common aim, though an individual differentiation.

Where does this leave us, then, with our commitment to Christianity? It cannot claim absolute validity, and it is not even at the top of a definable scale. Yet it is, and must be, true "for us." It is the religion through which we have been formed. "Its primary claim to validity is . . . the fact that only through it have we become what we are, and that only in it can we preserve the religious forces that we need. . . . We cannot live without a religion, yet the only religion we can endure is Christianity, for Christianity has grown up with us and has become a part of our very being" (pp. 54, 55). Obviously, Troeltsch adds,

Christianity could not be the religion of such a developed human group if it did not have powerful spiritual forces, if it were not in some sense "a manifestation of the Divine Life itself." For this, we have the evidence of "a profound inner experience." But that certifies only validity *for us*, and other groups can view their experience of the divine life as just as valid for them. Christianity "is final and unconditional for us, because we have nothing else, and because in what we have we can recognize the accents of the divine voice" (p. 55). With this Troeltsch has come to the recognition of a real religious pluralism.

The Historicity of Jesus

If the placement of Christianity in the context of other religions raises a question about any claim for its final validity, the same question emerges from the study of the history of Christianity itself. Troeltsch had made this point in *Die Absolutheit* as part of his basic argument that the deepest problems are raised by the historical method and consciousness rather than by (for example) the particularities of comparisons of religious ideas. But we need to take fuller account of the ways in which the question appears in a historical understanding of the development of the Christian religion. Two areas of Troeltsch's investigation must be noted: (1) his analysis of the significance of the question of the historicity of Jesus, and (2) his massive social history of Christianity, in which the ethical dimension comes most explicitly to the fore.

Troeltsch's view of the historical Jesus problem was developed especially in the lecture, *Die Bedeutung der Geschichtlichkeit Jesu für den Glauben* (Tübingen, 1911).[31] Troeltsch wrote this statement expressly in response to the recent claims of Arthur Drews that there was no adequate evidence for the existence of a historical figure behind the New Testament accounts. Troeltsch did not think the arguments of Drews worthy of serious scholarly attention, but he used the occasion to deal more generally with the question of the significance of historical research for the relation of Christian faith to Jesus. He thought that the overall picture of Jesus that emerged from historical

31. Citations in the text are from the translation in M&P, "The Significance of the Historical Existence of Jesus for Faith," pp. 182–207. The following treatment of Troeltsch needs to be read in the light of our long discussion of the Jesus of history/Christ of faith problem in chap. 5, above. See the excellent statement by Gerrish, "Jesus, Myth, and History."

criticism was reliable enough that we need not despair. But that is not quite the point. The question raised, even by Drews' bumbling attempt, is what one can say about the necessity of the historical figure for faith. Specifically,

> Is it still possible to speak of any inner, essential significance of Jesus for faith? . . . What can a picture of Jesus subject to and shaped by historical criticism mean for a faith that is by its very nature concerned with the eternal, timeless, unconditioned and supernatural? When it first formed its religious ideas, the primitive Christian community had already taken Jesus out of history and made him Logos and God, the eternal Christ appearing to us in historical form, one who is related in essence to the eternal Godhead and so not unnaturally the object of faith. But historical criticism, grown up in a world no longer dominated by the church, has returned him to history where all is finite and conditioned. (p. 182)

Does faith have an essential connection with Jesus? Earlier in the century, David Friedrich Strauss had said no and proposed that the predicates of the god-man, which are valid, be applied not to Jesus but to humanity as a whole. Drews had said no because we couldn't be sure there ever was a historical Jesus. But the church has always affirmed that there is an essential significance. The problem for us is how that connection can be described, assuming that a living faith in God is still possible.

On the basis of the traditional ideas of revelation, redemption, and church, one could speak of "a real inner necessity for the historical person of Christ for salvation" (p. 191). But only on that basis, which is no longer available to us if we wholeheartedly accept historical research into the gospel narratives (pace Kähler, though Troeltsch does not refer to him in the essay). The supernatural authority of Bible and church is not available as a guarantee of an essential connection. And "it is anything but obvious that the religious personality of the historical Jesus can be fully and clearly known and made directly and personally effective" (p. 188, pace Ritschl and Herrmann[32]). Our knowledge of Jesus is thoroughly relativized by historical criticism, and the "inner necessity" of the connection with him is "a very relative matter" (p. 192).

32. "Herrmann's talk about 'the fact of Christ' which, however, cannot be established like other facts but only seen by faith, is an obscure and mystical expression . . . [that] is almost incomprehensible to people who think historically and critically" (p. 192).

Yet for Troeltsch the connection cannot be given up. Not the individual details, but "the factuality of the total historical phenomenon of Jesus and the basic outline of his teaching and his religious personality . . . must be capable of being established by means of historical criticism as historical reality if the 'symbol of Christ' is to have a firm and strong inner basis in the 'fact' of Jesus" (p. 198). Troeltsch's way of dealing with the problem is to reject entirely the attempt to talk of the inseparability of faith and Jesus in terms of dogma or conceptual necessity, and to think instead in terms of social psychology. The model for understanding the relation of the Christian community to its founder is the same as the model for interpreting any religious community. Each requires a support, center, and symbol of its religious life (p. 202).

In this standpoint, Troeltsch has made a decisive shift in the categories of interpretation, namely, to the notions of community and cult. The importance of this change can hardly be overemphasized. "One perfectly clear result of the history and psychology of religion is that in all religion what really counts is not dogma and idea but cult and community" (p. 194). But if we make this shift, we have a viable way of affirming the central position of Christ. Christ is not a mere myth. We do need a basically reliable overall picture (thus historical criticism could have serious negative results for faith). But that we have, and by the general sociopsychological laws applicable to religion as to all human affairs, we can satisfy the need of Christianity "for a support, center and symbol of its religious life" (p. 202). This is the decisive point.[33] "As long as the peculiarly Christian-prophetic religion bearing within itself the Stoa, Platonism and various other elements continues, all possibilities of a community and cult, and so all real power and the extension of belief, will be tied to the central position of Christ for faith" (p. 205).

A SOCIAL HISTORY OF CHRISTIANITY

The thousand pages of Troeltsch's *Social Teaching of the Christian Churches* (*ST*) could be viewed as the complement, on a much larger scale, to his treatment of the specific problem of the historicity of Jesus. For if it is essential to understand the beginning of Christianity

---

33. Troeltsch notes that in fact, though in a concealed way, this kind of interpretation of the connection with Christ was employed by Schleiermacher, Ritschl, and Herrmann (p. 204).

fully in the context of the whole religiocultural situation of the time, it is at least equally important, from the standpoint of the historical consciousness, to look at the entire development of the Christian church in the light of the reciprocal relationship between Christianity and its social context. That is the task which Troeltsch set for himself in *Social Teaching*, which ought more properly to be called a social history of the churches, or, more specifically, a history of the social consciousness and sociological structures of Christianity in relation to the general society or societies of which it has been a part.[34]

The point of such an endeavor was of course nothing new for Troeltsch (see, for example, *GS*, 2:17–18, and *Die Absolutheit*, p. 70). From the beginning, the validity and identity in Christianity had to be seen in the light of Christianity's radical conditioning throughout its history by the historical situation and environment in which it found itself. But, as he noted in his autobiographical account (*GS*, 4:11–12), *Social Teaching* was a full-scale history of Christian church culture, a parallel to Harnack's *History of Dogma*. That parallel implies at least two things. First, it involved a conscious limitation to ideas, teachings, and theories in their contexts, in contrast to a full exploration of real practical conditions. Second, it involved a departure from Harnack's principle of judgment on the history of doctrine. Harnack, at the beginning of the *Dogmengeschichte*, had said that one either compares the history of dogma with the gospel or judges it according to the historical circumstances of the time and the results. Harnack chose the former alternative as appropriate for Protestantism. Troeltsch was much closer to the latter, and he took the step from church history to history of Christianity even more fully than Harnack. If the history of Christian doctrines cannot be dealt with apart from the influences of contemporary philosophies, as Harnack had clearly shown, neither can the story of the church or its institutions be understood except as an integral part of social history. Both the history of doctrine and church history have been changed by modern historical and nondogmatic ways of thought.

Further, in considering the problem of formulating "the world of Christian thought and life in frank relation to the modern world," Troeltsch said he had come to see that "the balance leaned to the side of the ethical. If Christianity is first and foremost a matter of practice

34. See the parallel of the problems of the Jesus of history/Christ of faith debate and of the rewriting of Christian history, as developed in chap. 5, above.

[and recall his judgment that cult and community count more than dogmas and ideas], then its main problems lie in the sphere of practical life, and it is from this realm that the most complicated difficulties and contrasts arise in opposition to the world of Christian life" (*ST*, pp. 19–20). Therefore Troeltsch's history had to focus on the social ethics of the churches, that is, on the social doctrines concerning the most important nonreligious social structures. This required a sociological formulation of the problem of the whole sweep of Christian history. It was both a methodological principle and a result of the inquiry that the entire world of Christian thought depends on fundamental sociological conditions and the social conceptions of the time (see *ST*, pp. 32, 992, 994). Alongside the "history of ideas" approach, specifically the "essentially ideological-dogmatic" presentation of Christianity by Harnack (and Seeberg), Troeltsch set a history that was "essentially sociological-realistic-ethical" (see *GS*, 3:369; also *ST*, p. 990).

In this connection, it is important to note the impact of Max Weber, with whom Troeltsch was in intimate contact in the decade following their trip together to a St. Louis congress in 1904. It was from Weber, he said, that he truly learned to appreciate the Marxist mode of questioning the sociological conditioning of Christianity and the extent to which Christianity itself operates as a sociological principle. He paid high tribute to Weber in his autobiographical sketch and in an obituary for him, and he reviewed Weber's major works at length in *Der Historismus*. Weber's ideas about Protestantism and the origin of capitalism were strongly represented in *Social Teaching* (and Troeltsch could say in *Protestantism and Progress*, p. 138, that Weber "has completely proved his case" about Calvinistic asceticism and the capitalistic spirit). Even more important, however, was Troeltsch's extensive employment of Weber's church/sect distinction in *Social Teaching* as a fundamental tool of interpretation.

The distinction between church and sect presupposed Weber's notion of ideal types, which was profoundly influential in sociology. Ideal types are not to be understood either as arbitrarily imposed constructs or as in themselves identical with the historical data (so that one might expect a historical reality to conform exactly to the ideal type). They are conceptual tools, analytical instruments, like Kantian concepts, arising out of the encounter between the present concerns of the interpreter and the historical data, whereby one can take account intelligibly of both the individual unique elements of reality and their causal interconnections and inner coherence. This view of the function of ideal types was taken over by Troeltsch, along with the church/sect distinction, as a means to the illumination of Christian history.

Yet Troeltsch differed significantly from Weber in defining the distinction. For Weber, the center of the distinction of the sect type from the church type was the voluntarism of the former, the freedom from compulsion. That element was also emphasized by Troeltsch, but he found the heart of the distinction in the differing attitudes toward the world, and eventually he added a third type, the mystical. The most extended systematic discussion in *Social Teaching* of the difference between church and sect appeared at the end of the treatment of medieval Catholicism (esp. pp. 331–49). The mystical type was analyzed in connection with the treatment of Protestantism (esp. pp. 729–802). The basic distinction of the three types of Christian thought in its sociological development was conveniently summarized in the conclusion (p. 993).

To put the matter briefly, the church type is open to the world and partially accepts the secular order. Its principle is universal, it seeks to include the whole life of humanity, and in its communication of grace and salvation it adjusts itself to the world. The whole of the secular order is a means and preparation for the supernatural aim. The developed church "utilizes the state and the ruling classes, and weaves these elements into her own life; she then becomes an integral part of the existing social order," both stabilizing the order and becoming dependent on the upper classes. Asceticism, expressed particularly in monasticism, is incorporated into the system as a special element of religious achievement, a means of acquiring virtue, notably through the repression of the senses. The church type is most grandly represented in medieval Catholicism, though it is also characteristic of the classical or main-line Reformation (hence, again, Troeltsch's view of Luther as belonging essentially to the medieval world). And we can say that this has been the mainstream of Christian development.

The sect type, represented in comparatively small voluntary groups that seek personal inward perfection and direct personal fellowship, gives up the idea of dominating or incorporating the world and its social institutions. It tends to separate itself from those institutions, either in indifference or toleration or hostility (and often in the creation of its own society). The sects are generally connected with the lower classes in their opposition to the state and society. Asceticism in the sect type is expressed in the detachment from the world, as in the refusal to take part in war, or to swear oaths, or to own property. The Sermon on the Mount, with its apparent contrast of the kingdom of God to all secular interests and institutions, is taken as the ideal.

Mysticism, which Troeltsch traces from the New Testament through modern thought (see pp. 729–802), is less a type of social organization than an insistence on direct inward and personal experience. It takes for granted the formal structures of religious life, but seeks to draw back from these (or to supplement them) in personal and living stimulus. It may create "special and more intimate mysteries, in which salvation is appropriated in a peculiarly inward manner" (p. 731), but it mainly "leads to the formation of groups on a purely personal basis, with no permanent form, which also tend to weaken the significance of forms of worship, doctrine, and the historical element" (p. 993).

The great achievement of Troeltsch, at which we can barely hint, was the way in which he applied this distinction of types to the whole of Christian history and illumined the complexity and interweaving of the several forms and attitudes relative to the church and the world. Yet while the church-sect-mysticism distinction is probably the feature of *Social Teaching* that is best known (and not unjustly so), its employment by Troeltsch was related to the systematic goals of understanding the essential nature of Christianity and of formulating "the world of Christian thought and life in frank relation to the modern world" (p. 19). To put the point most succinctly, Troeltsch showed, in a majestic and inclusive way, that the history of Christian thought and life, with its emergent structures, cannot be viewed simply as a uniform or unilinear development. In the broadest sense, one can say that from its origins in the free personal piety and intimacy of fellowship of the gospel of Jesus, Christianity developed gradually and dominantly along the lines of the church type, in medieval Catholicism and through the Reformation. But that type of synthesis or compromise has been brought fundamentally into question in the modern world with the collapse of the ecclesiastical spirit. And the distinct types and forms of relationship—church, sect, and mysticism—were foreshadowed from the beginning and have appeared alongside one another and interwoven through the whole history of Christianity. At every point the ideas and the forms of organization they shaped were determined "by the general conditions of civilization," so that for any given time the question has to be asked, "What was the relationship between the two forms of influence, and how did they mutually react upon one another?" (p. 992).

The upshot is that Christianity emerges as less *a* religion than a congeries of religions. The ideas of Christ, or redemption, and of toleration and relation to the state have all varied according to the type, and always as relative to historical situations in which they were expressed.

That poses the problem for contemporary life. Troeltsch could not give up the conviction that there was something of permanent value which could serve the present in the content of the Christian ethos. He saw certain enduring values contained in the "varied history of the Christian social doctrines": the conviction of personality and individuality; a "socialism" through the idea of the inclusive divine love; a way of resolving the problem of equality and inequality through the values of "mutual recognition, confidence, and care for others"; a charity that is indispensable in any social order; and a goal, in the idea of the kingdom of God, for social life and aspiration that lies "far beyond all the relativities of this earthly life" (pp. 1004–05).

The systematic question, then, is one of the best forms both of organization for Christian life and of how Christianity can be significant "for the solution of the social problem of the present day" (p. 1010; see p. 20). This is a new problem. The traditional types of Christian social philosophy found in medieval Catholicism and in ascetic Protestantism had lost their power. They were obsolete. Church culture had been crippled by the emergence of modern political, economic, and social conditions, and Troeltsch took no satisfaction in the various social gospels of recent times.[35] His hope was for new thoughts for a new situation, new compromises that had to be wrought out against the whole background of Christianity's history. As he concluded,

> Nowhere does there exist an absolute Christian ethic, which only awaits discovery; all that we can do is to learn to control the world-situation in its successive phases just as the earlier Christian ethic did in its own way. There is also no absolute ethical transformation of material life or of human nature; all that does exist is a constant

35. See pp. 20, 33–34, 1012, and Troeltsch's extensive critique of Herrmann's *Ethik* in the 1902 essay "Grundprobleme der Ethik," *GS*, 2:552–672.

wrestling with the problems which they raise. Thus a Christian ethic of the present day and of the future will also only be an adjustment to the world-situation, and it will only desire to achieve that which is practically possible. (p. 1013)

Relativity, *Kompromiss*, and Faith

It is evident from the passages just cited that Troeltsch was quite unwilling to give up the idea of a significant Christian ethic. He was equally unwilling to abandon the stance of faith. There was for him no way of being neutral about the claims of Christianity, for this involves our whole way of viewing the world. However impossible it may be to have an absolute view of the absolute, Troeltsch did not judge for a moment that one could be satisfied with substituting the reality of faith for the actuality of God. The symbols of faith have a cognitive value, and the referent of faith must be affirmed as a revelatory impulse. Contact with the divine life is possible and real. Troeltsch was expressing his conviction when he wrote in 1903 (and 1913) in the essay on the essence of Christianity that "no physics and no biology, no psychology and no theory of evolution can take from us our belief in the living, creative purpose of God, and . . . no anti-teleology, no brutality and no fortuitousness of nature, no contradiction between the ideal and the real, can take from us our belief in redemption as the destination of the whole world."[36] Similarly, as we saw, he argued for the indispensability of the historicity of Jesus for Christianity.

Yet it is equally evident that in Troeltsch the connections of faith, history, and ethics have become highly problematic. Their interrelation cannot be given up but can no longer be taken for granted and must be considered afresh. Ethics, like doctrine and like the historical relation to Jesus, is clearly relative. As Troeltsch put it in his final essays, "The entire domain of the ethical standard has itself been drawn, by Modern Psychology, by Historical Relativism, and by Evolutionism, into the flow of things, and been made part and parcel of this Historicism" (*CT*, p. 71).

We need to be quite clear at this point about what Troeltsch meant by relativism and relativity. He explicitly disclaimed what he called aimless or purposeless (zwecklos) or unlimited relativism, which

36. "What Does 'Essence of Christianity' Mean?," M&P, p. 159; *GS*, 2:427. See the assertion in *CT*, p. 55, that Christianity must be "in some degree, a manifestation of the Divine Life itself."

turns the elements of history into "an incalculable welter of evanes-
cent forms" and is utterly enervating. That might seem to be the result of historical thinking, but it is not. "Relativity simply means that
all historical phenomena are unique, individual configurations acted
on by influences from a universal context that comes to bear on them
in varying degrees of immediacy. . . . Relativity does not mean . . . denial of the values that appear in these individual configurations."[37]

A particular consequence of historical relativism for ethics, and indeed for all Christian thinking, is expressed in the theme of compromise (Kompromiss), a term that recurs throughout Troeltsch's writing. Compromise, here, is not an unworthy, illegitimate, or defensive
concession. Compromise is rather a positive term that describes the
historically inevitable relationship of Christianity to its context. The
history of Christianity is the story of a succession of compromises
creatively worked out in differing epochs and situations. In Reist's
apt phrase, compromise is "the phenomenology of involvement."[38]
The concept was most extensively employed by Troeltsch in *Social
Teaching* in interpreting the development of medieval Catholicism
out of the initial radical impulse of the gospel of the kingdom. Development and compromise are inevitably tied together. Compromise
also characterized the Reformers' protest, which was against the nature of the medieval compromise but not against the process, which
they continued in their own ways. Even the sect, which protests
against compromise, cannot escape the process (though that may
mean its dissolution as sect). The ethos of the gospel "is an ideal
which cannot be realized within this world apart from compromise.
Therefore the history of the Christian Ethos becomes the story of a
constantly renewed search for this compromise, and of fresh opposition to this spirit of compromise" (*ST*, pp. 999-1000).

Kompromiss is not only a category for historical interpretation; it
designates a task for the present, in the light of historical relativism.
The medieval churchly compromise has broken down. When the sect
gave up the idea of a supplement from the ethic of civilization, "it became uncultured and insignificant, while mysticism became complete
and solitary resignation." Today we are in a new state of civilization

---

37. *Die Absolutheit*, p. 89. See the whole eloquent argument of pp. 86–90. This is a relatively early statement by Troeltsch, but I do not see that the heightened importance of the
concept of individuality that appears in *Der Historismus* and in *Christian Thought* involves
any rejection of the judgment cited.
38. Reist, *Toward a Theology of Involvement*, p. 161.

and a new "supplementary process" is necessary. "In a permanent world the Christian ethos cannot live and be entirely self-sufficing. The question is simply this: How can this supplement be shaped today? The answer to this question constitutes an imperative demand for a new Christian ethic" (*ST*, pp. 1001–02). This will be an unending task. As Troeltsch put it in his last statements, writing more generally of the problem of ethics in "damming and controlling . . . the stream of historical life," the complexity and diversity of ethics in our world means that "the task of damming and controlling is therefore essentially incapable of completion and essentially unending; and yet it is always soluble and practicable in each new case" (*CT*, p. 145).

The task, furthermore, must now be undertaken with the recognition of genuine religious and ethical pluralism. The late-twentieth-century language of religious pluralism was not Troeltsch's. But the idea is implicit from the time of his early consideration of the problem of the absoluteness of Christianity. It was present, for example, in his description (in *Protestantism and Progress*) of the way modern Protestantism has had to recognize the coexistence of multiple religious convictions and denominations. The idea of a plurality of autonomous religious and cultural traditions was extensively articulated in his discussions of collective individualities in *Der Historismus*, and resulted, for example, in his judgment that there was no way of incorporating Islam into the cultural history of Europe (with which Troeltsch was always chiefly concerned). Islam has its own universal history, and there is no cultural synthesis between its world and the European world. The idea of pluralism was quite explicit in his final essays, in which the claim for supreme validity of Christianity (and in principle of any religion) had to be given up. There is no longer room for religious or cultural imperialism. Troeltsch could even speak of an "anarchy" in the present day in the religious and metaphysical sphere, and suggest that instead of seeking a single all-embracing common spirit, "one has only to resolve to let each complex go untroubled on its way, and to live in each according to its own special demands, without elevating any one of them monistically into a universal basis or a single all-determining accent. One can only demand for the most universal community, which is that of *Humanity*, a mutual understanding and tolerance, and a feeling of fundamental human obligation, without any very definite content" (*CT*, p. 139). There is, then, a pluralism of religions and a pluralism within Christianity.

In the face of these consequences of the historical consciousness, what can one say about social solutions, or ethical norms, or the certainties of faith? Here we come to the final point in our consideration of Troeltsch. Faith is for him a creative decision regarding standards of truth and value. It is in one sense subjective and individual—though one must defend Troeltsch against the charge of mere individualism by recalling his profound sense of the corporate character of religion as centering in cult and community, his insistence that individualities are always set in relationships, and his conviction that Christian redemption does not arise from autonomy but is received in history through the community. The central point is the decisional character of the act of faith, or the identification of normative value. One cannot help thinking here of Troeltsch in relation to William James's idea of responsible choice in the act of believing, and through him of the tradition of Pascal, Coleridge, and even Kierkegaard.

In the early essay on what "essence of Christianity" means, for example, Troeltsch reviewed the whole problem of how one determines what Christianity really is: the question of its integrity. The answer of dogmatic definition will obviously not suffice. Neither will the modern evolutionary history notion, out of which the idea of "essence" of Christianity has arisen. Nor will Harnack's notion of a permanent element that has persisted, in one way or another, through change. Rather, the question must be viewed in the light of the total history of Christianity as this is viewed by modern historical awareness. The consequence is that the essence of Christianity will always be determined by the engagement of the interpreter with the whole of history. The question of the essence as an ideal concept will always be answered, in responsibility to the objective historical foundation, by a subjective judgment, that is, a positive decision of the interpreter. This means it will be answered differently at different times and from different standpoints. It must always be answered anew. That is the "real knot" of the problem, and it cannot be undone. The combination of personal presuppositions and the contemporary perspective with the historical whole, in the interest of determining the essential, is always a "*creative act*, which can only be refuted or completed and amended by a more convincing and more deeply liberating act."[39]

---

39. M&P, p. 160; see pp. 156–81. See also the statement of the problem in "The Dogmatics of the 'Religionsgeschichtliche Schule.'"

If determining the real nature of Christianity is always a living decision, so also is every judgment about the normative in history. In Troeltsch's last statement about the validity of Christianity's impulse toward absolute truth, the acceptance of the claim of truth for us is still a decision. While Christianity is bound up with European civilization and is thus the only religion we can endure and the one binding on us, we affirm its validity as a choice arising from our situation. Troeltsch does not specifically use the language of decision in that statement, but decision is implicit. In speaking in the subsequent essays about ethics and the possibility of any synthesis of cultural values, he regularly recurs to the language of personal decision. There is, he says, "something objective and of a universal validity" in ethics, but "this objectivity is involved in a deep subjectivity and founded on personal resolve." In every system of cultural values, "it is faith that ultimately decides; and here, too, it is likewise faith that justifies" (And this faith proves itself by its fruits—see James again?) (CT, pp. 125–26, 120).

Faith as it seeks to be certain that it has laid hold of the divine source and the divine goal, faith as it is connected to the historical person at the beginning of Christianity, and faith as it is expressed in ethical decisions is in every case an act of responsible decision. In those decisions, faith in God, faith in Jesus Christ, and acceptance of the moral claim can be held together, but always as a venture fraught with inner tension, uncertainty, and temporality. Every such decision will be a relative decision, an assertion of validity for us in our particular present, and will always have to be made anew as a creative act. Historicism is not to be overcome by being abolished, but by our discovery of how to live creatively with a permanent problem. How to do this is the question Troeltsch left as an inescapable legacy to the theology of the twentieth century.

Bibliographic Notes

Chapter 1

Ritschl's earliest major work was on the origin of the old Catholic church, *Die Entstehung der altkatholischen Kirche: Eine kirchen- und dogmengeschichtliche Monographie* (Bonn, 1850; 2d ed., 1857), in the second edition of which he broke decisively with the interpretation of his teacher, F. C. Baur. Subsequent principal works include *Die christliche Lehre von der Rechtfertigung und Versöhnung*, in three volumes: 1: *Die Geschichte der Lehre* (Bonn, 1870; rev. ed., 1882 [cited in text as *R.u.V.*, 1]; trans. by J. S. Black as *A Critical History of the Christian Doctrine of Justification and Reconciliation* [Edinburgh, 1872]); 2: *Der biblische Stoff der Lehre* (Bonn, 1874; 3d ed., 1889 [cited as *R.u.V.*, 2]); 3: *Die positive Entwicklung der Lehre* (Bonn, 1874; 3d ed., 1888; trans. by H. R. Mackintosh and A. B. Macaulay as *The Christian Doctrine of Justification and Reconciliation* [Edinburgh, 1900; reprint, Clifton, N.J., 1966], cited in the text as *J&R*); *Die christliche Vollkommenheit* (Bonn, 1874); *Unterricht in der christlichen Religion* (Bonn, 1875; 3d ed., 1886; trans. Alice Swing as "Instruction in the Christian Religion," in Albert Swing, *The Theology of Albrecht Ritschl* [London, 1901]; the *Vollkommenheit* and the *Unterricht* were republished in a critical edition by C. Fabricius [Leipzig, 1924]); *Schleiermachers Reden über die Religion und ihre Nachwirkungen auf die evangelische Kirche Deutschlands* (Bonn, 1874); *Theologie und Metaphysik: Zur Verständigung und Abwehr* (Bonn, 1881; 2d ed., 1887); and *Geschichte des Pietismus*, 3 vols. (Bonn, 1880–86). *Theology and Metaphysics* (cited in the text as *T&M*) and the prolegomena to *History of Pietism* have been translated by Philip Hefner in *Albrecht Ritschl: Three Essays* (Philadelphia, 1972), along with a revision of the Swing translation of the *Unterricht*. References in the text to these three documents are to Hefner's translation.

The standard source for Ritschl's life is the biography by his son, Otto Ritschl, *Albrecht Ritschls Leben*, 2 vols. (Freiburg, 1892–96). Among the more recent estimates of Ritschl's thought, the following may particularly be noted: Karl Barth, *Die protestantische Theologie im 19. Jahrhundert* (Zurich, 1946); H. R. Niebuhr, *Christ and Culture* (New York, 1951), chap. 3; Hans Woelber, *Dogma und Ethos, Christentum und Humanismus von Ritschl bis Troeltsch* (Göttingen, 1950); Christoph Senft, *Wahrhaftigkeit und Wahrheit* (Tübingen, 1956); Paul Wrzecionko, *Die philosophischen Wurzeln der Theologie Albrecht Ritschls* (Berlin, 1964); Philip Hefner, *Faith and the Vitalities of History: A Theological Study Based on the Work of Albrecht Ritschl* (New York, 1966), and Hefner's introduction to *Three Essays*; Hermann Timm, *Theorie und Praxis in der Theologie Albrecht Ritschls und Wilhelm Herrmanns: Ein Beitrag zur Entwicklungsgeschichte des Kulturprotestantismus* (Gütersloh, 1967); Rolf Schaefer, *Ritschl: Grundlinien eines fast verschollenen dogmatischen Systems* (Tübingen, 1968); David L. Mueller, *An Introduction to the Theology of Albrecht Ritschl* (Philadelphia, 1969); David W. Lotz, *Ritschl and Luther* (Nashville, 1974); and James Richmond, *Ritschl: A Reappraisal* (London, 1978).

Extensive bibliographies are given by Hefner, Mueller, Lotz, and Schaefer, and, for the literature up to 1941, by Gøsta Høk, *Die elliptische Theologie Albrecht Ritschls nach Ursprung und innerem Zusammenhang* (Uppsala, 1942). Recent dissertations in English include William Barnett, "Historical Relativism and Christology in the Thought of Wilhelm Dilthey and Albrecht Ritschl" (University of Chicago, 1976); Darrell Jodock, "F. C. Baur and Albrecht Ritschl on Historical Theology" (Yale University, 1969); Gerald McCulloh, "Christ's Person and Lifework in the Theology of Albrecht Ritschl: With Special Attention to Munus Triplex" (University of Chicago, 1973); Joseph Pickle, "Epistemology and Soteriology: A Study in the Theologies of Albrecht Ritschl and Karl Barth" (University of Chicago, 1969); and Michael Ryan, "The Role of the Discipline of History in the Theological Interpretation of Albrecht Ritschl" (Drew University, 1967). See also Jodock, "Metaphysics and Theology in Albrecht Ritschl," AAR 19th Century Theology Working Group Papers (Berkeley, 1983), pp. 106–17.

Chapter 2

Herrmann. Herrmann's principal books were *Die Religion im Verhältnis zum Welterkennen und zur Sittlichkeit* (Halle, 1879); *Der Verkehr des Christen mit Gott* (Stuttgart, 1886; 7th ed., Tübingen, 1921); and *Ethik* (Tübingen, 1901; 6th ed., 1921). *Der Verkehr* was translated into English in two editions under the title *The Communion of the Christian with God*, the more important being the revision by R. W. Stewart (London, 1906) from the fourth German edition of 1903. It was even a standard textbook in the English-speaking world and has been reprinted (Philadelphia, 1971) with an introduction by Robert Voelkel. Page references in the text are to this edition. To these works may be added *Die Metaphysik in der Theologie* (Halle, 1876), and the posthumously published lectures, *Dogmatik* (Stuttgart, 1925), trans. N. Micklem and K. A. Saunders as *Systematic Theology* (New York, 1927).

An excellent selection from the many essays has been edited, with an introduction, by Peter Fischer-Appelt, *Schriften zur Grundlegung der Theologie*, 2 vols. (Munich, 1966, 1967). Fischer-Appelt has also published an exhaustive bibliography of Herrmann's writings in his *Metaphysik im Horizont der Theologie* (Munich, 1965). Other recent useful discussions of Herrmann's thought include Karl Barth, "The Principles of Dogmatics according to Wilhelm Herrmann," *Theology and Church*, trans. L. P. Smith (New York, 1962); Daniel L. Deegan, "Wilhelm Herrmann: A Reassessment," *Scottish Journal of Theology*, 19 (1966): 188–203; Dietz Lange, "Wahrhaftigkeit als sittliche Forderung und als theologisches Prinzip bei Wilhelm Herrmann," *Zeitschrift für Theologie und Kirche*, 66 (1969): 77–79; Theodor Mahlmann, "Das Axiom des Erlebnisses bei Wilhelm Herrmann," *Neue Zeitschrift für systematische Theologie und Religionsphilosophie*, 4 (1962): 11–88, and "Philosophie der Religion bei Wilhelm Herrmann," *Neue Zeitschrift für systematische Theologie und Religionsphilosophie*, 6 (1964): 70–107; Hermann Timm, *Theorie und Praxis in der Theologie Albrecht Ritschls und Wilhelm Herrmann* (Gütersloh, 1967); and Robert Voelkel, *The Shape of the Theological Task* (Philadelphia, 1968).

James. Among James's writings, the most immediately important for his views of religion are the 1896 address, "The Will to Believe," and the essays collected in

The Will to Believe, and Other Essays in Popular Philosophy (New York, 1897); the Gifford Lectures, *The Varieties of Religious Experience: A Study in Human Nature* (New York, 1902); *Pragmatism: A New Name for Some Old Ways of Thinking* (New York, 1907); and *A Pluralistic Universe* (New York, 1909). To these should be added, for any full understanding of the bases and development of James's religious thinking, his masterpiece (and only major work of *Strengwissenschaft*), *Principles of Psychology*, 2 vols. (New York, 1890), later abridged in a single volume, *Psychology (Briefer Course)* (New York, 1892).

Many of James's works have been reprinted in numerous editions and collections. A full list is found in a supplemented version of R. B. Perry's annotated bibliography, published in John J. McDermott, *The Writings of William James: A Comprehensive Edition* (Chicago, 1977), pp. 812–58. This volume is a useful selection of essays and chapters from James's entire work, organized chronologically under major topics; its major deficiency, in respect of James's thinking about religion, is that little of *Varieties* is included. A full critical edition, *The Works of William James* (Cambridge, Mass., 1975–), is in process.

The literature about James is enormous, including, for example, special studies of James in relation to Pascal, Kierkegaard, Emerson, Aquinas, Newman, Ritschl, H. R. Niebuhr, Otto, Unamuno, Bergson, Peirce, Royce, Dewey, Whitehead, Husserl, Starbuck, and of course his brother, Henry James. But for the whole of James's thought, particular note should be made of Ralph Barton Perry, *The Thought and Character of William James*, 2 vols. (Boston, 1935), abridged in a one-volume edition (Boston, 1948); and the biography by Gay Wilson Allen, *William James* (New York, 1967). For a generally appreciative interpretation of James, which nevertheless concludes that his defense of religion in the "Will to Believe" and other essays flounders in confusion, imprecision and contradiction, see Paul K. Conklin, *Puritans and Pragmatists* (New York, 1968), pp. 266–344.

Chapter 5

Adolf Harnack was born in 1851, the son of Theodosius Harnack, a Lutheran confessionalist of the Erlangen school, at the time professor of practical theology at the University of Dorpat. Adolf studied at Erlangen, Dorpat, and Leipzig, where he took his doctoral examination (1873) and habilitated (1874) with a thesis on Apelles, an early Gnostic writer. He began his teaching career at Leipzig in the latter year and conducted his seminar in church history for 108 consecutive semesters up to the year before his death in 1930. In 1879 he accepted a call to Giessen, then to Marburg in 1886, and finally to Berlin in 1888, where he was appointed by the new Kaiser Wilhelm II, on the unanimous recommendation of the faculty and the urging of Bismarck and the minister of education, but against the will of the ecclesiastical authorities. The ecclesiastical authorities opposed certain conclusions in the first volume of Harnack's history of dogma on the grounds of their incompatibility with orthodox doctrine. Hostility from the church authorities was a source of pain to Harnack for the rest of his career because he considered his entire work to be a service to the church, yet was not allowed to share in the ecclesiastical examinations of the thousands of students he taught.

Harnack was a founder, with Schürer, of the *Theologische Literaturzeitung* (1876) and its editor for twenty-nine years (1881–1910), and he initiated the famous series *Texte und Untersuchungen* in 1881–82. He published regularly in *Die christliche Welt*, founded in 1887 by Martin Rade and three other of Harnack's Leipzig students. In 1890 he was elected to the Prussian Academy of Sciences and wrote its bicentennial history (published in three volumes in 1900), a work that surveyed the whole history of modern scholarship. He was the organizer and chief editor of the *Critical Edition of the Greek-Christian Authors of the First Three Centuries*, begun in 1891. In the early years of the twentieth century he was president of the Evangelisch-Soziale Kongress for eight years; he was active in the Innere Mission and a cofounder and president of the Evangelische Union.

Harnack was an organizer and administrator as well as a prolific author (with 367 published items by the age of thirty-five—see Friedrich Smend, *Adolf von Harnack: Verzeichnis seiner Schriften* [Leipzig, 1931], which lists a total of 1,611 publications). His career after 1900 was nearly coextensive with the cultural life of Germany, and he exemplified the optimism of the German historian in the late nineteenth century (see George G. Iggers, *The German Conception of History* [Middletown, Conn., 1968], pp. 128–310). He was a prime organizer (and president from 1911 until his death) of the Kaiser Wilhelm Gesellschaft, which developed research institutes especially in the natural and medical sciences. Kaiser Wilhelm II, to whom he was a friend and confidant, raised him to the hereditary nobility in 1914—the last scholar to be so honored. He was also one of the ninety-three German intellectuals (including eleven other theologians) who signed the August 1914 manifesto in support of the war.

From his enormous list of writings, the following may be noted. Harnack's first major work, though unpublished, was a prize essay (at Dorpat, 1870) on Marcion, who was also the subject of his last major work, *Marcion: Das Evangelium vom fremden Gott* (Berlin, 1920; 2d ed., Leipzig, 1924). The classic *Lehrbuch der Dogmengeschichte* was first published in three volumes (Freiburg, 1886–90; 4th ed., 1909–10), and was followed by a one-volume summary, *Grundriss der Dogmengeschichte* (in two parts; Freiburg, 1889–91; authorized trans. by E. K. Mitchell, *Outlines of the History of Dogma* [London, 1893; reprint, Boston, 1957]); the N. Buchanan translation of the third edition of the *History of Dogma*, 7 vols. (London, 1896–99), is less usable.

Das Wesen des Christentums (Leipzig, 1900) appeared in fourteen printings and as many translations by 1927 (Eng. trans., T. B. Saunders, *What is Christianity?* [London, 1900]; cited as *WC* from the 1957 New York reprint). The *Geschichte der altchristlichen Literatur bis Eusebius*, 4 vols. (Leipzig, 1893–1904) became the foundation for subsequent critical studies in patristics.

See also the brief 1896 lecture *Das Christentum und die Geschichte* (Leipzig, 1896; 4th ed., 1897; trans. T. B. Saunders, *Christianity and History* [London, 1896]); *Geschichte der Mission und Ausbreitung des Christentums in den ersten drei Jahrhunderten*, 2 vols. (Leipzig, 1902; 2d rev. ed., 1906; trans. James Moffat, *The Mission and Expansion of Christianity in the First Three Centuries* [New York, 1908]); *Die Apostelgeschichte* (Leipzig, 1908; trans. J. R. Wilkinson, *The Acts of the Apostles* [New York, 1909]); *Entstehung und Entwicklung der Kirchenfassung und des Kirchenrechts in den zwei ersten Jahrhunderten* (Leipzig, 1910; trans. F. L. Pogson, ed. H. D. A. Major, *The Constitution and Law of the Church in the First Two Centuries* [New York, 1919]); *Reden und Aufsätze*, 2 vols. (Giessen, 1904); and *Reden und Aufsätze, Neue Folge*, 5 vols. (Giessen, 1911–30).

The standard biography is by Harnack's daughter, Agnes von Zahn-Harnack, *Adolf von Harnack* (Berlin, 1936; 2d ed., 1951). Useful studies in English include Wayne Glick, *The Reality of Christianity* (New York, 1967), and, more briefly, Wilhelm Pauck, *Harnack and Troeltsch* (New York, 1968).

Chapter 6

The literature on Darwin's work and its impact is enormous and has been greatly augmented since the centennial of 1959. Among recent responsible works, several are particularly worthy of note. *The Comparative Reception of Darwinism*, ed. Thomas F. Glick (Austin, 1972), contains especially useful accounts of the response to Darwin by scientists (mostly) in various countries, and I have relied on it at appropriate points. It also includes excellent bibliographical essays. Michael T. Ghiselin, *The Triumph of the Darwinian Method* (Berkeley, 1969), though marred by repetitive adulation of Darwin and an unduly systematized view of his method, is valuable for an understanding of what Darwin actually contributed, not only in the *Origin* but also in other works. Alvar Ellegård, *Darwin and the General Reader: The Reception of Darwin's Theory of Evolution in the British Periodical Press, 1859–72* (Göteborg, 1958), is as yet unparalleled by any study of the popular response in other countries.

On the problem of Darwin, evolution, and religion, James R. Moore, *The Post-Darwinian Controversies: A Study of the Protestant Struggle to Come to Terms with Darwin in Great Britain and America, 1870–1900* (Cambridge, Eng., and New York, 1979), is a detailed and reliable account with an extensive bibliography, which lays to rest many of the myths about the theological responses to Darwin and goes far to distinguish and explain their varieties. A lively and still useful historical study of the general impact of Darwin and Huxley in England is William Irvine, *Apes, Angels, and Victorians* (New York, 1955). Perceptive and balanced statements are also given by John Dillenberger, *Protestant Thought and Natural Science* (New York, 1960), and especially by Owen Chadwick, *The Secularization of the European Mind in the Nineteenth Century* (Cambridge, 1975), chap. 7. Chadwick is particularly helpful in setting the discussion of Darwin in the general social context.

Chapter 8

The two major works that Troeltsch published were *Die Soziallehren der christlichen Kirchen und Gruppen* (Tübingen, 1912 [some portions were published earlier]; trans. O. Wyon, *The Social Teaching of the Christian Churches*, 2 vols. [London, 1931]), and *Der Historismus und seine Probleme* (Tübingen, 1922). The latter great work has not been translated into English and, despite some recent ventures in that direction, it does not seem likely that it will happen soon. *Die Soziallehren* and *Der Historismus* are included as vols. 1 and 3 of *GS*. Vols. 2 and 4 include a large number of important monographs and articles: vol. 2 (essays from the Heidelberg years), *Zur religiösen Lage, Religionsphilosophie und Ethik* (Tübingen, 1913); and vol. 4 (other essays), *Aufsätze zur Geistesgeschichte und Religionssoziologie*, ed. Hans Baron (Tübingen, 1925).

In addition to the material in *GS*, special note should be made of *Die Absolutheit des Christentums und die Religionsgeschichte* (Tübingen, 1902; 2d ed., with a few changes, 1912; trans. David Reid, *The Absoluteness of Christianity and the History of*

Religions [Richmond, 1971]); *Die Bedeutung der Geschichtlichkeit Jesu für den Glauben* (Tübingen, 1911; trans. in Morgan and Pye, see below); *Die Bedeutung des Protestantismus für die Entstehung der modernen Welt* (Munich, 1906; 2d ed., 1911; trans. W. Montgomery with an unfortunate title, *Protestantism and Progress: A Historical Study of the Relation of Protestantism to the Modern World* [London, 1912; reprint, Boston, 1958; cited as *PP*]); *Christian Thought: Its History and Application*, ed. with intro. by F. von Hügel (London, 1923; lectures written for delivery in England and subsequently published in German as *Der Historismus und seine Ueberwindung* [Berlin, 1924]); "The Dogmatics of the 'religionsgeschichtliche Schule,'" written for *The American Journal of Theology* 17:1 (1913): 1–21 (German text, *GS*, 2:500–24); fifteen articles in the first edition of *Die Religion in Geschichte und Gegenwart (RGG)*, vols. 2, 3, 4, and 5 (Tübingen, 1910–13); and five articles in the *Encyclopedia of Religion and Ethics (ERE)*, vols. 4, 6, and 8 (Edinburgh, 1912–15).

A detailed, chronologically arranged bibliography of Troeltsch's writings is provided by Hans Baron in *GS*, 4:861–72. A list of recent editions (since 1960) of Troeltsch's works, an account of English translations, and an extensive bibliography of studies of Troeltsch, compiled by Jacob Klapwijk, may be found in *Ernst Troeltsch and the Future of Theology*, ed. John P. Clayton (Cambridge, 1976), pp. 196–214. This volume contains several excellent essays on aspects of Troeltsch's thought. One should note especially the translation, with a fine introduction by Morgan, of four important essays in *Ernst Troeltsch: Writings on Theology and Religion*, trans. and ed. Robert Morgan and Michael Pye (London and Atlanta, 1977), cited here as M&P. The essays included are: "Half a Century of Theology: A Review" (1908), "Religion and the Science of Religion" (1906), "What Does 'Essence of Christianity' Mean?" (1903, 1913), and "The Significance of the Historical Existence of Jesus for Faith" (1911). A still useful general introduction to Troeltsch in English is Benjamin A. Reist, *Toward a Theology of Involvement: The Thought of Ernst Troeltsch* (Philadelphia, 1966), though it is marred by the contention that Troeltsch's theology "collapsed." And one dissertation escaped Klapwijk's net, namely, Hiroshi Obayashi, "The Absoluteness of Christianity in the Thought of Ernst Troeltsch" (University of Pennsylvania, 1967), which has the special merit of showing the centrality and persistence of the problem of the absoluteness of Christianity in Troeltsch's thought. Other valuable secondary works are noted at appropriate places in the text. For the most complete, annotated list of Troeltsch's publications, see F. W. Graf and H. Ruddies, eds., *Ernst Troeltsch Bibliographie* (Tübingen, 1982).

Index